PRINCE
A SIGN O' THE TIMES

Play in the sunshine!

Turn all the lights up to Ken,

John M...

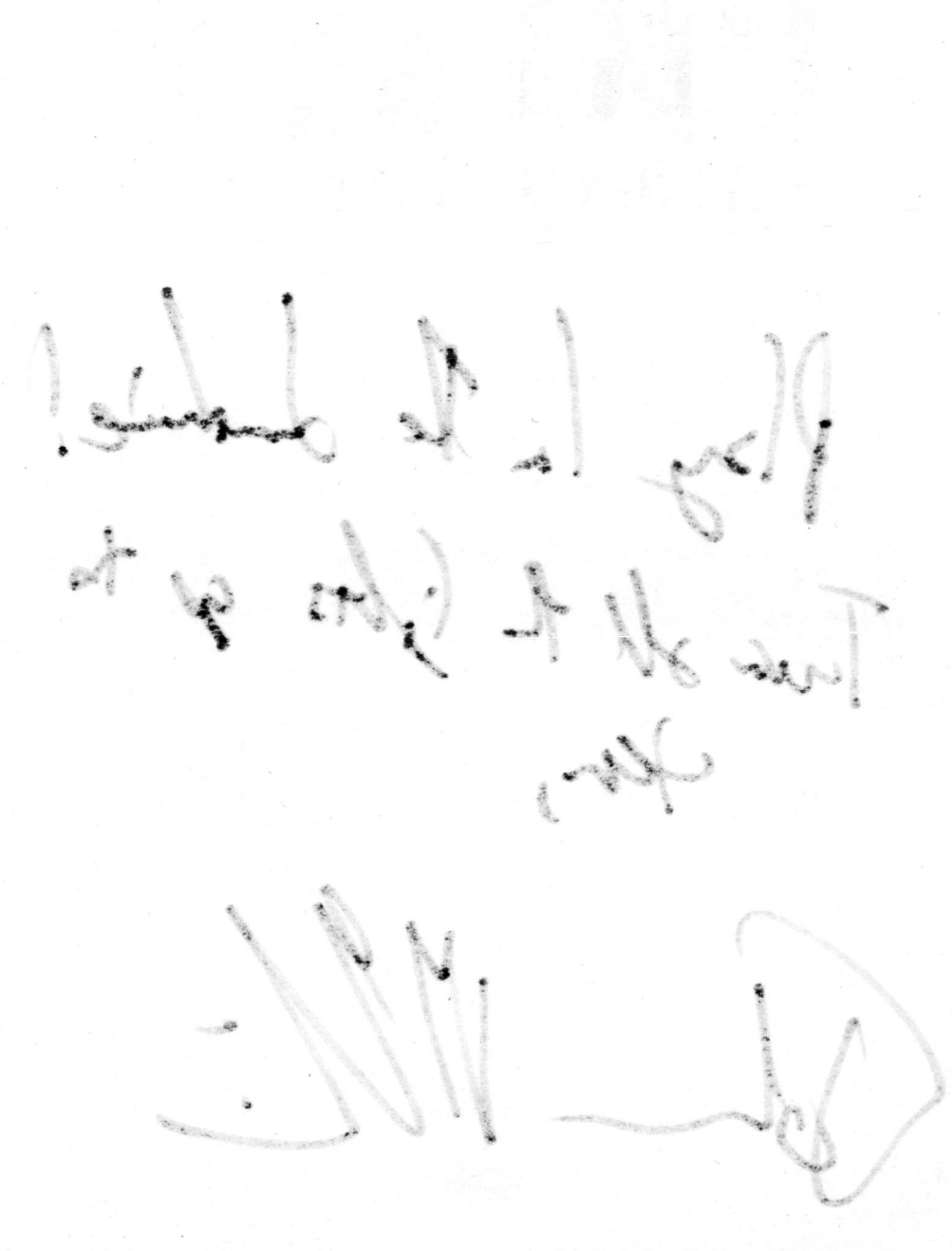

PRINCE

A SIGN O' THE TIMES

JOHN McKIE

First published in the UK in 2025 by Blink Publishing
An imprint of Bonnier Books UK
5th Floor, HYLO,
103–105 Bunhill Row,
London, EC1Y 8LZ

A CIP catalogue of this book is available from the British Library.

Hardback ISBN – 9781785121944
Trade Paperback ISBN – 9781785121968

Also available as an ebook and an audiobook

1 3 5 7 9 10 8 6 4 2

Design and Typeset by Envy Design Ltd
Printed and bound in Great Britain by Clays Ltd, Elcograf S.p.A.

The authorised representative in the EEA is
Bonnier Books UK (Ireland) Limited.
Registered office address: Floor 3, Block 3, Miesian Plaza,
Dublin 2, D02 Y754, Ireland
compliance@bonnierbooks.ie
www.bonnierbooks.co.uk

To Liz Ford. Forever In My Life, D.V.

CONTENTS

TIMELINE

7 June 1958 – Prince Rogers Nelson born in Minneapolis to musicians John L. Nelson and Mattie Della Shaw.

24 September 1968 – John and Mattie formally divorce having announced plans to separate in 1965.

1971 – Prince forms his band Grand Central while at high school with best friend André Anderson and cousin Charles 'Chazz' Smith on drums.

1976 – Prince leaves the band and works on demo tapes with Minneapolis producer Chris Moon.

1 September 1977 – The *St Paul Dispatch* reports that Prince has signed a record deal with Warner Brothers Records.

7 April 1978 – Prince's debut album *For You* is released.

8 October 1980 – The third album, *Dirty Mind*, with its provocative cover of Prince in suspenders and containing controversial songs 'Head' and 'Sister', is released.

10 December 1980 – Prince plays The Ritz in New York on the Dirty Mind tour. KISS, Andy Warhol and Nile Rodgers are in attendance.

22 March 1981 – Prince returns to The Ritz in New York, this time with Mick Jagger in the audience.

16 August 1981 – Prince starts recording at Sunset Sound Recorders in Los Angeles, working on the track 'Private Joy' from the forthcoming album *Controversy*.

9 October 1981 – Prince and his band, including bassist Mark Brown making his debut, support the Rolling Stones at the LA Coliseum and are booed off stage after three songs.

27 October 1982 (7 March 1983 in the UK) – Prince's fifth album *1999* is released, featuring the US hit singles 'Little Red Corvette', '1999' and 'Delirious'. It is the first to be credited to Prince and The Revolution.

25 June 1984 (13 July in the UK) – The soundtrack album *Purple Rain* is released, spawning three number-one singles and staying at number one on the Billboard album charts for 24 consecutive weeks.

27 July 1984 (31 August in the UK and Ireland) – The movie *Purple Rain* is released, grossing more than $70m.

4 November 1984   Prince begins his biggest tour to date of arenas and sports stadia.

28 January 1985 – Prince wins three American Music Awards in Los Angeles. Later that same night, in the same city, 'We Are the World' is recorded with some of the biggest names in the American music industry. Prince is absent.

25 March 1985 – Prince wins an Academy Award for Best Original Song Score for the *Purple Rain* soundtrack (but not Original Song, which is won by Stevie Wonder's 'I Just Called to Say I Love You').

7 April 1985 – Prince wraps up the Purple Rain tour at Miami's Orange (renamed Purple for the night) Bowl Stadium. It does not go any further than North America.

22 April 1985 – Prince releases his seventh album, *Around the World in a Day*.

5 February 1986 – The single 'Kiss' from *Parade*, the final album by Prince and the Revolution, is released and reaches number one on the Billboard Hot 100.

1 July 1986 – The film *Under the Cherry Moon* makes its world premiere in Sheridan, Wyoming, a day before its US release.

17 October 1986 – Prince's publicist issues a press release announcing that he has parted company with the Revolution.

30 March 1987 – *Sign o' the Times*, Prince's second double album and his first LP since *Controversy* to be released under solely his name, is released.

8 May 1987 – The Sign o' the Times tour opens in Stockholm's Isstadion after three weeks of rehearsals at Birmingham's NEC.

29 June 1987 – Prince plays the final date of the Sign o' the Times tour in Antwerp's SportPaleis arena. He later cancels proposed dates at Wembley Stadium and plans to take the tour home to North America.

11 September 1987 – Paisley Park Studios in Chanhassen in the Minneapolis suburbs is opened. Prince is absent, performing at the MTV Awards in LA.

29 October 1987 – The *Sign o' the Times* movie premieres in Detroit before being distributed nationwide the following month.

November 1987 – *The Black Album* is withdrawn from sale, at Prince's request after promotional copies have been sent out to select critics.

31 December 1987 – Prince and his new band play a homeless benefit at Paisley Park and are joined on stage by Miles Davis.

10 May 1988 – Prince releases *Lovesexy*, with his naked appearance on the cover and its continuous tracklist.

5 October 1992 – Prince's album featuring his new symbol is released across Europe (13 October in the US).

7 June 1993 – Prince turns 35 and decides to stop using his name, replacing it with an unpronouncable symbol.

16 August 1994 – 'Prince' releases his final album for Warner Brothers, *Come*.

14 February 1996 – Prince marries dancer Mayte Garcia.

16 October 1996 – Their son Amiir is born with type-2 Pfeiffer syndrome and dies six days later.

16 May 2000 – He stops using the symbol as his name and reverts back to Prince.

June 2000 – Divorce proceedings between Prince and Mayte Garcia begin.

December 2001 – Prince marries second wife, Manuela Testolini (reports suggest both Christmas Day and New Year's Eve, neither confirmed).

8 February 2004 – Prince duets with Beyoncé at the 46th Annual Grammys.

15 March 2004 – Prince and (posthumously) George Harrison are both inducted into the Rock'n'Roll Hall of Fame.

24 May 2006 – Divorce proceedings between Prince and Manuela Testolini begin.

4 February 2007 – Prince plays the half-time show at Super Bowl XLI at Miami Gardens, Florida.

1 August–21 September 2007 – Prince plays a record-breaking twenty-one nights at the O2 Arena in London with tickets priced at £31.21 each.

12 December 2015 – His thirty-ninth and final album, *HITnRUN Phase Two*, is released.

15 February 2016 – Prince collaborator Denise 'Vanity' Matthews dies from kidney failure. The following night, he pays tribute at the opening date of A Piano and Microphone tour in Melbourne.

14 April 2016 – The tour ends with a final date at the Fox Theatre in Atlanta, Georgia.

21 April 2016 – Prince is found dead at home at Paisley Park. NASA (through a telescopic image of the supernova remnant, Crab Nebula), London's Wembley Arena, the eight-lane I-35W Mississippi River bridge and Lowry Avenue Bridge (both in Minneapolis), and the *New Yorker* magazine front cover all turn purple. He doesn't leave a will.

INTRODUCTION

As far as anni mirabiles go, Prince had a few. Certainly 2004 wasn't too shabby: duetting at the Grammys with Beyoncé; a show-closing guest spot guitar solo at the Rock'n'Roll Hall of Fame so memorable that people had almost forgotten he was inducted into said hall earlier the same evening; and *Musicology*, for some fans his greatest twenty-first-century album, was released.

Then there was 2007, which started with a residency at the Rio in Las Vegas (where Prince had an adjoining suite to Sir Elton John); giving what, by common consent, is the greatest half-time Super Bowl show in history; a record-breaking twenty-one nights at London's O2, which included on-stage spots from guests Amy Winehouse and Sir Elton; and confounding the music industry by giving away his *Planet Earth* album free in the UK with the *Mail on Sunday* newspaper.

If you ask most casual observers what his finest hour was – and an hour of achievements in Prince world could mean twelve months in another artist's career – the popular choice would be 1984: the release of *Purple Rain* the movie; the soundtrack album; a tour of North American stadia; the writing of 'Manic Monday' and 'Nothing Compares 2 U'; finishing the recording of *Around the World in a Day* on Christmas Eve; and starting work with his long-time collaborator, the saxophonist Eric Leeds. On top of that, the combined forces of Chaka Khan, Grandmaster Melle Mel, Stevie Wonder (on harmonica) and producer Arif Mardin took Prince's 1979 song *I Feel For You* to number one in the UK, his first.

If you are a less than casual observer, here's another theory. He was never better than in 1987.

That year, he was coming off a flop movie, *Under the Cherry Moon*, but had made a great artistic leap forward with its soundtrack album, released as *Parade* (Eric Leeds calls it 'Sign o' the Times Part 1'). He then recorded a triple album, editing it down into a double. He and Sheila E assembled a brand-new band to replace the Revolution, arguably his most beloved musical sidekicks, before touring Europe – but not the US – in what tour manager Jeff Mason called 'the best tour the world never saw'. Prince directed and pretty much distributed a film, *Sign o' the Times*, bracketed alongside other classic concert movies like Jonathan Demme's *Stop Making Sense* and Martin Scorsese's *The Last Waltz*. He wrote and recorded another album (*The Black Album*) before shelving it at the eleventh hour, thus giving it a legend that even he – as the King of Mystery – couldn't have planned. He also opened his own working studio, and later home, Paisley Park; he wrote songs and recorded with Bonnie Raitt, Mavis Staples, Madonna and George Clinton; he conceived a new motion picture idea (albeit glossing over that, by 1990, he would lose interest in *Graffiti Bridge*); and he finished his year singing 'Auld Lang Syne' at a New Year's Eve party with Miles Davis for a $200-a-head homeless benefit. Even though it was their only US gig with that band, it was just another day. Even for Prince, it was quite the year.

Nothing about *Sign o' the Times* makes sense.

One of the few musicians in the popular music era who can and does play all his own instruments finally finds a band worthy and willing to go toe to toe with him, to challenge him creatively, to help him write hits and to join him in a film which makes him the biggest pop star in the world. Then he splits the band up.

He finds the first woman with whom he can live and, just as she helps him build a life, home and a band around her, both implode. He pulls the detonation chord himself.

Coming off a flop movie, and two albums which commercially underwhelmed after his biggest hit, he reacts not by retreating or retiring. He works on three, possibly five, albums. One of these albums is a triple.

Things were never straightforward in the Prince universe. Then again, neither was he.

That same triple album was nixed by the record company, after he himself abandoned another two, possibly four, album projects. If you're struggling to keep up, few could.

What happened next?

Sign o' the Times happened next.

When the double album was released in March 1987, critical consensus ruled that the man was at the peak of his powers.

That was masking trouble on several fronts. The woman he'd asked to marry had moved out for good. Band members with whom he'd forged most of his success had all gone (bar one). And he had just written and directed a film whose only award was a 'Razzie', the golden Raspberry for Worst Film of the Year, shared with *Howard the Duck*.

Out of that wreckage came one of the greatest albums of

its age, an album routinely hailed as one of modern music's game-changers.

Before the decade was out, *Time Out* would call *Sign...* the greatest of all time.

On its thirty-three-and-a-third anniversary, BBC Radio 6 Music played the entire album in full, with one BBC Culture online piece at the time asking: 'Is this the greatest album of all time?'

Of his thirty-nine studio albums, *Purple Rain* may have been his commercial peak, but *Sign o' the Times* has its own summit.

What kind of person made *Sign o' the Times*?

Without analysing his upbringing, his personality, his friends, his enemies, his contemporaries and his character, you can't understand how he got there.

Sign... doesn't happen the way it did without the Revolution splitting, and that possibly doesn't happen without the failure of Prince's second film *Under the Cherry Moon*, which doesn't happen without the success of his first film *Purple Rain*, which doesn't happen without being initially bankrolled by the Triple Threat Tour in support of *1999*. This in turn owes much of its existence to a finessing of the techniques and musical ideas first expressed on *Dirty Mind*, an album borne from Prince heading home to Minneapolis and making a shocking album sleeve dressed in suspenders.

That's before you pay due homage to those paving the way for Prince, from Sly Stone and Joni Mitchell to James Brown and Carlos Santana. To understand Prince without acknowledging his deep connections to these artists paints an incomplete picture.

How much did he rely on others' talent? And to what extent was the man who memorably started one of his most famous songs singing 'In this life, you're on your own' a solo artist?

He could sing over four octaves, write hit songs for himself and other artists, produce his own material and that of others, and play many instruments – drums, piano, bass, rhythm and lead guitar – and mastered all of them.

How did he do it?

Prince: A Sign o' the Times is an attempt to find out, in part, how.

The reason the answers are 'in part' is because Prince focused on creating his own universe and he liked to muddy the route to his process so that no one – journalists, bandmates, family members, girlfriends – could reach it.

As any music writer knows from the paucity of interviews, or the half-truths and evasions he uttered in the rare ones he did, Prince's music had mystery at the heart of it. This was very much by design.

Pretty much everything was by design.

*

This book is an attempt to uncover the parts of himself the most self-actualised pop star of all time was willing to reveal – and some parts he wasn't. He used to kid around in interviews. His statement 'If you want to know me, listen to my music' is as earnest as he often wanted to get. Some who spoke to him on a private basis about religion, or guitars, or the mistreatment of black artists by the music industry, or drum machines, found someone much chattier.

The book in some respects is based on, and inspired by, a failure on the part of its author.

Writing a feature for the BBC News website on the record's 30th anniversary led to some interesting discoveries – what the album meant to fans, how it had lasted, whom it had influenced, Prince's own working techniques – but the more sources I approached, the less clarity there was about the man who made it.

Every effort was made to reach those who were around when

Sign o' the Times was made, but it quickly became apparent that Prince can be understood by collaborators from his entire career, from his debut record *For You* to his passing in April 2016.

So while this work aims to focus on the era around *Sign...*, the lead-up to its creation and the near thirty years after that that he spent making music all help to signpost us to him.

It also touches on those moments where Prince played himself back into the centre of music's conversation – his performance at the George Harrison tribute at the 2004 Rock'n'Roll Hall of Fame and the 2007 half-time Super Bowl show. And the time Prince got the world talking about him because he refused to let them use his name.

What you're reading is about *Sign o' the Times*, and, yes, that's the wrong title. Unlike his own memoir, which used Prince-speak, the reader was considered, and so the CND symbol is replaced with an 'o' and, unlike Prince's song titles and written correspondences, 'eye', '2' and 'u' are spelt in the boring, conventional ways, and the English is spelt in British not American English.

This is a book about Prince and sadly limited by how much his voice can be used.

The people who were in and out of Prince's life, and some who weren't but have interesting things to say about the man or the music scene at the time, are part of his story. Bandmates, girlfriends, staff, shoemakers, admirers and acquaintances are featured, while an attempt to understand Prince is incomplete without an attempt to view his craft alongside other musical contemporaries and influences. Musicians who worked with James Brown, Miles Davis, Joni Mitchell, Sly Stone and David Bowie (for whom Prince threw a party the same year *Sign...* was released) also feature.

Starting during lockdown, the journey took in conversations

with interviewees in many outposts of Los Angeles and Minneapolis – the two cities where the record was predominantly made. (One song also involved Mississippi by way of Paris and Utrecht, a big place in Sign o' the Times lore.) There were also FaceTime or Zoom calls to Manchester, England; Brisbane, Australia; Las Vegas, Nevada; Knoxville, Tennessee; Las Cruces, New Mexico; San Antonio, Texas; Charlotte, North Carolina; Fountain Hills, Arizona; and Sheridan, Wyoming (another place with its own bookmark in Prince folklore), as well as Italy, Sweden and the Netherlands.

If you're playing Prince interview bingo, the following phrases are likely to come up before house is called.

'A musical virtuoso.'

'Working for him was like walking on eggshells.'

'I never saw him eat.'

'I never saw him sleep.'

'He always dressed as if he was about to go on stage.'

'His work ethic was like no other, and certainly no one who worked for him.'

'He loved women.'

'He was incredibly competitive.'

'He was a joker.'

All of these in one shape or another form the making of *Sign o' the Times*.

Prince has some devoted fans, many of whom were colleagues. Others were less keen.

Very few phrases are as instructive to the nature of Prince's personality as the one often heard from his friends, colleagues, girlfriends and bandmates – correction: ex-girlfriends and ex-bandmates: 'He moved on.'

Anniversary album reissues? Tours to celebrate the landmark of a decades-old album gone by? Acoustic reworkings of previous hits committed to a deluxe edition release? Not his style.

When he was in a hole, he just redirected his energies forward.

He met those two imposters of triumph and disaster the same way. In the white-hot heat of *Purple Rain*'s success, he and his band the Revolution already had written and recorded *Around the World in a Day*. When *Purple Rain* won him an Academy Award for Best Song collection on 25 March 1985, a brand-new album was out the following month.

In his personal relationships, where the fixed status of single or otherwise was, to put it politely, a little blurred, Prince was rarely without company.

It's hard to view the double album, its movie and tour as a masterplan as Prince didn't share plans.

As his indefatigable personal assistant at the time, Karen Krattinger, observes, she only knew about *Sign o' the Times'* existence when the album sleeve was being shot. The chapters serve as a guide around the sixteen tracks which showcase his music, his personality and his musical personality.

The book looks at the man who made this record, and the tour and movie that shaped a singular career – and how and why he did it.

CHAPTER I

SIGN O' THE TIMES

Following Purple Rain with a dampener ... Prince and Michael Jackson, two Midwest pop comets born in 1958 ... and another, Madonna ... and the sleeves that kept the world – and Prince's dad – guessing

Following Purple Rain with a dampener

Even for a light comedy, it was the wrong kind of laughter. *Under the Cherry Moon* was Prince's sequel to *Purple Rain*. After shooting in France, test screenings were scheduled for California and, during one scene where comic foil Jerome Benton's character Tricky had knelt down to pray for his wingman Christopher Tracy to be spared from death, laughter filled the cinema.

An upset Prince exited, quickly.

The laughter he heard was something he had grown up with after being teased at school for his height. This time, he couldn't disappear – because 1984's *Purple Rain* had turned Prince into one of the world's biggest stars and this was its follow-up.

When he walked out of the screening of Pasadena, filmgoers started following Prince out the theatre.

The box office returns for Prince's big sequel two years on were certainly not better. The 1984 film had grossed $68m, but 1986's *Under the Cherry Moon* stalled at $10m.

The film's romantic lead, Kristin Scott Thomas, had brought a date, her mother, to the premiere of her first-ever movie. Kristin recollected the evening on *The Graham Norton Show*. As the end credits rolled, Deborah Scott Thomas patted her daughter's knee and said: 'Don't worry, darling. It'll be better next time.'

The following year things would get worse for Prince before they got better – arguably better than they had been in his career.

He dispensed with the services of the Revolution, the band who had helped his rise to fame, and at the start of 1987 had split up with his fiancée, Susannah Melvoin.

It would not have been unrealistic at that point for Prince to have been written off. Instead, he released what most regard as his most ambitious and creatively satisfying record to date.

His career up until then was example after example of confounding expectations. Being five foot two would be a recurring sore throughout his childhood. His own name was one his father John chose for him based after his own jazz trio, which had performed to a high standard but not one high enough that John wouldn't have had to go and work full-time for Honeywell computers instead. His mother Mattie Della Shaw would also have to go from jazz singing to full-time social work. This drive to determine his own music career led to him teaching himself several instruments and the ways of production. He signed his first record deal aged seventeen.

Things didn't catch fire overnight.

After albums three and four gained some momentum, Prince

landed his big break with 1982's *1999* album before another huge leap forward a couple of years later.

Purple Rain would make him a global superstar with 25m sales and his first number-one singles, as well as Academy Awards and Grammys. Alongside the Revolution and Susannah, his first serious girlfriend, things were looking up.

The next two albums would not match these sales.

The before, during and after of *Sign o' the Times* is quite the rollercoaster. In early 1987, Prince was without his band and fiancée.

What followed was not just another leap forward, but his masterpiece.

And after *Sign o' the Times*?

Some of his most erratic decisions which would have derailed other careers.

An aborted album, leading to hundreds of thousands of records being pulled overnight.

A tour, some say his best ever, abruptly curtailed before it reached his home country.

And, before the year was out, the second flop movie in a row.

The opening to *Sign o' the Times*, the title track, would be thought of by many as Prince's most socially conscious song to date. When it was being created, the world was in a difficult place. Social and racial unrest, natural disasters and the implosion of the space programme (tied into the US's sense of itself) were all bubbling up.

Prince and Susannah hopped on a plane to LA on 13 March 1986. The *Minneapolis Star and Tribune* was running a series of articles about local murders. The main suspects were in a gang called the Disciples.

He headed to his then studio of choice, Sunset Sound. By Wednesday the 16th, after a ten-hour session at Studio 3, he had finished his new song with lyrics detailing all the above news stories, with the additional horror of Hurricane Annie destroying a church. In late June 1986, Hurricane Bonnie led to devastation on the Gulf Coast from Texas to Louisiana, with twenty-five homes, trailers and cabins in south-western Louisiana destroyed, resulting in about $1 million in damages. As both Prince's parents originally hailed from the Pelican State, you could speculate – but struggle to prove as he rarely discussed lyrics with anyone other than Susannah – that 'Bonnie' became 'Annie' here.

A West Coast visit in July with fiancée Susannah, his most serious relationship to this point, was cut short after an earthquake measuring 6.0 on the Richter scale. As the couple checked out of the Bellagio, a copy of the *LA Times* on the front desk delivered more bad news: the AIDS epidemic was out of control. 'He said "Something's happening to the world",' Susannah relayed to The Current podcast.

Indeed it was.

The opening track of *Sign...* starts with Prince shrieking 'Oh yeah', but that opening yelp of positivity is misleading. This is a funky record, but one with downbeat themes. It could even, lyrically at least, be categorised as blues.

No other big hitters in 1987 – not U2 with *The Joshua Tree*, not George Michael with *Faith*, certainly not Michael Jackson with *Bad*, not even Public Enemy with their debut *Yo! Bum Rush the Show* – would open their records with a song featuring AIDS, the Space Shuttle *Challenger* crash, crack addiction and gun crime among inner-city street gangs.

Prince goes from AIDS to heroin addiction and gang gun crime. And that's just the first verse. What had got into him? He had a lot on his mind.

The title track and first single opens the double album. Prince had never sung about AIDS before. Few pop stars had, even though actor Rock Hudson had died from AIDS two years previously. HIV was around Prince in the crew and his record company. 'I had an assistant in his early twenties,' relates Marylou Badeaux, an executive from Warners, 'and he got sick. My boss said, "I don't think he will be back. He has AIDS." I said, "What's that?" This wasn't that long before *Sign o' the Times*. When Prince spoke about it in that song, I understood what he was singing.'

'We had a couple of crew members who were living with AIDS,' confirms then bodyguard Harlan Austin. Prince's drummer Sheila E had a stylist who quietly left the crew, but no one knows how much that informed the lyrics. 'He died young and that would have been the first person [we knew],' recalls Prince's then tour manager Alan Leeds, 'but whether that influenced the song, I don't know. It was in the news.'

'He was an information junkie,' adds Austin. 'He would take on as much information as possible. You just listen to the lyrics on that particular song. He's talking about a lot of current events.' Nothing – relationships, the state of the world – was more important to Prince than his work.

The song displayed Prince's prowess in the studio, his virtuoso guitar skills and drum programming, and the mastery of his four-octave range. It is also noticeably spare for a hit single, another example of the singer's respect for the less-is-more principle. Just as he had with the opening and title track of *Dirty Mind*, he pared back with most of the song consisting of just a state-of-the-art Fairlight CMI synthesiser, Linn M-1 drum machine and guitar.

'It's such a simple, cut-down version of a song,' reflects Harald Michael Danker, his monitor engineer at the time. 'Linn drum machine, guitar, piano. It seems like often that's all he ever needed. Some of his greatest stuff was only a handful of tracks.

Records nowadays [are] fifty tracks, overdubs and overdubs. He was able to make this incredible music very simply.'

Around half a minute from the end, the song (also featured in the movie) features a battery of rhythm in the style of the drum-and-bugle corps marching band from Prince's childhood, transposed from Louisiana to Minneapolis, according to his cousin Chazz Smith.

'Me and Prince would be going "Look at those dudes drumming". And spinning the sticks and clicking on the side of the drum. We were going "We can't do that." These cats were trained. Prince just said, "I'm going to learn how this dude is doing this."'

The song ends on a hopeful note, with an exhortation to fall in love, get married and give birth. If it's a boy, the plan is he'll be called Nate. To bring a baby into a world with natural disasters, guns, drugs and AIDS shows a sunny disposition in a sky full of clouds. He was looking at grim headlines in the news, and his summer 1986 movie *Under the Cherry Moon* had just bombed, but Prince was used to being written off. 'Sign o' the Times' was the start of the fightback.

The song itself would go on to meet comparisons with Marvin Gaye's *What's Going On*. Unlike that record – which Berry Gordy famously begged the singer not to release, calling it 'the worst thing I've ever heard in my life' before it became the fastest-selling single in Motown's history – Prince's record company was keener.

Lenny Waronker, the A&R director at Warner Brothers, was invited to a meeting with Prince's management team. 'Bob [Cavallo, Prince's manager] said "Why don't you play Lenny the single?"' Waronker's first thought? 'He's gone to another level. Unbelievable.

'It must have been a month before the final album was done.

He played me "Sign o' the Times" and it killed me. It reminded me of "Papa Was a Rolling Stone". I looked at him and said, "That's a number one record". I suggested he add acoustic guitar on it, which would make it more country blues. He looked at me… "I don't think so.'"

The song would reach number three in the Billboard Hot 100, but topped the R&B charts and would go on to be covered by, among others, stadium rock acts Simple Minds and Muse, Chaka Khan (whose version was produced by Prince acolytes Jimmy Jam and Terry Lewis), Nina Simone (who waggishly sang 'We'll call her Nina / If she's a girl'), and jazz musicians pianist Robert Glasper and drummer Billy Cobham, the latter particularly tickling Chazz Smith.

'That was testimony to me. Here's this genius musician, here's another musician's work. He complimented Prince with that. That's dope. You have arrived when the drummer of all drummers covers you.'

And Nate? 'My hunch is that it's a name he liked,' says Prince's engineer at the time, Susan Rogers.

Writer Mi-Ling Stone Poole, who thinks seemingly with some justification that she may have been the inspiration for 'Little Red Corvette', dated Prince just after his debut album *For You* came out. He was from the north side of Minneapolis, she from the twin city of St Paul. 'The north side was dangerous. I dated Nate who lived in the north side, Phelps Park. When girls from St Paul would go to the north side, they didn't like it.' 'He [Prince] would see me at the club. Nate was the skinniest man I ever dated. This was the first time he'd picked me up and said "Who's that skinny guy I always used to see you with?" I remember the conversation as if it was yesterday. We used to laugh and joke all the time. "His name is Nate." He said, "Nate?" and gave this funny look.

The more likely Nate is the son of the model Janice Dickinson who married Simon Fields, the producer of Prince's videos and the *Sign o' the Times* movie, in 1987. When with his young son, Fields was hanging out with Prince in the early hours just after the song was released.'He [Nate] was really young and he [Prince] was really sweet with him,' recalls Fields. He asked Prince directly and received the usual raised eyebrow.

'Is this my Nate?'

'What do you think?... Yeah.'

Prince and Michael Jackson, two Midwest pop comets born in 1958

If Prince was under pressure that year, another pop star had an equally big target on his back.

Prince had delivered a movie sequel to *Purple Rain* in 1986, but by the autumn of 1987, Michael Jackson had to execute a much bigger music follow–up: to the biggest-selling album of all time. (In the meantime, as well as Prince, and stars like Madonna and Whitney Houston, Michael's little sister Janet had become the competition with her third album, 1986's *Control*.)

Back in the mists of 1982, Prince released the *1999* double album in October, with the title track and 'Little Red Corvette' breakthrough hits on MTV rotation and four million sales turning him into a bona-fide, *Rolling Stone* cover-fronting star. The following month, Michael followed up his 1979 solo debut *Off the Wall*. And, by 1983, Jackson moved into a field of one: the biggest star pop had ever witnessed.

In between *Thriller* (which sold 66 million copies) and its follow-up, 1987's *Bad*, Prince reeled off a hit movie with an Academy Award and 25m-selling soundtrack (*Purple Rain*), *Around the World in a Day*, *Parade* and, in March 1987, *Sign o' the Times.* Were the pair contemporaries or competitors? Friends or sworn rivals?

Yes, it seems, to all four.

Purple Rain in particular had got Jackson's attention. He wanted Prince to duet on the title track of his next album, *Bad*, which was five years in the making. He had been circling Prince for a while, and vice versa.

The offer from Jackson to duet preoccupied Prince a little less. Susannah Melvoin remembers his response. As she told writer Touré, Prince took the tape back to the studio, re-recorded his version and sent it back to Jackson's team, suggesting the song they should have recorded. This was not the last time he did this, but it was the last he heard of a Jackson–Prince duet.

The song's opening lines – 'Your butt is mine/Gonna take you right' – had not gone down well. Prince told Nandy McClean, a dancer with her sister Maya in early 2000s, 'I just read the first line and said "I'm out".'

While MJ was preoccupied by Prince, Prince's attitude to Michael, aside from the duet, could be summed up in stages: adulation, aspiration, exasperation, irritation, mild ridicule, bouts of disinterest and finally admiration and appreciation, which became more comfortable for him to express after Jackson's passing in 2009.

As a child, he adored him.

It is well known that Prince learned to play piano aged seven. He was in a band by twelve and had mastered guitar and drums the following year. What's less well known is why he picked up the guitar in the first place.

Albert Magnoli, the director of *Purple Rain*, explains: 'Prince told me when he saw Michael Jackson on television, it made an enormous impression on him. He told me that one of the reasons why he learned to play guitar the way he did was that it gave him something that Michael Jackson didn't have. He recognised that Michael Jackson could dance his butt off. "If I play guitar, it gets me in a different space from Michael Jackson." It was a calculated move.'

At fifteen, Prince and his band performed the Jackson 5's 'Dancing Machine' at an early outdoor park gig in St Paul. He studied him too. In the *Purple Rain* era, he, lighting director LeRoy Bennett and manager Steve Fargnoli flew by private jet to check out the Jacksons' Victory tour, recalls Bennett, 'just to see the opening night to make sure we knew our stuff before they even started'.

From the monumental success of *Thriller*, MJ had got under Prince's skin in the way few others had. This could be Prince's competitive instincts, but it could also be dated to a 1983 performance by James Brown at the Beverly Theatre in Los Angeles. Brown had Jackson on stage and Jackson spied Prince at the back of the auditorium, inviting him on stage to join one of his heroes. It would not be Prince's finest live moment as the unprepared Minnesotan was piggybacked down the aisle on bodyguard Chick Huntsberry's back and played a guitar with faulty sound, before giving up and dancing awkwardly, and then knocking over a stage prop of a lamp-post as he exited.

Jackson 1, Prince 0.

The original DVD footage omitted Prince's contribution, at his behest. Lisa Janzen, who then worked for Prince's management team, recalls a conversation between Prince's friend, on-off girlfriend and bandmate Sheila E and her friend Lionel Richie, who showed her the video. She recalls: 'Prince left the building and says, "As soon as that guy comes out, run him over."'

This may – or may not – have been a joke.

'He perceived that Michael had set him up with an out-of-tune guitar.'

Singer Anthony Hamilton says that, by the 2000s, Prince had mellowed and laughed at the clip on YouTube with guests at his home. Back in the mid-80s, things were more intense. Janzen was with Sheila at the Beverly Hills Hotel. 'He'd been asked to Michael's house and they made a deal. "Call me in an hour so if I need to get out of there…"'

One hour later, Sheila called Prince. His response? 'You thought *I* was crazy. Get me out of here…'

Around that time, Prince bailed from the recording of the charity single 'We are the World', co-ordinated by Lionel Richie, Quincy Jones and Michael Jackson. He sent Sheila E in his place. It frustrated his close lieutenants. 'All he needed was to show up with [Journey's] Steven Perry and Quincy Jones,' says longtime soundman Scottie Baldwin. 'That would have changed the entire trajectory of his career.'

Instead, that same night, Prince ventured out to Carlos N Charlies' nightclub on Sunset Boulevard, where his security fell out with paparazzi. Coverage of this would guarantee years of bad press. 'I still think it [passing on the collaboration] was a bad decision,' argues tour manager Alan Leeds. 'Even though he devoted another song to the album, the song ['4 The Tears in Your Eyes'] isn't remembered but 'We are the World' is. Musicologists will one day want to know why Prince wasn't in the room.'

Susan Rogers considers that Michael Jackson did not pre-occupy Prince's thoughts often. 'We checked out his work. We'd listen to it, we'd talk about it. Michael was his rival clearly, but I'm going to go out on a limb… I don't think Prince considered him to be a musical rival. I don't think he copied Michael. My hunch was that Michael was Prince's rival from the perspective of the public's love.'

Musically, they were in different lanes. 'It annoyed him,' says Lisa Janzen, 'when people would compare them. He didn't feel they were in the same hemisphere. He was a musician first and a performer second.'

Prince, with various instruments at his fingertips, was a more instinctive musician. Producer James 'Jam' Harris (henceforth Jimmy Jam), who worked with both men, says: 'Michael knew what he wanted to hear. He would go to the keyboard player and say "can you play it like this?" Prince was very spontaneous. Michael would spend four days deciding if the handclaps were loud enough."

Both men held an uneasy truce when editor Eva Gardos was mixing the sound at Teddeo Studios for 1986's *Under the Cherry Moon*. 'Michael Jackson came in and they played ping pong because there's a lot of down time. And Prince beat him solidly. He was a lot more macho than a guy like Michael.'

Lori Elle Werner, from Prince's early '90s *Diamonds & Pearls* era, had danced in Jackson's video for 'The Way You Make Me Feel'. 'He probably didn't love that,' admits Robia Scott, the 'Pearl' to Lori Elle's 'Diamond'. 'He hated us doing some other artist's video, especially Michael Jackson. If someone said "Michael Jackson", he would give that little look, that scowl – the same look he would give his bandmates if they played a wrong note.'

The *Bad* duet may not have happened but there was another near miss. Some time in the early '90s, the King of Pop made concrete plans to head for Paisley Park to collaborate. It was concrete in the sense that Sal Greco, in charge of logistics at the studio, was making phone calls about recording equipment. 'Prince and Michael were going to work together and we were talking to them and their trucks were going to leave and we were going to change consoles and he [Prince] said "Stop!". It was very close. We were talking to his people about what equipment they wanted. They were going to bring another console.'

Around 1993, Prince's then drummer, Michael Bland,

remembers 'packages [that] would show up at Paisley Park that just say "MJJ Productions". They just put them in mailboxes and Prince would put the video cassette in and call us to his office to watch VHS tapes of original real Jackson 5 concerts with the numbers rolling on it. Michael Jackson would just send these old video tapes of these old shows – Sly [Stone] on *Portrait of a Legend*, on *ABC Live*, on *Midnight Special*. That was exciting. Before the internet.'

Skip Johnson, Prince's tour manager in the early '90s, remembers 'more of a competitive atmosphere. Prince once told me he had the fax number of Michael's ranch and that he would have reviews and other accolades of Prince's work faxed over'. In 2007, as a guest of will.i.am, Jackson attended the 3121 tour residency in Las Vegas and Prince jumped on his table and played bass aggressively in his face.

For all that the rivalry of the stadium-selling two African-American pop stars would sell papers in the '80s, the mutual respect between both men existed. They also chatted backstage after the 2007 gig.

Shelby Johnson was introduced to Jackson on that 3121 tour before the singers disappeared to talk shop. '"Shelby, there's somebody I want you to meet." It was Michael standing there. He [Prince] had a lot of respect for his artistry.' But threatened? 'I don't think Prince was threatened by anybody.'

As someone who wrote and played all his music, Prince had the edge. But Michael Jackson had his own advantages. Business acumen, for one. Don Peake was the Jacksons' accountant for many years before performing the same function for Prince around the *Purple Rain* era. 'The one thing I admired about Michael was that he was very into the business side with his lawyers. Prince delegated that more to management committee. "I have my guys keep me up on the high points."

Michael sat in money meetings and I was impressed by his astuteness to business.'

Michael, like Prince, a student of Freddie Mercury's stage presence, had a magnetism which impressed everyone – even Prince. 'Nobody could hold a candle to Prince's performance level apart from Michael,' contends former Prince employee Craig Rice.

Both men were preoccupied with each other, despite the lack of public statements. Nandy McClean, whose dream, with sister Maya, was to dance for Michael (they danced with Prince in the '00s as the Twinz), remembers Prince occupying a certain amount of rent-free space in Jackson's head. 'I heard a story from a creative close to Michael Jackson that sometimes he would wake up in the middle of the night. Michael Jackson had called him saying "I have got to get this track down or they'll give it to Prince. The universe is dropping musical bombs."'

Prince acknowledged he was the McCleans' second choice. 'He did say to me and Maya "You guys are just working for me until Michael Jackson calls."'

Morris Hayes chuckles when he recalls his boss's reaction in the mid-'90s when they watched Michael on the History tour being shot from under the stage and suddenly appearing, eliciting audience exhilaration without moving. 'He stood there and didn't do nothing and people were falling out, passing out. He's just standing there like a statue.' Prince's reaction? '"You can't do nothing with this dude. You have got to let him have that. Only Michael can do that." He was right. That's respect.'

Photographer Ebet Roberts, who shot both men, places Jackson in a class of one for personal charisma. 'It was 1979, I had to fly to New Orleans. I was taken backstage to meet Michael. That guy's energy almost knocked me over. I have never felt an energy from anywhere else like that.'

Record sales, business smarts, stage presence… Michael may have also outstripped Prince when it came to competitiveness. After Prince played those record-breaking twenty-one nights at London's O2 in 2007, Michael Jackson followed suit; on 5 March 2009, he announced fifty dates at the same venue, scheduled to start on 13 July. But on 25 June, he died at his home in Holmby Hills, Los Angeles, with Propofol and other sedatives in his body.

Prince would pay tribute in the intervening years, playing 'Don't Stop 'Til You Get Enough' regularly in concerts and referring approvingly to MJ in his memoir *The Beautiful Ones* as an alpha. Talk show host Tavis Smiley recalled to Conan O' Brien in June 2016 an early morning-to-dawn conversation with Prince about his admiration for Jackson as an artist. 'The day Michael Jackson passed,' says Bland, 'Sonny [Thompson, guitarist] was with Prince and it had a profound effect on him. That's what Sonny told me.'

Prince clearly had a similarly powerful effect on the King of Pop. 'What's Michael Jackson's son's name?' asks rapper Talib Kweli in reference to his eldest, Michael Joseph Jackson Jr, born in 1997. But his youngest son, born in 2002 and also nicknamed 'Blanket', was christened Prince Michael Jackson Jr. 'Who else could Michael have named his son after but Prince? You mention Prince's name and that shows it all.'

Prince and Madonna

Any conversation about the two major pop stars of the era inevitably leads to a third, also born in the Midwest in 1958.

Madonna arguably had more in common with Prince: a good ear for a pop tune; both prolific workaholics; musical magpie minds; signed to Warner Brothers; and constantly fixed up strong, sexually provocative visual images which helped them get famous as MTV bloomed – and was replaced by a more demure emphasis on spirituality in the twenty-first century. At the start of 1987, they both won at the same award ceremony. Prince won Worst Actor for *Under the Cherry Moon* at the Golden Raspberry Awards (the Razzies), while Madonna was 'honoured' for *Shanghai Surprise*.

Although they both became global megastars with hit movies (Madonna after *Desperately Seeking Susan* in 1985), this was asymptomatic of their hit-and-mainly-miss cinematic track record. But when it came to music in the '80s, it was all gold. All killer, no filler, they took on *Thriller* and inevitably each other.

When the Purple Rain tour rolled into the Inglewood Forum in February 1985, Madonna – who had yet to go on the road – was paying close attention. 'She was sitting next to her choreographer and they were certainly taking notes,' observes Prince's then engineer Peggy McCreary, who was sitting next to her. 'It wasn't a night off.'

Devin DeVasquez, Prince's girlfriend at the time, remembers 'sitting next to Elizabeth Taylor and Madonna. Madonna was watching and studying him.'

'They were friends,' recalls Prince's publicist Robyn Riggs, 'but they were also competitors. Before the decade was out, they would become collaborators.'

'He's great when you get to know him,' Madonna told *Rolling Stone* of Prince in 1989, the year her album *Like a Prayer* was released. 'Charming and funny, in his own way. More than anything, he really comes alive when he's working.' His workaholic instincts would prove useful when they duetted on 'Love Song' from that album.

But although Chester Kamen is credited with the guitar solo on the title track, Prince played on a version which, Sal Greco believes, resides in his vault of unreleased music. 'I don't think she was in the room at the time,' he claims. 'I had to man the facility. Studio A and Studio B at Paisley, from what I remember. She would come in, they would work together.' Only Madonna can confirm what took place after that, says Greco. 'Prince would say "I'll call you". We would leave. She seemed friendly and nice, but I was working with *him*.'

Warner Brothers were delighted the pair were working together. Their then head of press Bob Merlis likens it to country music, where MCA Records would ask Conway Twitty and Loretta Lynn to duet. Fans were less enthused by the end results. 'Love Song' wasn't released as a single.

Paisley Park engineer Mike Kloster ended up having a mishap on a Prince–Madonna duet called 'Cookie Jar'. 'He had to re-record it. I erased half the song and Prince was really cool about that. We ended up having to pay for the studio time [for the re-record].'

Madonna claims she stopped working with him because Minneapolis was cold, even though she hailed from the hardly tropical Michigan. The truth is that two alphas were unlikely to work together too much. 'I never expected too much to come from that,' suggests Alan Leeds of their collaboration. 'They're very similar. They were determined to bump heads.' Leeds concedes that, unlike Prince, Madonna 'developed a personal life'.

In terms of musical talent and versatility, there was no one like Prince. Perhaps because he could do so much himself, one of his strengths was not always collaboration. Madonna would show herself to be a savvy operator in finding the right people to get her where she needed to be, from Nile Rodgers on 1984's *Like a Virgin* to William Orbit on 1998's *Ray of Light*. Her willingness to allow her music to be sculpted in part by collaborators like producers Jellybean Benitez, Babyface, Stuart Price and

Timbaland led to huge worldwide hits. It wasn't something Prince would have countenanced.

That collaboration difference extended to social settings. 'Whenever we went to one of her parties,' remembers hairstylist Max Pinnell, whose work with Herb Ritts helped define early '90s style (Pinnell and Ritts worked with both Madonna and Prince, as well as on the infamous Calvin Klein ad with Mark Wahlberg and Kate Moss), 'it was always her crew and her dancers. She liked her people around. Prince didn't. We were two of the few who were allowed to walk on set with him.'

That doesn't mean Prince didn't rate her, as his '90s drummer Michael Bland discovered in a conversation about her songs.

'Prince changed my opinion about Madonna as an artist. I used to think, like a factory, there was a collective that churned them out. Prince straightened me out about that. "The reason she is so successful is she has co-written almost all of her hits. She knows what she wants to hear." Working with her, she'd say "That's not the right chord" and Prince would hunt and pack until she'd say "That's it!" Her instincts have always been pure. Prince was like, "No, she understands music."'

Jimmy Jam agrees that all three '58 Midwest Comets had a clear idea of what they wanted to hear, and worked hard towards the result. "The thing that they have in common is that they breathe music. It was their oxygen."

Bill Stephney, the first president of Def Jam Recordings, feels she had the edge over Prince in one area. 'She's in the clubs with the Beastie Boys, she's at Danceteria, she's at Peppermint Lounge, she's at all of these places. She felt the sensibility of what other people were listening to. She's been a musical chameleon, she's in the middle of it. Punk, disco… It's amazing to think of what came out of all these faces that were in that stew. She was a part of it.

'You would find Jean-Michel Basquiat, Andy Warhol, Grandmaster Flash and Madonna in the same place.' Prince would go to nightclubs, but not those. Stephney points out that 'he's not going to make himself subordinate to a scene'.

Prince and Madonna nearly had their closest collaboration on celluloid in 1990 when she was selected to play the female lead in *Graffiti Bridge*, with dancer Cat Glover as her love rival. They met at Paisley Park to discuss it, a meeting which soon went south. 'The original script for *Graffiti Bridge* was me, Prince and Madonna, and Sheila E,' Glover told Prince podcast PodcastJuice.net. 'I got a call at the residence and Madonna was there and it was about two or three in the morning.

'They started arguing about the script, and then shoes. Madonna was wearing cowboy boot shoes up to her ankles and he said 'Look at *your* shoes'. Madonna said the script sucked and Prince said, "Cat, can you go to the kitchen and pop some popcorn?" Madonna loved popcorn. Madonna said "I'm going to leave, it's too cold in Minneapolis." He had a party planned for Madonna but Prince's chef made food for Madonna so we all proceeded to the kitchen and she saw all these candles and she said "Are we having a seance?" And she started laughing, and I started laughing. Then they recorded that song "Like a Prayer"and another song [most likely "Love Song"], and then she left.'

After Madonna, Prince's then girlfriend Kim Basinger was pencilled in for the role. 'He was seeing Kim and she was at Paisley a lot and then one day she was gone, which is what happens,' recalls engineer/producer Michael Koppelman.

Novi Novog, who played strings on 'Papa Don't Preach' and remembers her as 'very nice and down to earth', was in the studio with Prince when Madonna's tour was discussed. 'I remember at Sunset they were talking about Madonna's show having a bed on it.' Prince's previous tours and videos had a bed too – as did the room (Sunset Sound Studio 3) where the discussion was taking place.

Both artists, famous for wearing next to nothing in the videos which made them famous, would move their minds on to higher matters after the early '90s. Prince would clamp down on swearing around him and ask Larry Graham to join him to discuss ideas around the Jehovah's Witness religion, while Madonna was open about her enthusiasm for the Kabbalah religion, with her charity shelving plans to build a $15m school in Malawi in 2011.

'Once she got herself established,' suggests Brenda Bennett of Vanity 6, who themselves had a house uniform of lingerie, 'suddenly she wanted to be thought of as a different human being. She became respectable.'

Prince and Madonna would both spend the next quarter of a century selling out stadia with a string of hits, with the loudest singalongs reserved for music from the era when they were in each other's airspace.

Scottie Baldwin, who toured with both artists, argues: that 'when they leave from where they come from and they get to where they want, they end up going into protectionist mode. That could be said of most artists.'

Most artists, of course, were not Prince, Madonna or Michael Jackson.

The sleeves that kept the world – and Prince's dad – guessing

Prince liked to be inscrutable about his own personality. But even before you put the record on the turntable, his sleeves would still offer useful clues.

With his first four albums, he had tried to bare all – or at least the version of 'all' he wanted you to notice: blurry selfie for his '78 debut; a topless shot for the eponymous second album; an even more provocative image in suspenders and raincoat for 1980's *Dirty Mind*; and another arresting portrait flanked by newspaper headlines courting the *Controversy* promised in the title in 1981. By his first double album, *1999*, Prince drew his own cover (this drawing is also rumoured but not confirmed to be the work of his then girlfriend Denise 'Vanity' Matthews). *Purple Rain* established the wish fulfilment of the rock star on a Honda motorbike – he was too small for a Harley Davidson – and, by the following year, he commissioned Doug Henders to draw an animated world for *Around the World in a Day*, with Jeff Katz's black-and-white shots for *Parade* accompanying the black-and-white movie it soundtracked.

Where *Parade*, and the following record *The Black Album*, were minimal, *Sign…*'s sleeve would be more of a production. The record label's art director Laura LiPuma Nash was given licence by Prince to pick photographer Jeff Katz's monochrome cover shot for *Parade*. Although some of the tracks on *Sign…* date back to 1979, the sleeve would be done on the hoof.

'I never even knew he was making an album called *Sign o' the Times* until it was time to do a photoshoot,' remembers his assistant at the time, Karen Krattinger.

Make-up artist Robyn Lynch also got the call on a Sunday night, asking that Prince wanted to be shot against a backdrop of street scene and neon. 'So I made calls, including one of my girlfriends, who was a producer at Chanhassen Dinner Theatre and she was friends with Jessica Lange's sister [Ann], who was a set designer. Everybody started pulling stuff together.'

Karen Krattinger was sent to look at possible backdrops, while Jeff Katz, the in-house photographer, was called to the

Eden Prairie warehouse studio, where Prince was doing most of his work at the time.

'There was not a lot of stuff, apart from the movies, that was pre-planned. There was a spontaneity.' That planned spontaneity led Prince's assistant (Krattinger) to ask his make-up artist (Lynch) for tips. At the time, she was dating an employee of the Chanhassen Dinner Theatre. Tom Butsch would go on to work as an art director for the shows at Disney's parks in Tokyo and Florida, as well as TV shows like *Different Strokes* and *Silver Spoons* in Hollywood. In 1975 – from when the backdrop, which LeRoy Bennett would later adapt for the Sign tour, dates – he was working on shows for the four theatres at Chanhassen Dinner Theatre: Stephen Sondheim's *A Little Night Music, Man of La Mancha*, Peter Shaffer's *Sleuth*, and *Guys and Dolls*, 'so we were really busy.'

Based on a book by legendary Broadway scenic designer and seven-time Tony winner Jo Mielziner, Butsch painted a 30-foot by 16-foot muslin drop stretched out on the floor. 'It would take somebody four days to paint something like that. The advantage of painting on the floor is that your brushes are on sticks. You can have as many people [working] on it.'

He painted other drops, including Times Square and The Alley 'that was much darker with a couple of scenes in the district and this which we referred to as the street drop. It was a heightened New York atmosphere.'

This atmosphere – featuring night-time words like BAR GRILL, HOTEL ROOM, ARCADE, GIRLS! GIRLS! GIRLS! and (unexpectedly) SNOOKER – was selected by Krattinger as the backdrop for the stage. One of Prince's crew had found a blue Pontiac front end from the junk yard and left it in the warehouse. Prince kept it.

His then driver and general fixer Robbie Paster remembers

something missing. 'When he came in to look at the set, it was for the album cover shoot, the car didn't have a licence plate on it. So he comes up to me and says "Robbie, there's no licence plate", so I took the licence plate off my Volkswagen and put it on the thing. CKJ 505.' (For those requiring further details, Paster confirms it as a 'Volkswagen Rabbit, square body, four door, champagne, Burgundy interior... I wasn't making a lot of money.'

The set-up featured Prince's peach drum kit and keyboard on a stage festooned with flowers, the Pontiac front end, the Volkswagen Rabbit licence plate and Pierrot dolls and masks 'he liked at the time', according to LeRoy Bennett, his lighting director and friend. These would feature in the *Sign...* movie, with Prince's Cloud guitar on the floor. The instruments were all peach, a colour Prince would be wearing in a trouser suit with his custom black leather jacket knocked up by his wardrobe team. This would inform the following tour.

'He showed me pictures from the shoot,' remembers Bennett, 'and said "I want the stage to look like that". It was my interpretation of the cover. I understood the premise about bringing that backdrop to life. I wanted to incorporate lights into the set.' As for the artist himself, Prince walked towards the camera and Katz shot him out of focus. His Sunday nights, when he wrote the title track, were often him at his most contemplative. He told the photographer, 'Use that one.'

'He [Katz] had no idea what Prince would have in mind,' Laura LiPuma Nash adds. 'You don't art direct Prince.'

'It was a funky, crazy, urban vibe he was going for, a city vibe. He was into yellow and teal blue colour then [for British readers, this is more Manchester City than Chelsea].' On the floor was his Cloud guitar, peach to match the album's theme colour, designed by Dave Rusan.

LiPuma Nash did get involved again on the sleeve design.

'He didn't want any type on the cover.' Instead, she went with a blue sticker against the peach and black backdrop, informed by Prince's outfits at the time, and peach handwriting in its own font. Lipuma Nash found Prince's usual typographer Margot Chase was busy, so she asked Glenn Parsons.

'The Prince projects were handed around a little bit,' Parsons says now. 'Some people had difficulty dealing with him. They were handed off to various art directors depending on who was around and who dealt with Prince best. Laura got along with him better than anybody. One woman art director said "Don't give me a Prince art project."'

The designer was told to write *Sign o'* (the 'o' was a CND symbol surrounded by quotation marks) *the Times* in a new font. The font was all Prince, as was the direction, as Parsons recalls. 'Prince had his way with everything. It would have been Prince saying to her "Yes, I want this logo". That's the kind of stuff I wouldn't have decided on my own. It's not the kind of things – the peace sign – they would pass on to the creatives. That is something they would have passed along, so that was definitely from Prince. No question about it.'

Parsons, who would go on to redesign the Ozzy Osbourne and Journey logos, the font on Madonna's 'Borderline' single and work for DC Comics for fifteen years, was then charged to write the song titles in the font he had just created. He was looking forward to seeing his name on the sleeve. But that wouldn't materialise. That was all Prince too. 'Somebody must have said "That's the logo, now do everything else, all of the credits and all of the stuff that is on the cover."

'I went uncredited on the cover.' Lipuma Nash told him that 'Prince thinks there's too many credits on the cover. For ten or fifteen years, nobody knew that I did it.'

Robyn Lynch explains that Prince didn't get what he

wanted with this sleeve. He got something else. 'He was such a perfectionist that they would do a shoot and he would restage it. It was quite a long period of time. Sometimes it's exactly what he wants and sometimes it's maybe even better than what he wants.'

For the 'Sign'… single sleeve – a figure in a peach dress, a heart-shaped mirror and a guitar, Prince had just hired a new recruit, dancer Cat Glover, who was sent to pick up a dress intended for girlfriend Susannah Melvoin from Beverly Hills and fly over to Minneapolis.

'I get to Minneapolis and they gave me Prince's glasses. I had his guitar and we did the shoot. Then I had to hold the mirror which was heavy and made my muscles stand out. So that's probably part of the reason why people thought it was Prince in a dress. His dad called me and said "Is that really you wearing that dress?" I said "Yes, Mr Nelson".'

John Nelson's response? 'I thought my son had lost his mind.' Glover's own father 'kinda freaked out a bit'. For Prince, it was just another day at the office. 'He never told me this would be the cover at all.'

CHAPTER 2

PLAY IN THE SUNSHINE

*Prince's sense of competition ... Twin Cities, one focus ...
when and where it started (the music) ... signing for Warner
Brothers ... Piano and no Microphone ... the musician who
gave him a sense of Wonder ... Play in the Sunshine*

Prince's sense of competition

Joseph: 'I wish we could have a competition! Mozart
against some other virtuoso. Two keyboards in contest.
Wouldn't that be fun, Baron?'

Amadeus, Peter Shaffer (1980)

In terms of proximity and time spent together, few people were
as close to Prince as his engineers. In many aspects of his life,
he preferred female company.

One day in the early '80s, Sunset Sound Studios engineer
Peggy McCreary skipped into work one morning singing a
Culture Club song she had as an earworm. The boss wasn't
happy and told her to stop singing.

'Why? It's a great song.'

'It's the competition.'

Prince was competitive.

His engineer after McCreary at LA's Sunset Sound Recorders, Susan Rogers, where much of *Sign...* was recorded, gives another example of his one upmanship.

'We had just arrived to do work and the assistant engineer is picking up tapes and we were there in our control room. It was some rock band and he said to me "Open the box". I said "It's a violation of trust" and he's holding their track saying "Let's erase their bass. I will redo the bass and write 'Bass you should have played' on the label." He wasn't actually going to do it... There was a moment. We had to pull him back. That really tickled him.'

At the time, Prince was represented by the management firm Cavallo, Ruffalo and Fargnoli. Steve Fargnoli's then assistant Susan Hale gives another example. 'Right before *Sign...*, in the *Parade* era, when "Kiss" and "Addicted to Love" were vying for the number one spot on the Billboard Top 100, Prince asked me which song I liked better. I said "Addicted to Love" because it had a more driving beat and was more rock'n'roll, which was my preference. So the next thing I know, he goes into a studio here in LA, writes a rip-off song to "Addicted to Love" and comes back to the office, hands me a cassette, and says "I wrote this in one minute and it's better than 'Addicted to Love', and 'Kiss' should be number one" and then he stormed off. He always stormed off. And then he was back the next day.

'He was such a competitor, I think he was just shooting for first place and laying out his case to me. By the way, the song he wrote for me was fantastic. Maybe better than Robert Palmer. I, of course, lost it, or taped over it years later when I was in my mixtape-for-boyfriends phase. Something stupid. It never dawned on me that it might be worth something someday – not that I ever would sell anything of his.'

Just after signing to Warners, Prince had memorably announced to his A&R man Lenny Waronker the acts he wanted to be bracketed alongside. 'Fleetwood Mac. Eric Clapton. Sly and the Family Stone. Maybe Santana. He reeled it off. I understood it. You know when someone says something to you and you don't totally understand it, but you know it's important? That's what happened. This guy is so competitive, wants it so badly, is fearless.'

Was Prince competing against his chart contemporaries like Bruce Springsteen and Madonna and MJ or heritage artists with a series of classic albums behind them like Sly Stone, Joni Mitchell, Stevie Wonder and James Brown?

Interviewees seem to agree on the answer: all of the above.

Twin Cities, one focus

That competitive instinct had been forged in Minneapolis, where Prince Rogers Nelson was born on 7 April 1958. Madonna Louise Ciccone arrived on 16 August in Bay City, Michigan; Michael Joseph Jackson thirteen days later in Gary, Indiana.

Madonna would come to New York to seek fame and fortune and, after a spell as the drummer for the band The Breakfast Club, an introduction to producer John 'Jellybean' Benitez led the pair to date and work on 'Holiday', 'Borderline' and 'Lucky Star' together, firmly pushing her on the road to stardom.

Jackson's ambitious father Joe moved his family to Los Angeles in 1969 to bolster the Jackson 5's star wattage, after Berry Gordy had uprooted Motown's HQ west from Detroit.

Prince stayed exactly where he was.

His first two records were made in California, but it was his third album, *Dirty Mind*, recorded back home, which really fired the imagination of both the public and the press. He enjoyed spending time working and living near Hollywood in the winter, with parties at the start of the year around awards season. And, of course, he loved Sunset Sound Recorders, specifically Studio 3, on Sunset Boulevard, his West Coast recording base from 1981 onwards.

Between world tours and those spells in LA, the recurring theme was Minneapolis in the beginning, middle and end of his career. As well as being born in the city, and moving most of his recording to Paisley Park later in the *Sign...* year of 1987, he spent most of his hang time there too.

His first band was Grand Central who faced off against bands such as Flyte Tyme, the latter featuring Terry Lewis, Jimmy Jam, David Eiland and Cynthia Johnson. Johnson would leave Flyte Tyme for Lipps Inc (which also featured future Paisley Park stalwart David Z. Rivkin), whose 1980 hit *Funkytown* reached number one in twenty-eight countries. Johnson says she remembers Grand Central in the context of Battle of the Bands, a frequent fixture for musicians, particularly black groups, in Minneapolis.

That Battle of the Bands theme would go on to define not just the plot line of Prince's debut movie but would make up the tour (Prince and The Revolution vs his funk band the Time) that would provide the initial funding for that movie. That tight-knit community would be forged in a kiln of competition, although a heat metaphor is less than perfect, as his friend and protege, Taja Sevelle, who signed a contract at his record label the same year that *Sign...* came out, reflects.

'I love that Prince stayed in Minneapolis. I think, in the end, he knew what I also knew – that Minneapolis is a remarkable place. Minneapolis has cultivated many, many talented musicians, actors and artists. We have always joked around that this is because of the cold winters in which most musicians would "woodshed", meaning they would stay in and practise, playing music for hours on end.'

That cold weather meant that musicians in the Mill City had fewer distractions. Like Prince, they stayed home and rehearsed. And why would Prince need to call a session bassist, guitarist or drummer if he had learned those instruments himself?

'There's nothing else to do in Minnesota other than what it is you do,' laughs Michael Bland who, after his time with Prince, went on to drum with another of the city's big acts, Soul Asylum. 'There's only two seasons – there's spring and there's winter. With six, seven months of winter, that's also time to dig down, to figure out who you are artistically. You're going to write. You're going to work on your craft. We have a different type of discipline. There's always the beach in LA. There's always the nightlife in New York. In Minneapolis, all you got is "What am I doing with my time?" Minneapolis musicians, in my experience, we will work 'til it's done. Everybody's great.' When Prince shuttled musicians to the Land of 10,000 Lakes, Bland says, this was 'not an accident. At almost every turn, he knew what he was doing.'

Later in his career, his house since 1987 – Paisley Park – would be a hub for travelling musicians. The legends he signed to his Paisley Park label, such as Bonnie Raitt, Mavis Staples and George Clinton, would travel to the studios of that name to make their records.

Bobby Lyle and Hubert Ives made it before Prince. Northern Minnesotans Bob Dylan (Duluth) and Judy Garland (Partridge) had gone to Greenwich Village and Hollywood respectively to make their names. The opening line of 'Funkytown', with Prince's future collaborator David Z Rivkin on production and

Cynthia Johnson on vocals, would not have escaped Prince's notice: 'Got to make a move to a town that's right for me.'

Minneapolis was right for him. It's the rest of the world who would have to get with the programme. The mountain had to head to Mohammed.

Or, to be more geographically correct, Chanhassen.

Producer and engineer Dylan Dresdow, who also worked with Madonna and Michael Jackson, notes that 'a lot of these artists have their own climate. They all have their own hurricanes. Prince was very autonomous. He had his own recording studio, which was very private. He didn't have to worry about budget issues most of the time.

'All these people can call the shots. The difference with Prince is that it's always in house. If you're in Chanhassen, Minneapolis, you have to feel that you're on call all the time. There's not anything else you can do.'

Welcome 2 America engineer Jason Agel's memory of the area is being ferried from the airport to the Chanhassen branch of the hotel chain Country Inn & Suites where dancer Misty Copeland and Janelle Monáe had been recent guests. 'We're in the middle of nowhere with nothing to do,' Agel reflects. Again, the man who sent the cars set it up that way. 'Absolutely. There's nothing else for me to do besides Prince's music.'

For Prince, there was no place like home; not just for comfort but, unlike entertainment hubs like New York, LA, Nashville and London, there were fewer distractions. 'People always wonder "Why did Prince stay there?",' says Sotera Tschetter, a Dayton, Ohio native who helped him shape his logo. 'The work ethic is a little different. The Midwest as people work extremely hard.' Tschetter had grown up in a farming family, so working at 4 a.m. (as Prince often would) did not unsettle her.

Ultimately, control – especially at Paisley – was about Prince finding his happy place. Behind a mixing desk, in the vocal booth, with a guitar round his neck – all of these represented sources of contentment.

The area was also, if you were so minded, a useful barometer of Prince's steady girlfriends. Playboy model and ex-girlfriend Devin DeVasquez started dating Sylvester Stallone around the time that Prince and the Revolution left for Europe to tour *Parade*. The words of Carmen Electra, another of his many exes from the early '90s, still ring in her ear. 'There was always one leaving Minneapolis at the same time as someone was coming to Minneapolis.'

The chill outside may have led to Prince creating one of his most plaintive ballads in 'Sometimes It Snows in April' (from *Parade*), but it didn't suit all his employees, including personal assistant Karen Krattinger. 'I did a 360° on black ice, and all I could think was, *I'm going straight into the snow banks and they're going to find my body in the spring.*' Marie France, who hailed from France and worked with Prince on costume from just before *Purple Rain*, was equally distressed by the 'brutal' winters. 'Polar bears maybe don't mind them. I can't believe Prince didn't (mind them), as he used to wear such flimsy outfits.'

Prince adapted – be that frequent winter work trips to LA, world tours, and using home studios and studio warehouses before Paisley Park opened in 1987. He also used the climate in the Twin Cities to his benefit, as Albert Magnoli, the director of his breakthrough film, remembers looking up for inspiration.

'For me, the concept of "purple rain" was very specific in terms of the feeling you get just before the clouds would open up and gush raindrops. I learned that the entire area of Minneapolis, before a storm, the skies would turn this amazing blue-purple before the rain came. It was a phenomenon. Later on, when Prince and I were working at Paisley Park [Prince moved there in 1987], we would go outside prior to a rainstorm and just stand in the field, looking at the sky together, waiting for the rain to drop. And those skies went purple.'

The city's cultural climate, with its population spread and being around 10 per cent black, meant Prince listened not just to urban contemporary radio station KMOJ but also pop and rock stations, meaning Fleetwood Mac and Joni Mitchell influenced him alongside James Brown and Earth, Wind and Fire.

Minneapolis may have gone in and out of fashion, but Prince always thought his hometown was cool. 'Minneapolis is so far behind other major cities,' he said in 1980, 'it forces you to create your own sound.' By the year 1999, he was telling Larry King that 'Minneapolis always been the bomb. You don't have to go outside that.'

Alexander O'Neal, whose 1987 hits 'Fake' and 'Criticise' were produced by fellow Minnesotans Jimmy Jam and Terry Lewis, fell out with Prince when discussions about O'Neal becoming the lead singer of the Time dissolved over money. O'Neal concedes that one thing he appreciates about Prince is that he 'never gave up on Minnesota. He kept that connection with the state and artists like myself. The music community is tight-knit. We kept it simple and humble.'

When and where it started (the music)

Born – to two musicians originally from Louisiana – at Mount Sinai Hospital, Minneapolis on 7 June 1958, it's hard to carbon-date the moment Prince's musical die was cast. His father John Nelson was the bandleader for a group called the Prince Rogers Trio and, according to the Time's Jellybean Johnson, was 'a world-class musician'.

When Prince was a toddler, he was babysat by saxophone

player Morris Wilson, who had worked with Ike and Tina Turner, the Temptations and Muddy Waters, as well as with Prince's dad. The die could have been cast at Prince's first gig when he snuck into the hall of his dad's matinee performance in Austin, Minnesota when he was meant to be in the car.

Or you could place it to the original piano performances of the *Batman* theme (the first tune he learned on the keys) around the age of nine while in the fourth and fifth grade at John Hay Elementary. When the call came from Tim Burton to create music for the 1989 film, Prince would not be able to resist.

Or it could be that his relentless drive to become a musical prodigy was largely unrelated to music.

John was a jazz musician, but that didn't mean he was always encouraged. Prince was banned initially from his father's piano for not meeting the requisite standard, thus perhaps giving it an illicit cachet which would guarantee more of Prince's time spent practising.

John went on to work for Honeywell computers and Mattie as a social worker, so his parents' inability to hold down a full-time musical career – think many – contributed to his drive to make one of his own.

Prince had a complicated relationship with his own name, even decades before he commissioned designers to craft the squiggle logo or created 'The Artist Formerly Known as...' to thwart his record company in the '90s.

Mattie informally called her son Skipper (John pronounced it 'Skippah'). It could be because he skipped around, but there was another more damaging reason, according to his engineer during the early '80s, Peggy McCreary. 'His mother called him Skipper because she didn't like his name.' Her husband had given his jazz band the name the Prince Rogers Nelson trio.

'His family and his aunt and his mum would know him as

Skipper,' recalls Paul Mitchell, a close friend and classmate in their teenage years. 'He would hate it when she [Aunt Olivia, with whom he lived in his teens] would say 'Skipper! In here.' He was Prince to us. We called him Skipper as a joke. My sister used to tease him saying "Prince is a dog's name". He hated it.'

Aside from the obvious nickname Princess – 'Well, y'know, kids...' grimaces Jackson, referencing the way adolescent peer groups would hone in on weaknesses – and Butcher Dog (because other classmates thought he resembled a German Shepherd), his distinctive Afro led to another unintended nickname, as Terry Jackson recalls. 'One day Prince had a Michael Jackson Afro, but in the shadow, it looked like he had a big head on a little body like the character in *The Flintstones*, Gazoo.' This explains Prince's fondness for bestowing nicknames for others, as Gazoo – voiced by Harvey Korman, who would go on to play Hedley Lamarr in Mel Brooks' *Blazing Saddles* – became his.

His childhood was a point of bonding for him and Carole Davis, whom he tried to audition for Apollonia's part in *Purple Rain* (she turned it down) and who shared a co-writing credit for 'Slow Love' on *Sign o' the Times*. 'He told me he was very badly bullied at school for his size [Prince attended Bryant Junior High, then Central High) and that was something we had in common. When I was fourteen, I looked like I was ten. He opened up to me and we shared that. We had a long conversation about how we had both been bullied. It never leaves you. It is a deep wound of injustice.'

Prince's home life and musical career would be blurred from an early age. Even though he continued to live with Mattie after his parents' separation (at the time he was seven), his mother's new husband Hayward Baker did not meet with his approval. He writes in *The Beautiful Ones* that the day Mattie remarried was the day he left. When he says 'left', he means the family home of

2620 8th Avenue, north Minneapolis. He did not, and this was a constant throughout all his life, get out of his hometown.

Paul Mitchell suggests Prince's desire to win started before music came into his life. His height may have been a determining factor, while hanging out with six-foot-one Mitchell and six-foot-three half-brother Duane Nelson. 'Totally – the fact he couldn't play athletics the way he wanted. He played basketball and he had great hand-eye coordination where he could play, but his height didn't allow him to do it. You have got to have some size.

'I got a football scholarship, Duane had a basketball scholarship. The girls that he liked, liked me and Duane. All of that drove Prince's competitive drive. As he got older, I knew it drove him to say "Look at me now". By then, I couldn't care less as I was so proud of him. It probably drove him to the end with Michael Jackson and Madonna. That all continued to motivate him.'

After Hayward Baker moved in, Prince moved to 1244 Russell Avenue, the home of the Anderson family (mother Bernadette and Prince's best mate André), and two doors down from the Jackson family at 1248, including his friend Terry.

That didn't stop him playing. If anything, it accelerated it.

... Piano and no Microphone

Prince's performing life started and ended in front of black and white. His first big school concert he played piano. As friend and keyboard player Morris Hayes notes, his final tour 'Piano and a Microphone', featuring Prince and a custom-made Yamaha grand, was the first one he was guaranteed never to fine a band member.

The evening of 21 January 2016 saw his first of these gigs at

Paisley Park. Prince approached the keys, his narration reverting to his three-year-old self. 'Here comes Dad. Not supposed to touch it, and I wanna play it so bad… There goes Dad. Him and Mom are getting divorced now.' In the show, he fast-forwards to his parents' estrangement. 'I was only seven years old. But now: I can play anytime I want. Can't play the piano like Dad, though. How does Dad do that? Let me see… I wish I could sing.'

Prince's first public performance was behind the keys. To be strictly accurate, he played piano on his *second* public performance. The first – when he was 'around eight or nine', according to his childhood friend Terry Jackson – was at a talent show where he tap danced. That didn't go down too well with his classmates. By fifth grade the following year, at John Hay Elementary's talent show, he had practised and played the themes from *The Man from U.N.C.L.E.* and *Batman*. 'That helped him get a lot of friends.'

In a 1984 interview, his mother Mattie told the *Star Tribune* that 'he could hear music even from a very early age. When he was three or four, we'd go to the department store and he'd jump on the radio, the organ, any type of instrument there was. Mostly the piano and organ. I'd have to hunt for him, and that's where he'd be – in the music department.'

Prince told the same publication in 1978 that 'around the time I was eight, I had a pretty good idea what the piano was all about. I had one piano lesson and two guitar lessons as a kid. I was a poor student, because when a teacher would be trying to teach me how to play junky stuff, I would start playing my own songs. I'd usually get ridiculed for it, but I ended up doing my own thing. I can't read music. It hasn't gotten in the way yet. Maybe it will later, but I doubt it.'

His relationship with his father John's instrument of choice was almost as complicated as his relationship with his father.

John Nelson did not regard his son's playing as up to standard. 'My father was so hard on me,' he told talk show host Tavis Smiley in 2009. 'It was never good enough.'

Mattie was 'really strict' too, reflects Terry Jackson. 'Every time we would go over to his house, we were told we couldn't play on the furniture and couldn't play on the piano in the basement.'

By the time John and Mattie split (they separated in 1965 and divorced three years later when Prince was ten) and she remarried Hayward Baker, his friend remembers his stepdad didn't appreciate Prince's playing either. 'When his dad's piano stayed at his mum's, and when Hayward Baker moved in, he wasn't allowed to play the piano. The influence of his dad was definitely there.'

Whether this gave his father's piano a feeling of forbidden fruit, or meant Prince concentrated on his other instruments, particularly guitar, is open to conjecture. By high school, he was known locally to play piano with his right hand while playing a harmony on the guitar with his left.

He was certainly more comfortable using his piano and guitar as his musical voice than his actual voice. In an early interview, reported in Barney Hoskyns' book *Prince: Imp of the Perverse*, he explained that he 'never sang in talent shows... I never thought I could sing. My speaking voice was so deep it hurt to sing. I had to sing in a high voice, but Lord knows I didn't want to be laughed at so I would only sing in my boudoir.' That singing shyness would be replicated in his career; unusually, he recorded vocals on his own.

Prince couldn't read music. He took one theory class in high school and gave it up. That lack of formal training, coupled with the music in his head, meant him becoming a multi-instrumentalist was perhaps inevitable.

Prince himself laughed off the hype around his first album

at having played twenty-three instruments (sometimes listed elsewhere as twenty-seven). That number didn't matter as much as the proficiency of his playing – and being left to get on with things.

Signing for Warner Brothers

How did Prince go from playing bass in his own band Grand Central to securing his own record deal aged seventeen?

Playing more than bass was part of it.

Spotting a prodigious talent, Minneapolis businessman Owen Husney offered to manage him, while another Minneapolis musician, Chris Moon, set him up his studio time. Soon Husney was shopping this talent around to Columbia, Portrait, part of A&M and Warner Brothers records.

The approaches, remembers Warners rep Lenny Waronker, were as follows: 'Columbia's was "You're going to get a hit share". A&M had Quincy [Jones] and I knew he didn't want anybody to produce.'

Warners were ready to gamble. 'There are eight guys in A&R and every one has a strong feeling about him and what you're hearing is what the first album is going to sound like and we liked it. Why go against his wishes?

'If you're dealing with the real deal, and you have creative issues, and your vocabulary is able to point it out, you win some, you lose some. I was talking to the top lawyer in the company and he said "We could win this battle" and I said "What do you mean?" These are the things that separate us. I was betting on our ability to know someone who is gifted when you hear it. He wanted three albums from us. Nobody got that.

'Should we gamble? If it was me, I'd gamble. We caved on that. We won.'

Warners were at that stage run by Mo Ostin who formed Reprise Records with Frank Sinatra. Ol' Blue Eyes acquired his other nickname, the Chairman of the Board, by forming a company which would be artist-led. Control was also important to Prince from minute one – something his record company and Mo Ostin understood.

Jay Graydon, who often played sessions at Sunset Sound in LA while Prince was in the next studio, calls him 'a control freak. He always had to be there.' The guitarist compares this to Marvin Gaye, who skipped the session for 'I Want You' on which Graydon played. It seems unthinkable Prince would have done that.

That control would see him resist being marketed just to the black community. 'He didn't want to be pigeonholed because of the colour of his skin,' says Warners' Marylou Badeaux. 'There were three or four labels who were very interested in him but he wanted total creative control. That was a difficult one. An eighteen-year-old kid and people are wondering if he's capable. Under Mo Ostin, Warner Brothers was an incredibly artist-friendly company. It was also an employee-friendly company, so no one wanted to leave.'

Waronker had signed off on Prince being able to produce his debut album, *For You*. 'We were setting up for a bass overdub and he was sitting by the 24-track machine and I was walking towards the engineer. I was stepping over him and he looked down and he said "Don't make me black".'

Alexander O'Neal praises the racial integration that led to Prince's sound. 'We live in one of the most interracial areas of the US. I would say we're probably number one. I think that's what his music was designed to be.'

Because Waronker and Ostin allowed him to produce his debut album in his teens, it made him one of the last artists who enjoyed the freedom to make three albums before he started making waves and five before he made it big. Stars from the '90s onwards rarely had that latitude.

Insisting on producing his own records as well as playing all the instruments on them, even as a teenager, suggests a certain insistence on control. This extended even to how he got dressed in the morning. Scottie Baldwin – Prince's drum tech and then front of house engineer, who worked with him for two decades – calls him 'a man fully in control of how he looked at all times'.

Even in business meetings?

'Especially in business meetings. He would pendulum his head, sway out like that. He didn't just have faces. He had attitudes.'

That attitude would keep employees on their toes. That iron grip was easier to exert on staff as a bandleader rather than on girlfriends. He had a useful antecedent. Those present at either end of his career noticed who that was.

'His idol was James Brown, and that's pretty clear to anyone who watched him on set,' says Bill Reeves, who worked with him from the Controversy tour to *Lovesexy*. 'He wanted instantaneous control of what his band was doing – "turn it up and down", "speed it up", "slow it down" – with the smallest of gestures. He could lift his left eyebrow and that means everything is going to change.'

That insistence on control meant that money was no object in the pursuit of getting what he wanted. When Paisley Park was built in 1987, he angrily rang up engineer Sal Greco.

'I don't like how my live shows are sounding. Why can't it sound like my studio?'

'We tuned it…'

'Why can't we do that live?'

'You know how much that's gonna cost?'

'What am I, broke?'

'You're not broke. [pause] I will wake them [tech staff] up to work on it.'

Paisley Park – his living quarters and studio which would mark the full stop in the *Sign o' the Times* era and the start of another – was another expression of that desire for control.

The musician who gave Prince a sense of Wonder

James Brown is a useful template to understand Prince: the controlling bandleader, the dancer, the fashion maven, the activist and the party starter. Stevie Wonder was another key point of reference.

Both he and Stevie were child prodigies. Stevie had his first number-one hit aged thirteen. Prince had a record deal by eighteen. By seventeen, Stevie Wonder had a greatest hits album out.

Both multi-instrumentalists, it was not unusual for either man to write a song or more a day, or to disappear into the studio and emerge forty-eight hours later without a break. Both skipped over genres like puddles: Stevie playing at Nashville's Grand Ole Opry and reggae in Jamaica with Bob Marley, while Prince played at the ALMA Latin music awards in tribute to Sheila E and jammed to Led Zeppelin with Dave Grohl at a soundcheck.

The run of landmark albums Prince enjoyed from *1999* in '82 to *Sign o' the Times* five years later scaled dizzying heights. The streak Stevie Wonder delivered from 1970's *Music of My Mind* to the 1976 double album *Songs in the Key of Life* would have given even Prince vertigo. Only the Beatles can boast a comparable run.

Dave Hampton, who ran Paisley Park at Prince's request

between 2004 and 2007, has worked with some American modern greats, including Bill Withers and Herbie Hancock. 'Stevie's was dominance unlike any other,' he argues. 'Stevie's dominance overshadowed Prince's, if you ask me. Music was in a different place. The record business was in a different place.'

That dominance was exemplified by the Grammys that decade: *Innervisions* (1974's Album of the Year), *Fulfillingness' First Finale* (winner in 1975) and *Songs in the Key of Life* (1977). When Paul Simon won 1976's Album of the Year for *Still Crazy After All These Years*, he rounded off his speech with, 'And most of all, I'd like to thank Stevie Wonder, who didn't make an album this year.'

(Prince never won Album of the Year, losing to Lionel Richie's *Can't Slow Down* in '85 and U2's *The Joshua Tree* in '88. He also presented Beck with his in 2015.)

Prince, along with cousin Chazz Smith, watched the awards in his teens and was paying attention. 'We thought the Grammys were for the people who were the greatest of the greatest. When Stevie didn't get something, we would be bummed out. He gave one of his Grammys to the dude who wrote songs for Elvis Presley [Otis Blackwell, writer of *All Shook Up* and *Don't Be Cruel*, was mentioned in his 1976 speech for Best Male Vocalist]. We didn't know that so we would go and read about it.'

Stevie would be a guiding light throughout his career. Grand Central would play every track on *Talking Book*, with a special emphasis on 'Looking For a Pure Love', 'Superstition' and in particular 'Blame it on the Sun'. Stevie would also turn Prince on to Jeff Beck, who played on 'Superstition', originally written for him before Stevie stole it back.

Prince played guitar on 'So What the Fuss' from Stevie's 2005 album *A Time to Love*, while he and Sheila joined Stevie onstage to jam on 'Superstition' at The Bercy in Paris on 1 July

2010. Prince and Stevie also played at the White House at the Obamas' request in June 2015, but it was in private the two men really tapped into the other's musical energy.

Prince's '00s house parties were legendary and other musicians would be present – such as singer Anthony Hamilton, Herbie Hancock and keyboard player Frank McComb – and occasionally participating. Stevie would inevitably be tempted up on stage to jam with Prince's band.

Alan Leeds says he 'idolised' Wonder and purchased *Talking Book* again days before his death. The day following Prince's passing, Wonder appeared on *Good Morning America* to pay tribute and to sing 'Purple Rain'. On 10 July 2016 at London's Hyde Park, he played *Songs in the Key of Life* in full and for the encore – listed on the setlist sheet of paper as 'Superstition etc.' – Wonder announced he had changed his name to DJ Shake Shake Boom and dropped snippets of 'Kiss' and 'When Doves Cry' for the audience to sing along in tribute.

Both men developed musicians to thrive elsewhere. Ray Parker Jr, who played on *Talking Book* aged seventeen, testifies to Stevie's mentoring skills for teaching him how to play and produce. Like Prince, only the musically strong survive. 'He stays on piano and hums a line and you have to interpret it and play it back. For him, if you can't play, you're out anyway. He took me into the studio, showed me how to record a little bit and write songs. No surprise, a year later, I had my first hit record.'

There were subtle differences between the two. Stevie doesn't publicly play guitar, but his harmonica prowess would be his signature move, the way Prince's guitar solos would redefine how audiences often saw and heard him.

Prince famously recorded his vocals on his own. Stevie would want people in the room to whom he could react that would give him an inkling of how it was going.

Prince would start recording a song with the drums. Stevie, according to producer Andrew Watt (who worked with him), left the drums he played on his to the last.

When Stevie transitioned from child star 'Little' Stevie Wonder to one of Motown's big hitters in his twenties, he thrashed out his own contract and publishing deal with Berry Gordy so that artistic control was one negotiation he never need make again.

'Early in his career,' adds drummer Michael Bland, 'Prince had sought to be like Stevie in terms of being autonomous. Stevie was so in control of his vision, no pun intended. He wrote the song, he recorded the song.'

'One day,' remembers his final female engineer Lisa Chamblee, 'he asked me who my favourite artist was.' When she answered 'Stevie', he said 'Well, that's *everybody's* favourite.'

'Play in the Sunshine'

By being a multi-instrumentalist, Prince was in an elite bracket that included Stevie Wonder, Sly Stone, Frank Zappa, Paul McCartney and Todd Rundgren. As *Purple Rain* director Albert Magnoli notes, it put him in a place Michael Jackson couldn't reach.

This meant his musical vision would be translated at warp speed, according to Lisa Chamblee. 'He had a lot in his head. People who play a lot of different instruments, they feel a different purpose. I think he was happy that he was the most musical genius in our times. He knew that he was in competition with himself.'

Another reason for his versatility – according to Scott Thurston who played bass, lead guitar, keyboards and harmonica for (among others) Iggy and the Stooges, Bonnie Raitt and Tom Petty and the Heartbreakers – could be a lack of patience.

'People who are into music and have a talent learn the instruments not because they want to or because they're trying to show off. They just sort of have to. They hear the piano and they have to play that. It's not a choice they can make. It's all impatience. You just learn it because you have to. It takes you twice as long to teach it to someone else. By the time I have taught it to someone else, I have forgotten fifteen other things that I want to do. I think anyone who plays a lot of things is impatient. I know I am.'

Prince's ability to play all the instruments would come in handy for the second track on *Sign o' the Times*. The first germ of an idea for the title track, the first on the album, was when he was living with Susannah Melvoin in the early part of 1986. The apparently gleeful rock song, the second track on the album, was when things with Susannah were at a trickier pass.

'Play in the Sunshine' was the last recording session at Sunset in November 1986 where Susannah was present. Her twin sister Wendy had been part of the Revolution, whose services Prince had dispensed with the previous month.

He played all the instruments on 'Play in the Sunshine'; he was his own garage band before GarageBand. The Fairlight synthesiser which sampled dozens of sounds was a useful tool when his band had gone.

The lyrics for 'Play in the Sunshine' oozed the positivity he probably wasn't feeling at the time. 'Ooh doggies!' it begins, which was country-speak, if you believe Texan Coke Johnson, (a Sunset Sound employee) for 'it's getting slamming! It's getting really good. Whenever Prince would get behind the console and we did a session with [*Sign*-era bassist] Levi [Seacer Jr.] or the brass section where they would just play and jam, he would turn it up and say "That's bacon grease!" When it's getting really funky, he says "It's greasy". It's so funky, it's slippery.'(He references chicken grease later on *Sign...* on 'It's Gonna Be a Beautiful Night'.)

There follows a hymn to playing in the sunshine and being free, and echoing Prince's on-off puritanical stance with no assistance from either margaritas or ecstasy. He was focused on sounding like he was having fun, but more focused on the record working. The track was designed to be the glue which linked the opening track and 'Housequake', which was originally slated to be a single – to the extent he even recorded a segue between tracks one and two in January 1987. Plotting the order of his albums was important to him. Prince held a reverence for the format. When presenting Beck with the Grammy for *Morning Phase* a year before his death, he announced: 'Like books and black lives, albums still matter.'

'He always thought of albums as a whole instead of individual songs,' agrees Alan Leeds. Susan Rogers, one of the few individuals in the room at Sunset Sound's Studio 3 when *Sign...* was made, calls 'Play in the Sunshine' a 'segue song. Let me get from "Sign..." [into a happier place].' The dark underbelly of the title track had to be lifted, and even if Prince wasn't feeling it, he had to fake it while he would make it.

'Sequencing an album was really fun and we spent a great deal of time and thought on it,' Rogers continues. 'We'd have one song, we'd know we wanted it to fit out. Let's say when playing "Sign o' the Times", he and I would be taping. This would require edits with actual tape and questions like "Where is the next downbeat track? Where do you make the mark?" You take the razor blade and you make the mark and you play it and listen to that timing and you listen to that side and there's how it flows. I suppose it's a bit like editing a television programme. You pivot the scenes which need to be interesting and keep you from changing channels, but they can't be so dramatic before the end.'

'It isn't picking the best songs, it's what songs best go together,' adds Alan Leeds. 'That's just part of the process anybody has when they're cutting their material down. I haven't questioned that. It's his art, his vision.'

'Housequake', as the next chapter suggests, was a party in the studio with his then colleagues and a stuffed penguin.

CHAPTER 3

HOUSEQUAKE

Does anybody know 'bout the Quake? ... the room where it happened ... Dirty Mind, the first in a series of firsts ... You can't always get what you want ... Bring on the Revolution ... 'Wow, a little Sly and The Family Stone' ... another major influence ... 1999 – the latest great leap forward

Does anybody know 'bout the Quake?

Two other bandmembers arrived around the early '80s and remained key parts of the creation of *Sign o' the Times*, especially its third track, 'Housequake': the Linn drum machine and the Fairlight.

The fact Prince used the Linn LM-1 drum machine and the Fairlight CMI, which sampled a succession of varispeed voices to create what at one stage was going to be the second single released from the album, displayed how his editing instincts would serve him well through key periods of his career.

Prince had figured out how to get the black radio audience in 1980 with *Dirty Mind*, and to get the black radio department of his record company excited in the process. He first used the LM-1 on 'Private Joy', from 1981's *Controversy*, and it became a feature on many of the tracks on *Sign*...

The Fairlight, particularly the CMI, was a key arsenal in the decade's trailblazing pop. Susan Rogers remembers Prince playing Kate Bush's Fairlight-infused *Hounds of Love* in full while they were working together 'and talking about what an extraordinary record it was'. He also admired the work of Peter Gabriel, another Fairlight enthusiast.

In the summer of 1986, Prince bought one but needed help, particularly from a recent graduate. Fresh out of college, Todd Herreman decided he was interested in 'selling cool gear. I went to Chicago to sell $10,000, $20,000 keyboards and they paid me on commission. We could run up a system up to 30,000 bucks. I said "Why don't we sell a Fairlight?" [The CMI-2X model Prince favoured was then retailing around $35,000.] I listen to Herbie Hancock's "Rock It" and Peter Gabriel's "Sledgehammer". Kate Bush was a huge user. I was selling more Fairlights than Fairlights made. I was there when Prince wanted to buy a Fairlight. I got a call from Alan Leeds.

'"Prince got a delivery of a Fairlight and no one knows how to run it. Could you recommend someone?"

"That would be me."'

Herreman jumped aboard.

The Fairlight synthesiser was suited to those who loved to sample. But that, Susan Rogers notes, was not Prince. 'We didn't do sampling. We could have, we should have. Todd was there and could have shown us, but Prince worked so quickly, it would have meant taking the time to learn something new. It was the same thing with the Yamaha DM7X. He wasn't into that. He needed the pre-sets on a musical instrument. He loved the horn stabs and the orchestral stabs. They totally served him well. He loved some variety in his drum sounds. He loved that LM-1 drum machine. He wasn't going to give that up.'

Jellybean Johnson, drummer with Prince's spin-off band the Time, appreciates Prince's mastery of the Linn LM-1. 'He and [Time member and producer] Jimmy Jam are the greatest drum machine guys I have met in my life. He made it feel real and that's what Jimmy does. They make it feel like a drummer is playing it. And, being a drummer, I can appreciate that.'

The link between old school drummers and the LM-1 was closer than first appeared. Drummers programmed the beats, discloses Jimmy Jam. 'They [Linn] wanted to make sure musicians did not feel intimidated. One of them was [Tower of Power's] David Garibaldi. He programmed a beat into it. It was one of the last ten pre-beats.'

When hearing The Time's 777-9311, Jam was told by Morris Day: 'That's a David Garibaldi beat.'

The trusty Fairlight and Linn LM-1 would remain important to Prince throughout his career, but not as important as the musicians by his side on stage and, to a greater extent, in the studio.

On the third song of *Sign o' the Times*, Prince tells everyone to shut up, and to listen to the band.

One problem. The band were no more.

He had recorded 'Housequake' on his own, without the band who accompanied him from the *1999* era through to *Parade*: the Revolution. He had recorded much of the rest of *Sign...* with them and then re-recorded it without their parts. It was arguably when he assembled these talented musicians that his career took off.

Prince's capacity for stretching his employees – bodyguards would become bandmates on stage; assistants would become videographers and managers – extended to front-of-house soundman Rob 'Cubby' Colby when they were trying out the

Fairlight. He was asked to sing 'in this funky town' (a likely reference to Minneapolis band Lipps Inc) and then sampled it on the Fairlight. 'We were just testing and we thought we'd get rid of it. He looked at me the next day and said "I've got a new singing partner."'

Prince was especially fond of the kick drum on 'Housequake', likening it to the LA earthquake he and girlfriend Susannah had escaped in July. The kick drum, he would sing, is the fault.

Coke Johnson, that Sunset Sound engineer, has a memory of the song's construction beginning with 'a slamming drum track. It was the Linn machine. We had a Quantec effect with gated reverb which was causing that kick drum to go. We got all that slamming and there were a lot of people around the studio at that time. He had a whole entourage shouting and laughing and goofing and he had me go get 'em all. I set up two big mics in the recording space and got everybody out there and they were all going to sing the chorus. But, two bars in, I was sitting there behind the mixer and Prince said "You guys ready out there?" It made it sound like a whole bunch of people. They were just a bunch of friends like a party atmosphere. I had to go back and erase all the talking between the vocals. The whole Prince entourage was out there. Ten or twelve. More people and it might have had people who were out playing hoops in the court.'

The Revolution, save for keyboard player Matt Fink who stayed on, were no longer employed. Wendy and Lisa were long gone, so was childhood friend and drummer Bobby, and baby of the band, bassist Mark 'BrownMark' Brown.

Prince took direct action after missing his previous bandmates. He wanted brass on it, so called Matt Blistan and Eric Leeds. 'Atlanta Bliss', as he had been dubbed while living in Atlanta by his new bandleader, was actually back at his family home in

Pittsburgh for Thanksgiving when his phone rang. "'Prince wants you out in Los Angeles to record." I remember the first thing. "I want you to do a trumpet solo on this" and it was "Housequake". It was the first take I did it.

'Two minutes of recording. I flew all the way across the country and play a minute, and recording for a minute, and went home. This is rock'n'roll. Hit it and quit it.'

'There were some other songs which would have taken longer,' admits Todd Herreman. 'A lot of the time he would just use stock sounds on the synths. "Housequake" is almost all Fairlight.' By the time of recording, Herreman remembers a room full of buzz; as well as Eric Leeds and Matt Blistan's horns cameo, Prince was joined by engineers Coke Johnson and Susan Rogers (who were working in tandem), bodyguard Gilbert Davison, and techs Mike Soltys and Brad Marsh, all there and credited on the record, as well as The Penguin.

The... what?

Herreman takes up the story. 'There was this regal two-, three-feet stuffed penguin. Prince had given it to Sheila E.' Herreman, Soltys and Marsh assigned The Penguin toy a crucial task to liven up touring: They would perch it behind shoulders, explains Herreman, 'to catch Prince employees out when they were asleep on the job. They caught Gilbert [Davison, then bodyguard] and Mike [Soltys, bass technician]. They never caught me.'

The Penguin, which had its own flight case on tour, eventually came to the boss's attention.

'One day, he discovered about 30 Polaroids of his employees asleep with a penguin. "What the hell is going on?" He thought it was really funny.

'The next day, he's cutting vocals and it sounds quiet on there. He was face down with his arms spread on the console. We said "Shall we do it?"' The urge to take a Polaroid of a snoozing

Prince with The Penguin was strong. 'We were about to, and he said "Don't even think about it".

'One day he [The Penguin, not Prince] went missing and there was a ransom note. "If you don't deliver ten thousand pounds in cash or a case of Twix bars, you will never see The Penguin again." We figured out – because of the pounds and the Twix – that it was the British guy in our crew. One night, we had planned that The Penguin was going on stage until Alan [Leeds, the tour manager] found out, and told us it was the last show, and we were filming it.'

Prince retained his fondness for penguins. When producers of *Happy Feet* asked if they could use 'Kiss', he wrote 'The Song of the Heart' instead. It won 2007's Golden Globe for Best Song.

That childlike sense of play is shown in 'Housequake''s lyrics when Prince references Dr Seuss's menu of green eggs and ham. It also emanates from his actual childhood. 'Me and Prince used to record ourselves doing different voices,' says his cousin Chazz Smith. 'You hear these spot-on vocals he's doing on "Housequake". We used to do skits like that on cassette. My Aunt Della would say "You guys should have a show." Sometimes we got on each other's nerves.'

Susan Rogers doesn't remember such a fun atmosphere. By then, it's fair to say Prince could get on his engineers' nerves. They tell stories of not sleeping, finishing work at 5 a.m. and going back to hotels to brush their teeth before Prince called them back because he had another song idea.

Rogers took over from Peggy McCreary who left to have a personal life. Rogers would be denied this until she left Prince's employ in 1987. 'I remember it fairly well because I was going through a rough time myself. I had been overworked to a point of nearly breaking.

'Peggy would be there too and it was really helpful. It was

like working with a sister, but Peggy had gotten married and moved on. It wasn't the same without Peggy. I carried most of the weight at that time, and Prince was not noticing it and he was teasing me a little about it, but the subtext of that session [was] "If I can be optimistic, well you can too. This is what we do." He was very much about an "us". You focus on the bright side. You dance, you have fun, you like the joyful things in life. This helps explain why he was such a successful artist. He didn't wallow in self-pity. He hated it. He was always grateful – he was grateful for the way his hard work paid off.'

Years later, when Prince had stopped swearing, the song was still performed but Prince cut out the BS; that word in its purest form was no longer used in the refrain. As he told talk show host George Lopez in 2011, 'if I can stop swearing, everybody can stop swearing.'

'We didn't cuss around him,' reflects Shelby Johnson, a singer from his band through 2006 to 2014. 'It wasn't a control thing. It was a respect thing. He would change stuff. He would take that part out.'

Johnson fondly remembers Prince teaching her his inter-pretation of the 'jump up and down dance' a version of which she told him she self-taught as a teenager. Prince, by then resistant to the concept of time and therefore ageing (as a Jehovah's Witness, he didn't celebrate birthdays), groaned at the idea of the dimming of his youth, saying: 'I don't want to hear that.'

Back in 1986, saxophonist Eric Leeds feels Prince may been thinking about reconnecting with his black audience even if he wasn't. 'It did become an issue later, after the album was released, and black radio was anxious for "Housequake" to be released as a single, since that's what they were playing the most.' Prince was interested in hits, with many at Warners thinking 'Housequake' might make a single to help grow the album's sales.

He gave an early version to (adopted) brother Duane Nelson and told him: 'Don't let anybody hear it'. Mark Webster, Prince's friend dating back to his first album, has memories of being with Duane in a small Suzuki Jeep driving around Minnesota's lakes. Prince had spies everywhere.

'I told you not to play it!'

One unlikely fan of the song is Academy Award-winning composer and performer, Randy Newman. 'You can tell more about his sense of humour from "Housequake" and "If I Was Your Girlfriend". I pictured him telling these background singers and these big rough guys the words. The voice of that whole lady he does on "Housequake"… it's unheard of! That's great. That kind of sharpness is all over the place [on the record].'

Scottie Baldwin worked on Prince's sound for two decades before his death. 'He once told me that the kick drum from this period was the perfect kick drum.' They once had an argument over a drum sound in Japan. '"I can do that but it will take some time to tune," and he said "Can't you just use a sample? Just use it from "Housequake". That's the perfect kick drum. That's the best kick drum of all time."'

The song was also used by Prince to make a point to *Rolling Stone* magazine about his own individuality in 1988, when U2's *The Joshua Tree* trumped *Sign* for the Grammy Album of the Year. 'I'm not saying I'm better than anybody else. But you'll be sitting there at the Grammys, and U2 will beat you. And you say to yourself, Wait a minute. I can play that kind of music, too… But *you* will not do "Housequake".'

The room where it happened

Much of *Sign…* was made in a room he would regard as his second home from the start of the decade. Even if there was no place like Minneapolis for Prince, he certainly wasn't immune to the charms of Hollywood.

6650 Sunset Boulevard, to be precise.

His hangout was not a nightclub nor a restaurant, but where he made his music while he was on the West Coast – Sunset Sound Recorders. He even earmarked a special spot there.

It was where they'd made all sorts of classic albums. In Studio 1, the Stones did the overdubs for *Exile on Main Street* and the Doors cut *Light My Fire*. *Led Zeppelin IV* was completed in Studio 2.

Those two rooms had their own mythology.

Sunset Sound was where Brian Wilson tinkered with 'Good Vibrations', Eddie Van Halen tapped out the jam (in Studio 1) that would become 'Eruption' and, in May 1962, where Bobby 'Boris' Pickett and The Crypt Kickers recorded 'Monster Mash'.

'Sunset Sound is one of the few studios that had kept the consoles from '58/'59,' says Todd Herreman. 'Studio 2 was an old mechanics' garage. There was a basketball court. I was a foot taller than Prince, but he would kick my ass at basketball. We used to play ping pong and we had those slamfests. He has a three-piece suit and I'm in jeans.'

Toto and Van Halen were part of the fixtures and fittings. Toto's Steve Lukather remembers learning the intercom codes with bandmate Jeff Porcaro. 'I knew the codes to the intercom system. Studio 1 in front, Studio 2 off the back and Studio 3 is off to the side. I loved the sound of that place, knowing the Stones and the Doors had been there. I have never had a bad experience at Sunset – best sound, best headphones, best players, best engineers wanted to work there. They gave us Disneyland and we used it.' (Side note: Sunset Sound got its start as that's where the Disney animation soundtracks were recorded.)

'They were there all the time,' Sunset engineer Terry

Christian says of the Toto duo, 'whether it was their own records or whether it's other people's records. A lot of work was going through Sunset. Between Lukather and [Jeff] Porcaro, they were playing on anything.'

Grammy award-winning producer and guitarist Jay Graydon calls Studio 2 'one of the best studios in town… the best sound I ever heard.'

Studio 3 – where Fleetwood Mac worked on *Rumours* when their domestic dramas weren't unfolding six hours north west in Sausalito, and which was favoured by Earth Wind & Fire – would develop its own mythology, once Prince had made himself at home there, from 1981's *Controversy* to *Sign o' the Times*.

He would play in the same space as the session players of the day, like Lukather, Jeff and [brother] Steve Porcaro, John 'JR' Robinson – all of whom played extensively on *Thriller* – and Jay Graydon, whose resume spans the guitar solo on Steely Dan's *Peg* to a Grammy for co-writing Earth, Wind & Fire's 'After the Love Has Gone'. That song's producer David Foster, best known for his work with Chicago, songs like Whitney Houston's 'I Have Nothing' and writing the theme from *St. Elmo's Fire*, was at one stage juggling multiple rooms on site.

'You'd get people like Toto or Barbra Streisand or Neil Diamond or Cher and Prince out there, bumping into them or talking to them,' recalls Paul Camarata, who inherited the studio from father Tutti. 'This is the '80s.'

Terry Christian recalls one major difference between Toto's recordings and Prince's. 'There were always a lot of drugs and alcohol on these sessions. With Prince, never any drugs, never any alcohol.'

Studio 3 did feel like home for him. 'I just think he felt comfortable in that room,' intimates Camarata. 'It's kind of a segregated part of the facility. It offers complete privacy. The other studios you have to traverse through the lobby [to get to]. Studio 3 is self-contained. It has its own bathroom, its own lounge.'

'That was the room he loved,' agrees Susan Rogers, 'and he would always get the big room. His preferred way of working was to sit behind the console to move pretty quickly from instrument to instrument.'

Graydon remembers a more distant figure. 'Prince was like a ghost, kinda. You don't get near that guy unless he wants you to. Prince is the guy who's going to isolate himself from everybody apart from the guys he was to work with.'

The API custom-built Demedio console, constructed by Cuban émigré Frank Demedio, and the privacy afforded by Studio 3 – a basketball court away from Studios 1 and 2 – were both lures for him.

'It was the last room they built,' says Peggy McCreary, whose job at Sunset meant she inherited Prince. 'The performance room was big. It had a big isolation booth, its own private lounge, its own back door. He was cocooned in there – he didn't have to see anybody. He didn't want anybody in there that he didn't expect or know. He liked the safety of that studio.'

Prince booked the room out at $2,000 a day for months, whether he was in town or not. That block-booking afforded him the right to bring guests in to produce their own records, like his band the Time, Sheila E and Sheena Easton. He would also let 'his' studio be used while he was on tour or back home. 'It was Prince's inner sanctum,' says Coke Johnson. Studio 3 gave them the opportunity to 'be part of Prince's world even though Prince wasn't there. He was there in spirit.'

James Brown was one guest, who came with his manager, and four or five sheets of poster board with lyric cues of the kind Sid in *The Larry Sanders Show* used to hold up for Larry. 'He read the lyrics out on the poster board,' explained Johnson the in-house engineer. 'Kind of like a teleprompter. He didn't want to read lyrics in front of him. That way he could dance and sing and the manager was holding up the block letters.'

Other guests on time booked out on Prince's dime were Kenny Rogers and Dolly Parton, who recorded *Islands in the Stream* in Studio 3. Dolly Parton told Mike Kloster, the Sunset staff engineer working on the session, that he was 'about as nervous as a kitty cat in a room full of rocking chairs'. He confirms this to be true, adding 'I was surprised by how small and short she was.' (For those curious, Graydon adds that 'What you see on TV, that's Dolly all the time. She's one of the cats.')

Not everyone loved that studio, though. 'Studio 3 was the old accountants' office,' recalls Peggy McCreary. 'There was a story that a woman had died up there. If you were alone at three or four in the morning and could hear footsteps, you left.'

Initially, Prince would be at Sunset on his own or joined by bodyguard Chick Huntsberry. But sometime around the success of *1999* and *Purple Rain*, an entourage developed that included Jill Jones, Wendy & Lisa, Wendy's sister Susannah, Sheila E and the members of Vanity 6. 'A lot of people would be part of his thing,' says Christian, recalling the change in Studio 3's dynamic. 'As an engineer, I would feel a little uncomfortable.'

That discomfort could be not just due to a series of Prince's female friends but the presence of a bed in the studio itself. Mike Kloster feels that the legend 'has got so out of whack. I have heard some really strange stories about that bed. It was never used for anybody.'

Kloster actually bought the double bed. 'It wasn't a queen. I couldn't fit a queen in my Ford Ranger truck. Everybody thinks it was for Prince but he actually got that bed for Peggy so if she wanted to lay down, she could. The funny thing is nobody ever used it.' Sunset's studio manager Craig Hubler eventually told

Prince he had to get rid of it and he offered it back to Kloster, who gave it to his mother Barbra.

Prince relished playing basketball in the courtyard between Studios 2 and 3, which Kenny Rogers (but not Dolly Parton) also played. Those exiled from the studio when Prince chose to record vocals would be more likely to use the pinball machine in the lobby.

Prince was so impressed by Studio 3 that he hired Frank Demedio to recreate the console at his home studio at 7141 Galpin Boulevard, Chanhassen and acoustician George Augspurger to fit it out. He also had a Demedio console installed in Paisley Park.

For Camarata, who saw his guys flown out to Minneapolis to fit out rooms at Galpin Boulevard and then Paisley, Studio 3 has its own legacy which endures. In an era where the big recording studio has been an endangered species, and albums are composed on iPads, bands born and brought up in LA (for instance, Haim) and visitors from Sheffield, England (Arctic Monkeys) continue to work at Sunset.

Camarata keeps hearing the same request. 'A lot of people call up. "I wanna use the Prince room."'

Dirty Mind, the first in a series of firsts

Back in 1978, when making his debut record, Warner Brothers was understandably concerned about an eighteen-year-old let loose in the Record Plant in Sausalito, California producing his first album, *For You*. Some execs on arriving asked 'Where's the band?' The skinny kid with the Afro *was* the band, the whole band, and he proceeded to prove it by playing all the instruments on the record to a level expected of players two decades his senior.

He had the ambition. He had the talent. He had the cojones.

And a three-album deal with Warner Brothers. The scene was set. This strong-willed, competitive, exceptionally talented player was ready to become top dog in music.

Except that's not quite what happened.

By 1980, Prince's three-album deal with Warner Brothers was two albums in, albums which had been made entirely in California. Although *For You* had caused some ripples on the radio – and the label's Lenny Waronker recalls the second album *Prince* selling 'close to 900,000 copies' – by 8 October, the release date of *Dirty Mind*, many still didn't know who Prince was.

He was keen for that to change.

Dirty Mind would be different because it had to be. One of his wisest counsels, Alan Leeds, suggests 'there wasn't too much Prince did that wasn't pre-meditated.' By this stage, every decision was deliberate. He turned up to a photographer and friend Allen Beaulieu's studio in Minneapolis at ten o'clock at night, ready to be photographed.

'He just comes in the studio. When he was in the studio, it was just me and him. I didn't even have an assistant. So he would come up in a trench coat and leg warmers. He would wear anything. Nobody knew who he was.'

So Prince put his plan, one outside of music, into operation.

The provocative look of trench coat, underpants, female suspenders, thigh-length boots and a neckerchief was not an accident. 'That was a major move,' says Waronker now. 'The panties, the title.' The record exec calls it a pay-attention-to-me statement, demonstrating Prince's 'courage and relentless belief in himself'.

Prince delivered his message to Beaulieu. '"I just want to shock people." That's pretty much what he said. That wasn't him every day. That was just for that cover. The next one [*Controversy*] was a brown coat and the next one [the back sleeve of *1999*] was purple. Grey coat cover, brown coat, purple by 1999… every time he got slicker.'

After two topless album sleeves, author and Prince fan Edgar Kruize points out 'Dirty Mind is Prince getting dressed for the first time'. For Dirty Mind, everything, not just the cover, was stripped down.

At a point where some believed Warner Brothers could be willing to say goodbye – it was, after all, a three-album deal – he didn't throw everything at his career. He went back to basics.

His debut album cover was blurry. People weren't paying attention. He disrobed for the second album for a topless head and shoulders shot. Still no attention.

Craig Rice, who worked with Prince from 1984 until 1994, is blunter about where he was after his second album. 'He had to do something radical. They were going to drop him.' (Other Warners executives strenuously dispute this.) For example, the choice of album title and cuts like 'Head', about oral sex, and 'Sister', about incest showed his intent to shift the needle.

He returned east to a studio at his rented home on North Arm Drive in Orono, Minnesota, largely recording on his own with only key lieutenants for company. As well as best friend André Cymone on bass and drummer Bobby Z (the two were thanked as 'heaven-sent helpers' by Prince on the Prince credits), keyboard player Lisa Coleman sang on 'Head' and Matt Fink played a punchy keyboard riff on the title track (and lead single), which would give him a rare writing credit. Cymone threw in a bassline for 'Uptown' and was a source of support in the studio as the drummer for Grand Central, while Morris Day offered the song 'Partyup'. Prince would be credited as its author, in exchange for helping Morris start a new band further down the track.

Released in October 1980, Dirty Mind went gold, with sales

in excess of 500,000. By contrast, Michael Jackson's fifth album, *Off the Wall*, would go on to sell more than two million by 1979. Prince wasn't where he wanted to be yet, but he was finding an audience, with admirers at his record company and his records on black radio.

'Between that and [Prince's fourth album in October 1981] *Controversy*,' remembers Waronker, 'there started to be an incredible vibe about him. *Rolling Stone* were writing about him. The guys who were really into Prince were the urban promotion guys and when they heard *Dirty Mind*, they freaked out. He didn't want to be typecast. Once he did *Dirty Mind*, it came together.' In terms of imagery, Vernon Reid of rock band Living Colour observed to *Record Collector* magazine that, with *Dirty Mind*, Prince 'did something really interesting. He became the pimp and whore in the same body.'

Many critics see the album as the start of Prince's imperial period. It certainly saw some firsts. It was the first, but not the last, album Prince would make at home in Minnesota. It was the first sense of a band, where Matt Fink, Lisa Coleman (both on keyboards), guitarist Dez Dickerson, Bobby Z were brought forward; just after its release, in 1981, he played his first gigs outside the US – in Amsterdam, London and Paris. And it was the first time that the fluidity of Prince's masculine and feminine personalities was expressed in its boldest form.

But for all the critics, the urban department of Warner Brothers and black radio were now paying attention, Prince had one eye on the pop audience, with songs like 'When You Were Mine', later covered by Cyndi Lauper on her 1983 breakthrough album, *She's So Unusual*. 'He had worked out his tactics for career success,' Susan Rogers thinks. 'It was sugary and saccharine, but it was still Prince. He'd been listening to Blondie, the Cars and Talking Heads.'

It was actually the *Dirty Mind* imagery which, decades later, would be the start of the praise for Prince for blurring distinctions between black and white music, and male and female presentation. The title track of the following year's album *Controversy* featured Prince railing against conjecture about his racial politics, about his sexuality and his tempestuous relationship with his father, but this conjecture had been manufactured by him in the rare interviews he did.

Allen Beaulieu confirms that the bold *Dirty Mind* cover was black and white for a reason. 'He definitely wanted black and white, I wanted colour. So we did black and white.'

Dirty Mind was a risk that paid off critically and, to a lesser extent, commercially.

Matt Fink has no doubt of the album's importance. 'It didn't catch on fire. To this day, it hasn't reached platinum status [it reached forty-five on the Billboard Hot 100]. From a critical and growth standpoint, that was a real step forward. Anything after that was just gravy.'

You can't always get what you want

Things were changing in Prince's world. After *Dirty Mind* and *Controversy*, towards the end of 1981, he had momentum.

That didn't smooth out all the bumps in the road.

The former host of *The Tonight Show*, Conan O' Brien, once said: 'The beauty is that through disappointment you can gain clarity, and with clarity comes conviction and true originality.' That's easy for him to say. He never had a bag of fried chicken hit him in the face on stage in front of 90,000 Stones fans at the LA Coliseum.

It was bassist Mark 'BrownMark' Brown's first gig with Prince's band as support to the Stones; he told Matt Fink on the plane over he didn't know anything about them. Their fans, a few at that time from the Hell's Angels fraternity, were not minded to embrace the tight funk Prince and his band were serving up.

The keyboard player winces at the memory of getting 'beaned in the right temple by one of those waxy Coca Cola cups. They threw it hard. They were throwing baggies that had food in them like chicken wings. They were throwing fifths of whiskey bottles and that whistled by Prince's head.'

As well as BrownMark, it was drum tech Brad Marsh's first gig. His memory? 'One guy in the front row who had a paper bag of raw chicken parts.'

Donnie Graves, the *Purple Rain*-era tour accountant, brought the subject up in front of his new boss on that tour. 'I wouldn't say all the blood drained out [Prince's] face but he became visibly shaken up. I could see he went back to that. I could tell that it was soul-crushing and embarrassing to him. After they got through throwing their shoes at him, there were people urinating in cups and throwing it at him.'

Prince was not minded to stay on stage at the Coliseum.

'After he got booed off in the middle of the third song,' Marsh recalls, 'he walked back to his hotel and went home.'

Legendary promoter Bill Graham berated the crowd. Mick Jagger took more direct action to ensure Prince would return. 'Jagger phoned him the day off, which was the Saturday,' remembers Matt Fink. 'He contacted me and Dez [Dickerson] and Bobby [Z], and said "Can you guys get me through to Prince?" Jagger managed to talk him into coming back on the Sunday show. The same thing happened all over again. With that said, we played over half the set and then he cut it short. He shrugged it off. He wasn't angry about it. 'That's their audience, not ours.'''

He might not have shown anger but clearly it had an impact.

Graves says he 'got the impression that there had been some apologies from The Rolling Stones and Prince didn't think they were sincere.'

Andrew Watt, the producer of the last Stones album, 2023's *Hackney Diamonds*, was wearing a Prince T-shirt when he worked with Mick Jagger, which caused the singer to reflect on how upset Prince had been. 'He got beer thrown at him. His heart broken,' Watt remembers being told. 'He says to Mick Jagger backstage "They hate me!" Mick told him, "if you're going to play to a crowd this big, you have to have a rock band. You have got to have a big sound."'

Watt, who has helped acts from Dua Lipa and Miley Cyrus to Elton John and Stevie Nicks construct hits enjoys the benefit of hindsight. As a fan and musician, he has studied the journey Prince traversed with his own sound. His early hits, records like 'Soft and Wet' and 'I Wanna Be Your Lover', are, reasons Watt, 'small on purpose'. He continues: 'Think about Prince watching the Stones from the side of the stage. [Prince is said to have flown straight home after the third song so this could be apocryphal.] If you listen to the drum sound versus the earlier albums, the drums are huge. It's a bigger sound.' Prince's disappointing reception led to clarity, and with that came conviction and his own true originality. The sound would have to get bigger. So would the audience.

By the time Donnie Graves worked with Prince, he had eclipsed Michael Jackson, Bruce Springsteen and Madonna. The accountant speculates the Coliseum gig 'drove him to a place to achieve heights he might not have. That's how self-aware the guy was, that's how pissed off the guy was. I don't think he would have reached the level he reached without that level of humiliation.'

Prince uttered four words when Graves was 'just enough of

an idiot' to raise the Stones debacle at the height of his global domination:

'That's why I'm here.'

Simon Fields, who supervised Prince's pop videos at the height of his fame, is positive about the experience. 'It gave them a lot of press. When your artistry is put under question, that's when you're put to the test and he comes up with excellence.'

Bring on the Revolution

The excellence came in the form of 1982's double album *1999*, which saw Prince go from planning to execution.

This period of his career was key in building the groundwork for *Purple Rain* and, if you look far enough into the distance of nearly five years later, the creative wellspring of his second double album, the *Sign o' the Times* record.

Drummer Michael Bland acknowledges that *Sign...* is 'the album most fans hold up to be the masterpiece. To me, *1999* is where it all came together. The decision to take the world by storm ... he singlehandedly made that record. He couldn't explain to the others what he wanted to do. *1999* – that's the template. His consciousness aligned with pop culture at that time. The stylist walked into the room with the purple coat. Now it's showbiz. Still Prince, but pop music.'

Prince's cousin Chazz Smith and best friend André [Cymone, his contemporary as musician and producer] first heard all eight minutes and eighteen seconds of *1999*'s 'D.M.S.R.' and the musicians were inspired and depressed in equal measure. 'Our mouths just dropped,' laughs Chazz. 'A double album [of which we] said "That reminds us of *Electric Ladyland*." Me and André, we've got to go back to the drawing board.'

Around *1999* (released in October '82, the same calendar

month as the previous two albums), a group of new musicians – Lisa Coleman and Matt Fink on keyboards, drummer Bobby Z and guitarist Dez Dickerson – joined Mark Brown on bass. Prince had an established band, who committed the cardinal sin of skipping a soundcheck. By 1982, Coleman would be singing back-up vocals on a *1999* track ('Free') and be playing on stage with Prince's band the following August.

That doesn't mean they overly informed the sound of the record.

Prince was producing and playing instruments from his first album, with the next two representing a culmination of his writing (and editing) of power pop, and his proficiency of technology came to fruition around Album #4, *1999*. The ambition to move into the mainstream didn't stop there. *1999* was a double album – not by masterplan; Prince just told reporters he couldn't stop writing. He got himself a band proper, didn't really use them as he continued to play most of the record, formed a girl band and created an R&B band and wrote and played on their songs too. Then he took them all on tour.

If you thought there wasn't a Minneapolis music scene before Prince, he took out the insurance of creating the scene himself. 'He created his own competition,' suggests engineer Susan Rogers, so it could appear that there was a scene emanating from Minneapolis, when in reality it was one man.

'I can't think of any popular music artist who could rival Prince. They couldn't play musical instruments or run their business as well as he did. He was a one of a kind artist in so many ways.'

Prince may have been one of a kind, but between The Stones gig in October 1981 and August 1983, when Wendy Melvoin came aboard, he was creating a crew – specifically his own band, the Revolution. The words 'and the Revolution' were written backwards on the *1999* credits, while the sleeve of *Purple Rain* would feature the words 'produced, arranged, composed and performed by Prince and the Revolution'.

'As musicians, the Rolling Stones were not the best,' muses Prince's soundman at the time, Rob 'Cubby' Colby, 'but as a band they were unbelievable. As musicians, they [the Revolution] were good. As a band, they were just unbelievable and I think he kinda felt that and knew it too. He knew we would take care of him and give our best. He would say "It will never be perfect, so don't try and make it perfect."'

For many, the combination Prince assembled with the Revolution was close to perfect. With friends from back home, talented musicians who could push Prince forward to new heights, the leader had assembled his cabinet.

'Wow, a little Sly and the Family Stone'

There is someone else, with whom Prince was frequently compared, particularly around that era, who was another one-off.

Many of Prince's legendary tracks started off with him and his trusty Linn LM-1.

Sly Stone made chart history with 'Family Affair', believed to be the first US number one with a drum machine.

Both men had mixed-race, mixed-sex bands, leading to criticism and misunderstanding in each of their eras.

'He was really into Sly,' adds Prince's A&R at Warner Brothers, Lenny Waronker, 'and that affected him in terms of the different characters who surrounded him and made music with him.'

'Prince was like a huge, huge fan of Sly,' recalls his *Sign*-era keyboard tech David Rule. 'Sly and the Family Stone was like the holy grail to him. His three favourite bands were Sly and the Family Stone, Grand Funk Railroad and Joni Mitchell.'

Both men produced everything themselves, both were bandleaders, both sung socially conscious anthems (*Everyday People, Sign o' the Times*), both criss-crossed genres.

'We used to do a lot of different genres, even country and western,' says Sly and The Family Stone's drummer, Greg Errico. 'I have heard Prince do big band jazz. When we started the group in 1966, it was a conscious effort to include everything! Just music. There was no black and white and that's what the music turned out to be.'

For all Prince's similarities in spirit with Joni and James Brown, you could argue the closest to him musically was Sly. The men did not fraternise, but both were at the Jacksons' last-ever show on the Victory tour at the LA Dodgers' stadium in December 1984, where backstage 'in the catacombs of the stadium', Sly broke Prince's heart, according to Errico. 'It was already established and well known the influence of Sly Stone on Prince, and we knew Prince wanted to meet Sly Stone so badly.

'Me, Sly and my brother are walking in one direction, and Prince is walking in another direction. He had a long-stem rose in his mouth and I understood that he's walking to greet Sly. They passed and Sly didn't even make eye contact. Prince just stopped and melted [about the fact] that that had just happened. He had given his heart to Sly and had a rose in his mouth, but that was that. That was the last encounter.' Errico puts this behaviour down to 'Sly being an asshole. This was the rascal side of Sly. He was like that.'

Privately, Stone admired him. 'Rufus and Sly Stone did a [January 2010] tour in Japan,' recalls Rufus's guitarist Tony Maiden. 'We talked about Prince. Sly was a fan.'

There were areas where the men were different. By 2011, Sly was reported to be living out of a campervan. Prince stayed in control and on top throughout his career. Sly had problems with drugs – plenty of problems – and Errico feels that 'Prince looked at the trail that existed there and said "I don't wanna do that". All the important and influential acts of the late '60s, there's a lot of casualties and, of the acts later on, a big percentage were forewarned.'

Another of Sly's drummers, Andy Newmark, who played with Stone later in his career on 1973's *Fresh* album, noted the difference. 'When I worked with Sly, he wasn't functioning much as bandleader, or anything else. He was just going through the motions on stage and getting high the rest of the time. I seem to recall that Prince never got high or did any drugs. He worked 24/7 and it showed.'

Prince's moodiness was less chemically related, notes Errico. 'Prince was very different, more guarded, moody, could switch in the blink of an eye. Sly wasn't necessarily like that until the drugs heavily influenced him.'

A face-to-face discussion about collaborating, according to Michael Bland who played drums for Prince from 1989–96, had not gone well. 'That predated my work but that was my understanding. Just that it was not a productive meeting. He [Sly] was just too far into whatever it was he was into.'

Ruth Arzate, Prince's manager in the '00s, says that he had also tried in vain to reach out. 'He tried to help Sly Stone financially, but Sly wouldn't accept it. We couldn't find him. He was living in a trailer home at the time.' Sly Stone died on 9 June 2025.

But there was one important lesson which Prince learned in the 1999 era. 'He figured out who his audience was,' Bobby Z told The Current. '"I'm going to take the Stones audience and I'm going to take the Rick James audience and make it one big 'my audience."'

Around that time, Greg Errico recalls an early incarnation of the Revolution. 'I remember the first time I saw the group on

TV and I'm thinking to myself, *Wow, a little Sly and the Family Stone*. Black, white, male, female, the funky music – everything exuded us. He obviously touted Sly as a big influence. He wasn't shy about it. He wore it.'

The Time's Jimmy Jam sums up Sly and The Family Stone as 'Prince's whole blueprint for putting a band together.'

The comparisons really started around the *1999* album.

Dan The Automator, who has worked with Gorillaz and Depeche Mode and scored the film *Booksmart*, calls the album 'his true Sly & The Family Stone moment', adding that it is Prince's 'I'm a black rock band' statement. 'I think that was a Sly thing that never really got recaptured until Prince did it. He was right there at the moment but using a distinctive sound. That's why that moment was so big for him. Stevie was making soul records with synths but Prince – it's black rock with synthesisers. So revolutionary.'

A whole new audience

There was another thing he did in that era, perhaps the most important thing.

He delivered hits.

1999's title track, 'Little Red Corvette' and 'Delirious' all made the Billboard Top 20. The title track, with female and male members, was reminiscent of what Sly used to deliver with the Family Stone. Intended backing vocals from Dez Dickerson, Lisa Coleman and Jill Jones were pulled up in the mix to open the song, jointly leading with Prince.

The song was born after a stop at a hotel which had a 'free HBO' sign where a documentary about Nostradamus (most likely *The Man Who Saw Tomorrow*, narrated by Orson Welles) was showing. 'We were all blown away by this,' drummer Bobby

Z told The Current's Jim McGuinn. The next morning 'the water cooler talk is "Did you see…?" Prince had written a song.'

More than that, *1999* had songs that were working across radio sectors. 'White pop music in the '80s was so protectionist,' points out Bill Stephney, president of Def Jam Recordings in 1987. 'Black radio was playing Malcolm McLaren.' Mainstream FM radio was less enlightened. R&B hits by Cherrelle, the Gap Band and the System were not getting played on white radio. Covers of the same tunes by Robert Palmer would be.

Stephney, part of the team behind Public Enemy, was well aware of the band's crossover instincts. 'We were pro black but we were on tour with the Beastie Boys, with Anthrax, with U2. We were sampling Slayer. There is no Public Enemy without me seeing the Clash at Bonds International Casino.

'We were just trying to do the Clash and hip hop. Our minds were incredibly open. The guy who did bridge all of that, who did get played on rock radio, was Prince. "Little Red Corvette" got played, "1999" got played, "Purple Rain" got played. "Lady Cab Driver" (from the *1999* album) got played by the more progressive stations.'

It was the first of these which was Prince's biggest crossover hit to date, and proof he could reach a white audience. He was sitting in Lisa Coleman's pink 1964 Ford Mercury Montclair when the melody of 'Little Red Corvette' came to him. The lyrics about a promiscuous woman who was out of his league, whom he wondered if he had enough class to date – may have germinated from a previous girlfriend from 1979, Mi-Ling Stone Poole, from St Paul. Prince hailed from grittier north Minneapolis. 'I first met him at a party on New Year's Eve 1976 in Bloomington, Minnesota.'

A friend made introductions and told them 'I thought you'd be cute together because you're both short.' Prince may have wondered if he had enough class but two days after his gig at the Capri Theatre, they started dating. 'He was shocked that I had talked to him. He had given the DJ [a copy of his first single] 'Soft and Wet' and we would dance to 'Le Freak' by Chic.

'The song is that the girl is older but I was more mature. He was not the Prince that he was when he was dating Vanity, Jill Jones and all the other women at the same time. It was when he was shy and not that sure of himself. When he came to my house, he saw all these [photos of] jocks on my wall.'

Mi-Ling Stone Poole got married in November 1983 and didn't properly hear the song and join the dots with the lyrics until 1985. The pictures of jockeys on the wall in her room when they got together had made her rethink the lyrics. 'When I first heard it, I said "Are you kidding me?!?" I had no idea the song was about me.'

She is operating on timing and instinct because if the song is about her, the man who wrote it would be the last person to confirm it. 'He liked it that way. Every girl thought she was the "Little Red Corvette".

'When we were together, it was passionate. He respected the fact that I wasn't a fun girl. My parents had divorced, I was in school working two jobs and my support system was me and my sister. I had my own car.'

'Little Red Corvette' was the record Stevie Nicks heard when driving on her honeymoon, which inspired her song 'Stand Back', on which she asked Prince to play at Sunset Sound. 'I played the skank Michael Jackson part. They were looking for that "Billie Jean" kind of thing,' chuckles Steve Lukather who took Jimmy Iovine's call after other guitarists – including David Williams, who actually played the 'Billie Jean' riff – hadn't delivered what they wanted. 'They needed something to make it dance. One take, it was done.'

In 1981, Prince got booed off stage supporting the Rolling Stones. In 2016, the band chose 'Little Red Corvette' to play as a tribute to him.

The one-two punch of the title track and 'Little Red Corvette' expanded the group of Prince fans dramatically.

Prince was using his band but working on his own: having his cake and eating it. The lyrical themes of partying through nuclear apocalypse would develop into more mature themes by *Sign o' the Times'* laments around earthly problems.

Christian McBride, the director of the Newport Jazz Festival, who came within a whisker – or a phone call from John Blackwell Jr – of playing bass for Prince in the twenty-first century, calls *1999* 'as much of a masterpiece as *Sign o' the Times*. I don't think it sounds like any other African-American artist at the time. It sounds like nothing else that was on the market. He combined all these new wave and funk and jazz abstractions. I just thought he was so incredibly creative and different. It wasn't just weird. It had a real gravitational force. Being a Weather Report fan, I could see many comparisons to Weather Report on *1999*.'

In terms of Prince's audience, Allen Beaulieu puts it more bluntly. '[With] *1999*, he started getting white girls.' That audience, increasingly whiter and more mainstream, was built and grown off ninety-eight gigs of the 1999 tour, also known as the Triple Threat tour. With *1999*, Prince created an audience, and a tour with two new bands he had constructed. Prince paid for *Purple Rain* with the profits from that tour.

On *Sign o' the Times*, Prince had the tech down, a band close at hand, and was fleshing out his musical ideas across various genres. *1999* was where he had really started assembling the building blocks.

And back in 1982, the sky was turning purple and Prince had a film idea in his head, which would need funding.

CHAPTER 4

THE BALLAD OF DOROTHY PARKER

*The Ballad of Dorothy Parker … the happy accident …
Prince and Joni … The individual voice …. Making the
band … Making another band. Time for the Time …
Why build two bands when you can build three?*

The Ballad of Dorothy Parker

Morris Hayes, Prince's bandmate of two decades, once asked the multi-instrumentalist/singer-songwriter/producer/ businessman/filmmaker/fashion template/logo consultant/ what he thought he was best at.

'You know what, man, I'm a songwriter, I'm a poet. Nobody reads anymore.'

'Prince had a library at his house in Beverley Hills. Most of the books were [about] psychology. He had all kinds of poetry. He was very well-read. He had a stack of magazines and books. [He would say] "People don't read."'

Prince saw his lyrics as the strongest part of his arsenal. He thought of himself first and foremost as a musical storyteller. It's what U2's Bono paid tribute to in a 2020 fan letter, pointing out that many of his songs ('When Doves Cry', 'Raspberry Beret', 'Kiss') start with a set-up line letting you know what the song is about, calling him 'the master of the establishing shot' (what cinematographers frame to help directors set a scene) and 'the most cinematic of musical geniuses'.

The most unusual track on *Sign o' the Times*, the one reflecting a bunch of different Princes – 'The Ballad of Dorothy Parker' – is a story song. It's the result of a technical mishap and it sounds like nothing that could be played on pop radio. Plus, for all his subsequent investment in a library, it's widely considered that his then fiancée Susannah Melvoin had to tell him who Dorothy Parker was.

Bill Stephney calls it 'one of the Prince songs you really wanna sample'. He asked if it could be sampled on Trouble Funk's 1993 album 'but we got a no. We understood.' The song may have impressed the hip hop elite, but the narrator in the song who asks for a 'fruit cocktail' is hardly speaking the parlance of rappers. As Susan Rogers suggested, Prince's idiosyncrasies marked him out. 'He was not interested in being a stereotype,' she told the BBC in 2020. 'In the words of Thelonious Monk, the genius is the man who is most himself.'

The song's narrator – we are assuming Prince – tells the story of Dorothy, a waitress on the promenade working a night shift, whose response to 'Prince' ordering a fruit cocktail is that he sounds masculine – 'a real man' – and offers to take a bath with him. As infidelity songs go, it's more unusual than John Lennon's 'Norwegian Wood' or Billy Paul's 'Me & Mrs Jones'.

Once the waitress turns on the radio to hear Joni Mitchell's 'Help Me' (her only Billboard Top 10 hit from 1974's *Court and Spark*), Prince mimics a phone ring sound effect and agrees to take a bath, but with his trousers on because he is with someone else. The song then takes another handbrake turn.

The waitress hadn't seen a film adaptation because she hasn't read the book, and claims to have been blinded because of a witch's curse and Prince takes another bubble bath. So the lyrics say.

Prince has not said whether this is based on a true story and neither Susan Rogers nor the Melvoins had at the time of writing. What Rogers does know is that, sonically, a mistake is at the heart of it. Sal Greco rather ungallantly says of his fellow engineer that it was 'Susan's fault'.

Cuban émigré Frank Demedio had just installed the console in Prince's home studio, but Rogers the in-house engineer (almost literally, considering the hours she kept) was fitting the wires in April 1986 when Prince arrived. She was figuring out the console's positive and negative supplies when he breezed in ready to work. She now says she thought, *How did he not hear that there's no high end on this?* 'I like this new console,' he said on leaving later. 'It sounds kinda dull.'

Greco remembers Prince's fondness for this kind of sound manipulation. 'He liked to saturate the tape. Too much distortion is bad, [but] some is good. We had more headroom. I got one more and he pushed the faders up to ten. So you would make it [what he wanted] happen.'

Rogers says now that Prince 'used that fate intervening in order to make art out of it.' The mistake – in this case, the dullness from the Demedio console – would work in his favour.

Jazz musician Christian McBride likens Prince to his former bandmate Herbie Hancock. 'He's so wide open. He's open to everything. He loves these moments that are so-called mistakes. He wants that. He never gives you too many rules. He enjoys the challenge of being in that grey area.'

'If you have the mindset that there are no mistakes,' reasons Miles Davis's drummer Jack DeJohnette, who knew all about playing in the grey areas, 'there aren't wrong notes. Only wrong resolutions. He [Davis] never hears it as wrong. He was able to use what the band came up with. A lot of band members and bandleaders do that.'

Jay Graydon, a session player for everyone from Dolly Parton to George Benson, has a craftier method. 'If I play a note that is too far from the chord changes, I will play the note as a pattern. I will play it again to make you believe I meant to play it the first time.'

There were plenty of accidents on purpose happening in Prince's world by the time he was recording *Sign o' the Times*. 'At that stage,' recalls Coke Johnson, then working at Sunset Sound, 'he was doing a lot of experimental stuff. Different sounds on different effects pedals. That may be why he got away from the Revolution, because he wanted to change his sound.'

'I hate the word experiment,' Prince told *Rolling Stone* in 1990. 'It sounds like something you didn't finish.' When he thought a track was finished and an engineer spotted a mistake, he made sure to finish.

'He would usually just say "God wanted it that way",' says another engineer, Michael Koppelman. 'If there was a mistake, if it wasn't something brutal, he would just let it go. The performance is more important than the actual aspect, the groove – if it's not a glaring technical glitch or a really bad note. He wasn't the only artist like that.'

The happy accident

There are mistakes on *Sign...*, as experts might understand them: the repeating backing vocals on 'Forever in My Life', the flat sound in 'The Ballad of Dorothy Parker' and accidentally distorted voice on the recording of 'If I Was Your Girlfriend'.

Prince embraced those as part of the wider picture. He would do this live too, according to Morris Hayes. 'He was great at that. That was the thing Prince could always do. If I messed up, he would always say "What did you just do?" He could do it over again and play it. Even when I played some wrong notes, I would say, "Prince, let me fix that solo." He would have the horn players play a note and then it worked.'

Michael Bland, his drummer in the '90s, adds that 'there's no such thing as an accident. Whatever it is, he found a way to use it. He was playing an organ and he leaned over to play and his necklace with the symbol on it hit a key and he made some kind of riff out of it. He never passed on an opportunity to try something.'

The singer Patrice Rushen knows this method all too well. 'That's how it happens sometimes – not to be afraid, to embrace something and to be able to hear or see a diamond in the rough, or "Wait a minute, right there". That's a unique talent to have that some people have. They can filter what's good from what's great.'

This happened to Rushen herself making 'Forget Me Nots', her biggest hit, where bassist Freddie Washington played notes not on the page and which were quickly seized upon. 'The listener and the person who's playing will discover. That's the stuff that good producers used to be made for.'

Prince was happy with the final version of 'The Ballad of Dorothy Parker'. Another rendition, with Eric Leeds on horns, was ditched and resurfaced on the 2020 reissues. Clare Fischer added strings on one version, but the spare one without both horns and strings is what has endured.

Different people love different things about the track. Tionne 'T-Boz' Watkins of TLC loves it because, as she told the BBC in 2017, 'it's not set up from top to bottom like a regular song. I love "If I Was Your Girlfriend" and "Adore", but there's something about that song that's the perfect song. You can do everything to that song – clean the house, have sex, drive.'

Alan Leeds calls it 'a boutique record'; Todd Herreman 'a left turn'. James Poyser of the Roots argues of the song that 'only he could have done that. The sonics of that thing, the way the drums sound, the weird chord progression.' The song could only have come out of Prince's imperfect imagination – and a malfunctioning mixing desk.

Prince gave his best buddy André Cymone a playback of the record, and he admitted to Ryan Bethea that he was 'blown away' by this track. Rashida, Prince's DJ in the '00s, says her calling card was being known as 'the girl who played "The Ballad of Dorothy Parker" on a Friday night.' She described the reaction she received at playing such an unconventional song for the dancefloor as 'Really?!? Are you tripping?'

Singer-songwriter Ani DiFranco feels the song reveals him to be 'a song crafter as well as a funk master. Sometimes it was a social commentary about saying something. All those different song natures are mashed up. See how many writers are in there – [a] deeply feeling, deeply vulnerable human being. All things that he felt came through and made many of us feel less alone – to feel seen and to feel heard.'

For all that critics referenced the Beatles during Prince's *Around the World in a Day* period, this might be the closest he came to one of Lennon and McCartney's story songs.

Prince and Joni

'The Ballad of Dorothy Parker' would be the first song Prince recorded at his home studios in Galpin Boulevard. It would be like no other song he recorded before or since. And, of course, it name-checked Joni Mitchell.

The effect Joni had on him ran deep.

Part of the reason he hired nineteen-year-old Wendy Melvoin to the ranks of the Revolution was her open chord playing – what Joni called her own 'chords of enquiry' – he overheard while walking past her bedroom. 'It was Wendy and Lisa that turned him on to Joni Mitchell,' confirms LeRoy Bennett, Prince's lighting director.

Prince's cousin Charles 'Chazz' Smith suggests a fandom from childhood, referring to what is believed to be his favourite Joni album, *The Hissing of Summer Lawns*. 'We would wear that album out and if you listen to "For You", you can hear a lot of those vocal improvisations. We tripped hard on Joni Mitchell.' Prince would cover 'A Case of You' from her 1971 album *Blue* throughout his career. Listening to that album would, claims his Purple Rain-era tour accountant Donnie Graves, reduce Prince to tears 'dozens of times'.

By the time of his heyday, Joni became attached to Prince too, attending a listening party for *Around the World in a Day* and visiting his Eden Prairie rehearsal space, as well as the *Under the Cherry Moon* world premiere and the show in Denver shortly afterwards (2 July 1986), where engineer Todd Herreman recalls 'Joni came out to sing back-ups on *Purple Rain*. They met a lot.'

As people and artists, they had plenty in common. Joni was dedicated to jazz, to the extent she devoted an album to Charlie Mingus, and played with Wayne Shorter, Jaco Pastorius and Herbie Hancock among others. Hancock was asked by Prince to bring Joni to a party Prince threw in LA. He saw Hancock and Joni Mitchell. 'He was shocked to see Joni,' he admitted to the BBC's Colin Paterson. 'I don't think he paid attention to me. He was almost in tears – he admired Joni Mitchell so much. I had never known that before. He loved her lyrics, he loved her music, he loved her.'

Prince's parents were jazz musicians and he wrote material for Miles Davis, and dabbled around jazz in 1987 with his Madhouse fusion project.

Brian Blade, who played drums for Joni earlier this century, remembers her talent for recruiting, similar to Prince and Miles. 'She had that gift that Miles had of spotting this person's gift. "If I get together with my own or these others, then this magic will come." Music will come and become something more than images – having the right people in your life at the right time.'

Perhaps the deepest musical connection was that both Joni and Prince were dedicated to being their own producer. Earth, Wind & Fire's Verdine White was attached – and then, swiftly, at his Highness's demand, unattached – to produce Prince's 1978 debut, *For You*. Joni's first album was produced by David Crosby, but only to the extent, she told writer Barney Hoskyns, 'that he'd keep producers off me. For the most part, producers are spirit-bruisers. They're formula people who usually only know what's been before.'

On Joni's second record, the proposed producer went away for a fortnight. Joni turned to engineer Henry Lewy and asked 'Could we get it done in two weeks before he gets back?' 'Henry and I made thirteen albums without a producer. I didn't need a babysitter. I worked in a focused way in the studio, so I didn't need somebody reeling me in.'

Both experienced serious childhood illnesses – Joni contracting polio when she was nine, Prince suffering epileptic seizures until he was seven – which could have fed into this shared forward motion with their music, passing on the chance to commemorate their older records, or reel out nothing but the hits live. They would be partying together into the twenty-first century.

Although Prince was the 'star of stars' (the words of his then backing singer Shelby Johnson) at the Hollywood parties he would throw in the mid-'00s, Sam Jennings ponders whether Prince acted to anyone with deference. 'The closest was with Joni Mitchell. He was very excited. He wanted to talk music with her. There was someone special. She was in awe of him too. She deferred to him a lot. She recognised who he was.' Joni was spotted at these parties, staying up to chat over pancakes at breakfast. While Stevie Wonder, Herbie Hancock and Prince jammed on stage, she was playing pool. 'Prince came over and started playing her at pool,' laughs Ruth Arzate, his manager around the *3121* era. 'I think he let her win, I don't remember. We didn't allow smoking in the house. She went outside and smoked and Prince didn't say a word. That's how much he loved her.'

The individual voice

Ultimately, Prince respected two things about both peers and up-and-comers: a work ethic and a sound of their own.

One thing in particular he was seeking was artists inspired by other artists in unusual ways, so that they preserved their own personality. 'Guitarists should listen to singers for solo ideas – especially women singers,' he told *Guitar Player* magazine in 2004, the same year as he called the Grammys to ask to duet with Beyoncé (the pair sang 'Purple Rain', 'Baby I'm a Star', 'Crazy in Love' and 'Let's Go Crazy'). 'Women haven't had a chance to run the world yet, so you still hear the blues in their singing. Try to play one of the runs that Beyoncé or Ella Fitzgerald does and you will surely learn something.'

Dave Hampton, who ran Paisley Park in the '00s, says his boss 'thought highly of Beyoncé and who she was and how she was delivering her artistry. Madonna had her uniqueness. All artists have their own way of being.'

Carlos Alomar played guitar for David Bowie between 1974

and 1987, and argues that 'David Bowie and Prince were extremely curious individuals. It's a redeeming characteristic. It keeps you young. You have so many artists that stagnate in their own realm comparing themselves to everybody. There are going to be one or two artists who just say "the hell with it". When you do meet somebody that does that, don't you want to find out more? We have something that you like. We call it a signature look.'

As well as his music making him a one-off, the way Prince did things was singular, to put it mildly.

Making the band

While Prince's vision was often singular, his working methods could be collaborative – never more so than when he got his band together. With all due respect to the *Sign*-era band Sheila put together, to the New Power Generation (1990–2013) and to 3rdEyeGirl (2013–2016), the band which normally follows 'Prince &...' in the wider consciousness is the Revolution. As Prince had looked to reject Warners' positioning purely in the R&B lane, part of being considered as a rock star would mean his own merry men – and, crucially, women.

Keyboard players Matt Fink and Lisa Coleman and drummer Bobby Z Rivkin, brother of another studio associate David Z Rivkin, had been helping Prince since *Dirty Mind*, bassist Mark Brown had come on board to replace André Cymone at the Rolling Stones gig in October 1981 and, when Prince heard Wendy Melvoin playing in her girlfriend Lisa Coleman's bedroom aged nineteen, he hired her on the spot.

So the Revolution were born complete with requisite Prince nicknames. Wendy & Lisa didn't need one as they had a musical telepathy borne from their relationship and their musical families.

Brown became BrownMark, Bobby Z Rivkin's surname was dropped and Matt Fink was soon referred to as Dr Fink after a costume change into medical scrubs one night in Chicago.

Prince's albums, from *1999* to *Parade*, were released as Prince and the Revolution. The influence the band had on him ran deep. Wendy and Lisa were huge Joni Mitchell fans. 'I can hear my influence in "Purple Rain" in the harmony, but I don't know if that's coming from him or Wendy and Lisa,' Joni said in a 1988 interview, 'because they've also assimilated some of the modality of the open tunings.'

Matt Fink would be by Prince's side from 1979 until 1991, while Mark Brown's band Mazarati was the creative wellspring that would lead to *Kiss*.

Together, though, was where the Revolution scored. Working with Prince day in and day out – being drilled in rehearsals to play his ideas and bring along theirs – produced arguably the most creative and fruitful spell of his career. Gradually, they came onboard and Prince kicked on at lightning speed. When he was writing and recording as many as three songs in a day, he would also work these songs out in rehearsals alongside his closest musical foils. That was where the Revolution helped. But, even then, they couldn't keep up with the songs Prince was writing. Few could.

Making another band. Time for the Time

When you're writing as many songs as Prince was in the late '70s and early '80s, recruiting another band couldn't hurt in managing the workload. A separate entity could perform the songs which he and the Revolution didn't have time to record and release. Only, in some cases, it was like Superman inventing his own Kryptonite.

Prince's cousin Charles 'Chazz' Smith had been drumming in Grand Central when he took Morris Day, who was in his photography class in freshman year at North High School, round to meet his new other band, the Time. Day took a turn on the sticks. Prince let his cousin go.

Morris Day would later write the groove for 'Partyup' for Prince in 1981 and was given a straight choice. Credit for the song, or his own band.

He chose wisely.

Jimmy Jam and Terry Lewis had been making music with their own bands like Flyte Tyme and the Family when they got together with keyboardist Monte Moir and singer Alexander O'Neal. This was the Time.

They would go on to usher in three hit albums, but drama too. In 1981, before the band had played a show, Prince fired singer O'Neal, replacing him with Day, and later sacked Jam and Lewis, who would go on to become one of the most successful production teams in late twentieth-century music history. One night in Cincinnati, the band threw food at Prince – quite a lot more food than the raw chicken he'd faced supporting the Stones.

'He would get you outside of your box,' laughs Terra Hinrichs, a make-up artist on tours with the Time and the Revolution. 'He never settled for little bits of you. He wanted all of you and then some. It's like the boot camp of life. Jimmy and Terry were talking – "Do this, now dance and do that" – and then they ended up being this [amazing] band.'

O'Neal, being a bit older, was not prepared to be pushed around and wanted specifics around payment. The confrontation where he brought up the subject, he now reflects, 'wasn't that type of dramatic situation. I had some questions in reference to the business interview that was required of me.

'Sometimes you have the talent to be a great musician, but you're not in a position to make great business decisions. When you have the expectations of a company like Warner Brothers and you're playing everything, that's way out there. I think he could have been more relaxed about it.' O'Neal points out he was 24, but that 'Prince couldn't have been more than twenty. I thought at the time he could maybe be a little more humble. Sometimes when you come from a simple environment – and Prince was in his Warner Brothers, Hollywood family – all of a sudden life gets a little different.'

Once Prince and O'Neal fell out over money and the latter was jettisoned, a new singer was required. 'Morris Day didn't want to be a frontman at all,' recalls *Dirty Mind* photographer Allen Beaulieu. 'Prince had to show him how to be up front, but once he got in a frame of mind, it took him hours. It wasn't [that] he just walked on stage and became a front guy. So he's not that person.'

Prince was unsurprisingly in charge of every last detail, which didn't always make for the most nurturing atmosphere. If he wanted credit for the Time, perhaps Prince also had to take some of the blame for the chaos.

The preening peacock with his own mirror was work-shopped, Beaulieu adds. He describes Prince's autocratic bandleader style in the vein of his hero, not just for one band but three.

'Prince came up with all that James Brown-y stuff. During the tour Prince would supervise all three bands, playing behind the curtain for the first two, and joining the Revolution on stage as their bandleader. No one got off lightly.'

Engineer Michael Koppelman is not alone in observing that Day's over the top personality wasn't exclusively his own. 'Prince was exactly like the Morris Day character in *Purple Rain*.

Prince would laugh and joke like that and make fun of people but Morris was completely quiet at least when I saw him.'

Prince's childhood friend Terry Jackson is a little less charitable. 'Morris got really lucky. Alexander O'Neal let Prince know he wasn't going to put up with any of his nonsense. He had all these songs with no vocals on them.'

'The Time were a formidable performance group,' remembers *Purple Rain* director Albert Magnoli. 'Live, they kicked your butt. They had the production and visual and performance chops. He knew they were really, really good. He worked with them to put the band together.'

Prince may have created his own competition, but that created rivalry he didn't enjoy. From the Time's perspective, treating them mean didn't always keep them keen. 'My cheque was for $150 a week,' remembers drummer Jellybean Johnson. 'At the end of the tour, our bonus was $250. We weren't getting paid that much, so our only solace was whupping his ass on stage.'

Sixty-one dates on the Controversy tour from November 1981 to March 1982 with the Time, Prince and the Revolution and third act Zapp had led to a rivalry between Prince and his band which spilled over. Tour manager Bill Reeves characterises him as 'a very autocratic ruler'. Drummer Jellybean Johnson calls the Time 'his Frankenstein moment. He created us. He couldn't kill us because we *killed*.'

Prince himself chose another monster analogy when discussing the group with Detroit DJ The Electrifying Mojo on 7 June 1986, his twenty-eighth birthday. 'They were, to be perfectly honest, the only band I was afraid of. And they were turning into, like, Godzilla.'

Prince was learning on the job himself but supervising all three bands.

If the Time were under pressure, so was he.

The Time were slaying every night, says Jimmy Jam, 'but he would also think "I have got to go out and play". He loved it but he knew that it would make it harder for him.

'Our stage would get smaller and smaller, we would have less and less of the lighting rig. He was very competitive.

'Prince taught us the best work ethic. He would rehearse our band for six hours, then he would rehearse The Revolution for six hours and then go into the studio and write songs and present it to the band the next day. He made us the best we could possibly be.'

An example of his mentoring came when Jam was being taught to play the Time's 777-9311. 'Jimmy Jam. [Prince always called him Jimmy Jam.] What are you doing with your left hand? Do Monte [Moir]'s part. It's got to be bigger than the record.

'Jimmy Jam. Why are you not singing? It's got to be bigger than the record.

'Jimmy Jam. Why are you not doing the choreography? You should be able to do the dance.'

Jam admits that, at first, he 'couldn't do it.' The next day, Prince called 777.

'We start playing and a minute in, I realise, I'm playing with both hands, doing the choreography, and I'm playing with my handkerchief and doing extra. He sees me better than I see myself. He knew I could do it. '

Both tours – Controversy, from November '81 until March '82, and Triple Threat, from November '82 until April '83 – headed for the critic-packed entertainment coastal capitals of Los Angeles and New York, but the Time were only playing behind the curtain for third act Vanity 6, about whom more later. Prince kept the Time off the bill, leading to tears backstage.

'It was heartbreaking,' says Jellybean Johnson. 'LA and

New York, he purposely took us off and he made us play for Vanity 6. It was so heartbreaking because these are the two meccas of entertainment. Every famous person known to man was backstage. The most famous prominent film actors and basketball players wanted to see the Time and were wondering why we didn't play.'

For Jimmy Jam and Terry Lewis, there were consolations. 'Prince always got good reviews,' reflects Jimmy Jam. *'Prince was good but you have got to see the Time ...* We kind of quoted him the reviews and that couldn't happen in the big cities which were New York and LA. We were purposely kept off those shows.

'We didn't play Madison Square Garden and we didn't play The (LA) Forum. We did play Long Beach and that was where we met Janet.'

That would work out all right for them, and her. (Jam and Lewis produced Janet Jackson's multi-platinum albums from 1986's *Control*).

Back on 14 March 1982, simmering band tensions came to a head in Cincinnati. The Time were in the middle of 'Cool' when they noticed their sidekick (and Morris's valet) Jerome Benton was missing, as was guitarist Jesse Johnson. 'Big Chick [Huntsberry, Prince's bodyguard] had taken Jesse off the stage,' explains Jellybean Johnson, 'and they took him back to the Revolution's dressing room where they handcuffed him to a rail and poured eggs all over him.' Jeff Sharp recalls another food fight at New Jersey's Capitol Theatre, where the crew enabled Prince to be rigged up to drop out the ceiling on to the stage interrupting the Time's set.

'When that happens,' continues Jellybean Johnson, 'Prince gets up and jams on guitar at the Time. The audience is tripping about this. We finish the set, thinking "This is war". Jesse was so outraged he literally tore the handrail off the wall. There were eggs, all sorts of food flying everywhere. It was crazy, man.

'He has been taken off the stage and handcuffed by a huge guy. The only problem they [the Revolution] have is that they have got to go and perform. We decided to take our suits off and put on clothes we didn't care got messed up, put garbage bags on top of those. We sent someone out, they got a bunch of eggs. We went down underneath the stage, and sat in front of Prince and the Revolution. They saw we had taken our suits off. And we waited.

'The final song, Chick comes and gets Prince with a big umbrella, and when they came back off the stage, all hell broke loose. We were messing them up. We got 'em good. Bobby and Matt, Morris was throwing eggs at them. We egged him 'cos Big Chick couldn't stop us. This went on for a good hour.'

'What the Time did, literally, that afternoon,' recounts the Revolution's Matt Fink, '[was] they had their management people run out and get hefty garbage bags and shower caps, cut holes and they had the shower caps on and cut holes for arms, they bought dozens of eggs and waited offstage for us. As soon as we left the stage, they pelted us with eggs. They just nailed me. Anybody in the band was fair game. They were throwing them hard. It was stinging. During our show, they were tossing eggs on stage and some of them hit the monitor mixing board off to the right of the stage.' This enraged sound engineer Rob 'Cubby' Colby who was aware of the cost to the equipment.

The ultimate question. Who won?

'Prince won,' says one of his closest aides, Alan Leeds. 'One deciding factor. Big Chick could have taken on five of us. Prince signed their pay cheques.'

'I would have called it a draw,' suggests Bill Reeves. 'Food fights eventually always come out a draw because you run out of stuff to throw. Honestly, I think the Time was my first reaction. My sense of it would have been the Time.' Matt Fink judges the winner as 'nobody. At one point, I felt The Time had a little bit of an upper hand.'

Of course, if you're keeping score, it was probably Prince 1 Morris Day 0.

'Prince always got mad because I said in later years "We definitely won the food fight",' laughs Johnson now. 'He made Morris pay for the damage to all of the rig and it ran into thousands of dollars.'

The Time's Jimmy Jam picks up the story: 'Prince won because we got fined for the damage. Zapp's drum kit got kicked off stage and broke. Even if we won the actual fight, we were the losers because we had to pay the bill.'

Zapp's Roger Troutman was unimpressed. On saying goodbye at the end of the tour, he looked at Matt Fink, shook his head and sighed 'Grown men...' Zapp were replaced on the next tour, Triple Threat, by another group – Vanity 6 – and an even more brutal schedule of eighty-seven dates.

That didn't stop Prince's fondness for the Time. 'Ultimately he did love us', says Jimmy Jam, 'and later in life, he was very complimentary and proud of us.'

The snarky one-liners of Morris Day were also useful cover for Prince, whose profile was on the rise. 'A lot of humour that Morris did on the Time,' argues Jimmy Jam, 'was written by Prince - things Prince couldn't say as himself. He could give them to Morris.'

In 1986, after comparing them to Godzilla, he admitted: 'I still love all those guys and hope they get back together, because I want some competition, you know?'

Why build two bands when you can build three?

If the internal dynamics between the Time and Prince were complicated, Vanity 6 was something else entirely.

The Time were built in Minneapolis, but Prince's other group started to take shape the day after a famous night in music history in December 1980 when Prince played the Ritz in New York in front of KISS, Andy Warhol and Nile Rodgers.

It was also the night Prince met Brenda Bennett, in inauspicious circumstances.

'I'm in the elevator going down to the Ritz,' she recalls. Prince was due to play a gig there the following night, 10 December. 'Roy [Prince's lighting director LeRoy Bennett] wanted me to meet him and chat with him. The elevator stops and some of the crew got in and said "Did you hear what happened last night?"'

As John Lennon was her idol, and she was in New York, it is a day she is unlikely to forget.

Roy had invited his then girlfriend to see Prince at the Ritz, telling her: 'I think he's incredible and he's going to be a huge star.' Soon after, they married and, a little time later, Bennett had to go on tour. But he wanted Brenda with him.

She took on 'four or five jobs, two of them were for Prince. One of them was taking care of his wardrobe, the other was filming the shows.' She took over from Morris Day on filming. Prince is believed to have all his shows videoed from the early '80s, often screening them for his band in the early hours to point out errors to individuals.

Going on the road was no big deal to Brenda, who had toured the States in the '70s with Mott the Hoople and Queen as part of Ken Lyon and the Tombstone Blues Band. One day, a few years later, 'out in the Midwest somewhere', she was preparing things in Prince's dressing room when the boss entered and started working on his make-up. 'He put a cassette tape on the player and it was a rough edit of Stevie Nicks' "Stand Back". This was a song which had been inspired by the Fleetwood Mac singer driving in Santa Barbara with "Little Red Corvette" on the radio. Prince had added a keyboard part.

'When you're a singer, you sing. I've been singing all my life, I started harmonising with her and he's looking at me in the mirror with that look. His hands are in the air with the curling iron. "I didn't know you could sing." He put the curling iron down and said "You could be the other hooker".'

This was a compliment.

Prince had recently watched Barbra Streisand's *A Star is Born* and the movie's all-female trio the Oreos had got him thinking. (He loved rags-to-riches movies; 1980's *The Idolmaker* is said by some to be the impetus for *Purple Rain*.) Prince's version of The Oreos had an early working title of The Hookers, then Vagina 6.

At the time of the group's inception, he was dating Trinidadian Susan Moonsie. Considering his penchant for mixing work with the personal – for him, work *was* personal – she was in the band. Her sister Loreen and his then personal assistant Jamie Shoop were also to be in the band, until they weren't. And a former Canadian glamour model called Denise Matthews had started hanging out on tour after coming to Prince's attention – and tapping into his competitive instincts – when she was Rick James' date at the 1981 American Music Awards. Prince asked her a question he often asked of women he found attractive: 'Can you sing?'

Brenda and Susan, only sixteen at the time, were less than impressed. 'She has started a relationship with Prince,' says Brenda, '[and] she was singing with this girl group never having done it. I was a little bit "Wait a minute". Susan was along for the ride, coming from a totally different background. It wasn't that big of a deal to her.'

Brenda's husband wasn't thrilled either, according to Simon Fields, who produced Prince's pop videos. 'Prince wanted the lighting director's wife in the band. He was a disrupter. Roy wouldn't talk to Prince for a while.'

Brenda claimed the Supremes may have been more than an influence, but with only Lisa Coleman in the early phase of the Revolution, and the Time as a support act, Prince wanted to offer his audience something else. 'Lisa at that time was the only female in Prince's band,' she notes, reflecting on his thinking. 'Everyone else was guys. The Time had no girls. What about providing something for the guys?'

Denise, whom Prince renamed Vanity, had been in a couple of B-movies and, says Bennett, 'considered herself an actress and model. She was used to being around the publications, being on a movie set naked sometimes, so this was nothing for her. Prince put me in charge of the girls' group because I had had experience of being on the road and recording.'

Soon, after Denise nixed the name Vagina 6, Vanity 6 were performing in front of a pink scrim curtain with the Time backing them behind it. As was the problem for many working with Prince, they were doing what they were told but feeling under-appreciated. Worse, their backing band was the competition, competition that Prince had created.

'We didn't count off the song,' recalls Bennett. 'The Time counted off the song. Sometimes 1, 2, 3, 4. It's almost as if they were trying to sabotage us or test us. They may have felt they weren't getting paid enough for what they were asked to do. We're all on tour together, we're doing well, there are a lot of egos flying around, there's a lot of whining. But we had fun too at the same time. They sort of helped us by being a great sounding band.'

That didn't mean Prince was receptive to his other bands writing for others.

A snowstorm had caused the Time's Jimmy Jam and Terry Lewis to miss their flight and a San Antonio performance during the second tour. Preparing for the future marked the beginning of the end for the Time. Jam and Lewis had gone to Atlanta to record the song 'Just Be Good to Me' with the S.O.S. Band. In 1983, the pair were summoned to Sunset Sound Studio 3. 'It was me, Terry, Prince, Jesse [Johnson] and Morris," recalls Jam. 'Prince goes "I told you not to produce other bands, you produced The S.O.S Band, so you're fired." So I got up and walked out the room. Terry tried to reason with him.'

Jam and Lewis headed ten minutes up the road to Larrabee Studios to meet engineer Steve Hodge, who told them: 'I don't think you have anything to worry about because this song's a smash!' and pressed play on The S.O.S Band's worldwide hit. The Time would change personnel and, in the process (according to Jam), break Morris Day's heart. 'It devastated Morris. He went down a really bad path. All his favourite bands stayed together, and he didn't want a revolving door situation.'

A month after Jam and Lewis's exit, Moir left the group. Jesse Johnson soon followed. Paul Peterson and two other members were drafted in but, he says, he was not a popular recruit. 'All the guys didn't want to have me in it. I understand that now, thirty-five years later.' The group eventually disbanded in 1985 with the departure of Day; Prince would make other plans for Peterson.

Prince didn't ease up on the Time in the studio, where he was keen to let them know who was in charge. (Clue: it wasn't Morris.)

'On the [1984] *Ice Cream Castle* record,' remembers engineer Terry Christian, 'my time on that was him basically taking a live performance on tape. He would listen to what had been live and then he would replay it. He would replace the parts and, while this was going on, the band would be in the lounge watching TV. They wouldn't come in. Prince did rule with an iron fist. I didn't hear any conversation, but it seemed very clear to me that the band wasn't invited in, although I never heard that said. The only people in the control room were me and Prince. He was very competitive with the guys in the Time. We knew how talented those guys are, but he wanted them to be sure that they knew he was more talented.'

Three groups, but, adds Bill Reeves, the tour manager for the second half of the tour, essentially one man.

'There were ostensibly three different groups on that tour but in reality, it was one big group. He didn't really write with anybody. We would have these three-hour soundchecks on the 1999 tour and what they were was him working on his next set of tunes. That [1999 tour] eventually became tunes from *Purple Rain*. I can't say that he wrote with anybody. He would collaborate when he had a thought of a song and BrownMark might contribute a bassline or Lisa might contribute a keyboard part, but I don't know if he was writing with a band. The thing as a whole came from Prince's brain. There might be a musician that thought differently – "I'm the one who came up with that melody" – but, no, it was all him.'

With Vanity 6, Prince's vice-like hold on a band featuring two of his girlfriends would involve delegation – to Brenda Bennett. She was charged with keeping her bandmates in line, but one of them, Vanity, was then dating the boss of the touring company and imagined herself as Vanity 6's de facto leader. 'She didn't feel she needed to take direction from anybody but Prince.'

Allen Beaulieu chronicles Prince's Vanity 6 love interest – between '82 and '83 – as 'Susan at the beginning and Denise at the end.' But dating two women in his first all-female group was not a problem, says the tour's production manager Tom Marzullo, because Prince was 'so good at compartmentalising that I never knew. His day-to-day personality was reserved.'

It says something for his energy levels that Prince was juggling three bands, all of whom he would accompany on occasion, as well as prepping to star in a motion picture whose soundtrack he would write. With one of these three bands, he was dating two out of three members. With another (the Revolution) the guitarist's twin sister was soon to be Prince's girlfriend. The main theme was hard work with a side order of domestic drama.

'It was pretty brutal,' recalls Murielle Hodler-Hamilton, the manager of the first half of the tour. 'Six days out of seven. We went back around the United States. Some cities we hit them about three times. Every night we got on the bus, maybe you have a hotel room to take a shower and then you're back in the afternoon doing a soundcheck.'

'He really was the Energiser Bunny,' Hodler-Hamilton adds. 'If we went to a city where we had a day off, he would have a studio booked and a recording engineer waiting for him and he would write and record. That's not even mentioning the pick-up games of basketball. We might go to a club after a concert, and there might be a band and he might sit in on drums, then move to the bass and start playing guitar after that.'

Throughout the Triple Threat dates, Prince, as so often, had an eye on his next project. The proceeds from that same tour would be funnelled into funds for a new movie.

CHAPTER 5

IT

*Time to get a movie made ... Prince + movies = music ...
Covering all basses ... 'It' isn't the next single ... How he
marches to his own beats ...The Bodyguard: not the movie*

Time to get a movie made

Some are born with stardom, some achieve stardom and some have stardom thrust upon them. Despite his regal name, Prince definitely belongs in the second category.

The path from major recording artist to biggest star in the world – which is what Prince became after *Purple Rain* won an Academy Award, American Music Awards and Grammys, and took him from theatres and arenas to football stadia – was carefully plotted.

Prince was ready to negotiate with his management firm Cavallo, Ruffalo and Fargnoli after *1999*'s hits propelled him into being an MTV mainstay. You can stay, he told them, on one condition: get me a movie. He was savvy enough to understand that he needed to move on from a double album into a different territory. Only the big screen could be bigger than MTV.

The film would not be so much a bargaining chip as every single one in the casino. Warner Brothers' music division was warming to Prince after *1999*. Warner Brothers' movie division was somewhat cooler. Having planned to pay for the film using funds raised from the Triple Threat tour, even before that, Prince had booked acting classes with Minneapolis actor Don Amendolia, with the star pupil of the group being no surprise. 'The cast were not actors,' says Amendolia. 'In fact, they were shy about "performing" in front of each other. Prince was a natural. He fully participated and seemed eager to learn. Keep in mind, we had not seen a script. In fact, it wasn't until I saw the movie that I knew the story.

'Pretty much the entire group was receptive and worked in the class, with the exception of Morris Day and Jesse Johnson. They were decidedly not cooperative and were ultimately barred from class.' That, Amendolia hints, was Prince's call.

William Blinn had written a screenplay *Dreams*, before film school graduate Albert Magnoli (the editor for *Reckless* director James Foley, who turned it down) rewrote it. After Magnoli spent time with Prince, it was soon discarded for a more personal tale. The story concerns 'The Kid' Prince who, with his own musicians (played by the Revolution) compete against a rival Minneapolis band, the Time (played by the Time).

Denise 'Vanity' Matthews had been slated to star as his romantic love interest, but Patricia 'Apollonia' Kotero ended up as the female lead. Carole Davis, who would have a co-writing credit on 'Slow Love' from *Sign o' the Times*, was also auditioned; Jennifer Beals of *Flashdance* was another considered. Prince's father was played by Clarence Williams and his mother by Greek actor Olga Karlatos, who appeared in Sergio Leone's *Once Upon a Time in America* the same year.

Filming mainly took place in Prince's hometown over forty-two days from October 1983. Albert Magnoli was directing his first movie and took inspiration from another American director and choreographer. 'Bob Fosse was in my eyeline. I love the way he shot music, I loved *Cabaret*, I watched it 100 times just to get the groove. He saw *Purple Rain* and he says to me "I hear you did the music in seven days". He said "It took me months to do the video in *Cabaret*". I told him "I had to".'

Although the movie took forty-two days of filming, the songs themselves were a longer work in progress. There is evidence suggesting Prince never considered the music on his albums quite as meticulously as he did on the soundtrack album for the film which would make his name.

Prince + movie = music

As Prince says in 'Let's Go Crazy', in this life, we are on our own.

Well, yes and no.

Barring a handful of co-writing credits to Chris Moon ('Soft and Wet'), Matt Fink on *Dirty Mind*'s title track and Morris Day on 'Partyup', *Purple Rain*'s soundtrack album is the first where Prince shares the limelight. Sort of.

The words 'and the Revolution' were written backwards on the hand-drawn *1999* sleeve. By the follow-up, his best-selling album, *Purple Rain*, the back sleeve credit read 'Produced, arranged, composed and performed by Prince and the Revolution'. But Susan Rogers suggests that 'he made the majority of *Purple Rain* without the Revolution'.

There was some collaboration, particularly on 'Computer Blue', while the instrumental lament at the heart of 'Father's Song' was given to him by his father John. Lisa Coleman, Wendy Melvoin and Matt Fink all fed in too.

The title track took seven studio sessions, including two for the movie version. In the film, he describes 'Purple Rain' as 'a song the girls in the band wrote, Wendy and Lisa', but it's nothing of the sort. It was a calculated attempt to write an anthem which would appeal to middle America. Prince and Matt Fink had discussed how Prince could create a rock anthem for his growing, increasingly white, audience.

'When I heard "Purple Rain", I thought "He's got it". What was great about '"Purple Rain"' is that he had the chord progression, he had the lyrics, [but] they weren't finished. He took the song into rehearsal and we're jamming it and we're running through the chord progression and I'm playing the high singing part with the right hand and next thing you know he's singing along to it. That's part of the song.'

Prince had been paying attention to other big acts, but the idea and the song were almost exclusively his. The big sound he had been building since the Stones gig at the Coliseum had its biggest theme yet. Inspired by the skyline of Minneapolis, which could turn purple when overcast, this was designed to cross over. This was rare for a black act in the MTV era, criss-crossing across genres (country, rock, soul, blues), just as *Sign*'s title track (blues, funk, stadium rock) would be three years later.

'*Purple Rain* is a white rock album and it was a total break from tradition,' says David Z. Rivkin. 'I remember going to his first concert and seeing the audience. That hasn't happened since Sly and the Family Stone or Jimi Hendrix before that.'

The title track had formed in his own head.

It was around midnight in August 1983 when he asked for a favour from engineer Peggy McCreary.

When we say 'asked'…

'One time he called for a string section at midnight.'

"For tomorrow?"

"*Now.*"

Luckily, McCreary had an orchestra contact, Novi Novog, whom she called. Novog remembers it well, partly because she was in her 'giant T-shirt' PJs and it was a school night. 'I was just getting ready to snooze off, watching the television, and I got the call. It was either now or never.

'"Say, do you wanna come up and play on a Prince song? And do you know a cello player...?'

'She [Suzie Katayama] said yeah! They were impossible things but you just did it for him. We picked it up as we went along. When we recorded it, we didn't even hear the lyrics. We heard the chords so we could be part of the track.'

Novog remembers Prince in the control room, with Wendy & Lisa, Apollonia, Susannah, Peggy 'and a couple of other people' asking if she wanted a soda or crisps. 'I remember we would be at the studio for hours starving and there were Doritos and coffee.' The studio was decorated with candles and, three and a half years before they would feature on the *Sign...* sleeve, the Pierrot dolls, beloved of French pantomime and David Bowie in his 'Ashes to Ashes' video.

Just before she finished at three or four in the morning 'feeling exhilarated' and drove back to her home in West Van Nuys in the Valley, Novog had a question.

'This is a beautiful song. What's it for?'

'We filmed a movie called *Purple Rain*.'

Brenda Bennett, who sang in her share of country and rock bands, calls it 'a bluesy song. Country being white man's blues. We have always gravitated back to the blues. From the heart, you're going to hear funk, blues, country.'

It would become many people's favourite Prince song. He did however, according to future mid-'00s-period dancer Nandy McClean, have a stock response for anyone who told him this: 'Dig a little deeper.'

Slower than usual, Prince was putting the pieces together. 'Take Me With U' was a song for Apollonia 6 (the new incarnation of Vanity 6) until it wasn't. He had 'Let's Go Crazy' in his back pocket after being inspired by a riff that photographer Allen Beaulieu had played on his Les Paul Junior, which he'd 'borrowed' in exchange for an advance copy of *1999*. Beaulieu maintains he remains happy with the deal to this day.

Sometimes the song had been worked out in advance. The live shows or the soundcheck would help, which impressed his tour manager Bill Reeves. 'Some musicians sit around with the band and work on their songs, and their input influences and guides the primary musician. I don't think he's that guy. The thing I used to marvel at, particularly on *Purple Rain* and *1999*, was he would come in for a soundcheck and have a song pretty much completely done in his head. He would teach it to the band, they would work on it, he would make little tweaks to the performance, maybe change the drums or a different bassline. He would come in with the song fully formed. It was a pretty much fully developed production when he introduced it at soundcheck.'

Rob 'Cubby' Colby, Prince's front-of-house sound engineer at the time, remembers the '30-minute, 40-minute, one-hour jam' which 'would just get whittled down when it was recorded. What we heard from that day was turned into a song. He loved this side. He had a lyric, he had an idea, he had a concept and we just followed with him. I believe that happened more than fifty times. That fifteen-minute jam, half-hour jam, would turn into a recorded song. "I Would Die 4 U" was a line he heard from one of the crew when he was walking in.'

David Z Rivkin, a close confidant of Prince's in the studio, points out that the jamming he did in early career led to the Revolution where 'he incorporated his touring band into his recording band'. He adds that 'Purple Rain' and 'Kiss' were collaborations. 'I think he did his best work with other people.'

Prince wasn't doing interviews, which was unusual for a star expected to promote his first movie as well as a soundtrack album and an Apollonia 6 album. If he was going to let the music do the talking for him, he simply had to get the lead-off single right. All the rest of the soundtrack had been written. Save for some late edits, largely recorded too. He had known how he wanted it to sound, and even subsequently hired one of the men behind it.

David Tickle worked as a sound engineer for Peter Gabriel. Tickle had been told that Wendy & Lisa brought Prince to one of Gabriel's shows [most likely LA's Greek Theatre in August '83]. 'He was knocked out by the sound. Heavily gaited snare drum and reverb. This really stuck in Prince's head and that night he went back to wherever he was staying and recorded "When Doves Cry".' That gaited reverb, in much of Prince's sound in the intervening years including on *Sign...*, had been the result of an accident. Engineer Hugh Padgham, retelling the story to Music Radar in 2020, opened a microphone to speak to Phil Collins, while he was playing on Gabriel's 1979 track 'Intruder', 'to hear what he was saying while he was still playing the drums and out came the most unbelievable sound. Everyone went, "That sounds incredible".' Producers in the '80s – and in subsequent decades – of clean-sounding pop from Duran Duran to Carly Rae Jepsen and Haim would agree. Collins did too, as the gaited reverb gave much of the space to his Padgham-produced 1981 song 'In the Air Tonight'.

Prince once again had his ears open.

Tickle, who would work with Prince from the Purple Rain tour onwards until *Parade*, was told his new boss had said: 'I have got to get that guy who did Peter Gabriel's sound.'

Prince had been, for a while, working on a lyric about a man struggling with his relationship with his girlfriend and his father – not, at that point in his life, a lyrical stretch. Often with songs, he would walk into the recording studio with it in his head and leave when it had been played, recorded and mixed in one session. And he wouldn't restrict a session to just one song either.

While 'When Doves Cry' didn't exactly take the kind of time 'Born to Run' had (Bruce Springsteen famously spent six months writing and six months recording the anthem that would make him famous), this process was different. For a man who liked to only leave the studio with the song recorded and mixed within a day, 'When Doves Cry' tested him. He threw the kitchen sink at it, recalls Peggy McCreary. 'That was a two-day song.'

Three, actually: 1–3 March 1984. It was the final track Prince laid down for the album, but the first to launch it.

He taught Matt Fink a hypnotic keyboard part, which was a challenge as he had recorded it using the old George Martin trick of slowing the tape down to record it with vari-speed, then asking Fink to play it in real time.

'It was a wall of sound,' says McCreary. The engineer actually left the room, such was the pressure around getting the song right. 'It was so overproduced and, as the night went on, it started getting less and less. He started taking stuff off until he took the bass out. He said to me: "Ain't nobody gonna believe I did this!" It was 7:30 in the morning when he left.'

Peggy McCreary didn't leave. She waited until Sunset Sound's receptionist Susanne Edgren arrived for work. McCreary rushed up to her with the tape still warm.

'You have *got* to listen to this song.'

Prince stood out in an industry of people-pleasers, trend-chasers and insecure second-guessers for knowing his own mind. Brenda Bennett calls it 'a no brainer that the movie was going to do really well'.

Others around Prince weren't necessarily convinced. He played 'When Doves Cry' for Morris Day on his car stereo. The Time's frontman told WUSB FM's Tom Needham that he had said: 'Next time play something funky', slammed the door and skedaddled.

Prince wasn't convinced either. His confidence in his own ability could waver.

He was staying in the same New York hotel as Patrice Rushen, the singer-songwriter he was rumoured to have written *I Wanna Be Your Lover* about five years earlier. 'We had a conversation just before *Purple Rain* came out. I happened to be in New York doing some promotion and he said:

"I'm in the restaurant. Can you come down?"

"How you doing? What's going on?"

"Well, I may have bitten off more than I can chew. I have got this movie coming out and I don't know how it's going to go."

"Did you do your best in what you were hoping you could do? That's all you can do."

"From your lips to God's ears."

'You know what happened. He was really worried about it. What I got from this conversation was that he did not express himself to that many people but because our conversations had been about music – face value, no agenda. I thought that was a moment that says a lot.'

Prince was also, even if he didn't say it out loud, anxious that his record company was happy with the song that would lead the soundtrack. He went to see one of his few label confidants, Lenny Waronker, who recalls the meeting clearly.

'He knew the last song was "When Doves Cry" and he knew that was going to be the single. That might be part of the campaign for the movie. I get a call from his management saying "Prince wants to see you" and I think, *What does he want?*

'Prince comes in looking great, shiny as hell, black and white shirt.

"What's up?"

"You know when I make these records and I start, and I keep going, and when I think it's done, I stop."

"Yeah, so?"

"This thing has no bass on it."

'He was worried about it. He knew what was riding on it. My feeling was that knowing how thorough he was if he stopped, that meant it was right artistically for him. But he hadn't made up his mind.'

The record exec settled back in his office with 'two small speakers, two larger speakers and two big speakers' to listen to the most important record in the twenty-six-year-old artist's life. It was pretty vital for the label too. They had gambled on letting the then teenager produce his own records, the first two of which had commercially underdelivered, and its movie division was now paying for the film.

Waronker was ready to listen out for the bottom end 'but I couldn't pay attention because the record was so good. I got lost.'

"'If you want, put a bass on it. If it was me, I'd leave it alone."

'That's what he wanted to hear. That's one of the first records of that kind that didn't have a bass. As soon as he walked out, I thought, *What did I just do?* But the record company very quickly got it on the radio and I thought [hearing it] *This is unbelievable.* Not only was it a unique record, it was a unique-sounding record.'

Singer-songwriter Sananda Maitreya's first reaction on hearing it was 'Dude, who the hell are you and where on earth did you come from? Up to that point in time (and still), there was simply nothing as bold, audacious, stark and original as that, not to mention intimately poetic.'

Its nature was so revolutionary, contends Grammy-winning

producer Andrew Watt, that although Prince never reached the commercial heights of *Purple Rain* again, the sense of 'That was my idea and I did it and it works. Maybe I'm going to do a similar thing again' fuelled extra confidence in him. 'Whether it was conscious or not conscious, that has a lot to do with the sound of *Sign o' the Times*. It's his drums and his melody and it signals to you where the chords should go where there aren't any chords. That's the greatest song. It's so sexy.

'He invented that for himself on "When Doves Cry". He is in his own lane. Once he did something and did it to the nines, he didn't do it again. He kept pushing sound. He kept pushing instruments, getting new instruments built for him.'

Covering all basses

'When Doves Cry' enjoys an entry in pop folklore for Prince's removal of the bassline – at the time, a daring move in music.

That doesn't mean he didn't have the instrument down cold.

It was bass he played with his first band, Grand Central. In the studio, he sometimes let Sheila drum on the record or Wendy play guitar, but he always found his way back to the bass when it came to recording – and often live too, borrowing the bass of 3rdEyeGirl's Ida Nielsen (and other bassists before her).

His guitar tech Joel Bernstein had worked with Dylan, Joni and Crosby, Stills, Nash & Young and once declared to friend Jeff Gold that 'Prince is one of the greatest bass players who ever lived'.

Prince had fun on the bass. 'I'm always trying to work in the bass notes when I'm playing funk rhythms,' he told *Guitar Player* in 2004. 'It's the same way that [Sly's guitarist and brother] Freddie Stone would always play the same parts as [bassist] Larry Graham, but just a tad higher. Kids don't learn to play the right way anymore. When the Jackson Five came up, they had to go through Smokey Robinson and the Funk Brothers, and that's how they got it down.'

Prince loved bassists, not just Funk Brother James Jamerson, one of the originators of the Motown sound. He used to ask his valet Robbie Paster, who played bass, his preference: Stanley Clarke or Jaco Pastorius, both giants in the jazz fusion space. One of the many things Prince appreciated about Wendy Melvoin and long-term guitarist Sonny Thompson was that they could both play bass.

'His favourite bassist is Larry Graham,' says another of Prince's former bassists, Rhonda Smith. 'Absolutely,' agrees Nik West, who jammed on bass with his band at Paisley Park. 'Larry was his number-one guy. "I need to call Larry. He needs to meet you." The first person he wanted to talk about.'

Larry and Tina Graham would move near Prince's house in Minneapolis for many years. Shelby Johnson, who sang with Prince between 2006 and 2014, recalls his special name for Larry: 'The Trunk of the Funk Tree'.

Larry and Tina were devout Jehovah's Witness followers and were frequent visitors with Prince to Kingdom Hall in Minneapolis. When Prince would discuss his faith in interviews in the late '90s and early '00s, he would often call Larry into the discussion to back up his views.

Greg Errico played as part of the Family Stone rhythm section with Graham (who's arguably better known now as Drake's uncle) and 'didn't see any significant influences in Prince's recordings or performances that exuded Larry's influence. It was kind of mixed into the soup and even in his behaviour. He did look up to Larry, but Prince was very independent and did his own thing. He would be influenced by Sly and Hendrix but it was still Prince.'

Jellybean Johnson feels that the bassist's influence on helping Prince clean up his act was not desirable. 'Larry changed him for the worse. It was the last person he needed in his life. The Prince I grew up with cussed, was gangsta and was a snotty-nosed north-side kid like me. When Larry got a hold of him, I lost all of that. You can't tell a man not to cuss on his own stage. He fell out with Larry at the end.' Prince had set up Larry and Tina in accommodation near him in Chanhassen but, as was Prince's wont, he moved on and they moved out.

Hans-Martin Buff, a Paisley Park engineer between 1995 and 2001, disagrees that Larry's friendship didn't benefit Prince. 'Larry is one of the people that should convince you to join their church because he just lives it. The European approach to religion is kind of apologetic. None of that with Larry. She [Tina] was so in love with God and she brought Larry on board and he brought him [Prince] on board. He didn't treat me any different from [how he treated] Prince.'

Musically, Larry Graham and Prince were tight too. When Prince's band rehearsed at Paisley Park in his later years, sessions would last from 2 p.m. until midnight, at which point musicians would go and Larry Graham would come in and jam with Prince.

Prince and Paul Peterson (from the Time and then the Family) had made up in the years before Prince's passing and were talking music and mentors after a Victor Wooten concert in Minneapolis.

'Do you have someone you look up to?'

'I have four brothers and sisters, so sure.'

'You should. Larry Graham is my mentor.'

Prince's influence on basslines was hard to replicate. He would play along with a keyboard bass, just as Marcus Miller, Miles' collaborator on *Tutu*, had. But it wasn't just on 'When Doves Cry' that he spared listeners his bassline. The 'space between the notes' philosophy expressed and practised by Miles was not lost on Prince. He seemed to adhere to Jeff Goldblum's character's approach in *Jurassic Park*. 'Just because you can, doesn't mean you should,' he would tell Nik West. 'Just because you can play a note, doesn't mean you should. Just let it breathe. When you listen to the groove, you listen to the groove.'

Prince had very specific ideas of what the bass should do, a joy in repetition to use one of his song titles. 'He thought the bass should do a lot of that as well as discipline,' explains Rhonda Smith, his main bassist from 1996–2004. '"Play the same four notes again." He would come over and say, "I know you wanna change, but don't." The pole was the bass – that was having the structure. He built from inside and there were certain things that should stay stagnant. It's like anything else. If you don't have a strong foundation, you don't have a strong structure.'

Simplicity with the basslines was, according to Nik West, the secret of his success. She worked out that 'the songs that are hits are like third-grade basslines'. Andrew Gouché, another of Prince's bassists, who played between 2011 and 2013, sums up his own philosophy as 'I only want to play music that people who don't play music can understand'. He believes Prince shared that.

The bass would remain Prince's power move. When Michael Jackson came to his 3121 Vegas residency in February 2007, Prince did not pluck lead guitar or sing, but played bass in his face.

Dywane 'MonoNeon' Thomas, no slouch on the same instrument, describes Prince's bass playing as 'otherworldly funky. I do wish he would've played some bass when I was with him, but his rhythm guitar stuff was definitely enough for me to realise I need to work on my guitar playing. Prince is one of the reasons why I started playing guitar more.'

Some accomplished bass players still couldn't take their eyes off him. Rhonda Smith describes his technique as 'a frustrated guitar player's technique. You can tell he was a guitar player when he played bass. Kind of a messy way if you were school-taught. And look at what he was doing with his hands. You could see that's not right, but it doesn't matter in the way he played because he had a sound that was particularly "his". He would show me some things that he would do wrong technically, but that's why he sounded the way he did.'

The self-taught method would serve him well when he was teaching other musicians, such as Smith, whose fretless bass he admired, and Josh Dunham, a bassist around the 3121 era. 'The only time he picked up the bass to show me something,' says Dunham, 'my eyes were glued to his hands. Larry would come and sit in and we would all be playing.'

In the mid-'80s, a decade before Roni Size and LTJ Bukem came to prominence, Prince was telling Susan Rogers at the Flying Cloud Warehouse that 'the future of music is drum and bass'.

'It' isn't the next single

The spareness of how Prince worked was apparent when he was recording *Sign o' the Times*, a couple of years after *Purple Rain*'s release.

'It', recorded after deeply personal 'The Ballad of Dorothy Parker' and 'Starfish and Coffee' at Sunset Sound on 11 May 1986, was due to be the fifth track on *Dream Factory*, Prince and the Revolution's slated, but unreleased follow-up to *Parade*, and instead became the fifth track on double album *Sign o' the Times*.

Prince clearly always saw 'It' as a bridge song. Others in his team thought it had to be released first before any other song. Perhaps not others, plural. It reminded his former protection officer Harlan 'Hucky' Austin of Duran Duran. 'It was one of the few times we got into an argument. I thought "It" was the most incredible song and it reminded me of a song they did and I told him he should make it the lead-off single.'

Prince gave a typically cutting response to the bodyguard. 'He looked at me and said, "What do you do for me again?" And that was that.'

It would be few people's choices for the album's first single. As Todd Herreman, who sold Prince the Fairlight Page-R sequencer on which its drum pattern was recorded, notes, 'there's a strange bombastic vocal to "It". It's really all over the map.' Also, the lyrics are not overly nuanced. But 'Slow Love' co-writer Carole Davis, for one, admires the way he wrote about sex. 'His finest work was sexual in nature. The lyrics when you got into it were very refined. The religiosity and repression made him that much more of a genius when he wrote about sexuality. That's the effervescence of who he was.'

'If you listen to shows from the time of '86,' reveals Herreman, 'he took the drum sequence for "It" from "When Doves Cry".' Herreman had to sneak behind Lisa Coleman when she played the song to help out on the Fairlight, leading to the crew nicknaming him 'Dove Head'.

Prince's '90s drummer Michael Bland had a moment when spotting Kate Bush backstage at a Wembley gig. 'It was like Mary Poppins walked in. I was so into *Hounds of Love* when it came out. The English always got the technology first. She and Peter Gabriel had the Synclavier, as well as the Fairlight, and that's what made Prince want to get them.'

Prince's engineer in the early '90s, Sylvia Massy, adds that he remained 'most interested in the latest and greatest gear that he needed to know about'. This was relevant when it came to the heartbeat of each song.

How he marches to his own beats

John 'JR' Robinson was drumming in the band Rufus when he met Roger Linn in 1978. 'Rufus and Roger came by with a little cassette player. I made it my point to master all the [technical details] so that I would not be replaced.'

Smart move.

Robinson eventually become the most-recorded drummer in recording history. That's what happens when you play on *Off the Wall*, *Thriller*, Madonna's 'Express Yourself', Rufus and Chaka Khan's 'Ain't Nobody', Steve Winwood's 'Higher Love', Lionel Richie's 'All Night Long (All Night)' and 'We Are The World'.

Prince also mastered all the details of the Linn drum machine, specifically the LM-1, starting with *Controversy*'s 'Private Joy'. There is a strange science, best explained by his engineers, as to how Prince programmed beats. It is hard to demystify, even to trained audio professionals. Sylvia Massy, his engineer around *Diamond and Pearls*, explains it thus.

'He would use his left hand to play the drum machine live and he would play it by tapping the kick drum with his thumb and the snare drum with his index finger and the hi-hat with his pinky.' His right hand? That was playing lines on the keyboard.

Eric 'Vietnam' Sadler of Public Enemy's production team, the Bomb Squad, describes Prince's tendency to lower the sound. 'Usually you use drum machines, you can hear what they're doing. He would tune 'em down, he would add different reverb and he was triggering them to work while he was playing real drums.'

'Prince made beats that were iconic,' says David Z Rivkin, sibling of Revolution drummer Bobby. '*Purple Rain* was real drums triggering the drum machine. My brother played the drums and the drums had hot dots that triggered the machine. It was human-machine led.' His drumming chops were well-honed and his drummers, including Bobby Z and Sheila E, would play at the same time he did. Sheila put Bose guitar pedals on hers.

It's possible that Prince's use of the LM-1 took on an intensity of its own in 1986 (the year most of *Sign o' the Times* was recorded) with the success of Michael Jackson's little sister Janet and her *Control* album.

It was her third album, but the one which made her a star, helped in no small part by her producers, Jimmy Jam and Terry Lewis.

Jam and Lewis had their ears to the music in the clubs playing both R&B and hip hop and found a new way to programme beats. Public Enemy producer Bill Stephney argues that 'from a hip hop producer or from a hip hop fan standpoint, I don't think Prince ever worked out what made the music appeal to him. Jimmy Jam and Terry Lewis coming from the same birthday cake, they had a better sense.'

Scottie Baldwin, Prince's friend and colleague of two decades' standing, admits that their success 'had to get under his skin. We never talked about it. He let Terry and Jimmy go. Terry and Jimmy knew what they were doing because they were musicians. They were on to something. They took Prince's sound and put a new twist on it. I am sure that ate at Prince but I don't know. Jimmy and Terry are talented. That was all based on Prince foundationally. Foundationally, who I am as a sound engineer is based on Prince.'

Jimmy Jam admits that Prince 'never told me he was proud of it. He covered [in the 2010s] "What Have You Done For Me Lately?" He would say "Who wrote that?" It was his contention that he wrote that.' Jam also recounted a tale he heard, unverified, that Prince listened to *Control* in his car and threw the CD out the window.

Paul Peterson, no stranger to run-ins with Prince, feels he would have been 'pleasantly surprised' by Jam and Lewis' success and, in fact, aided them. 'He could spot talent a mile away. He didn't coddle them or give them pastoral care. He said "You're fired" and that helped them both out.'

At some point in the early '90s, Prince moved on from the LM-1. 'Part of the reason he put that machine away,' argues Bland, was because 'it had been overused by everybody else.'

Jimmy Jam, no slouch with the drum machine himself, admires Prince's counterintuitive instincts. "When everybody got into drum machines and sampling, Prince would go back into live horns. He was a step ahead in that sense. Even at live shows, Bobby played to a drum machine."

Before he mastered the drum machine, Prince would master the detail of the drums themselves. 'If I went to the toilet or to get a cup of tea,' Ringo Starr told Stephen Colbert in 2020, 'one of them would be on the kit. John, Paul or George banging on the drums. Every guitarist wants to be a drummer. Every band member wants to be the drummer.'

The list of musicians who understand the importance of drumming is longer than the arms of Animal from *The Muppets*. Marvin Gaye started his musical career as a session drummer. Steven Tyler, Bobby Gillespie, Don Henley, the Whites (both Jack and Barry), Teddy Pendergrass, Glen Campbell, Lauren Mayberry and Donny Hathaway all spent time on the sticks. Before she moved up front, Madonna played drums for her group the Breakfast Club. The beat that kicks off 'Superstition' is played by Stevie Wonder. 'Uptown Funk' started as a jam session with producer Mark Ronson on guitar, Jeff Bhasker on keys and Bruno Mars behind the kit.

The difference with Prince is that it's possible, unlike the sarcastic quip about Ringo Starr misattributed to John Lennon, he really was the best drummer in his band. He was considered a 'light hitter' by former drum tech Scottie Baldwin; 'very creative … incredible pocket' by Michael Bland, referencing the in-the-pocket nature required of funk players; and 'sloppy but funky' by his '80s drum tech Brad Marsh. Prince played drums on most of his records including, the legend goes, the first four tracks on *Parade* in sequence.

'He's playing to music in his head,' Susan Rogers recalled to Prince podcast PodcastJuice.net. 'That's how the *Parade* album started. It would be Peggy, me and Prince. He said put up fresh tape in the machine and said "Don't stop the tape between songs. I'm just gonna go 1, 2, 3, 4. I'll play the first four tracks." We had to cut things later.' That next-level skill was not something he advertised. Michael Bland listened and figured out he'd played *Parade's* four tracks in sequence. "'I can tell. Did you play all those in a row?" He always seemed a little upset when I figured things out.'

Prince's sense of musicality was so pronounced that he didn't even require the usual studio guide of a click track, the metronomic cues to help out musicians. Furthermore, the kit could be set up for a left-hander, but Prince would proceed and play anyway. David Tickle recalls another snapshot of his skills. 'He would record the drums from the beginning to end, he had the song in his head, he knew where all the fills were and he would get it down and say "Turn the tape over and play it backwards". The track would play perfectly forwards and backwards. He would do these things to blow you away and it would stretch him. "Keep the tape rolling." I have witnessed.'

Jimmy Jam knew Prince in their school days as a piano player. 'My first professional gig when I met Prince was at Bryant Junior High, we took a piano class together and at the end of the lessons we were asked "who wants to be in the band? What do you want to play?" He said guitar and I said drums. I go to the bathroom and Prince is kicking it on the drums.'

Prince loved drummers. He talked up John Bonham in interviews, while his cousin Chazz (also a drummer) says he adored Santana's other drummer, Michael Ceriff. When working on 'Cream', he told Bland to 'play it more like Charlie Watts when he was good'. 'I knew what he meant by that. He meant *Sticky Fingers, Exile [On Main Street]*, early-mid-'70s. He didn't want "Paint It Black".'

David Garibaldi, of Oakland funk band Tower of Power, is considered by several interviewees to be Prince's favourite drummer. 'A student of Garibaldi for sure,' contends Bland, citing 'Tambourine' (from *Around the World in a Day*) as an example. Garibaldi – an inspiration for Morris Day too (which probably landed him his first job for Prince) – feels that Prince was 'not so much a drummer' because 'he understood all the parts of a rhythm section. I could tell from the quality of his recordings, the content of his recordings, what he understood about music. It was very evident. A deep guy.'

He loved working with drummers. When Dave Grohl came to a soundcheck at the LA Forum in 2011, they jammed on 'Whole Lotta Love', Prince giving him the option of where to play. Grohl opted for where he played with Nirvana: behind the kit.

And, of course, there was Sheila.

Jimmy Jam argues that 'other than Sheila, Prince's favourite drummer was Morris [Day].'

From replacing his cousin Chazz with Morris Day, and the hiring of Bobby Z, Michael Bland, Cora Dunham, John Blackwell Jr and Hannah Ford for his bands to his twenty-year work with Sheila E (who had played percussion with George Duke, Billy Cobham and Marvin Gaye), where he would drum and she added percussion or vocals, Prince loved keeping time with great drummers. Sheila is the closest Prince got to riding shotgun over a period of time with another musician around his own age (Larry Graham, Sonny Thompson, Chaka Khan, Stevie Wonder and Miles Davis were all senior to him in years).

Sheila E would enjoy the long-service award, unusual for Prince's musical collaborators. 'There was no doubt in my mind,' says Eric Leeds, 'that Sheila was going to end up being the drummer in the band.'

That didn't mean that Prince let her have the final musical word. David Tickle's example of him playing the drums for a whole album in his head, including one track backwards, was, he says, for an album Prince produced for Sheila E.

The Bodyguard: not the movie

For Prince watchers, there was a before and after with *Purple Rain* best defined by his relationship with bodyguard Chick Huntsberry, the Hell's Angel-lookalike bodyguard who towered over five-foot-two Prince. After being spotted in Columbus, Ohio, where he had carried Angus Young on his shoulders through the crowd while the AC/DC man played guitar, 'Big Chick' (who stood six foot seven in his cowboy boots) was hired for the *Dirty Mind* tour. He and Prince would become inseparable, with Huntsberry accompanying Prince on stage at awards shows (which would lead Cyndi Lauper to bring an old wrestling buddy on stage when she won one).

Huntsberry's family moved from Tennessee to Minneapolis. 'When not touring, he would be with Prince in LA while recording at Sunset Sound or making *Purple Rain*,' remembers his daughter Tina Huntsberry Kahn. 'Dad lived out there with him. He taught Prince how to ride a motorcycle for the movie [it's a customised 1981 Honda CM400 Hondamatic you see on the soundtrack sleeve] and they would ride all over Minneapolis together. Prince would come to our house for 4th of July picnics, Thanksgiving, Christmas or just to stop in.'

They spent Christmas Eve 1984 together, with Prince at Big Chick's new family home, where Tina's sister Melissa got him a purple furry monster that he took to a party that same evening. 'You could put it on your finger and bounce up and down and it made a noise,' Melissa recalls.

'Prince was always good to my family,' she adds. 'The more famous Prince got, the busier he got. He got a little bossier towards Dad. Dad said he was shorter with him. I think it was people invading his space when he went out. Prince liked his privacy. I think it was pressure – from fame and being tired.' Huntsberry left Prince's employ in 1985 with a *National Enquirer* interview with the bodyguard sealing the fallout before the pair were reconciled before Huntsberry's death in 1990.

The film, propelled by its music, was a smash. It took $70m at the box office and Prince would grace the cover of *Time* and *Newsweek*. And his life would never be the same again.

But, as publicist Robyn Riggs points out, 'when you get that level of success, it's hard'. Prince was about to find out how hard. Up until then, his default setting had been forward momentum. This time, he went in a different direction. Not so much sideways but somewhere with clouds on it.

CHAPTER 6

STARFISH AND COFFEE

Starfish and Coffee ... The man with the child in his eyes ...
Prince and Susannah ... Prince and Sheila ... the two brothers
who helped Prince change course ... Meet the Family

Starfish and Coffee

Dreams were important to Prince.

As well as *Dreams* being the original working title to *Purple Rain*, he claims at the start of *1999* that he was in his slumbers when he wrote the title track, while his 'Manic Monday' started at six (presumably a.m.) just as he was in the middle of another dream.

Once he had an intense working relationship, revolving around very little sleep, the gap between making music and what was on his mind when he slept would inevitably blur.

After one phone call at a reliably unsociable hour, engineer Peggy McCreary was summoned with the words: 'I said if I dreamed another verse, I would come in.' She admits that she 'used to dream about him, and sit bolt upright in bed [thinking] *He's in town*. Sure enough, he was.'

He admitted to her, 'I dream about you too.'

On the subject of those dreams, though, McCreary 'never asked him and he never asked me. It was very interesting.'

Such was the intimate nature of relationships Prince enjoyed with his female engineers (male ones are less likely to detail such an exchange) that there was an inevitable closeness. There was always a danger male engineers wanted to be their boss. There was less rivalry with his four female engineers (Peggy McCreary, Susan Rogers, Sylvia Massy and Lisa Chamblee-Hampton) with whom, it is noted, Prince enjoyed his biggest hits and, all four note, did not get romantically involved. That didn't always make it fun for them either, as another studio consiglierie, David Z Rivkin, explains. 'Susan Rogers suffered the worst. She was in there any hour of the day when he wanted her. She was a very good engineer and he put her through the mill. He put her through the wringer. He wore her out. He was non-stop. Never saw him sleep. The rumour was that he slept in his limo from his house to the studio. I even lived in the same house as him for a while [in Sausalito, recording *For You*] and never saw him sleep.'

Brent Fischer, who, with father Clare, arranged the strings for Prince's records from *Parade* onwards (but not *Sign...*) says: 'Both he and I will write music, so ideas will come to us in our dreams, and you get up in the morning and write them out.' Childhood friend Terry Jackson recalls seeing Prince's pupils dilate while he slept, thought to be some form of Rapid Eye Movement, the sleep-dream process that gave the band from Athens, Georgia its name. (Incidentally, R.E.M. were one of the early clients at Paisley Park, there in 1990 to record *Out of Time*.) Other friends and ex-girlfriends say that they never saw him sleep – or, if they did, it was rare it would exceed four hours.

'Starfish and Coffee' is another song on *Sign...* which doesn't feel typical of other music of the time and has Prince's finger-prints writ large over it. Not just his fingerprints. He wrote the music and recorded the song while his co-writer Susannah Melvoin was asleep, quite possibly just in the middle of a dream.

Todd Herreman remembers doing 'that whole thing at his house. (Galpin Blvd). I remember Susannah being there, and I thought they were kind of carefree, funny lyrics.' The song, with a nursery rhyme element, is based around tales his then girlfriend had told her about her school days.

Remembering Susannah being there is an understatement. Prince had remembered a conversation with his girlfriend about a classmate of hers at LA's Highland Park High. He asked Susannah to write down the story of Cynthia Rose. Susannah recounted the details from memory. The fact that the classmate, an autistic girl, 'was exactly the same as she was when she was eleven' (as she told The Current podcast) and they'd kept in touch meant memories were fresh.

When in teacher Kathy Smith's class, alongside classmates Kevin and Lucy, Susannah recounted to The Current's Andrea Swensson that Cynthia's favourite number was twenty – to keep in line with the safe speed limit which would keep her calm – and when asked what she had for breakfast at the start time of quarter to eight, she recalled 'starfish and peepee'. As Susannah slept, Prince took some artistic license, adding butterscotch clouds, tangerine – clearly still working in peach mode – and a side order of ham for her breakfast.

When Susannah woke, he beckoned her to hear his new song, albeit with one slight change. 'He points to the page and says "Do you mind if I change that to coffee?" He stabs at the board and presses play and there it is.'

'Starfish and Coffee' it was, and the tribute to Cynthia Rose became the inspiration for naming cafes (from Brighton, England through Painesville, Ohio to Port Denison, Western Australia), a proposed but undeveloped animated series for Jim Henson, and one of the two songs Prince performed in September 1997 when he guested on *Muppets Tonight*. The puppet of Cynthia was the only pupil in colour, the Henson team's tribute to how autistic children see the world. Prince, who would go on to play a 2015 gig for the Autism Rocks charity, understood.

Susannah, who received a co-credit for the song as well as a credit for background vocals, added to The Current: 'I still love my starfish because they're transformative. A brain that lives in the unconscious. She [Cynthia] has such a fascinating mind. Prince had an ability to be that creative.'

That creativity came from a childlike place.

The man with the child in his eyes

Prince had one child with first wife Mayte Garcia. Their son Aamir was born a month premature on 16 October 1996 and died after six days, diagnosed with a rare genetic disorder of the skull called Pfeiffer's Syndrome, Type 2.

For someone who had no more children, who had been playing the piano from five and who had mastered Hendrix on the guitar by twelve, you might think that Prince was too focused on music to allow children anywhere near the studio or backstage.

Not so.

The child within never left Prince.

Being a parent had always been part of the plan. He talked family and children with girlfriends, including one of his first known serious relationships, with Mi-Ling Stone Poole. His on-off girlfriend Robin Power Royal, whom he dated for three years from 1989, was told 'you would look beautiful pregnant'.

From playing free concerts for Marva Collins's school in

Chicago and to 500 deaf children in Dallas to playing volleyball – in heels – at the height of the *Purple Rain* stardom in Big Chick Huntsberry's back garden with the bodyguard's daughters and members of the Revolution, he gravitated to childlike energy. That extended to backstage too.

In the late '80s, the stepdaughter of Sal Greco, the technical engineer at Paisley Park, then aged four, turned up to work one day and said within earshot of the owner: 'He's really weird.' His reaction? 'He started laughing. He loved kids.' *Sign*-era make-up artist Terri Hinrichs also remembers him laughing backstage with Boni Boyer's niece.

As he got older, and after his two divorces (he was married to Mayte Garcia between 1996 and 1999, and to Manuela Testolini from 2001 until 2006), his attitude to children never waned, but it did slightly adjust.

'From '98 onwards,' observes Hayley Drinkall, a friend of Prince's since the '90s, referring to the year before he split from Mayte, 'he mellowed a little. It was only about eighteen months after he had lost his child with Mayte. Then he lost his mum and his dad, and then he lost his mum's twin sister, Aunt Edna Mae. Not that he talked about the elders, as he called them. [But] something different changed for him there.' Robin Power Royal goes further. 'It's when Prince's baby died – that's when Prince completely changed. He became more introverted for long periods of time.'

Elisa Fiorillo occupies a unique space in the Prince story. She was an aspiring solo singer being produced by David Z at Paisley Park in 1990 when she met Prince, who worked on some of her tracks. They would end up dating for a few months around that time. She remembers a man who drove straight into his work. 'I think when he lost his child, he didn't really deal with that. He pushed it under the carpet and kept making music. I totally related to it. When he had problems, [it was] "I don't want to hear it. It's music, music, music.'"

Later on in 2009, Fiorillo returned to sing back-up at his request. There was a time to play by the time she returned in his final six years to sing back-up for him. 'He loved the energy. "Come to rehearsals and bring your daughter." We had dinner and my nanny had to come.' Everyone was thrilled to see her three-year-old girl, except perhaps the staff member sent out at 11:30pm to find a frame for the picture she had drawn of her Mum's boss.

In the 2010s, Prince insisted on Brenda Bennett's young son coming on the third night in Boston with another Vanity 6 member, and ex-girlfriend, Susan Moonsie. 'He sent a limousine, put us up in a hotel. He loved my son. Susan and I didn't exist. He liked to be goofy.'

Jason Agel, who engineered Prince's 2010 album *Welcome 2 America*, recalls him dating a mother with young children at the time. 'The kids would come to the studio and he was sweet with them and would carry them around. He seemed happy to have them [there].'

On Prince's passing, photographer Afshin Shahidi was contacted by Paisley Park, which made him 'both smile and weep. We hadn't worked together for a number of years.' Prince's estate was getting in touch about an autographed picture by Prince's desk. 'She had signed it "To Mr Prince, love Yara." My daughter made a film when she was seven and Prince rented out the movie theatre in Chanhassen and took whoever was around. He loved children. They probably reminded him of easier days.'

'He didn't have the opportunity to expand his family,' reflects former manager Ruth Arzate, 'but he would have been an amazing father. He was so gentle. The epicentre of creativity begins when you are a child. You don't look at something and say "This is dumb". You say "Look what I made". There's only joy when you're creating and that part of Prince's personality has always been dominant. "Look what I made." There's always joy in his courage. That effervescence really speaks to it and his childhood qualities are where he comes to life. It's about always being present and doing what he loves to do. His connection with children is not just that – he wanted to have children. They have a simplicity and joy before the world has got to them.'

Some close to Prince say he would never recover from losing Aamir. Apart from a TV conversation with Oprah Winfrey, where he denied there was anything wrong days after losing his son on 23 October 1996, he rarely talked about it.

Within a year, on 13 September 1997, to be precise, he was back at work, performing 'Starfish and Coffee' on *Muppets Tonight*.

Prince and Susannah

Sign o' the Times takes in several lyrical themes and musical genres, but when asked if there was one theme which resonates throughout all sixteen tracks, Scottie Baldwin, the front-of-house engineer who worked with Prince across two decades, says: 'I have a guess. That it was Susannah. She's all over the place there. That relationship was hugely important to him and one he didn't get over, even though he had [married] Mayte and Mani [Manuela].'

To say that Prince and Susannah Melvoin were involved ahead of the *Sign o' the Times* double album is an understatement. She had been the first girlfriend to live with him; she was picked to be the lead singer in his new band the Family; she was cast as his romantic lead in his follow-up to *Under the Cherry Moon*; and she happened to be the twin sister of Wendy, the guitarist in his band, the Revolution.

All of this would fall apart.

The permanent contribution, the thread which held from *Purple Rain* to *Sign...*, was Susannah. She is widely considered to be the subject matter of 'Forever in My Life', 'Adore' and 'If I Was Your Girlfriend' (Prince never confirmed these things) and was by his side when he wrote the double album's title track, 'Sign o' the Times'.

In some respects, the coming-together of Prince and Susannah Melvoin was inevitable. She and Wendy, like Prince, were the offspring of accomplished musicians; their father Mike played upright piano on the Beach Boys' 'Good Vibrations' as part of legendary session musicians the Wrecking Crew. Like Prince, Susannah sang and had a strong sense of personal style. And he once reminded her (as she told Variety): 'You remember my mom was a twin, right?' They had kinship on many levels.

They were friends first, when Prince used to stay at Wendy & Lisa's house in LA. On day he pushed her against a wall, kissed her and said 'I can't stop thinking about you', before leaving the room. Luckily, she felt the same and, after becoming an item, Prince wanted to work with her on all fronts; as singer in his new band the Family, as the lead in his next film, she was by her sister's side and Prince's too.

Prince's musical collaboration, his business, his personal life would not be easily compartmentalised. Where he would go, Susannah would follow, and he would follow her too – to LA, NYC and she was often back home in Minneapolis before he was.

'The Ballad of Dorothy Parker' was the first track Prince recorded at the downstairs studio at 7141 Galpin Boulevard in Minneapolis. Susannah fixed the place up while he was either on tour or making *Under the Cherry Moon* in Europe. Susan Rogers, who arguably spent more time there than even Susannah, remembers the home studio as being 'absolutely gorgeous. It was a basement studio, but the front of the house was higher than the back of the house. In that basement, the back wall was stained glass, like you'd see in a church, and you could look out on to a big piece of property. The carpeting was a really royal purple, but the panelling was a pale oak. There was a nice contrast and a fairly high ceiling. There was a bathroom there and an adjacent room, where you could record drums, which had glass doors that would slide open. There was a den with a pool table and, along one wall, was where Susannah had done a mural.' Prince had sung 'As soldiers draw of swords of sorrow' while his lover draws 'pictures of sex' on his song 'Crystal Ball', but in the interests of accuracy, Susannah had drawn winged fairies on those walls.

Susannah had been by Prince's side since he rocketed to fame, as had her twin sister. But as things began to fissure between Prince and the Revolution from the spring to the autumn of 1986, so too did they with Prince and Susannah. As she went back home to her sister in LA, he would bring company back to Minneapolis.

There was further Melvoin family business in the mid-'80s. Karen Krattinger was Prince's personal assistant and Susannah's friend – an awkward position to be in. 'I know how much he loved Susannah. He was just not ready to make any sort of commitment. He wasn't such a rock star, but he was playing that role with women. It was hard watching it. She was so incredibly in love with him and dedicated to him and good for him. He would want me to take her somewhere, say "Go to New York and represent me at the MTV Awards, and hey, fly this other chick in." She didn't know any of that.'

If this sounds disrespectful, Krattinger is tactful. 'He was always just Prince. He always said please and thank you. That shows appreciation, I think. As far as romantic relationships, I have never seen Susannah so happy as when things are good and so miserable when they weren't. I think he toyed with their emotions to such a degree that they were willing to take what they got and hope he chose them. I think he did realise his own power with women.'

'Susannah is one of my best friends,' Krattinger continues. 'It was very difficult for me when he didn't treat her correctly or I knew he was flying in some girl behind her back. I loved her, but I loved him – and he was my boss. She understood.'

The 'some girl' was often one individual – a talented one at that.

Prince and Sheila

For all that his relationship with Susannah was durable, Prince and Sheila Cecilia Escovedo went way back. To the Circle Star Theatre concert in San Carlos, California in January 1980, to be specific. She introduced herself as he stared in his dressing room mirror. 'I know who you are' – the same five words he frequently said when others introduced themselves.

And, according to Prince's personal assistant at the time, Sheila 'was the one he was flying in'.

Sheila E and Prince went way beyond boyfriend and girlfriend, and way beyond bandmates. They were, to misuse drummers' parlance, in each other's pocket for the best part of two decades. For someone like Prince, whose ultimate love language was music, Sheila would prove irresistible.

Paul Peterson, the Family's singer, grew up with both parents and a brother who were musicians, and Sheila's father and brother were too. 'Those of us who grew up in music families had a jump start on those who didn't.' This applied to Wendy (and therefore Susannah) and it applied to Lisa, whose respective fathers Mike Melvoin and Gary L Coleman were fixtures of the Wrecking Crew. Sheila was something else, though: Latin music royalty.

She was the daughter of Pete Escovedo, the legendary Mexican-American percussionist, while her uncle Coke played in Santana (as did Sheila herself, along with dating Carlos) and formed Latin rock legends Azteca with Pete. Her godfather was legendary bandleader Tito Puente, the man dubbed 'the musical pope'. Sheila played alongside her brothers Juan and Pete, also percussionists, and was asked to join George Duke's band before she was 21. She also played on Marvin Gaye's Midnight Love tour, as well as enjoying spells keeping rhythm for Lionel Richie, Herbie Hancock and jazz royalty Billy Cobham.

So Prince knew who she was.

'She had been around [music] longer than he had,' points out Alan Leeds. 'She had been on the circuit and knew tons of musicians and she had some idea of what she wanted. She was terrific.'

Sheila spent time first as a solo support act, then on percussion with Prince around the Purple Rain tour. 'He and Sheila had fun,' recalls Peggy McCreary. 'That was the first real collaboration I saw. That was the first time I ever saw him relax. He liked it when she played the drums and he could play something else.'

By the mid-'80s, Prince decided to help Sheila become a pop star, writing, producing and performing on her albums and two Billboard Top 20 hits, 'The Glamorous Life' and 'A Love Bizarre'. They would continue to perform these songs together two decades later.

In 1986, bandleader Sheila had assembled a crack unit behind Lionel Richie on his Dancing on the Ceiling tour: Boni Boyer from Sheila's home base of Oakland on keyboards; Norbert

Stachel from nearby El Cerrito on sax; Levi Seacer Jr from Richmond (twelve miles from Oakland) on guitar; Timothy Christian on drums and Raphael Saadiq on bass (who would go on to form Tony! Toni! Toné!, as well as collaborating with artists from Rick Ross and Amy Winehouse to Elton John). Sheila would also bring in guitarist Miko Weaver from Berkeley, five miles from Oakland.

The band's tightness was not lost on Prince, who was considering making his own changes. He needed help with his band. Switching from singing hits at the peak of her pop-star years to playing drums for someone else seems like an unusual move. Not for Sheila. 'She stopped pursuing her career as a drummer to be in his band,' suggests Lisa Janzen from his management team and a friend of Sheila. 'I spoke to him about it. They spoke to each other about ten times a day. I see Sheila's perspective. She's a huge name in Latin jazz. Probably the best music director. She was great at putting a band together. He would steal her band all the time – Levi Seacer, Boni Boyer. She's the brother and he's the sister.'

Norbert Stachel feels that heading back behind the drum kit would lead to a few misgivings on Sheila's part. 'She would think of it as being her own bandleader and having her own band playing music of her own choice. That's a hard thing for any artist and when you're at the beck and call of another artist, you have to give up that because Prince talked her into it.'

Mychael Gabriel, godson of both Prince and Sheila and now her musical director, calls it 'very organic. I know for Sheila, she really missed playing drums. It's almost like two friends just chatting. "You wanna come play drums for me?" In a way, it was as simple as that.'

Their romantic connection may have played on Sheila's mind. Musically, more so. The fact she hailed from Oakland, home of Tower of Power and near to Sly and the Family Stone and Graham Central Station can't have hurt in Prince's eyes (or ears). 'Prince was already up on the Oakland funk thing,' attests Eddie Miller, one of the *Lovesexy* engineers.

Sheila and Prince were becoming close. She was being produced by him as a solo artist in 1984, and the end of the Revolution in 1986 predated Sheila joining his band. The romantic lines were less clearly stated, but the musical connection was solid.

While dating each other and working together, musically 'every time they were on stage together, you saw and felt the bond,' says trombonist Greg Boyer. 'Indescribable, unbreakable.'

'I met Sheila when she was a teenager,' recalls another great Oakland drummer, Tower of Power's David Garibaldi. 'A fabulous musician. Her dad and her Uncle Coke, they were Bay Area legends, their pedigree was incredible. She's really representative of the Oakland thing. A very specific drum language comes out of this place. Coming up in the Bay Area, it was always a very diverse musical landscape. We heard all the great rock music, any kind of world music, Latin music, funk, jazz, classical music. It was this great mix and the guys when they played, it was everything. It was fusion before it was fusion. The East Bay scene was always about funk.'

Sal Greco remembers the same virtuoso instincts. 'Watching her play drums, she could play independently, so her two arms could play something differently from her two legs.'

Musically, few kept pace with Prince. He was a bandleader. So was Sheila. He was a musical virtuoso on guitar, bass, keys and drums. Sheila – virtuosic on all areas of percussion and someone who had sung hits too – was the same. Sheila was a quintuple threat, says Coke Johnson. 'She can dance, she can sing, she can pretty much play all instruments, she can play guitar, I even saw her play trumpet one day. He would make up wardrobe for the whole band, but she always looked like she could be his sister and she's pretty.'

Eric Leeds marvels at her being able to sync her parts on a Charlie Parker tune to footage shot for the *Sign o' the Times* movie. 'Sheila even re-recorded parts of all of her drum solo on "Now's The Time". *That* was a neat trick.'

Prince also skipped across genres but, in Susan Rogers' phrase, 'the street where he lived' was funk. Sheila's street was Latin.

Prince had the chops to drum the entire Sheila album he wrote and produced from his head. Sheila had the edge in a different way. While Prince was self-taught, Sheila was schooled with both a dad and uncle who would guide her in Latin and an Oakland funk scene which was even more embedded than the music in Minneapolis.

Prince and Sheila would end up very quickly finishing each other's drum patterns. 'Her playing is more precise than Prince's,' adds Eddie Miller. 'You can also hear how she's influenced by Prince. Her technique was impeccable. Prince's wasn't like that [some interviewees called his drumming 'sloppy'], but it didn't matter. Generally, when he's working on music, he would start on drums.'

No one disputes Alan Leeds' judgement of Sheila as 'one of a handful of the best musicians he [Prince] ever worked with. She's not just a skilled percussionist, she's also a remarkably savvy bandleader. She's a versatile musician that can play Latin or jazz or fusion or R&B or pop. She's a performer with great skills. She's a sweet person. She didn't grow up in LA with Wendy & Lisa. She didn't grow up in Minneapolis with Bobby and Matt Fink and she was an outsider to the rest of them. They bought into this concept that the Revolution was the Beatles and not to be tampered with.'

Those around Susannah are hardly likely to be effusive in their praise of Sheila, Prince's on-off girlfriend at a time that he and Wendy's sister had been expected to marry. Some interviewees were upset about Sheila's comments of closeness to Prince after he died at what they felt was to the exclusion of others.

Others regard her as a sweet, humble girl descended from musical royalty who was a master at jazz, funk, fusion, Latin and rock'n'roll.

In terms of WAG status, Sheila E never married Prince and did not enjoy the same kind of deep romantic relationship with him as Susannah or his two wives Mayte Garcia and Manuela Testolini had. But, in terms of musical partners, she was there near the beginning, right in the thick of it, at the forefront of the *Sign...* tour and movie, and with him in the decade of his death.

Lisa Jordan, Sheila's friend and designer of her clothes on the *Sign...* tour, says they worked together 'right up until the end. She was touring with him when he played with a cane.' Sheila would tell interviewers after his death that she had a musical kinship with Prince like no other.

Because she probably did.

The two brothers who helped Prince change course

There was another example of Prince's ears being open to talent in late December 1983, seven months before the release of the *Purple Rain* film and two months before Prince would start working on the first of three solo Sheila E albums.

Around 8 a.m., Sunset Sound engineer Bill Jackson was awoken with a phone call. 'He is coming in with the band.'

Jackson had only been working with Prince for a month, but he saw the seeds of something new, a decidedly left-field turn. 'I needed to be there by nine, so I just started grabbing microphones.' The engineer couldn't put his finger on it – Prince normally started at '10 a.m. or later' – but couldn't shake the feeling that something important was happening.

In a way, it wasn't.

'Nothing that day was really relevant to that album, but the people who were there became relevant to that album.'

It was important in other ways. Most of Prince's music involved him walking into the studio, with a purpose, an idea or a set of lyrics and only an engineer for company. But sometimes, with talented musicians with him, he would jam and discover something new. 'It was a jam session that eventually, obtusely, went into that album,' explains Jackson.

The band was the Revolution, but Wendy Melvoin had brought her brother Jonathan and Lisa Coleman her sibling David. David Coleman played a series of instruments, including cello, finger cymbals and the oud, a short-necked Arabic lute. Prince tuned in.

Jackson struggled to keep up as the band played. 'I'm moving the mics around as I'm bringing the faders up and bringing the EQ and even still adjusting things. It's a little groove rocking.'

Prince didn't use the material, but patterns were emerging of what his new sound would be – and it was quite a gear change from his biggest-selling album. Soon after, he gifted Jonathan and David a free day of recording at Sunset Sound. This was to prove crucial, according to Jackson. 'They were two different distinct things.'

The first was the jam session which 'as far as I know, was never released as anything. Somewhere I have a cassette of it. Then it was the birthday gift of the studio for a day and that's when we did the two brothers doing a song. That ended up being 1985's *Around the World in a Day* title track. It was just a jam with sitar, Indian tablas, Sheila E on drums, Prince on bass, Wendy and Lisa on keys and the two brothers.

'Prince was at that period in 1984 working on Sheila's record [*The Glamorous Life* album, released in June], but it just seemed like they were having fun and it didn't seem like they were trying to accomplish something specific. If they were, I didn't notice that. But that next time, when it was just the brothers, they were really excited and they were so happy about doing that.'

Prince gave Coleman and father John (not present) a writing credit on that title track. The Arabic sound and multi-instrumental skills of Wendy and Lisa's brothers – Jonathan played keys, drums and percussion and would briefly be a member of the Family – had sparked a fire in Prince on what direction his new music could take.

'David Coleman's influence on *Around the World in a Day* is felt on almost every track,' argues Prince's soundman of two decades, Scottie Baldwin. David Tickle, who worked with Prince on the record during the *Purple Rain* tour (which hosted venues with audiences from 34,000-129,000), agrees on the brothers' influence. Prince would tell him: 'I don't really want to do big places [anymore]. I only want to do twenty-, thirty-thousand seaters. Always have a studio available for me, David.'

Tickle would keep two or three studios for each city on hold, proof that money and manpower would be no roadblock in the face of Prince's constantly rolling muse. 'After a gig, he would say "Let's go to the studio". Other times "Let's go party". I'd be in the truck, he'd be teaching the band parts and I recorded whatever he was doing. That's how we recorded *Around the World in a Day*.

'David [Coleman] played cello and violin, string instruments. We were still in Minneapolis and although we were getting ready to do the live shows, six weeks in a big hall, there was this other band which David was part of in the rehearsal studio and they were working all sorts of different things. Prince got influenced by them.'

Jonathan Melvoin would die of a heroin overdose in 1996 and David Coleman of a heart-related problem in 2004. But their influence and mastery of instruments would live on in Prince's follow-up to his biggest record.

A new visual direction would also be required. He had artist Doug Henders, who painted the backdrop of the eyes on the 'When Doves Cry' video, with him on tour as a camera operator. 'I had just left art school as a neo-Marxist punk rocker who was more interested in the Clash than [Sheila E's first solo album] *The Glamorous Life*.' He gave Prince music by influential hard-rock band Bad Brains, along with David Byrne and Brian Eno's *My Life in the Bush of Ghosts* album. 'He said they were an epiphany and thanked me.'

The ballad 'Condition of the Heart' was another track which, for some Prince admirers, also represented an epiphany. Guitarist Steve Vai's then girlfriend brought home a copy of the album and it was this song which tipped him over into fandom. 'I was deeply moved and felt as though I discovered a new treasure. It was uplifting, ethereal, inspired and retained a perfect balance of an exceptionally gifted instrumentalist and brilliant songwriting craftsman. But it was his unabashed confidence in his choice to be nothing but authentically himself that carried the greatest impact for me. I was hooked.'

Just as he would record *Around the World in a Day* on tour, Prince asked Henders to paint him a cover. 'I made management buy the painting its own seat on airplanes.'

Prince finished the album on Christmas Eve 1984, before the *Purple Rain* tour was done and before he had won his Grammys and Academy Awards in 1985, respectively for *Purple Rain*'s soundtrack. He was ready to move on again.

Henders, alongside the Revolution, his management and Warner Brother execs, was summoned to an office space in

Burbank, California. 'Prince showed up with his dad wearing matching paisley bathrobes and pyjamas. We all sat on the floor of the empty carpeted room and he played the entire album from beginning to end for everyone to hear for the first time. Everyone was blown away and baffled that it was so different from *Purple Rain*.' 'Baffled' might be polite; 'blown away' might be generous. Warner Brothers employees may well have been horrified with this peculiar follow-up.

The psychedelic work, with the cartoon depictions of Prince, his band and other members of his party, was immediately compared to the Beatles' *Sgt Pepper* era, but it was something else. It was his latest gear change, perhaps the most dramatic since the *Dirty Mind* cover, but the first one that, commercially anyway, hadn't grown his sales more than the previous record since *Controversy* in 1981. It sold three million to the previous album's ten million.

Prince had let his label and the rest of the world know that he would be doing things his way.

Meet the Family

Even though *Purple Rain*'s movie release was on 27 July 1984, by early August – when two of his bands, the Time and Vanity 6, were in a state of breakdown – Prince reacted as you might expect. He formed another band.

Such was the intimacy of Prince's inner circle, its name – the Family – felt appropriate, even if Prince may well have borrowed it from Sonny Thompson's original late '70s band of the same name.

Rehearsals for the Family started in Minneapolis with the Time's Jellybean Johnson on drums and Jerome Benton on backing vocals, as well as new saxophonist Eric Leeds and

Miko Weaver on guitar from Sheila E's band, plus, for live shows, Minneapolis bassist Allen Flowers and jazz pianist Bill Carrothers.

They were also poppy. Blond, handsome Paul Peterson, actual family (brother) to keyboardist Ricky from a later line-up of the Time, would front the enterprise with another musical sibling, Wendy Melvoin's twin Susannah.

Prince's intentions were clear. 'We gotta go after some of that Duran Duran money!' he was heard to tell David Rivkin.

The Duran dollar, suggests Eric Leeds, meant Prince opted for 'The Screams of Passion' ahead of the funkier 'High Fashion' as lead-off single. 'That decision was his way of saying that he wanted to get the "pop" market on board before he hit them with a more obviously funk/R&B song. So perhaps Duran Duran was just his metaphor for that.'

They were glamorous. The video for 'The Screams of Passion' featured an orchestra and the band clad in silk pyjamas on a Santa Monica beach. The visuals were in line with the old-school movie glamour Prince had been mining for *Under the Cherry Moon*. Susannah told the Beautiful Night blog website in 2013 that their look 'was inspired by mid-to-late 1940s noir films with smoking jackets, fast dialogue and black-and-white glamour.

'It was Prince's concept to put us together. The reason [the band] was called the Family was because we had all been working within the Prince organisation. I was the staff singer. [Peterson] was the keyboard player for the Time. [Johnson] was the drummer for the Time and [Leeds] was a horn player for Prince.'

Marie France, from the wardrobe department, remembers 'an amazing photo shoot' with the Family with legendary fashion photographer Horst P Horst. 'That's where you feel the influence that Prince had for Hollywood of the '30s and '40s. Horst came in, one assistant, one light.'

Prince told David Z Rivkin that he was going to be the producer, while Peterson's and Melvoin's good looks couldn't hurt. Rehearsal film from Prince's Flying Cloud Drive warehouse was FedExed to him while *Under the Cherry Moon* was filming in the south of France. 'Everything was just going perfectly,' remembers Allen Flowers.

Prince had big ideas for Paul Peterson. 'He was training me to be in an upcoming movie. He had me taking singing, dancing and acting lessons in California.' Rivkin notes that 'he was developing a white artist to do his bidding, which was always successful'.

And then…

Paul quits, recalls Flowers, who played at the band's only gig. 'He puts the kibosh on the whole thing.' 'Paul Peterson unfortunately,' reflects Rivkin, 'had bad advice. He had a lawyer who was whispering in his ear and people believe their own hype.'

A firm six-figure contract offer from MCA Records as well as an offer from A&M 'to produce Janet Jackson before she was Janet' (meaning before the global success of *Control*) – as opposed to radio silence for months from Prince while he was directing in the south of France – was hardly conducive to building up confidence and loyalty in a restless eighteen-year-old.

The masterplan in Prince's head was never verbally articulated and wasn't worth the paper on which he didn't write it. There followed a series of furious phone calls between Prince in Nice and the man he dubbed at subsequent gigs 'St. Paul, Punk of the Month' at his place in Oakwood Apartments in Los Angeles.

'Paul had big eyes, he had so much talent,' says his brother Ricky. He calls his sibling 'a freak. Prince wanted to put him on a leash and say "This is my protegé". Paul was kind of like me.

I can do this on my own.'

'Those phone calls were not fun,' Paul Peterson sighs now.

"You want a house? You're going to have to work."

"I'm going to leave. I'm getting a better offer. I'm sorry to disappoint you."'

When asked how Prince responded, Peterson groans. 'Lawsuits. I can't believe I made it through that period of time. It was really stressful. I was under the gun and had to write, produce and record a great record for MCA. The rest of the band understood why I left.'

Peterson's own response? 'I got my own lawyers.'

As would be expected – because Prince worked with Paul's brother Ricky and the three men stayed in Minneapolis making music – an equilibrium settled. The 'St. Paul, Punk of the Month' chant Prince had started live was, Susannah told writer Touré, clearly a joke.

Paul is more reflective now. 'One of the biggest reasons I left the Family,' he says. 'was because there was no promotion, there was no contract, the money was not what it should have been. There was no one to talk to. Prince said "Talk to my manager".

'I remember doing a very little bit of promotion, and even then I understood that this was Prince's show. He's going to promote it the way he's going to promote it. [But] he wasn't promoting it, that's why I was upset. He did that with the Time.

'I rehearsed with the Family for a year. We did one gig and that was it. He went off. I went to LA. He was grooming me to be in the next movie.' The plot? 'He never let me in on that stuff. He worked on a need-to-know basis.'

Shortly after the 13 August 1985 gig at First Avenue organised by Prince, Allen Flowers' phone rang. 'Three or four days later, Alan Leeds called me and said it was defunct. He told me the whole story but it didn't matter because that's all I heard – that it was over. He didn't sign Paul because he didn't believe in contracts. Somebody else offered him a deal and Paul went.' It would be their first and last gig in that incarnation.

'After Paul Peterson quit,' says pianist Bill Carrothers, 'most of the live band was fired. I went back to playing jazz.'

It is easy to pin the blame for the Family not working out on an eighteen-year-old's defection, but Prince's focus on a black-and-white movie in the south of France, where his proposed co-star was also the band's singer, was probably more of a factor. 'Prince derailed them a little bit,' argues Lisa Janzen, who was working for Cavallo, Ruffalo and Fargnoli at the time. 'He was really good at that.' She cites the aborted plan 'that Susannah was going to be a movie star. She was out there nine months. The same thing happened to [another singer in his band] Jill Jones. I was in New York putting her band together to go out on tour and then the tour got cancelled.'

'It's been heartbreaking, a lot of it,' reflects drummer Jellybean Johnson who would go on to work with producers Jam and Lewis. 'He had me and Paul and Jesse and Susannah and Jerome and he didn't have us in a lock-and-key contract. He and Jerome ran off to do *Under the Cherry Moon*. By this time, the Family had been rehearsing nine months straight with the idea that we were going to tour with him. All of a sudden, he runs off with Jerome and Susannah is engaged to him.

'Prince calls me out the sky blue and says "Bean, I want you to join the Revolution". Bobby is already there. I said, "Prince, that's cool, but what are you going to do about the Family?" He hung up the phone. The next thing I know, my accountant called to say my salary was going to be cut. So I'm freaking the hell out and that is when I joined Jimmy and Terry and that is when they were able to give me a salary.'

Another song on the Family's album went on to global

recognition in 1990, thanks to Sinead O'Connor. Covers of songs normally had to cleared by the songwriter, but her then manager Steve Fargnoli had recently parted company with Prince and, it is rumoured, didn't check first. It was perhaps the reason Prince would be snippy about the version and start reclaiming it with his own live shows in the '90s.

Some thought the Family's version of 'Nothing Compares 2 U' was an instant smash, including Allen Flowers. 'Right away, man. Absolutely! Because it's such great material. All you got to do is listen. Coming from Prince, anything he touched was triple-platinum.'

'Nothing Compares 2 U' was just an album track on yet another Paisley Park project which hadn't flown commercially, thanks in no small part to the singer bolting. Prince had started using Clare Fischer for strings on *Parade*. 'When Dad did the string arrangement for "Nothing Compares 2 U",' recalls his son Brent, 'that was originally a band playing and Dad added orchestra. Prince liked the orchestra so much that he kept it with a synthesiser. So it was more like the Prince live version of "Nothing Compares 2 U". That's how my father heard it.'

The song is said to be either about Susannah (although it was recorded in July 1984 while they were still together) or Prince's departed housekeeper Sandy Scipioni, who left his staff after her father's death; it was rare he would confirm things such as this publicly – or even privately to friends. Paul Peterson feels the song attained much of its power through Fischer's work. 'It was a great ballad. I listened to it on my kitchen table, but all I heard was bass, drums, guitar, keyboard. No strings. When Clare Fischer put the strings on it, and David Z stripped everything away from it, Prince wrote the best song and I was lucky enough to get to sing it.'

The Family would continue to record. 'He [Prince] and

Susannah were having problems,' recalls Jellybean Johnson, 'and that just complicated the whole dynamic. If he was mad at her, it made it easier for him to be mad at the Family. Finally, she just left and that pissed him off more.'

St Paul and Susannah would reunite musically in the 2010s and both made personal entreaties to use the group name, which Prince owned – ironic, as it had been used elsewhere first. So fDeluxe was born.

'He was nothing but difficult the whole time,' adds Jellybean Johnson. 'Paul and Susannah called him and said "We're thinking of getting back together" and he just ripped their heads off. He wouldn't let us have the name.'

The Time, the Family, the Revolution… Prince was moving through bands at a rate of knots. 'Bean,' Jellybean Johnson remembers his old boss saying, 'I change bands like suits.'

CHAPTER 7

SLOW LOVE

'Slow Love' ... Credit where it's due ... The end of the Revolution ... Prince's secret weapon: Oakland ... Money don't matter tonight ... Dig if you will the moving picture

'Slow Love'

Prince collaborations could be brutal for some.

There are three co-writing credits on *Sign o' the Times*. One was given freely, to Susannah for 'Starfish and Coffee', based on that conversation about a classmate of her and Wendy's, Cynthia Rose.

'It's Gonna Be a Beautiful Night' features credits for Eric Leeds and Matt Fink based on a band live session.

The other co-writing credit was not freely given, as Carole Davis was to discover.

Her working relationship with Prince started around the time his romantic relationship with Denise 'Vanity' Matthews ended in 1983. Vanity had been slated to star in *Purple Rain* and Prince was aware of Carole Davis, an aspiring actress who would go on to star in *Mannequin* and *Sex and the City*, as a replacement. He flew her over to his purple home on Lake Riley on the south-west outskirts of Minneapolis.

'He was interviewing me not only for my singing and my acting,' she remembers. 'He wanted to hear me sing live and he realised that we could gel musically. That's when I realised he was auditioning for a girlfriend as he was asking me very personal questions. Today, I would probably call up the Screen Actors Guild if I had that kind of meeting now. He got too close to me and in my physical space.

'He became very angry and sullen and pouted like a four-year-old child when I told him I didn't believe in Jesus. I was there for about two nights. There were no agents or managers there. That was totally inappropriate. There was this guy who was his bodyguard [Big Chick Huntsberry] who brought me to the studio. He [Prince] was really angry with me right before I left that morning. I opened the door to one of the bathrooms and he was standing there in his heels with his curling iron on. I knew that was a sight I should never have seen. Half of his hair was curled and the other half was a mess.'

Not many predicted great things for *Purple Rain*, a movie from an aspiring musician with zero acting credits to his name. Davis, after being leaned on by her agents, opted instead to star in Garry Marshall's *The Flamingo Kid* with Matt Dillon. 'I regret not doing the movie. I should have done the movie. It was a mistake on my part to let my agents and managers and publicists talk me out of it.'

But something clicked, perhaps because of Davis's own musical talent – she would go on to become a recording artist for Warner Brothers, with an album *Heart of Gold*, produced by Nile Rodgers. She and Prince remained friends. 'I always found him to be amusing from a sociological viewpoint. It was a character study for me. There was nobody like him. What a fun opportunity that he would ring me when he would come through New York. He would never announce himself. He would call and say "Hi. It's me. Wanna hang out?" He would always behave in a weird kind of way. His persona was so carefully crafted. I had never seen anyone so self-conscious in my whole life.'

Some of the cultural blind spots Prince had at that point would be filled in later life. But a trip to New York's American Museum of Natural History with Davis was not a success. 'He knew nothing about anything cultural. He was spectacularly ignorant. It was either Biblical or sexual for him.' Others would talk in later life of Prince's cultural interests, such as ballet (he was dance trained from childhood) and literature, but not that many in the '80s. At that point, it was mainly music and film.

A song of Davis, which she recorded for *Heart of Gold*, had stuck with Prince. She and he had worked slightly on the bridge, but the song was mainly hers. A couple of years after the *Purple Rain* meeting, the phone rang. Prince had taken a fancy to this song she had played him: 'Slow Love'.

'I got a call years later from some lawyer just before it was released saying "We wanna buy the song from you outright for $25,000." I immediately said no. The lawyer said, "You might wanna reconsider. If you're not going to sell the song, it's not going on the album."

'The gentlemen's agreement when you write a song is that 50/50 is fair. He [Prince] didn't want my name on the album. He didn't make himself available even to discuss it. He made his team unavailable to my team. I remain angry about that to this day.

'I would say I wrote more than 98 per cent of the song. He made some very minor changes. At that time, if you co-wrote a song, it's a professional courtesy to share the song 50/50, and I would have done that but my lawyers were faced with some heavy paperwork. I was not happy with what the lawyers had done but at least I didn't sell the song for $25,000. If I had, I wouldn't be speaking to you.

'I wouldn't have been able to record my own song. He would have made the money from my album. This is the great conundrum of Prince. Everything he railed against he did to others.'

'Slow Love' was a song Prince loved, but he didn't own it. He would eventually give Davis a writing credit leading to regular payments when they actually materialised. To record it, he even roped in the Revolution – Wendy & Lisa on backing vocals, Wendy on guitar, and Eric Leeds and Matt Blistan on horns –for a session at Sunset. 'You could tell that was going to be a pop hit,' says Blistan. 'It was a good love song with a good message to it.'

The record was made between the West Coast and the Midwest. Susan Rogers arranged for the master tapes of the song to be shuttled 'to where Prince was, to the airport. Send it air cargo. Box it up, air cargo, [and] somebody who worked for his management would go to LAX and take it back to Sunset Sound.' The air cargo also once took him a meal from Rudolph's BBQ in his hometown and flew it to LA. 'You could do that if you had a load of money.'

'Slow Love' would continue to be performed sporadically live by Prince. It also provides an insight into how he taught musicians.

'One time we played "Slow Love",' says Adrian Crutchfield, a saxophonist who worked with Prince in the 2010s, 'we came up with horn lines on the spot. But I remember he came to me and he sang to me the horn lines that they played on the song. For the next four or five nights, he would show me different horn lines. 'I didn't actually hear that song until a year ago. *Oh! This is what he was trying to tell me. Why didn't he just tell me to listen to the record?*'

For Carole Davis, memories of the song and the man under whose name it was recorded, remain bittersweet. 'He tried to screw me out of my own songwriting. For years and years, I had to struggle to get paid for that song. I couldn't sue because I thought he would end up owning my house. He was so powerful.

'He paid me for quite a few years and then he got a new publishing company and for a while I tried to get my money and I couldn't. He never returned my call and I saw one printing of the record where my name wasn't on it.

'I knew he really loved that song. Why would someone like Prince be desperate for my song? He's a musical genius. I don't come close to him in that area. After he died, I went after the estate and I'm beginning to get cheques.

'I felt that my life was enriched having known him. I also feel that it's a mistake not to have done the movie. It's a very complex relationship. I might be one of the few women who have turned him down. We were mutually fascinated with each other. I remember having great laughs with him. I remember him, warts and all. He was very silly and giggly – very childlike and pathetically insecure as a man. I think it was linked to his height. He wanted to be all powerful and macho. It didn't work for me.'

Credit where it's due

Carole Davis was neither the first nor the last person to fall out with Prince over credits.

One of Prince's earlier hits, 'Do Me Baby', is widely believed to have been originated from Prince's then bandmate and best friend, André Cymone. Terry Jackson remembers a conversation with André when he was living in north Minneapolis at 1248 Russell Avenue and André was two doors down at 1244.

'At the time, Prince is living at the Blue House at 50th and France [in the city's south-west suburbs], where he has a four-track reel-to-reel. André plays me this song "Do Me Baby" and says "I just wrote that". A couple of weeks later, I hear it and tell him "I heard your song on the radio". André is dead silent. André says "It's not my song and I'm not in the band anymore."

'He heard the song the band was playing. "He told us to learn it." André is hot, he's pissed, he's mad. Prince shows up.

"What are you doing with my song?"

'Prince turned around to him. "I'm a star, you're not" – this is a direct quote – and he walks away. I asked André "What did you do?" "I left and quit the band."'

Allen Beaulieu, Prince's friend and the photographer behind his early sleeves, remembers a riff he was playing in the autumn of 1982 on his Les Paul Junior in Prince's basement. More to the point, so did Prince. 'We were jamming at three o'clock at night and he heard that riff and he logged straight into his recording board. "Play that riff so I can copy it. How much you want for it?"' Beaulieu settled for a copy of the record. The next spring, with the riff as a jumping-off point, Prince recorded 'Let's Go Crazy'.

Of course, if you're talking straight-up theft, Prince stole Sheila E's band for the Sign tour – not that they minded playing the bigger venues. He would do that in the future by recruiting Shelby Johnson from Anthony Hamilton's band and Josh and Cora Dunham from Frank McComb's crew, among others.

Sometimes, not often, Prince had to bow the knee.

The end of the Revolution, part 1

It's hard to carbon-date the moment the sands began to shift on the elite band Prince had assembled in the Revolution.

One pivotal point could be between 14–16 November 1984. The place was Greensboro, North Carolina. Saxophonist Eric Leeds joined the band on stage on one of the three dates, and was then invited by Prince to watch the show afterwards on video (he liked to have his performances taped). It's fair to say the Revolution dynamic shifted slightly. Sheila's appearances on stage at the end of the *Parade* tour had already disrupted things further.

Leeds would be asked to solo by Prince on some of the key songs, replacing solos that the others, particularly Wendy Melvoin, might previously have been invited to play. Prince, who had been working on Sheila E's album from the start of the year, had her as support and she would occasionally join the Revolution on stage.

'You have Eric, who can play an instrument that none of them can play,' his brother Alan reflects, 'and then you have got Sheila and she's the girlfriend. So it wasn't just somebody in there. They were losing their power. They were losing their access.'

The personnel was changing at Sunset Sound in LA too. Coke Johnson, who engineered on *Sign...* there, remembers 'Sheila and then Levi [Seacer, her band's guitarist] started coming down. Prince and Sheila's on-off dating status and friendship meant, Johnson notes, that Prince 'had a social interaction with her he wasn't getting with the Revolution. They got on amazing. She was really fun and she could make him laugh at the drop of a hat. She was really good at keeping him on the live side and on the funky side.'

The end of the Revolution, part 2

One of the patterns of Prince's career was that he was always in charge, his decisions were quick and the perspective he had on an employee often stretched beyond what they thought their potential was. These roles would often not be in their future, until he asked them to take them on. Saying no to Prince often meant, with him, no future.

Engineers would go on to produce other acts. Dancers would go on to duet with him or embark on solo careers. Photographers would be creative directors. Assistants would go on to manage him. Most improbable of all, bodyguards would become bandmates.

Just after *Purple Rain*, and the departure of Big Chick Huntsberry, Prince's much-cherished security detail grew to include Wally Safford, Jerome Benton and Greg Brooks. Brooks takes up the story of a soundcheck at Prince and the Revolution's homecoming Christmas gigs in 1984.

'He's on the piano and I'm singing what he's doing to the music and he sees that. "Brooks, go get on my mic." Me, never being a shy person, that happened and then the band came up. After soundcheck, he came over and said, "Brooks, I didn't know you could sing." "Hell, man, I do it all."'

Soon, Brooks and his fellow security guard Benton started joining in tour routines for 'Baby I'm a Star'. 'We rehearsed it every soundcheck. We started doing it on the show.' When the tour ended in Miami in April 1985, he called Brooks and Wally Safford to his room.

'I want you and Wally to be in the group the Family.'

Benton had been chosen for the Family and then, believes Brooks, deselected because he had appeared in a Jam & Lewis video. Brooks was summoned to France where Prince had been filming. 'When Paul Peterson went haywire, we started rehearsals for the Family in Minneapolis. When Prince went back overseas to make *Under the Cherry Moon*, I went back to Detroit. The office called to say "We want you over in France to do some videos". I'm thinking it's a video for the Family. Once I get there, I go over to the set and Prince says, "Brooks, ride with me. The Family is no longer a group.'"

This was late 1985 and, by then, the tight-knit unit of the Revolution was already being added to by their boss – not just with talented musicians, but bodyguards dancing on stage. Consummate virtuoso composers and performers from impeccable musical stock like Wendy and Lisa were unlikely to open their arms with enthusiasm.

The end of the Revolution, part 3

In 1986, after Prince chose not to tour *Purple Rain* outside North America, or *Around the World in a Day* anywhere, changes were afoot.

The previous tour had been the *Purple Rain* juggernaut: ninety-eight shows in arenas and sports stadia selling 1.7m tickets. After that, a rest was required. Or for Prince, who didn't really do rests, a reset.

Jeff Mason had been production manager since *Dirty Mind*. 'After *Purple Rain*, there was a big break and everything went away for three years. Everybody knew there was going to be a chunk of time that everything was dismantled.'

The Purple Rain tour ended in Miami on 7 April 1985 and, within a year, Mason was told to stand by his phone. He was even flown to the south of France where Prince had been making *Under the Cherry Moon*. 'Somewhere in the two- to four-week range, I get a call. "We're doing a show in Boston [at Metro, a 600-capacity club]. Would you like to come and see what's going on? Show's at eight o'clock. Come an hour before."'

Prince wanted to move his music back from arenas to theatres but his choice of how he toured was unconventional. 'For the next eight or ten weeks, we are doing our 'dart' shows. On a Tuesday night, he would throw a dart at a map of the US and would play a show where the dart landed. We would be playing 500-seater theatres. These were the days when he was so close to people. He had a ball.'

After Matt Blistan and Eric Leeds had been more of a permanent fixture on the horns, Prince had already augmented the Revolution with his security guards Greg Brooks and Wally Safford, while Sheila's guitarist Miko Weaver was recruited to give the band a funkier edge.

Wendy & Lisa and BrownMark, who was working on a contract basis after the Purple Rain tour anyway, had tried to quit before Europe until Bobby Z talked them round at the airport. 'Right before the tour,' Matt Fink explains, 'Wendy and Lisa decided to quit the group. The next day, they'd quit and were heading back to LA and they literally went to head them off at the kerb while they were unloading their luggage, like something from a movie. "Hey, you guys. Prince wants to apologise for what happened. He doesn't want you to leave and there are too many people depending on us to do the tour – crew people, management, booking agents." In their hearts, they really didn't want to quit.'

Wendy & Lisa, who around that time had been looking at houses in Minneapolis, were cautiously optimistic their earlier decision to leave might have gone unnoticed by Prince, who sent his team to stop them before *Parade* was promoted.

'I think in their minds,' Fink adds, 'maybe things have been smoothed over. Then we do the tour and, a month later, he fires them probably due to what he probably considered to be their insubordination.'

Prince was big on loyalty, but not as a two-way street.

By September in Japan, things were at a sticky pass. Jerome

Benton told Bobby Z on the bullet train that Sheila was to replace him. On the last night of the tour on 9 September in Yokohama, Wendy & Lisa both recall Prince smashing up two guitars during a particularly impassioned rendition of 'Purple Rain'.

Matt Fink doesn't. 'I have no recollections of him breaking the guitars. Everybody else did after the fact. I never saw any smashing. Wendy and Lisa knew right away that that was the end. Bobby did too.'

Like much of Prince's timeline, recollections are a little hazy, but things moved fast. On return from Yokohama, Wendy, Lisa and Bobby were summoned to Prince's LA rental and told their services were no longer required. Bobby and Prince would remain friends; Wendy & Lisa and Prince would have a more complicated relationship, although Prince did reunite with them occasionally in later years.

On 3 October, Lionel Richie's Dancing on the Ceiling tour – featuring Sheila E's band, including her friend from Oakland, Boni Boyer on vocals and keys, and Levi Seacer Jr – rolled into St Paul Civic Centre. 'Prince was really jealous of how good Sheila's band was at the end of the Lionel Richie tour,' recalls her saxophonist Norbert Stachel. So jealous that, straight after that concert, Prince was already on manoeuvres.

'Prince booked some rooms at the Minneapolis hotel for himself,' says Stachel. 'Four in the morning, Levi calls me. "Sorry to disturb you. I just joined Prince's band. Prince's bodyguard wants you to go to his room. Don't look at Prince in the eye. He's going to answer your question and you have to ask if you can be in his band.'

Stachel, who now admits regretting the decision, passed on Prince. He cites his 'Napoleon complex' and his 'habit of mistreating people and demeaning people a lot. He would belittle people all the time unless he couldn't get away with it.

Prince had a need to boss people around, dominate people, and I hated it.'

Stachel feels Prince's spoiling tactics also informed his decision. 'One of his reasons for hiring Levi and Sheila was to break up Sheila's band. He couldn't handle Sheila having a successful band that had nothing to do with him.'

Alan Leeds who had been with Prince on the road since 1983 had become accustomed to the plate-spinning. 'Prince was a charmer. He knew how to work people's loyalty. He was a master at manipulating people to get their dedication and involvement and he wanted everybody to share in it.'

The 'written, arranged and performed by the Revolution' credit on *Purple Rain*, carried onto the subsequent two albums, had been a moment where Prince's gang was established and acclaimed. But, unbeknown to the five members, Prince liked revolutions and understood their constantly spinning nature. The rock band model of The Last Gang in Town meant they were, to him, just his last gang before the next one.

'He had convinced them they were part of it,' adds Alan Leeds. 'Every one of them was a movie star. They had their own fan club. Wendy had become an icon for every girl who wanted to play an instrument.

'It was important his vision was a mixed-race, mixed-sex band. It made a lot of sense. To Prince, they were always hired hands and, once their usefulness expired, it was always easy for Prince to move on to the next. It was hard for the original five. They had an emotional belief, if not an intellectual belief, that they were a self-contained group that didn't need to be tampered with.

'Wendy would tell anybody who listened that he screwed up the greatest thing that had happened since the Beatles. Her inability to get it wasn't musical. It was personal. The fact Prince casually tossed it away when it was over [meant] there was a reaction that he had bamboozled them and they took it harder than they should have.'

Prince, feels Leeds, would have seen that sadness as 'a sign of weakness'. Cat Glover, a dancer on the Sign… and Lovesexy tours, told him 'firing them like he did was just cold when I knew him a little better, but I guess that's kinda how *Sign o' the Times* came about'.

Miles Davis' son Erin, a Prince fan, says his father 'thought it was cool that Prince could wake up and decide to get rid of the whole band. I thought that was horrifying.' Matt Larson, perhaps because he only joined Prince's touring crew that year, was matter of fact about their departure. 'It wasn't that big of a deal. We would tour and the tour ended. Sheila had been hanging around. Eric [Leeds] and Matt Blistan were part of the band. Suddenly the girls are gone, and Bobby has gone and Mark has gone.'

Prince's secret weapon: Oakland

If Minneapolis is the most important place attributed to the sound of the *Sign o' the Times* period, particularly live, and if LA – because of the work at Sunset and the contributions of Angelenos Wendy and Susannah – is second, Oakland deserves the bronze medal.

Lisa Jordan from Prince's Sign tour wardrobe team was also friends with Sheila E. 'Oakland's got a shoot load of musicians. She always just had people. She grew up in a musical family and had incredible contacts. She was as picky as Prince when it came to being spot on.'

Rose Ann Dimalanta, who played keyboards in both Prince and Sheila's bands, also hails from Oakland, calling it 'a lot more blue-collar. There is a vibe. Sly Stone comes from El Cerrito [15 minutes away]. There is a whole parade of great musicians. If you wanna play music here, there's a trinity of music you need to know – one is jazz, one is funk and R&B, and one is Latin. If you want to be a working musician, you have to have those in your toolbox. That [training] made you play hard. You couldn't fake it.'

Sheila knew all sorts of musicians back home and the boss wanted to tour the *Sign o' the Times* album. So after he said goodbye to the Revolution and retained the services of Matt Fink (and Eric Leeds and Matt Blistan on horns from the *Parade*/dart tour), Sheila called in guitarists Weaver and Seacer, the latter dragooned to play bass, and Boni Boyer on vocals and keyboards. Sheila would play drums and help Prince work up his new band. Sheila always just had people.

'Sheila and Prince played together for twenty years,' Lisa Jordan adds. 'Both had bandleader minds.'

According to the connective tissue in both Prince bands, Matt Fink, Sheila and Prince whipped the new group into shape in a matter of weeks. 'They were all very professional and experienced players,' Fink explains, 'and good at what they did, so it really didn't take too long for them to step up to the plate.' And not a mention from the boss of the transition. 'He never talked about it. Totally forward momentum.'

Money don't matter tonight

One thing Prince had in common with the Godfather of Soul was that James Brown paid people what he thought they were worth.

Prince wasn't quite on the same level as Brown – who told his bandmates to bury their money in the backyard rather than leave it with the banks – but ask ex-employees of Prince if they were well-reimbursed for what they did, and the answers vary.

For a boss with a keen appreciation of how black musicians of the past had not been paid fairly for their work – to the extent he wrote 'SLAVE' on his face in the '90s – Prince paid employees in a way that went beyond informal into, on occasion, the frankly unaccountable.

In the early stages of his career, he was careful with money. Allen Beaulieu, the photographer behind his early sleeves, says the two men 'never had a deal. It was just a handshake. I thought I was well paid. I called Michael Jackson's photographer and he wouldn't even talk to me so I could get a ballpark figure.

'The first shoot he booked me for three days. "I will give you 150 bucks a day." I think I got $10,000 for the [*Dirty Mind*] cover. It should have been $20,000 by now, but that's a lot of money to me. He was always good to me. He was always a real nice guy. We became friends.'

Whether Prince paid you well or not depended on your expectations. Brenda Bennett, one third of Vanity 6 who went on tour with Prince and the Revolution, feels 'sure we didn't get paid as much as anybody else. I would be looking to be paid more.'

The Time were on the same Triple Threat tour with a weekly pay cheque of $150. ($117 for those band members without children, who paid tax on it.)

It's clear Prince's fame and salary rocketed when the Revolution came on board, but theirs didn't. They too were on a weekly salary while playing arenas and sports stadia. By the time of *Parade*, he was aware Wendy & Lisa had made plans to leave (before being talked out of it at the airport), that Mark hadn't been happy since the filming of *Purple Rain* and that Sheila E was champing at the bit to be his drummer, so Bobby

Z was on borrowed time too. Matt Fink stayed and Prince was big on loyalty.

The Revolution, on a flat fee of $2,200 a week, got through the gruelling ninety-eight-date Purple Rain tour and were promised a bonus at the end of it. With the tour having sold 1.7m tickets, they had some figures in mind. But they weren't the $15,000 Prince reportedly gave them.

'It wasn't the greatest situation financially,' admits Fink, 'but he had us on a retainer whenever we weren't touring, so we were always getting paid a salary. In late '85, right after the tour, we were telling management that we'd like to have a better relationship financially. What can we do here? They agreed. We all signed a three-year contract going forward, which established a really decent salary, plus royalties. It definitely equalled a minimum of $1.2m which everyone could make and which didn't include tour salaries. We weren't writing that much and we were hired guns to be his sidemen, so it was a decent deal in my opinion. It was generous. Could it have been better? Probably.

'The only caveat was that if he decided to fire you, the contract was set up in a way that he could fire you with two weeks' notice and negate the contract. If he didn't fire you and you stayed on as a loyal member, you would see that contract fulfilled for those next three years. Unfortunately, Wendy and Lisa didn't even see the first year of that contract. They should have but didn't. Neither did Bobby or Mark.'

Prince's idea of payment, with himself as the benevolent paymaster, worked for him, but not everyone on the payroll. His former assistant Ruth Arzate thinks growing up poor in the US, like his idol James Brown, weighed heavy on him. 'Being poor in America is basically a disease. As you approach from the outskirts of what America looks like, black America has always been that way. There is a reason he wrote "SLAVE" on his face.'

Arzate also reckons his parents' experience of working full-time jobs to supplement any income they received from music informed his thinking. 'I am sure he got a lot of information from his father, a jazz musician, as his mother was, and a lot of information from his father travelled down from them. John probably talked about how he wanted a record deal and they were not paying him enough at the club. That lends itself to how Prince saw things.'

In the twenty-first century, Prince became more generous. Dave Hampton, who ran Paisley Park in the '00s, says Prince 'compensated me more than well'. Musician Frank McComb played quite a few private parties around the *3121* era. 'I was never shortchanged. He always took really good care of me. There were a couple of times I wanted an amount of money and I would get more.'

Scottie Baldwin worked with Prince for two decades until his death. When asked if he was well recompensed, he felt that 'all of us could all be paid more. When I learned what the Revolution were making per week, I was embarrassed for what I was making. It was ten times more. That question to me is about me.'

In 2009, Prince asked Elisa Fiorillo to sing back-up and, having produced her as a solo act around twenty years previously, she knew what to say – or what not to. 'I never spoke money with him. When I first joined the band, I had no idea how much money I'm getting paid. Don't ask. Give him your bank account information and you will get what you want. I never made so much money in my life. There was $50,000 in there. I never signed a paper or signed a contract.'

Prince could be stingy with payment or credit, but also extravagant in his generosity.

In the mid-'80s, luthier Roger Sadowsky was asked, and

refused, not to put his name on the headstock of the guitar he designed. 'Not so much frustrating as insulting… if I wasn't getting paid well. He was even paying for a first-class seat for the guitar. They flew me and the guitar out first-class from New York.'

Engineer David Tickle also understood how Prince was with credit when he was delighted with his work on '4 The Tears in Your Eyes' (a song Prince contributed to USA For Africa after not singing on 1995's 'We are the World'). He asked him to join his band and offered him a production credit on his next record. Sort of.

Prince asked him to work on it, said he'd be back and then, five hours later, Tickle gave it to one of his security detail.

'"Prince wants to see you."

'What have I done?

'I go up to his suite.

'"David, that's so amazing, that's good, I can't believe it. You are now officially the producer… the sixth member of the Revolution."

'Parade came out and I'm looking for my name. There! It's there. "Produced by Prince and the Revolution." Thank you.

'He treated me well. Wendy and Lisa found out how much I was getting paid.'

Among the many reasons the two had sought to leave the Revolution, that lack of respect, as manifested in their salary, could be one. The lack of communication from Prince about future plans, an experience not unique to them, could be another.

Prince controlled pay to the extent he liked to sign cheques, particularly when he had a small staff. But through neglect or choice, he was not always mindful to pay what was owed. Matt Fink and Carole Davis were not alone in having to chase up songwriting royalties.

"Beth Sidla's life."

① {Clover}

1. Jumpsuit no cutouts – white ~~eleven~~ buttons
   Medium size turtleneck.
   Pleated-back waistcoat
   Boots

② {Sapphire}
   Stove-pipe pants
   pleated-back waistcoat
   Boots

③ {Lacquer Red}
   Jumpsuit with cutouts
   Long turtleneck
   Waistcoat
   boots

④ Mint
   Jumpsuit no cutouts
   Medium turtleneck
   ~~Blue~~ Boots

⑤ Amber

over →

Design sketches for the 'Sign o' the Times' tour.

Medium turtleneck
Jumpsuit with holes white buttons
Boots

6) Pewter
Stove-pipe pants with black buttons
Waist-coat
boots

7) Rose
Stove-pipe pants/w rose-buttons
Waistcoat
boots

note: please send
lightweight plaid swatches

8) Sandalwood
Medium turtleneck
Jumpsuit no cutouts
Boots

Design sketches for the 'Sign o' the Times' tour.

Left: Artwork for Prince's 1980 album *Dirty Mind*.

Right: Prince at The Ritzy gig in NYC, March 1981.

The Time, standing around a pool table in Minneapolis, October 1990.

Vanity 6, performing on the TV show *Solid Gold* in October 1983.

Prince in a lace outfit performing in Detroit, November 1984.

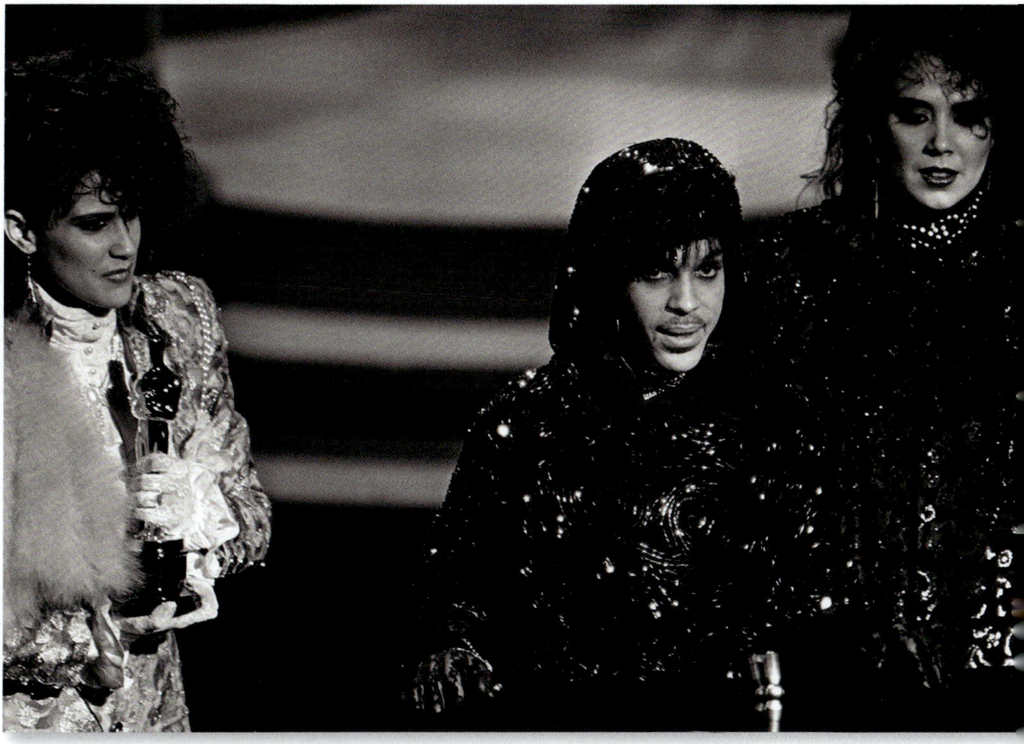

© HARMS/AFP/Getty

© Maximum Film/Alamy

© Warner Brother/Getty

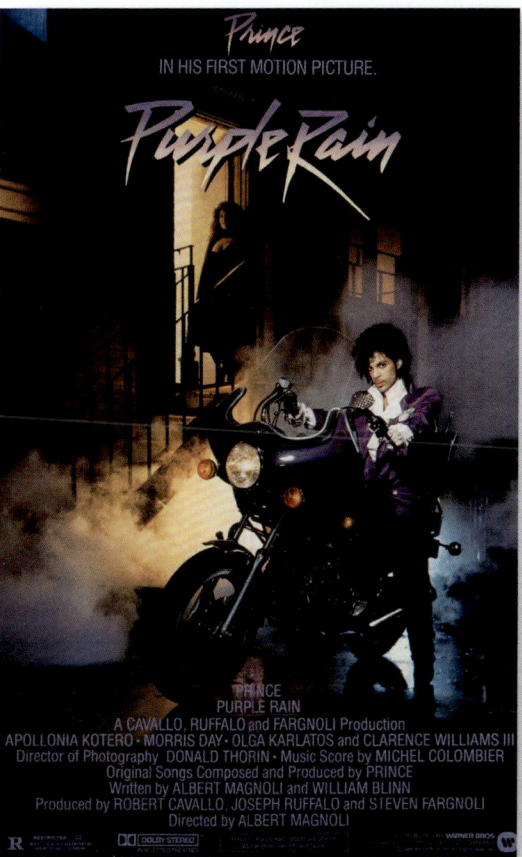

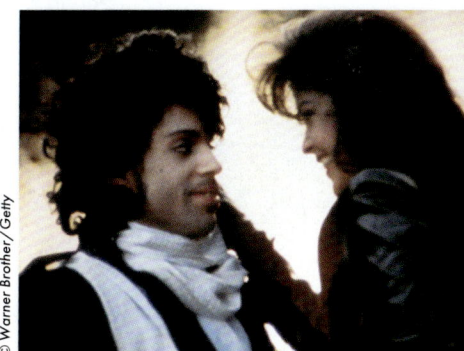

Top: Prince at the 1985 Academy Awards in a beaded hood outfit with Wendy and Lisa.

Above right: Prince and Apollonia Kotero in *Purple Rain*.

Left: *Purple Rain* movie poster.

Around the World in a Day, 1985.

Under the Cherry Moon movie poster.

Prince and Kristin Scott Thomas in *Under the Cherry Moon*.

Prince with Lisa Barber, winner of MTV's '*Under the Cherry Moon* to be Hosted in Your Home Town' competition in Sheridan, Wyoming, July 1986.

© Michael Putland / Getty

© FG / Bauer-Griffin / Getty

© Rob Verhorst / Getty

Top: Prince doing the splits at Wembley, London, 1986.

Above right: Prince with Cat and Sheila E, 1988.

Left: Prince performs on stage with Cat Glover in Utrecht, Netherlands, 1987.

'There were times Prince stopped paying people for years,' Fink says. 'We would have to go after our royalties and get them reinstated. He left Warner Brothers Publishing and, for several years, he stopped paying people. He'd gone to Universal. And another gentleman, Chris Moon, who'd co-written the song 'Soft and Wet' on the first album, and I went after our royalties in the year 2000 and it took two years of haggling with the correct people directly until the president said "You gotta reinstate people's royalties". Prince didn't want to do it with his accountants because it cost him money. Universal did it and they would take 15 per cent of our royalties. That went on until 2012 when Prince took his publishing in-house. So he stopped paying people and it took until his passing to get things reinstated properly for people.'

Prince admired musicians who would sell their own material like Frank McComb. After one show in 2005 he saw Mr & Mrs McComb packaging their own CDs in his dressing room (he approved) and he also admired Ani DiFranco, who in 1990 formed her own record company, Righteous Babe. 'He would turn up at my shows,' she laughs. 'I remember the one or two shows after I saw him play. I got completely red-carpet treatment, shagpile on the floor of the limo. He'd come to my shows and he'd be sitting by the stage on a case.'

'It [their relationship] started in the era when he was trying to get off Warners while I'm hitting the mainstream with my indie label. He told me at the time he dug that record. I remember the way I had confronted the music industry was an inspiration.

'I was on tour with Maceo [Parker] playing in Minneapolis. He was coming into town. [They talked, and Prince told DiFranco] "Warner Brothers is telling me I owe them something, that's insane?!?" It's no wonder he wrote "SLAVE" across his cheek. I was the straw that activated the camel's back.'

Prince never stopped paying attention to the discrepancies between high earners in the music industry who didn't perform and low earners who did. 'He was very aware of that,' says Ian Boxill, one of his mid-'00s engineers. 'Because of what he went through with Warner Brothers, he thought they were ripping off artists and managing control of their masters. He thought they treated artists poorly in general. When he's up at three in the morning making music, none of these record executives is up, they're sleeping. So he doesn't know why they made so much money out of record sales.' This particularly as, ever since *Dirty Mind*, Prince hadn't sought an advance to pay for the production of his own music (although Warners would make a sizeable contribution to the building of Paisley Park).

In the early '00s, Sam Jennings helped Prince start the NPG Music Club through which he could sell his own music. He admits how rare it is that an artist was across so many aspects of his career. 'He never had a manager in all the time I was there. He wanted to know where all the money was going, what was getting paid out. Artists normally brush off to their people but that wasn't him. I was getting paid out of the NPG Music Club, so he really liked that I made my own money. I ended up paying myself and he liked that.'

The more Prince ran his own not-so-small business, the more he admired those who did.

Dig if you will the moving picture

On 17 October 1986, Prince's publicists announced that he would move forward without the Revolution, the day before he started moving forward with 'Housequake'.

'Housequake' was meant to be a single, which would have

required a video. That was perhaps one contributory factor why he lagged behind Madonna and Michael Jackson in some aspects of popularity in the '80s.

His career in music video would not be a model of consistency. He had strong ideas about some of his videos, but not all of those worked.

Jackson would collaborate with established directors like John Landis, Martin Scorsese and John Singleton, while Madonna hired video directors who would go on to film success like Mark Romanek and David Fincher. Even though friend and collaborator Spike Lee directed 'Money Don't Matter Tonight' in 1991 and the posthumous 'Mary Don't You Weep' in 2018, Prince was less inclined to hire a big-name film-maker to tell him what to do.

Of the songs for which he chose to make a video, most were live performances from him and his band. Of the ones which are not, he didn't always decide to make things easy for himself. When he decided he wanted a video for 'Alphabet Street', the only song from 1988's *Lovesexy* to hit the US chart, it was on a Sunday. He wanted to make the video *that* Sunday, the same day that a huge snowstorm hit Minneapolis. This made it the only clip on MTV rotation filmed by public access camera crews, as opposed to film professionals.

It was a far cry from the video for 'Kiss', with dancer Monique Mannen, model Kara Young and commercials director Rebecca Blake. That was shot over two days on the same sound stage in Culver City where some of *Gone With the Wind* had been shot. 'He was always on,' remembers Mannen. Louis Falco was choreographer but Prince made significant input on the moves too. 'The split was Louis but the walk was Prince.' Young, kissed at the end of the video, was behind a veil, sunglasses and a glass screen. 'He didn't want you to see my face,' she laughs. 'He wanted to be the prettiest person in the video. He was aware of himself.' And Prince stood on a couple of apple boxes to kiss the five-foot-eight model.

In 1985, Prince oversaw three videos in a three-day period. He did pretty much everything. These were the videos for 'The Screams of Passion', the lead-off single from the Family's album, 'Raspberry Beret' and '4 The Tears in Your Eyes'.

This three-day run was not planned weeks or months in advance. Instead, Lisa Janzen, a week into working for management firm Cavallo, Ruffalo and Fargnoli, had quite the baptism of fire within her first ten days in the job.

'I got asked to assist on the beach at Santa Monica [for 'The Screams of Passion' video] and was told he needed to have a twelve-piece string section in silk pyjamas by 10 a.m. I called my mom, who was luckily a former opera singer, who told me to call the musicians' union [to get the players] and I maxed out my credit card in Nordstrom [to buy the Ralph Lauren pyjamas]. Marie France sewed on the shoulder pads.'

As part of Prince's in-house wardrobe department who knocked up clothes to order, Marie France was used to this flexible working. Janzen was not. 'Fargnoli says "He's decided to shoot 'Raspberry Beret'". Jamie [Shoop, her colleague] went out and cast extras for the dancers and decided to choreograph them, and filmed "Raspberry Beret" in the evening. By one or two in the morning, I thought we were done, but I'm told he wants to do one more, which is "4 The Tears In Your Eyes". We got out of there by three in the morning.'

'Raspberry Beret' was a high concept affair. It contained animation (the use of which came six months before it helped A-ha to number one around the world with their 'Take On Me' promo), choreography and extras, who included Pat Smear (later of the Foo Fighters) first at the invitation of a casting director and then of Prince, who liked his hair. Prince directed, wearing a cloud suit.

'One time, Steve Fargnoli called me at three in the morning,' continues Janzen. 'Since that phone call, I turned off my phone at night. Prince had decided he wants 300 raspberry berets as we were going to shoot the "Raspberry Beret" video the next day and I said "What do you think I'm going to do about it? Why don't you let me sleep?" So in the morning, I called Western Costume and asked if they had any raspberry berets. They told me the Tasmanian Army wears those colours. So I got a whole box of Tasmanian raspberry berets. In the end, they used one.'

According to producer Simon Fields, who was given latitude by Prince to let him choose directors, this scorched earth policy was typical. 'Warner Brothers spent all that money on a Japanese animator [for "Raspberry Beret"], they asked me to use it as a backdrop. He wanted to get extras as dancers and he wanted my accountant to choreograph them. He was a deconstructionist and he liked to break things into pieces.'

Steve Purcell had edited a few Prince videos and would go on to edit the *Sign...* movie. He was asked to direct 'Glam Slam', the second single from 1988's *Lovesexy*, and when he arrived on set, he got a surprise. 'It was basically a performance video and when I got there, he had on a blindfold. I asked why and he said "Anybody can go out and perform". He wanted to show that he couldn't see anybody on stage but everything was so well-rehearsed that he could do it.'

'Another thing he didn't tell us!' laughs Tim Clawson, who produced many of Prince's videos. He remembers the demands ahead of the same shoot. '"I want a theatre in the round, I want an orchestra." He comes out in a blindfold and we were looking at each other going "How did he do this?" That's what he would do. He would surprise you all the time. He was looking for ways to be new and innovative. He may have thought of that walking from the dressing room to the stage. He was impulsive that way.'

Other videos heralded in huge moments in the life of Prince. 'Gett Off' in 1991 saw a prototype of the logo which would become synonymous with his subsequent image. Five years later, his cover of the Stylistics' 'Betcha By Golly, Wow' would feature footage of Prince rushing a pregnant Mayte to hospital. The song's release would come a month after the death of his son Aamir.

Only two videos proper, relatively muted by that decade's standards, were made for *Sign o' the Times*. The second and fourth singles, 'If I Was Your Girlfriend' and 'I Could Never Take the Place of Your Man', are live performances from the *Sign* movie, with the latter used as a video. The third single, 'U Got the Look', is dropped into the middle of the movie, but was filmed between European tour shows in Paris on Bastille Day (July 14th), other shows in Nuremberg, and over three nights between shows at the Bercy.

He asked dancer Cat Glover to choreograph it. She asked if she would get paid to do so. She would, so she agreed. Then she set to work on the dancers in Paris, none of whom spoke a word of English. Glover's French was far from heck-a-slammin'.

'I talked to Cat more than anybody else on set,' explains 'U Got the Look' director Dave Hogan. 'Prince had asked her to choreograph. She told him: "Well, pay me more." This was an extra job on top of being in the band.

'We worked it out together in rehearsal. She had a loose idea of what she wanted on set. We're taking about a tight show. Three nights, a two-night shoot, most of the crew came from London. The [camera] operator came from Paris. Trying to communicate with the French was tough as they argue with each other. That was a little frustrating, but we got it done.'

A little bit more than frustrating, according to Cat Glover. 'I couldn't speak French so he [Hogan] got me an interpreter. We had 300 dancers that he wanted me to audition, so I would have to go back and forth with the interpreter until we got it down to about a dozen or so dancers, but it came out well on film in the end. I had to make sure that the band could play their instruments and dance at the same time. Sheena Easton was a sweetheart, but she couldn't move too well. I don't think she'd had intense choreography before, so I had her flicking her hair and hands on hips to try and get some kind of attitude like "Oh please" and sexiness to complement Prince's moves in the video. Prince could move and you could choreograph him too. If he dug it, we kept it.'

Hogan describes Prince's wardrobe department – the 'U Got the Look' video opens with Helen Hiatt from that department ironing one of Prince's shirts – as 'like a machine. They were making new clothes on demand. It was like a fashion show. I was thoroughly impressed. Sheena was very cooperative, took direction. That was another outfit they built on the day.'

The video was a strong peach-and-black statement from Prince, with the fashion representing the colour palette chosen for the album. 'It's all him,' says Hiatt. 'I really didn't know. "I want peach clothes. Make it peach."'

Hiatt remembers that the outfit for Sheena Easton 'was conjured up at Paisley Park.' Some were custom-made, one purchased. 'I went shopping. I remember shopping for the night gowns we bought in Venice. We were up all night. I had choices.' It is customary for a singer to have their own sense of style or, failing that, their own stylist. In this instance, the Scot had fewer options.

'Prince told her to wear it. There you go. I'm sure Prince was putting his charm on her. He's a very persuasive guy. He'd do it to women, he'd do it to guys to get what he wanted, from the guitar tech, or from the soundman or from his manager.'

The performance video, which uses Paris landmarks and the set from the tour, features a love triangle where Cat is dragging Prince away from Sheena. 'That was Prince's idea,' adds Hogan. 'Kind of like an opera.' The movie, of which more later, would feature a different love triangle, this time with bodyguard-turned-dancer Greg Brooks, Cat Glover and Prince. 'Prince wanted this whole story of me and Brooks,' remembers Cat, 'and this Brooks-wants-me-but-Prince-does-too kinda thing. But then, of course, I'm distracted by Prince because Brooks had this other girl, but it played out more in the movie.'

There were rumours of disquiet between Sheila E and Cat Glover on set, but Hogan claims that he 'never saw any conflicts. It was very smooth. They were like marines running the beach.' The shoot finished up at 4 a.m. 'He just patted me on the back, we just walked away from the monitor and he said "It's a wrap".'

Prince, not the director, said 'Cut' on set.

The video for *Sign o' the Times* was not choreographed in French or English, but in Times New Roman. A strategic plan would be required in the MTV age for the lead single for Prince's first double album in four years. 'It was a fluke,' says its director, Bill Konersman. 'My sister was a video producer. She got a call from Prince's label that they wanted a video and everyone was under a time constraint because it was for European release. Prince specified that it must be the lyrics.'

The video was the lyrics, and nothing but the lyrics, minimal in an age of big-budget promos. The title track's lyrics were punched out on peach and black ('a happy accident,' says Konersman who had no idea of the album's cover scheme) as well as flashes of red, white and blue, and purple. 'That was improvised, but purple and Prince go together.'

Konersman, a graphic designer and an early adopter of Apple technology, was at that time teaching typography at UCLA. He was given the job 'because there wasn't any time'. And got together with two guys with a Bosch 4000 computer.

'It was the size of a refrigerator and it took twenty-four hours to reboot. It produced the style that you saw on the video. We could make a shape and we could outline a shape and turn it around, but it was still a 2D shape. Since I was a typography guy, I asked them "Do you have Garamond?"

"No."

"Do you have Universe?"

"No."

"Do you have Baskerville?"

"No."

"Do you have Times New Roman?"

"Yeah. We got that!"

'We walk in the office and I saw them on blow-up Letraset.'

This would take days to digitise. 'My heart sank. There was no concept. It looked like it was made out of construction paper, but that's what I had to work on.'

In an era of big spending, dance troupes, sexy outfits and non-outfits, this was considered the first 'lyric video', a trend which would be followed in the next five years by (among others) Talking Heads and George Michael, and, in the twenty-first century, by most artists for whom it could garner pre-release anticipation before releasing a video proper – or, in the age when MTV moved from pop promos to programming, not bothering.

Konersman got the verdict from Prince via his sister. 'He loved it.'

Simon Fields explains that the lyric video was chosen 'because the words were important. He wanted the words to lead.

It [the song's subject matter – drug abuse, gang warfare, AIDS] was a worldwide calamity.'

Typography got easier too. With his profits from the video, Konersman bought his own $20,000 computer, taught himself animation on it and got himself as far away from the music industry as he could. 'They're so flakey. If you didn't like cocaine, you had no business being there.' At the time of writing, Konersman's employers are the Ministry of Defense in Arlington, where he works on a training simulator for the US Air Force in a job where everybody still wants to fly.

CHAPTER 8

HOT THING

Prince's Paris match ... Under the Cherry Moon ... 'Sign o'
the Times Part 1' ... I want my MTV ... James Brown –
this is a certain man's world. That man is Prince

Prince's Paris match

I t was the first foreign city Miles Davis visited. He ended up
hanging out there with Pablo Picasso and Jean-Paul Sartre,
and it would be where he and Juliette Gréco fell in love. Quincy
Jones studied composition and theory there, with conductor
Nadia Boulanger giving him the confidence to work with Frank
Sinatra a year later when he was just twenty-five. Grace Jones'
modelling career took off in the city, flat-sharing with Jerry Hall
and Jessica Lange. And it was where Josephine Baker had her
big break, the city adopted as her home and where she died.

Like many other African-American musicians, Prince had a
strong Paris match. It was love at first sight, says his then make-
up artist Robyn Lynch. 'He liked the romance of it. The texture
of it. The history. He was drawn to things which were different
from what he had grown up with.'

Sometime in 1985 or 1986 (he played two gigs in Paris each
year), he made his latest impulse buy, a ninety-nine-year lease

on a 5,000-square-foot place in the 7th Arrondissement. He quickly sold it.

The problem was that Parisians, who were getting used to seeing him as he made *Under the Cherry Moon* in France in 1985, loved Prince back, almost as much. 'He loved Paris, but every time he tried to stay there, everybody found out where he was,' observes his friend Hayley Drinkall, who saw him regularly over many European tours. He would chat to photographer Mathieu Bitton about Paris in the 2010s, the city where Bitton had hidden in the bushes, three decades prior, as a teenager to meet him.

The love for Paris was reciprocated. 'At that time,' says video director Dave Hogan, 'they were turning the lights off in the monuments around midnight. Prince's people called the mayor of Paris and they left them on all night for us, including the Eiffel Tower.'

Under the Cherry Moon

The follow-up to a film which couldn't have taken place anywhere other than Minneapolis was set a few hundred miles south of the French capital in Nice. Prince had got used to the good life after *Purple Rain*. Ray Parker Jr travelled to the south of France to visit him. His accommodation 'was where President Kennedy hung out. They gave me a driver and a car.' He was told that Prince was 'staying at a place down the street. The place JFK stayed wasn't good enough for him.'

Prince's costumes, made by a tailor in Nice, were overseen by Marie France, who was herself a graduate of the Sorbonne in Paris. She worked with fabrics that would look good in monochrome. Gone were the lace gloves, frilly shirts and bold purple trenchcoats. In came black leather jackets and white cashmere. 'The white cashmere on Prince's coat is the same white cashmere that's used for the Pope,' explains France. 'That's what the tailor in Nice told me where I purchased the fabric.'

Old movies and pop rivals were preoccupying Prince. He hired Mary Lambert – the woman who filtered Madonna's 'Material Girl' video through a *Gentlemen Prefer Blondes* lens – to direct (it was actually her video for Sheila E's *The Glamorous Life* which had caught his attention) and girlfriend Susannah would play the romantic lead.

The black-and-white movies of the past informed this black-and-white movie of 1986, according to France. 'We did camera tests to see what worked best for black and white. It was great to do *Under the Cherry Moon* for the fabric. At that time, for people working in films, TV and videos, you could access on the Paramount lot a large warehouse of fabric films left from the '30s, '40's... There would be some of the fabrics we used for him [Prince] and Kristin [Scott Thomas] and Jerome [Benton], which would correspond to the feeling of that film. We wanted it to be reminiscent of the great days and glamour of Hollywood in the '30s and '40s. That's what inspired me. We never did have a formal discussion. We were on the same page somehow. I don't remember having a formal discussion with Prince, but I talked with Mary Lambert about the look and showed her sketches, ideas and fabric swatches during prep.'

Under the Cherry Moon wasn't a sequel to *Purple Rain*, but all the important people – from those funding it to most of its intended audience – were waiting for *Purple Rain II: This Time It's in France*. Warner Brothers – who had provided the money upfront (unlike the earlier movie) – were, like audiences and critics, expecting another musical extravaganza as Prince essentially played another version of himself.

Prince had his own ideas.

'He was confident,' remembers the film's editor Eva Gardos.

'We would look at stuff and he would say "It would really be good to put a piece of music in here" and he would go to the studio that night and bring back a piece of music. That was fun.'

Purple Rain had contained a small bit of incidental music from film composer Michel Colombier. By the time of *Under the Cherry Moon*, Prince was adept enough to go home that evening and write, play, record and fill in what was required on a film that, unlike its predecessor, he was directing. For all that *Under the Cherry Moon* was intended to reflect that fun on-screen, Prince seemed to be taking film-making much more seriously.

His on-off girlfriend Devin DeVasquez, whose career was being guided by his management team, had also been slated to star – by her manager Steve Fargnoli, also Prince's then manager. 'Towards the end of 1985, someone told me "You're going to be in the next Prince movie." I asked what it was about. "I don't know yet." I said no to him when he asked me to come. It was the peak of my modelling career. [She appeared on the *Playboy* cover in June of that year.] I wasn't going to drop everything to come to Nice.'

This was before any of the Revolution would join him for the music, but his focus was making the film. The band was across the Atlantic, at Prince's warehouse at 6953 Washington Avenue South in the Minneapolis suburb of Edina, rehearsing with the tapes being FedExed to Prince in Nice (he was still monitoring their performance while directing). Susannah was scheduled to be with him on set, but Prince was facing opposition.

'Susannah was supposed to be cast as the girlfriend,' says Emmanuelle Sallet, one of the film's stars, 'but Mary Lambert early on convinced Prince he needed a real actress and when Kristin [Scott Thomas] auditioned for a small role, she caught the attention of the director and was finally cast as the lead.' (Because it was black and white, Susannah told Prince he'd need the cinematographer from *Raging Bull*, Michael Ballhaus, who was duly hired.)

Everything about the movie was a little out of whack. It was assumed Prince and Susannah were to co-star, with Lambert directing. Neither of these things happened. Prince had to break the news to Susannah. He decided to let her know she would no longer be his romantic lead in a Hollywood film at the same time that he asked her to be his fiancée.

Susannah recalled it in a podcast interview with the writer Touré.

'Three in the morning, looking out over the Arc de Triomphe.

"How would you feel if you didn't do the movie?"

"Hmm."

"I don't want you to do the film. I want you to be my wife."

'He's looking at me and he's so reserved and sweet about it.

"Of course. I'd love to be your wife."

'From then on, we were an engaged couple.'

Scott Thomas and Prince were an odd couple on screen. They would stay in touch into the twenty-first century, as she had with the film's editor, Eva Gardos. Onlookers deny any romance, which didn't stop speculation. 'She laughed, they had stayed in touch and she went to his concert in Paris,' says Gardos. 'I would be surprised if there was anything off-screen.' The photographer Ebet Roberts, who did a photoshoot with the actor after the premiere, agrees. 'I didn't get a sense. It never occurred to me even to think it.'

In 2009, by which time Scott Thomas had secured BAFTA, Academy Award, Golden Globe and Cesar nominations, Prince would release 'Better With Time' from his thirty-fourth studio album *MPL Sound*. He told *LA Times* writer Ann Powers that the song, comparing its subject to fine wine, was dedicated to the actor.

There was another plot twist a week into filming. The film Prince wanted made would become the film Prince wanted to make. The director who dispensed with his girlfriend was quietly dispensed with herself.

'Mary Lambert was fired over a weekend and we were asked to not ask questions,' says Emanuelle Sallet.

Eva Gardos suggests Prince deliberately let Lambert do all the lead-up work. 'I think that Prince really wanted to direct but he didn't have the personality or wherewithal to cast the movie. He was not really big at interacting with people. Pre-production of a movie is a lot of meeting and casting people. He used Mary to set up the film. What happened between the two of them, I don't know. I don't think they had disagreements – he just wanted to do it. It might have been purposeful.' In other words, it was a plan Prince had in mind once all the casting work involving people skills had been negotiated.

Personal assistant Karen Krattinger had arranged for VHS tapes of classic black-and-white movies to be sent to his Minneapolis home. The film he had in mind, says Sallet, was not Lambert's. 'I think he was going for the 1920s silent black-and-white burlesque-ish movie style. She had a different vision.'

'Someone once told me that he loved *Bringing Up Baby* and stuff like that,' adds Gardos, 'and I never realised that was the kind of movie he was trying to make.' Brent Fischer, who worked with both his father Clare and Prince on putting strings on his music, received a clue to the film Prince planned when he saw music marked for his attention titled 'The Marx Brothers Project'.

The rapport Prince enjoyed with Jerome Benton in the film, as with the Time's Morris Day in *Purple Rain* and Greg Brooks in the *Sign* movie, represented a pattern of carefully selected 'comic foils', says his video producer Simon Fields.

'They were like a comic troupe around him. It was very 1930s. He loved movies.'

His record company knew he wanted to direct. With Warners' movie division funding things, Prince's A&R director Lenny Waronker remembers internal foreboding. 'We had a conversation and one thing we said was "You can't let him direct". In *Purple Rain*, he had somebody he listened to enough to get it done.'

That person, *Purple Rain* director Albert Magnoli, says he was called by Prince's manager Bob Cavallo both before and after Lambert was sacked. 'Cavallo calls and says "I need you to do this movie" and I said "I'm not going to do it". When the first director was fired, I got another phone call.'

Once in the chair, the cast and crew relaxed into working with their new boss. 'I felt that Prince was very comfortable being the director of the film,' says Sallet. 'He assumed that role very well and was well-behaved on set, not only with the talent but also with the crew. I remember him being in control of everything he did and always very confident about his ability to handle things, even if foreign to him.'

Steven Berkoff, a last-minute replacement for Terence Stamp as the film's villain, reflects that 'Prince was very precise and always used to watch on the monitor and seemed very professional'. Castmate Pamela Ludwig agrees: 'he was very comfortable giving actors direction'.

Prince may have seemed relaxed to the actors, but not to his guest in Nice, Ray Parker Jr, who had been invited over by Prince for a week's fun. 'I was eating the good food and partying. I went to the film set and he was signing cheques on the back of his guitar, screaming and yelling.' Parker Jr had an all-expenses paid week at JFK's Nice hideaway and on his mate's 140-foot Benetti yacht, while Prince worked. 'I went back on the boat.

He was making a film. That's why I got the yacht with the eight-man crew and chef.'

The movie centred around a glamorous Riviera summer where entitled playboy Christopher Tracy (played by Prince) and his best friend Tricky (Benton) wreak havoc together at the expense of ice queen heiress Mary Sharon (Scott Thomas) whose heart he eventually melts. Off-screen, though, the atmosphere off-set was a little less light than the intended on-screen comedy. 'Prince wasn't very good at communicating,' reflects Gardos.

Prince and entourage had arrived in August, but it was October by the time they were shooting and December before they were done. Make-up artist Robyn Lynch has negative memories. 'Sunday was the only day off. Everything was shut apart from the hotel grooming parlours. I found myself buying and shopping for clothes that were warmer. There were some challenges. There was one TV station, the Sky channel. Everything was bad Eurodisco. It was insufferable.'

Prince, staying at Saint Paul De Vence, half an hour from Nice, had his moments of boredom too. By this stage, a big star and the captain of a ship he hadn't been expected to steer, he started ringing up his co-stars. 'One late night,' laughs Sallet, 'he called Kristin and me and asked to come by for a sleepover. She and I shared a house in Antibes. He came by, barely hung out with us and went straight to the guest bedroom.

'The next morning at 6 a.m., he was staring at the phone at a loss, not knowing his own home phone number as he wanted to call Gilbert [Davison, his then bodyguard] to come pick him up. I offered him a ride and he was insisting on closing the top of the convertible for fear of people recognising him without Gilbert to protect him. I laughed very hard and explained to him that, at six on this beautiful morning, I am not closing the top. The only people out – older housewives going to the early open-air farmers' market – would never know who he is.

'He enjoyed it so much and told me that he missed being able to do stuff like that or going to the market on his own to buy his own junk food. He was missing being anonymous.' Once filming was done, Prince returned to his comfort blanket of Minneapolis.

He originally planned *Under the Cherry Moon* reshoots with editor Eva Gardos at *Amadeus* producer Saul Zaentz's place in Berkeley, California before moving closer to Beverly Hills, handily close to Sunset Sound. Wendy and Lisa, rehearsing back in Minnesota at the Eden Prairie Warehouse, had prepared material for him which emerged on the end credits. 'They had filmed the movie,' says Matt Blistan, 'and that's when they got back to Minneapolis and when we came up with 'Mountains'. Because he liked the song, he took us back to Nice, where we recorded the video.'

The limitations of the movie were apparent to many of those working on it. 'The script was what it was,' says Robyn Lynch pointedly. Steven Berkoff is more direct. 'The story was weak and it would take a genius to make it exciting.' Another of Prince's on-off girlfriends of the time, Maneca Lightner, had seen rough cuts of the movie. 'I thought it was hilarious. The more I saw it, the more it grew on me. Prince said "This is funny but kind of corny."'

Once it was ready, Prince was ready to test the waters. Lisa Janzen from his management team calls Prince 'notorious for testing things in the middle of nowhere. He loved Detroit and he loved Minneapolis. I always got the idea that he was not a huge fan of American audiences which is why he toured Europe so often.' Cue the disastrous test screening and the even more disastrous box office.

'I think he shrugged off [its reception] with me,' reflects Maneca Lightner. 'He didn't seem fazed one way or the other, but it has to affect you. He put a lot of effort into it but he didn't discuss it.'

There were repercussions. 'Because so much money was lost on *Under the Cherry Moon* – *Purple Rain* cost $7m and made ten times that, *Under the Cherry Moon* cost $12m and only made $10m domestically – they had to cut projects and that's why the last Madhouse album [his jazz fusion outfit's *24*, on the cover of which the model appears] was not released.'

To this day, the film has its admirers. Jeymes Samuel, director of *The Harder They Fall* and *The Book of Clarence*, feels he 'could give a whole seminar on that movie. It might not be the greatest acting, but if you ask a Prince fan [for] their favourite movies, it's *Citizen Kane*, *The Godfather*, *Under the Cherry Moon*, *The Godfather Part II*... If you're a Prince fan, *Under the Cherry Moon* is the greatest piece of cinematic swag.' Prince's friend Sananda Maitreya calls it 'a very prescient, striking and impressive work' and feels that the weight of expectations sunk it. 'How dare he make a film that wasn't what we were "expecting" him to make? My wife Francesca and I spend a lot of time in that particular part of the south of France, and I cannot go there without being reminded of that film. I rewatched it after he passed through from this dimension of physicality and it is brilliant. Period. End of story. And the sly social commentary of the predilections and mores of rich European high society is spot on. And it's funny.'

Lenny Waronker, whose label at that time had been overseeing various major albums, including Madonna's *True Blue* and Van Halen's *5150*, admits the making of the movie had run away from Warners. 'I didn't follow it closely at that point. It shouldn't have happened. Maybe it had to.'

Sign o' the Times, part 1

Under the Cherry Moon's soundtrack album – *Parade* – is more fondly remembered by critics than the movie. Nonetheless, it remains a hard record to categorise.

It reflected The Artist Previously Known as Rock Star now settling into the role of The Artist. Its monochrome sleeve was selected by the record label's art director Laura LiPuma Nash; she says Prince let her pick the image from photographer Jeff Katz, who shot the sleeve.

Eric Leeds sums up *Parade* as '*Sign o' the Times Part 1*'. Keyboard player Matt Fink, who also featured on both tours, agrees. The saxophonist sees the songs of the 1986 album, which skip across jazz, funk, pop, playful French fancies and confessional ballads, as not just the precursor to 1987's double, but an insistence to avoid *Purple Rain Part 2* in sound as well as vision. 'Prince was determined to not repeat himself and wanted to concentrate on expanding his musical "mission" and not be concerned with just making hits. I think *Around the World in a Day*, *Parade* and *Sign o' the Times* reflect that.' Because of its idiosyncrasies, it is many Prince fans' favourite of his albums.

He was certainly expanding his horizons; there was more instrumental music than on the previous album, with string arrangements from Clare Fischer, the start of a career-long association. His musicality was coming on in leaps and bounds.

'At that point,' remembers Clare's son Brent, 'he [Clare] hired me to transcribe everything. I would take the time to give him extreme detail – not just chord changes but the exact notes, so that the keyboard player is playing drum fills. I notated everything in really graphic detail so he had something fine-tuned as the basis of his score. He [Prince] could address every detail in the arrangement. After the *Parade* album, we just continued.'

Mainly for the next three decades.

Prince was operating musically at warp speed but, Clare and Brent Fischer aside, he still had help. Eric Leeds points out that 'much of *Sign o' the Times* was recorded during 1986 when Wendy & Lisa were still involved, so it reflects the continuation of his musical involvement starting with *Around the World...* In fact, the original three-album version of *Sign...* might even include some things dating back to '85.' That meant Wendy & Lisa were feeding into – and, in some cases (particularly the single 'Mountains'), originating – musical ideas on *Parade*. The opening track 'Christopher Tracy's Parade' had the band initially singing the working title 'Little Wendy's Parade'.

The closing track on the album was recorded at Sunset Sound's Studio 3 on 21 April 1985, a Sunday – the day of the week that, according to some engineers, Prince wrote and recorded his most reflective material. It was the day after he recorded 'Old Friends 4 Sale', one of his most contemplative songs and one widely considered to be about betrayal.

'Sometimes it Snows in April' originally featured orchestral arrangement from Clare Fischer, but Prince chose not to use that, instead only featuring Lisa Coleman's piano, Wendy Melvoin's guitar and his own contribution. Sunset engineer Coke Johnson was present that day, expecting 'some funky music. That day he comes in and goes to the piano and just starts playing this melancholy melody. I was really disappointed, but I didn't know where he was coming from. The more he worked on it, the better it got. Now it's hard for me to listen to that song without bringing me chill bumps and a tear to my eye. Especially as he died in April.'

Parade's most audacious – and most successful – track arguably involved the highest levels of collaboration and was intended for another act. The pathway where his musical instincts and ability to take from elsewhere intersect are perhaps best displayed through *Kiss*.

Three people are at the heart of the creation of that song. Producer David Z. Rivkin and Revolution bassist BrownMark both stayed up all night crafting an album track written by Prince for BrownMark's side project, Mazarati, due to be executive-produced (again) by him.

Coke Johnson, who worked between Studios 2 & 3 at Sunset on Prince and Mazarati records, says 'Prince had given me the cassette of him playing an acoustic guitar and singing the rough vocal and David Z. and BrownMark reworked it until three in the morning.'

'What he gave me sounded like a folk song,' recalls David Z. 'We turned it into a groove and we'd been working all night. I borrowed the piano from an old song by Bo Diddley called "Say Man" and the background vocals that Mazarati did from Brenda Lee.' He synced the acoustic guitar to a hi-hat and ran it through the LM-1 machine. 'I kept it playing a rhythm that it's almost impossible to do because it's a machine that's playing. People were trying to play it and learn it. It's not something you learn because the rhythm changes every time. It created a complex rhythm pattern that was funky as hell.' (This partly explains why Prince's live versions of 'Kiss', across three decades, could sound markedly different from the record.)

Sunset engineer Coke Johnson remembers Prince coming next door to Studio 2 at eleven o'clock the next morning. 'I gave him a cassette of what we had done to that little song "Kiss" and he had me go get the multi-track from Mazarati's studio. "Coke, this is too good for Mazarati. I'm going to have to re-use this one." He muted all the vocals and put some guitars on there and re-sang the whole thing.'

By the time Rivkin returned, Prince 'had already added his

voice on it and his guitar intro and leads from "Papa's Got a Brand New Bag". The whole song is stolen and assembled into its own unique thing and then we mixed it right there.' Rivkin marvels at Prince's editing process. 'He turned off the bass fader and the piano fader. "You don't need this, you don't need that." I snuck some of the piano back in there. We mixed it in five or six minutes. It was recorded so there was not much we had to do.'

Warner Brothers didn't get it.

'It was not like anything else on the radio,' adds Rivkin. 'A lot of corporate rock had a lot of reverb on it. Warner Brothers didn't like it. The A&R guy said "You can't put that out. Prince screwed up." It sounded like a demo and they weren't going to put it out. Prince had the power to say "If you don't put that out, I'm not giving you anything else because that's the single." They were not happy about it, but all of a sudden, it was a huge hit.

'Just goes to show you, change comes from musicians not from record companies. A year later, Warner Brothers were trying to sign any acts that sounded like "Kiss".'

Rivkin had hoped for a production credit. BrownMark had hoped for a writing credit. Neither was granted, hastening Brown's departure. He decided to leave Prince's payroll rather than be forced to leave. Rivkin played the long game. 'Prince felt I was ruining my chances as a producer. I didn't want to push it too hard.'

There are two ways of looking at 'Kiss', both of which could be true. One is that he swooped in on the hard work of others to take the credit for a solo track intended for another act who needed the hit more than he did. The other is that he played guitar and vocals on what he thought would be an album track by a side project on Paisley Park Records and had the foresight to prune the extraneous parts and turn it into his own Grammy-winning song which would top the Billboard Top 100.

He recognised its potential, even when one of the world's most successful record labels didn't realise what they had. The musical magpie may steal trinkets, but it's still useful if you can tell the difference between tin and gold.

Craig Rice, who worked with Prince for ten years from 1983, intimates that a writing credit was never on the cards. 'This was his song. Nobody talked about it until after he was gone. It's Prince's party, you're just invited. You can bring some stuff to it, but when it's time to go, it's time to go. If you think it's your party, you're in trouble.'

Having said that, when BrownMark helped write the song, to put his bandmate Wendy as the only other musician in the video, says Rice, 'was a double-hurt. Prince always made sure Mark was in the dark. It's just competition. He was tall, good looking. Even in the movie [*Purple Rain*], Mark has no lines.'

I want my MTV

Back in 1986, there was one last roll of the dice between the Pasadena screening of *Under the Cherry Moon* and the nationwide opening; one that would reunite Prince with the Revolution and one that wasn't in the south of France. Nor was it back home in Minneapolis, or the usual world premiere settings of London, NYC or LA. It did, however, enjoy the backing of one major player.

Maybe *the* major player in pop music in the '80s. That wasn't Michael Jackson, who sold the most records. Or Madonna with her groundbreaking visual presentation. It wasn't Bruce Springsteen, Whitney Houston, Lionel Richie or Boy George.

It was Music Television.

The 24-hour world of pop music videos created its own

schedule, its own audience, its own set of new music stars and even its own words.

Les Garland had spent the early part of his career in music radio and Atlantic Records when the era-defining question 'Why don't we put music videos on television?' occurred. He would become the station's new programming head.

While MTV had given him a leg-up with its rise coinciding with his most hit-packed albums to date in *1999* and *Purple Rain*, Prince still had to pay homage to the emperors, known as VJs. MTV spawned this new word, this new job title. The video jockeys were on air as much as the pop stars whose videos filled up the round-the-clock content.

There's no doubt the stars, if they could tap into the right videos, scored big. Michael Jackson insisted on calling his clips 'short films', but another African-American man who wanted to be a rock star and not play by the traditional rules of genre would also benefit. 'Prince was part of that,' says one VJ, Martha Quinn. 'This was a new kind of rock star. Like Boy George. This was not Paul McCartney. This was not Mick Jagger. This was not even punk.' When asked if she thought Prince watched MTV, Quinn doesn't waver. 'Of course! *Bob Dylan* watched MTV.'

MTV Europe launched in 1987, the first video shown being Dire Straits' 'Money for Nothing' from the 1985 album *Brothers in Arms*, the first to sell more than a million on the new compact disc format by the following year. The song opens with Sting singing the refrain 'I want my MTV', an indication of how quickly a station's clarion call could be turned into the introduction of a pop song and be re-used by both parties for their own marketing slogan.

With his young, good-looking group and provocative imagery, Prince was in a position to be one of the early beneficiaries of

MTV. The urban myth, repeated in his autobiography, that Epic Records' Walter Yetnikoff had leaned on the station to play videos by black artists, is dismissed as 'a lie' by Les Garland. The station started screening Michael Jackson's videos from 1982's *Thriller* as soon as it could. The same year, Prince hit big with '1999' and 'Little Red Corvette'. He was well-equipped to take advantage.

Garland points out MTV had played 'so many videos by black artists', but had to contend with a major problem. 'The record companies didn't give their black artists money to make videos.' His radio programming background had taught him the importance of broadening playlists beyond rock'n'roll. 'I was convinced we needed to widen our vision. Whether or not we would play Michael Jackson was never a question.'

Garland, who went on to enjoy success with The Box, the interactive station whose viewing figures would top those of MTV, sees Prince and Jackson as 'two of the most important artists of the time. They had their own category.' If the two were competing in something of a pop decathlon, Jackson's specialist event would be music videos. MTV would establish their Video Music Awards in 1984 and, within seven years, there would be a category named 'the Michael Jackson Video Vanguard Award'.

Being bigger than big, MTV took advantage of its status with money-can't-buy competitions in the '80s. Garland – the man who talked Jagger into screaming 'I want my MTV' for channel promos for a grand fee of ten dollars – refers to these as 'stunts'. They included winning Jon Bon Jovi's childhood home, enjoying a night out with Van Halen or having Huey Lewis and the News playing a gig in your hometown.

Sometimes the winner got very lucky indeed. The victor of the 'Shoot a home-made video for Madonna's "True Blue"' contest – a Miami student called Angel Gracia – ended up being hired to direct commercials for Honda, Coca Cola and Mastercard, and landed a job with Ridley Scott.

Sometimes they didn't get lucky. Van Halen greeted the recipient of their MTV shindig with filet mignon, cocaine and Jack Daniels before Eddie Van Halen told him to shotgun a 16-ounce beer. The guitarist was unaware of brain trauma the winner had suffered two years previously from falling down a stairwell. He blacked out.

The winner of a 1989 competition to win Michael Keaton's Batmobile got a visit from the IRS when the car was valued at $300,000. 'We tried to find a way that we could pay that for him but we couldn't,' says Garland. 'I offered the Batmobile to the IRS, but they didn't want it.'

The discarded Batmobile had the station smelling of roses compared to the stunt inspired by John Cougar Mellencamp's 1984 hit *Little Pink Houses*. The channel gave away a house in Bloomington, Indiana, which the winner had to paint pink. The MTV researchers weren't that diligent. 'The first one we discovered before the contest,' recalls Garland. 'It was on a dump area that was contaminated. We got it from [Mellencamp's] wife who was in real estate. Back in those days, this was $100,000. That was the whole contest: you will win a whole house.' MTV, who couldn't get the first house off their books for five years, bought a second for the winner – who sold it two days later.

In 1986, Garland came up with the stunt to end all stunts. The 10,000th person to call up would host the world premiere of the follow-up to *Purple Rain* – which had, lest we forget, made him the world's biggest star – in their hometown. 'How wild would it be for MTV to host Prince's new movie and premiere in your home city? I'd love the winner to be from LA, Chicago or New York.'

The fact Prince felt inclined to sell *Under the Cherry Moon* in this way illustrates the muscle MTV could flex in the mid-'80s. MTV, Warner Brothers and Prince's entourage were all expecting a big city winner.

The 'dart tour' (as no one outside Prince's inner circle called it) halted for a week and then, one Friday afternoon – with 'no warning', as he recalls – production manager Jeff Mason received notice that 'the 10,000th caller to MTV would get a concert in their town, a concert by Prince'. By late Sunday night, he was told where this would be.

The rock'n'roll hotbed of Sheridan, Wyoming.

Lisa Barber, then a twenty-year-old motel chambermaid, had picked up the phone. 'My friend and I were watching it,' she remembers. 'I was the 10,000th caller. I think they [MTV] were glad. [They] thought it was going to be some snooty girl from New York.'

Culturally, Lisa was about as far from Park Avenue as Prince's bodyguards were from the Royal Ballet. Sheridan, Wyoming had received Her Majesty Queen Elizabeth II for a holiday in 1984, but its new royal visitor was much less private. With its history of ranching and its own rodeo week, a small town in the Equality State was not a natural fit for the world premiere of a light comedy filmed in monochrome about a sexually indeterminate playboy in the south of France.

But a 10,000th call is a 10,000th call, and Prince's team had to get their own metaphorical spurs on.

Security guard and future band member Greg Brooks sums up the prevailing mood in camp: 'Of all the places!' Prince's assistant Karen Krattinger and her good friend Robyn Riggs, then his publicist, quickly went into full-on prep mode. Commercial flights had to be arranged, multiple ones, from LA to Denver and then on to Billings. All sixty-five rooms in Sheridan's Holiday Inn were booked. That venue would, despite its low ceilings, also have to be the only place which would suffice for an after-party.

Flights to Billings carried Warners royalty, including Joni Mitchell and her then husband Larry Klein, Rosanna Arquette (fresh from *Desperately Seeking Susan*) for movie star glamour, *Ghostbusters* theme tune singer Ray Parker Jr, and stars of the film Jerome Benton, Kristin Scott Thomas and Emmanuelle Sallet, as well as Prince and the Revolution and their support act, Mazarati.

MTV had a party of four on their private jet 'a day or two earlier'. The prep had already been done and Garland's approach was optimistic. 'It was just mind-blowing to be a part of something that over the top – even for the '80s.'

Matt Fink remembers it well. 'We flew into Denver, then we had to get into these rickety old DC8 prop planes. They were old planes. The name of the airline is called Mountain Aid, puddle-jumper craft. Flying over the Rockies, literally just over the peak. They would catch the thermals coming over the mountain. People were freaking out on the planes because the turbulence was so bad. It was totally like that scene in *Almost Famous*. The terminal is the size of a typical middle-class home, no more than 25,000 feet. The grasshoppers were landing on top of us. We were in the sticks, in the middle of the mountains. Totally cowboy country.'

Susan Hale – working for Prince's manager Steve Fargnoli, who had taken his own private jet – didn't have an easier journey. 'My only memory is being in a private plane, having to take off for Sheridan during the great American air traffic controllers' strike. I was literally in the back seat behind Steve and my "job" was to monitor the left exterior window for oncoming planes. I was twenty-three.'

Landing in Wyoming to capture the all-important stills was unusual for Ebet Roberts, a photographer who came to prominence in the late '70s shooting the Sex Pistols and Blondie at NYC club CBGBs. She'd been coaxed west by publicist Robyn Riggs and remembers 'a red carpet in an airfield. Where the plane landed in the long field was literally covered in grasshoppers.' For Roberts, the whole circus was '100% Hollywood comes to Sheridan, Wyoming. The Queen had come here to look at horses to buy and that was their great claim to fame until Prince turned up.'

When they got into town, the Warner Brothers contingent ran into some local difficulties. 'The whole thing was absolute hilarity,' recalls label employee Marylou Badeaux, who remembers a traffic hold-up from the airport at Billings to the hotel. 'The next thing I know, there's a re-enactment of Custer's Last Stand.'

'They didn't even tell me they were going to have horses at the premiere,' laughs Roberts. 'The horses led the car that Prince was in.' The Buick convertible from the movie drove through town and was part of the first road trip for Prince's new employee, his valet Robbie Paster. Paster also had the responsibility of getting Prince's favoured piano into the after-show venue, as he remembers.

'They didn't have an elevator. Karen Krattinger and I said "What are you going to do? Have a crane through the patio door?"' That's what Paster did. (He would repeat the feat at London's Chelsea Harbour hotel in the '90s.)

The wardrobe team had issues too. Sheridan, recalls wardrobe chief Helen Hiatt, 'was the only place we had a serious dry-cleaning snafu' – specifically a problem concerning the trousers of Prince's white, four-ply silk suit. 'They shrunk. We were able to find a spare pair on the afternoon of the show. I just remember the horror of the pants shrinking.'

Hiatt and her team did their best to keep Prince in line, and occasionally managed. Krattinger remembers his arrival off the plane on the grasshopper-infested red carpet. 'He pretended to throw his coat to the people when his Lear Jet landed, but he had been reprimanded by the wardrobe team. "Do you know how long it took us to make one of those, so every time you throw one of those away, it's gone?"'

MTV's pre-Prince build-up played into Wyoming's cowboy heritage as a man in checked shirt and ten-gallon hat announced to camera: 'I told Darlene if I break in another horse, I'm gonna call it Prince.' Another sign from Sheridan read: 'Welcome to cow country. EAT BEEF.'

At this stage, Prince had not yet gone vegetarian.

Although inevitably linked with his co-star Kristin Scott Thomas, a role originally earmarked for girlfriend Susannah Melvoin, he invited other girlfriends along: Sheila E, plus models Devin DeVasquez and Maneca Lightner. Lightner had to contend with a case of mistaken identity, reminding 'a long line of people wanting my autograph' that she was not in fact Janet Jackson.

The evening was really about two things: giving the competition winner the night of her life and selling the film. On the first, mission accomplished. 'I had to invite 500 people,' Lisa Barber, now working in childcare with toddlers, recalls. 'I didn't know that many people. I got calls from all over the place and emails until the movie came out. They were happy. My mom got called by someone who told her he was her illegitimate son.' Mrs Barber's response? 'That might work on a guy. It doesn't work on me.'

Robyn Riggs arrived early and she and her friend Sheila E had dinner with Barber the night before. 'We were just like old friends,' Barber remembers. 'She was really easy to talk to.'

The night itself passed by in a flash. The Buick convertible took Prince and Lisa Barber from her home to the premiere at the Centennial 20 cinema, while a stretch Cadillac limousine transported the other celebrities. 'He was very respectful,' Barber says of Prince. 'He kissed my hand and opened the car door.' Jerome Benton was in the car too. 'Hilarious. He's just like that in person. Cracking jokes. Kristin Scott Thomas was super nice. Everyone was.'

Halfway through the screening, Prince departed for the Holiday Inn show. Leaving his date early sounds cruel, but staying may have been more cruel for Barber, sitting next to the director of a movie that was emerging as a stiff.

The director and star – whose mood earlier in the day was described by Ebet Roberts as being 'effervescent and flirtatious' – would later become distracted. 'It was one of those "Queen for a Day" things, then the caravan moves on,' the photographer adds. 'The only time I was around him, he was very sweet with her [Barber]. Those moments were few and far between.'

For Prince, selling the movie around the world starting with a day in Sheridan, Wyoming would be trickier. Lisa Janzen sat next to another of Prince's managers, Bob Cavallo. 'It was the most painful thing I have seen in my life.' Bob Merlis, from the Warner Brothers press department, remembers 'watching with the contest winner and the contest winner's friends, and I thought "This is a disaster. It's so mannered and self-indulgent."'

The director probably knew too; he didn't want to be around. 'I didn't have any down time with Prince,' adds Roberts. 'He disappeared a lot. He often wasn't around during that week.' When asked, she was told: 'He is in his cave. I think he wanted to get away from the circus.'

What did go well was Prince back in his comfort zone: the live music. The VJ assigned to present on the night, Martha Quinn, agrees. 'Watching him on stage, I think he was fired up by the presence of MTV. They [the local residents] were comparing it with the visit of Queen Elizabeth. Even for Prince to have MTV in that small town, and he had that stage, I almost feel like it fired him up more. He was more determined than ever to show that his brilliance was not limited to big arenas. He could be frickin' brilliant at a Holiday Inn in Sheridan, Wyoming.'

For MTV, he walked on stage, shouted 'All right, you cowboys!' and launched into what the Prince Vault site records as a six-song set ('Raspberry Beret', 'Delirious', 'Controversy', the Family track 'Mutiny', 'Do Me Baby' and 'Purple Rain'), accompanied by a hybrid of new band (Miko Weaver, Wally Safford, Greg Brooks, Eric Leeds, Matt Blistan) and the Revolution. Curiously, not one song was performed from *Parade*, the film's soundtrack album.

Matt Fink's main memory was how low the Holiday Inn ballroom's ceiling was, compared to normal gigs. 'They were too low and it was super-hot. That really stood out in a six-song set.'

'We were up on risers,' adds Matt Blistan, 'and we were very close to the big lights four or five feet from us. Normally, these lights are up to ten feet away. The crowd was incredible. Going out there, that's some great country.' The roof had a couple of holes drilled in it by David Rule, the guitar and keyboard tech, to fit in steep poles to hang lights. 'The roof wouldn't hold the weight,' he remembers. The show would go on.

Wendy Melvoin displeased her boss after the show by having a beer with Joni Mitchell. Prince felt this kind of casual kicking-back was not suitably on-brand. Relations with the band were straining. Susannah had been cut out the movie too. The aftermath of the show led to a few bumpy moments, but not for Barber who was taken home by limousine around 2 a.m. having had 'the time of my life'.

The following day, Robyn Riggs had to field calls from local press about a disturbing rumour surfacing about MTV's competition winner: that she 'was more of a Mötley Crüe fan'. Prince, Barber says, found that funny and had been taken with Sheridan on the whole. 'He loved the mountains.'

The Warner Brothers contingent went off ranching; another Prince associate, Craig Rice, enjoyed the rhythm of the visit. 'I found it incredibly exciting. When you're on the road, you check in, you do the gig, you check out. That's why they [rock stars] have this "If it's Thursday, it must be Cleveland" statement. There was a period we were in town, we met people, we went to her house, and I thought it was just endearing. It doesn't happen very often in this business when you get to hang out with the town people. This was crazy.'

Lisa Barber and Prince would never meet again, but she was his guest two days after the premiere at his show at Denver's McNichols Arena.

James Brown – this is a certain man's world. That man is Prince

In the post-Revolution era, when he could have been feeling vulnerable and alone, Prince went to his happy place. And his happy place often sounded like James Brown.

Alan Leeds should know.

Prince hired the tour manager in 1983 on the basis of his previous employer and, after a couple of weeks of the usual shy silence, he approached Leeds with the opening salvo: 'Tell me some James Brown stories.'

The small collection of people that Prince loved Leeds lists as 'James Brown, Stevie [Wonder, although he was fond of Nicks and Fleetwood Mac], Santana, Sly, Larry Graham.' (Joni should also feature.)

Who was top of that list? Almost certainly the Godfather of Soul.

Why?

Because even if Prince was a one-off, the most self-actualised pop star who ever walked the stage in heels, the template closest to any he modelled was built by Mr. Dynamite.

Prince got the JB bug early – at the age of ten to be precise. After his death, footage surfaced of Prince dancing on stage at a James Brown gig in Austin, Minnesota. His reasons for fandom were not particularly cerebral. 'The reason I like James Brown so much,' he told MTV, 'is, on my way out, I saw some of the finest dancing girls I'd seen in my life. I think in that respect he influenced me by his control of his group of dancing girls.'

Prince was on a roll when he recorded 'Hot Thing' at his home studio in Galpin Boulevard on 6 August 1986. The following day 'Forever in My Life' was cut. It's a high-energy funk track intended to reconnect him with both his black audience and the dancefloor. It was released as a promo single and is notable as the first material Prince allowed to be remixed by an outside source: Shep Pettibone, who had remixed many of Madonna's hits.

It was high-intensity in performance too. Although it has echoes of Prince's hero Brown, Eric Leeds' horn lines are one of a kind. 'I suspect the primary horn line was suggested by Prince and I just interpreted that along with a sax solo,' the saxophonist recalled in 2017. Later, in 2020, he expanded on this. 'Prince had the track completed and just needed to "plug me in" – a few parts here and there, and a couple of solo spots. He had a pretty complete idea of what he wanted me to play. In and out in an hour or so.'

Leeds' partner in brass, trumpeter Matt Blistan, gives him

more credit. 'Those were Eric's horns that he wrote. He writes great horn parts. A lot of those horn parts Prince did in rehearsals, he would sing, so between him and Eric, they more or less wrote the horn parts.'

Todd Herreman, in the engineer's chair for part of recording, recalls Eric as 'very adept and quick, a hot improviser and Prince really admired him'.

CHAPTER 9

FOREVER IN MY LIFE

Forever in My Life ... Prince goes Dutch ...
'Broken-hearted' ... Prince's ever-changing moods ...
Miss me? ... the end of Prince and Susannah ...
How Come U Don't Employ Me Anymore

Forever in My Life

'Forever in My Life', the final track on disc one, side two of *Sign...* (before CDs changed the concept of double albums) was recorded in one of the most remarkable weeks in Prince's career. It is a song which marks the push and pull of his desire to settle down and is best exemplified by the first week of August 1986. The weekend of 2 and 3 August was filled by two sell-out dates in Madison Square Garden with the Revolution. Then back home to Minneapolis and, by Wednesday 6, a quick call to saxophonist Eric Leeds to help him finish 'Hot Thing', an up-tempo jam about a girl looking for big fun.

Two days later, still at home, Prince had his mind away from short-term fun and on something deeper. The lyrics of 'Forever in My Life' speak for themselves. He sings seemingly from the heart, a man not just at a crossroads in his personal life, but someone apparently clear which fork in the road he was going to take. He was already living a life of domesticity in Galpin Boulevard, a place Susannah had fixed up while he was on tour. He was as settled as a man like Prince was ever going to be (prior to his two marriages in the '90s and '00s anyway).

'My job,' girlfriend/fiancée Susannah Melvoin told The Current's *Sign o' the Times* podcast, 'was to create a home for us while he was away. I kept the fires stoked at home. Lots of pastels, put it that way.' It was a home where she had installed a 'beautiful enormous teardrop chandelier' and he had his home studio. And it was in that studio where, on 8 August, he recorded the song. He sang about wanting to be a one-woman man because, since late November of the previous year, he had been living with Susannah.

It was the closest he had come to domestic bliss where he could live to work and work to live. 'The Ballad of Dorothy Parker' was the first thing he had recorded there. 'Forever in My Life' and 'Starfish and Coffee' followed, two songs inspired by Susannah because she was right under the same roof when he made them.

'Forever in My Life' was the latest in a series of songs on the album which could be filed under 'happy accident'. An early version, which resurfaced on the 2020 reissue, had piano and guitar higher in the mix, but Prince's mastery of minimalism saw a final stripped-down version with him, the Linn drum machine and an absent-minded backing vocal – *la da de da da* – recorded by accident running throughout the track.

He realised the error would make an effective counter to the chorus, stripped away some of the instrumentation and let the lyrics speak for themselves as a confessional to end side two of the first disc, just as 'Adore', a more sensual hymn of love, ended side two of the second. Both songs are widely considered to share the same subject matter.

Prince heard the accident and realised it worked, but by then, says the only other person in the room, his engineer Susan Rogers, 'it was a little bit lonely. He was so excited about "Forever in My Life", four bars out of sync. When we were doing a song by ourselves, he would call them [Wendy & Lisa] and say "Come to the studio" as he had just finished a song. I was no match for them. I wouldn't be able to do my job if I were. It wasn't my job to be his friend. It wasn't my job to be his confidant.'

Onlookers suggest Prince processed this quickly, moving on to his new band.

Prince goes Dutch

It's at this point in the story you may be wondering about Prince's windmill.

A full-size replica working windmill had been installed sometime in the mid-'80s in the grounds of his Galpin Boulevard home he made with Susannah and then again at Paisley Park.

Sal Greco, a chief technical engineer at Paisley Park, takes up the story. 'He was living in Kiowa Trail [in Chanhassen], but he gave that house to his Dad. He moved to the house at Galpin Boulevard. That had a much nicer home studio. In that basement, the back wall was stained glass like you'd see in a church and you could look out on to a big piece of property, and a windmill.' The purchase of the windmill – 'fifty feet-tall blades, fifty feet wide' from Greco's memory; 'from his kitchen it looks like it's five inches' – was inspired by Prince's trips to the Netherlands.

The Netherlands was where, on 29 May 1981, he first played live outside the US. By 1987, it was where he would choose to have the *Sign* movie filmed. Driving from his Amsterdam hotel to those three shows in Rotterdam, past the A4 Highway, he would say to anyone who would listen: 'I want a windmill.'

As Mike Soltys, who also helped set up technical logistics at Paisley, laughs, 'That never goes over well – saying no.' His team hired a retired GM engineer. 'We built a beautiful window,' remembers Soltys after hearing the boss ask if the windmill could face the house. Bret Thoeny, the architect for Paisley Park, was contacted about his company building the working full-scale windmill, 'per Prince's request, 10–12m tall' with 'pumped water for the pond'. The working windmill, with a spiral staircase, was to Prince's specifications, but others were attracted to it – mainly the local raccoons. 'There was racoon poop everywhere,' says Paisley maintenance man Buzz Goodchild. This would be cleaned up mainly by Michelle Schwartzbauer, Prince's housekeeper, who was then dating his half-brother Duane. Goodchild also 'had to deal with woodchucks. They chased me around the yard for a while.'

The colour of the windmill is a topic of dispute. Susan Rogers calls it 'pastel, peach, pale blue, it was all different colours. It was beautiful.' Greco says 'four pastel colours – blue, yellow, pink, some kind of rose.' Mike Soltys says 'mostly yellow. Fuchsia. The house was blue and fuchsia and then it was yellow.' Matt Larson, who worked with Prince's touring company from 1987, says 'there was a point he painted things peach'.

Pest control had been called, the pond and the windmill in Prince's back garden were aligned and he could see it from his window. All good.

Then one day, disaster.

Prince's then personal assistant Therese Stoulil, his manager and many of the Paisley staff had to get involved, as Larson recalls.

'He called Therese.

"What can I do for you?"

"We have a problem."

"What's the problem?"

"It's the windmill. It's facing the wrong direction.'"

It was at this point Stoulil advised that changing the wind might not be possible.

"We'll see about that.'"

Sal Greco called the surveyor who told him to tell Prince: 'It's pointed the right way. The blades are always supposed to be pointed to the house. His manager explained to him.'

The blades were digging into land and some flew into Lake Ann. The windmill had to be dismantled and the surveyor called for something called a hydraulic accumulator, as wind battered the base of the building.

The Department of Justice was also contacted, which was not what Prince had in mind when he and the female guest he was entertaining in the windmill raised the alarm.

Danny Soltys adds: 'The blades were forty feet across and they were stuck in the ground like a crucifix. There was a four-foot drop shaft, it was cut through like butter. We repaired it and we started taking the blades off and we would wrap them in tarp because the winds are so strong here in winter. We ended up locking it with a brake.'

Some might quibble with Prince's complaints about the direction the wind was blowing. Matt Larson didn't. 'Within a day or two, it was welded in the other direction the way he wanted. I agree with this because it was an artistic statement rather than a working windmill.'

That didn't stop a regular windmill malfunction in Galpin Boulevard and then at Paisley Park in Audubon Road, Chanhassen.

Buzz Goodchild bore the brunt of the repair responsibility. 'I brought an engineer out and he brought an engineer out to the top of the windmill. "Figure this out." I found the blueprints and gave it to them and he said "I got it."'

Goodchild and Greco both remember the blades rotating into the ground and churning up the land. 'We sent my landscape operator up there with a can of oil and he dropped oil into the shaft,' laughs Goodchild. 'I hear after I left that it fell out for the final time.'

One day, just like one of Prince's girlfriends, the windmill was gone.

'I think they got tired of fixing it and it quit working,' adds Mike Soltys. Even sadder, the house where Prince wrote and recorded much of the *Sign o' the Times* record has also gone. 'The whole place has been bulldozed and turned into a housing development now. 150 acres and a private lake.'

Prince, as was often the case, had moved on.

'Broken-hearted'

The Revolution had been crucial in helping Prince on *Parade* and were in the middle of a project called *Dream Factory*, which turned into *Sign o' the Times*. Many of the tracks on *Sign...* had the Revolution play on them before all but one of their members (Matt Fink) left Prince's employ abruptly. Prince would re-record the tracks so that the credit and the music went almost solely to him.

You may conclude for an album which finishes regularly in best-of polls that the Revolution were harshly treated. 'For sure,' reckons his soundman of two decades, Scottie Baldwin. 'Susannah *and* the Revolution. That is a Prince and the Revolution record. All the Revolution members were hugely important to the making of *Sign o' the Times*. It's not just those who play on the record, it's who is being influenced. The Revolution have a huge impact on that record. He short-changed them. I think he had moved on to Sheila's band. When it was time to press the record, he said "It's a Prince record". It should have been a Prince and the Revolution album. The Revolution inspired the record and cut a load of it. He took a new band out on tour. So he got the best of both worlds.'

The *Sign...* double album – with co-writes for Susannah ('Starfish and Coffee'), Matt Fink and Eric Leeds on 'It's Gonna Be a Beautiful Night' and Carole Davis for 'Slow Love' – credited Prince on the sleeve with a 'thank you to Wendy & Lisa'.

Wendy Melvoin told The Current's podcast of her mood on seeing those words. 'Broken-hearted. Because we looked at the credits and the last credit said "Thank you, Wendy and Lisa". The very last credit. We had done so much work on that record. It was very painful. We understood. It hurt like hell but life goes on.'

Their ability to move on, even with their own solo material, would be more of an uphill struggle than it was for their old boss. Even then, although he did some songs from scratch like 'U Got the Look', the pain of completing the album was raw enough to be visible to those closest to him.

'It was him losing a family again,' his then friend and lighting director LeRoy Bennett says now. 'He and Wendy & Lisa and that relationship with Susannah. It was all that. The girls participated a lot in helping to write songs and the frustration in not getting the credit when credit was due, you could see that all building up. He had a fascination with twins and the whole thing with Susannah and Wendy... It all got too weird.'

If you follow Samuel Goldwyn's maxim that if you find something you love, you never have to work again, Prince had found two things – Susannah and his music. It seemed he had found intrinsic comfort in both. These were only interrupted by the other tricky aspects of work that come with being an international rock star, and Karen Krattinger his assistant at the time was across most of those.

'I would say [to Susan Rogers] "Susan, let Prince know that I need to talk to him about a few things". I would talk to him about everything that was going on. I would have to wait until he had finished playback on a track. One morning, it was probably around two or three, he called me at home, "I just wrote a song. Will you come over and listen to it?" I sat down on the floor. It was just me and him, Susan was there, and he played 'Forever in Your Life'. It was my new favourite song, end of conversation.'

Krattinger, a close friend of Susannah Melvoin's, felt the song's subject matter was 'obvious. I'm sure I told her that. I would listen to that song every day.' Being friends with the boss' fiancée didn't have to be a bad thing, but for Krattinger, it was painful. 'I would love for them to have gotten married, but he wasn't ready, and I was too privy to all the shenanigans going on.'

Those shenanigans were, like the man himself, hard to pin down.

'It was a game and Prince liked the conquest,' says Krattinger. 'She had developed a relationship with Prince through Wendy & Lisa. I don't think anybody has had a longer and more enduring relationship with him. I believe she was the love of his life. Things would have been a lot different had he been mature enough to make the commitment.'

'I wish he had married her,' reflects Matt Fink. 'She would have made a tremendous wife for him and support person for him. I always felt he made a big mistake not committing to her. I really loved Susannah very much. She's a wonderful person. Very kind, generous. She would have been the perfect person to be his soulmate and I think he missed out on that one.'

Prince's ever-changing moods

Some, including engineer of the time Eddie Miller, felt that the *Sign* band was the best one Prince ever had. But members of the Revolution felt that dancing bodyguards, with the James Brown-style soul revue ambience, wasn't Prince's finest on-stage incarnation. Wendy Melvoin was especially scathing towards the end of the Revolution. Susan Rogers is more diplomatic. 'Sheila's band did not bring out the pop aspects of Prince's music the way that the Revolution had. These folks could really play but stylistically, they weren't as broad as Wendy and Lisa. Sheila E didn't draw from as many styles as the Revolution.'

'He had already started creating a divide between him and the Revolution,' notices Coke Johnson, who engineered at Sunset Sound around the *Sign* era. 'That was kinda Prince's nature. Every three or four years, he would change management companies. He would change his accountant. He would get new lawyers. He would hire new people who worked for him.

'If he lost people, the people who would come in and fill their shoes would try even harder. Once they started getting comfortable and feeling like they were in control, he would take that control away from them and give it to somebody else. I don't know if it was a trust issue or whether he liked new faces, but that seemed to follow him throughout his career.'

Prince's supreme leadership led to a blistering tour of Europe, accompanied by security men-turned-dancers-turned-comic foils Wally Safford and Gregory Allen Brooks, the latter easy to spot for the fur hat on his head. The hat belonged to his father Jimmy, a DJ-turned-music executive.

'I always went on tour in the winter because Prince wanted to get out of Minneapolis,' Brooks recalls. 'I wore the hat all the time.' Brooks, complete with Soviet-style hat, stayed on stage with Safford.

'Everyone says "Why is he wearing that hat?" Prince says "Why *isn't* he wearing that hat?"'

Miss me?

Opinion is divided on how much (artistically) Prince was missing the Revolution. Emotionally, say many interviewees, he wasn't missing them at all.

David Rule, his one-time guitar tech who then helped Wendy, claims 'the story I heard was that he invited them over to dinner and fired them by dessert. Nobody was expecting that.'

It's possible some of the band were.

Mark Brown had expressed interest in leaving after *Purple Rain* and stayed under contract until *Parade*. 'There are people who stopped playing with Prince who regret it,' says longtime Prince associate Craig Rice, who managed Brown's band Mazarati. 'But Mark didn't.'

Bobby Z and Prince had ended on good terms (according to Bobby) and the drummer was replaced by Prince's on-off girlfriend Sheila E. Matt Fink had stayed with the band. Wendy and Lisa were summoned to Prince's LA residence where they were fired. Susan Rogers points out that 'losing Wendy and Lisa is a big blow. Miko was a good guitarist, but he doesn't have that Joni Mitchell and Beatles musicality to his music. To lose Lisa Coleman, who has a great sense of melody, I don't think it's losses you can shrug off.'

Front-of-house sound engineer Rob 'Cubby' Colby feels he kept the momentum going. 'When Sheila came in, she was a cool drummer, Miko and Levi were a funkier bunch. They're all great players in their own way. I really feel he never took a step backwards. To lose musicians as talented as the Revolution would have sunk a lot of artists. Failure was not an option.'

Prince reacted as he had throughout his career. He assembled a new band.

The end of Prince and Susannah

Susannah was an even bigger influence. Susannah is believed to be the inspiration for 'Hot Thing', 'Starfish and Coffee', 'Forever in My Life', 'If I Was Your Girlfriend' and 'Adore'. She was with Prince at the Bellagio Hotel when the earthquake which prompted 'Housequake' was written, as well as having read the hotel lobby's copy of the *LA Times* that covered the news of Ronald Reagan's Star Wars programme and an increase in instances of AIDS.

In the spring of 1987. Susannah and Prince parted for good. 'We stayed together for six or eight months after the Revolution split [in September 1986]' she told *Variety*. 'He was very dependent on me at that time, but he was keeping me away from my sister and Lisa. We went back to Minneapolis, and the seclusion and isolation became way too much for me to bear. I couldn't do it anymore.'

Wendy and Susannah Melvoin's harmonious and close rapport would have messed with Prince's idea of control. It was not what he had grown up with, according to his cousin Chazz Smith. 'He loved Edna Mae. Prince's mum and her sister never got along – polar opposites like you wouldn't believe. Edna Mae would shoot you with a gun, Mattie Della [Prince's mum] was the sweetest woman you could ever know. That went on as adults.'

The '80s saw Prince's most significant relationships with women – musically at least. 'I think the special tracks on the album [*Sign*] were Revolution-flavoured,' argues Scottie Baldwin.

'Susannah influenced most tracks.' Even after Susannah had gone, 'Forever in My Life' retained its power.

Elizabeth Dorr (Sidla as was), from Prince's wardrobe department, had just got married at St Clara's Church in Stockholm to his rigger David Dorr. For one of the Swedish shows on the Sign tour in May 1987, she wore her wedding dress. At the show, Prince picked up his acoustic guitar from tech Joel Bernstein, nodded to his colleague in the wardrobe department and announced 'This one's for you' before launching into 'Forever in My Life'.

It was in the Netherlands where the song set another concert phenomenon in motion. The acoustic guitar and spare rhythm track set by Sheila E encouraged fans to stick their lighters in the air. Prince was heard saying 'That's a neat trick'. And what happened in Utrecht was then replicated in Rotterdam and Antwerp.

'A day later the word had spread,' says Edgar Kruize, author of *Prince: The Dutch Experience*, 'so when "Forever in My Life" started on June 20 (the second night in Utrecht), the lights were already flickering.'

By the twenty-first century, cellphones would replace lighters but a trend had been set.

How Come U Don't Employ Me Anymore

The split with the Revolution was a little earthquake against which subsequent band or other staff departures would be felt as light breezes. Certainly, the Revolution five, the basic unit who lasted four years, were worthy of a gold clock compared with other employees.

Job security and Prince went together like starfish and Earl Grey.

How did you get fired from Prince's team? That could be for something as simple as looking at him the wrong way.

The question of how you kept your job was trickier. Bevla Reeves, Prince's hair stylist for two years around the *Sign...* era when his regular stylist Earl Jones was unwell, remembers going on staff at the same time as... well, no one. 'I was hired at the same time as a designer and a chef were. We had a running gag with each other that if he didn't like us, he would send us home, or we wouldn't get to see Europe. The designer didn't even get to meet Prince. He saw his portfolio. He was eliminated straightaway.'

The chef? 'She didn't last that long either. Two weeks.'

He didn't always delegate when it came to sacking. 'Prince did it,' recalls Karen Krattinger. 'He would say "Book a flight for Miko". He would call and go "Here's Cat, and here's Boni."'

Sometimes he would delegate and expect close lieutenants to serve them their papers. 'When I was in charge,' says Jacqui Thompson, who ran Prince's operations in the early '00s, 'he would come to me and say "Boom, boom, boom" and I would have to do that. I hated it but it's my job.'

Sal Greco remembers it well, if not fondly. 'He was a guy about whom we used to say, if he woke up and his socks were on wrong, you could get fired. It's like the Foreign Legion. It makes you one of the meanest out there. If you live.'

Skip Johnson, a tour and production manager in the early '90s, remembers 'a time I had three different monitor engineers on the road at the same time. He would say "Get the next guy" and I would have five minutes to set up and if that didn't work out, I would get the third guy.'

Studio engineers showed an ability to bond with the boss, utilising discretion, talent, persistence and hard work. Without those, they wouldn't have been allowed in Prince's house, where many of his studios were. Lisa Chamblee, an engineer who worked for him between 2004 and 2005, remembers that 'probably with other teams, he would have somebody tell them "Don't come back". If I remember correctly, he would never say that. He'd leave if he just wasn't feeling the vibe and he didn't like the studio person.'

When assembling a roster of engineers at the start of Paisley Park, only the strongest survived. The blasé could look elsewhere. Prince didn't just give short shrift to those who didn't give him their best, he looked out and made sure his employees would give equally short shrift.

Greco remembers a conversation with another engineer. He had requested a mix on behalf of Prince. It wasn't ready.

'"Why not?"

"It's not my record."

"Well, go and listen to it."'

Prince was listening elsewhere (he did that).

'He was waiting on the phone.

"I don't like this, what are you going to do about it?"

"I will wake the engineer up."

"Wrong answer."

"I will put him on a plane and send him home."

"Right answer."'

Click.

By the time another engineer was appointed, Greco knew the drill. One defended his work not being up to standard thus: 'I didn't want to give him my best work so that I had somewhere else to go.'

Greco's answer: 'You do. The airport.'

Making it past what engineer Chris James called Prince's 'trial by fire' would require elements of cunning, knowing when to say no but, above all, the two four-letter words which had made their boss famous: hard work.

Lisa Chamblee suggests it was about his gut instinct for people. 'I'd seen him fire people if he didn't like their vibe. "Does he have to be here?" he'd say. That was Prince code for "I don't want him here". He was always at his best, so you had to be at your best.

'You had to be yourself. He didn't like fakeness. He could see through it if you were like yes people. I think he was always hyper-aware of what people wanted from him, if it was a woman or if it was a guy. He liked psychological games.'

As an engineer during the *Sign* era, Eddie Miller talks of '120–140-hour weeks. At the end of the day, as hard as I was working, he was working harder. You can't be mad at a boss like that.' When recording, he didn't mellow, as Chris James from the class of 2014 confims. 'I don't think Prince wanted to be told what to do. He was definitely tough. When it comes to labour laws, let's say they didn't apply.'

Other employees, such as Karen Krattinger and LeRoy Bennett, conserved energy by asking if they could skip the after-show parties which could run into breakfast time.

Marylou Badeaux, who worked with him at Warner Brothers from the '70s to the '90s, once said no to him around the time of *Graffiti Bridge* – and managed to catch Prince's self-knowledge in the wild. 'At one point, he asked me to come work for him. I knew he didn't like the word "no", so I said: "I'm more used to you at Warners and also… can I be honest with you? If I get a pay cheque from you, and I'm honest with you, and you don't like it, I would be gone." At that point, he flipped his hands in the air, turned round in his heels – he was always in heels – and said "I knew you were smart" and walked away.'

Humour was a good way to disarm Prince. If you were female and attractive to him, that didn't hurt either.

Those most often in through the out door, according to Sal Greco, were the ones in charge of looking after Prince's guitars on tour. 'We used to remember guitar techs by number and we used to wonder how long they would last. Takumi [Suetsugu, one of the few who lasted years] used to ask me "Why does everybody call me No 40?" One arrived at 9 a.m. He was back on the plane by 5 p.m.'

Morris Hayes, a rare bird in that he lasted two decades under Prince's employment, has the rundown of the most endangered species. 'There are four positions for Prince – guitar tech, soundman, security man and accountant – which you wouldn't wish for your worst enemy. They lived an eggshell kind of life.' Karen Krattinger recalls another endangered tricky role. 'If you had a family, being his housekeeper was impossible. They would often quit. He would call them to come round at ten o'clock at night.'

Prince regularly dated women who worked for him – his dancer Mayte, and Sheila E and Susannah to name three. Or he put women who were with him to work. Second wife Manuela Testolini would be tasked to run his charity.

In general, if you worked for him, you did your homework. The instruments in the studio had to be laid out. The songs had to be learnt. The clothes had to be tailored. The piano had to be craned into the hotel suite before he arrived. And so on. Musicians had it roughest of all, as their boss and bandleader could, horn players aside, play whatever they played.

Matt Fink found this out to his cost when he turned up to rehearsals without being au fait with all the material. 'The way he would operate [would be] "Here's the tape, learn the parts and we're going to run through the song". If you showed up at rehearsal and you weren't prepared, you would be called out in front of everyone.

'"How come you don't know it? What you been doing? OK, everyone, leave the room and let Matt learn his parts." Everybody would walk out and leave and you'd be sitting there on your own listening to the stuff for about an hour. You'd have to go back and say "OK, Prince, I'm ready now". That happened to me once during *Sign o' the Times* era. The Revolution was gone. It happened to me once on the *Purple Rain* rehearsals. He didn't like the fact I wasn't prepared. It was my fault because I was lazy. I hadn't prepared it the night before. His work ethic was so amazing. "I'm preparing the stuff every day, I'm writing it, you're not writing it."

'He didn't take that from anybody else.' He didn't bawl at his bands, Fink says. 'He would be sarcastic and try to humiliate you to shame you for not doing it. It happened to everybody at one time or another. Even Sheila once. Everybody had their turn with that.'

There was no hiding place, even if you were on stage with him. Andrew Gouché, a bassist in the 2010s, recalls a 2013 gig in Montreux. 'I messed up once and it was absolutely the worst feeling. Four-bar drum break, and I thought it was an eight-bar drum break. "Ladies and gentlemen, on bass, it's Andrew Gouché, and he's four bars late." He didn't fine me but he made me feel so small.'

Rose Ann Dimalanta, who played keyboards for him in the '00s and now plays with Sheila E, recalls him leading by example when one bandmate wasn't taking notes. "'You aren't taking notes? I'm not a genius, I need to write this down and take notes.'"

If you could summon the courage to be honest with him, that would help, as hair stylist Bevla Reeves notes. 'I didn't have to work with him if he was going to be nasty to me. I had a job back home. I let him know that early on and I think he appreciated it. He wanted what he wanted.' Susan Hale from his management team agrees. 'I never fawned over him and I think that's why we bonded back in the day.'

Accountant Donald Peake explains Alan Leeds' acknowledged status as the Prince whisperer. 'Alan could go one on one with Prince and just be honest with him. That's one of the few people he heard "no" from. He respected Alan enough not to sack him.' Leeds certainly knew what to expect. 'I had five years plus with James Brown, so I knew what that was like. Basically, your job depended on it. You work for the artist and your responsibility is to help them with their vision. At the end of the day, it's their name on the record and their name on the marquee.'

Helen Hiatt, among others, attributes Prince's trigger-happy moments to 'a little bit of the short guy problem', while childhood friend Terry Jackson is even less kind ('A lot of people in the community referred to him as Little Hitler'. But Albert Magnoli, the director of *Purple Rain* and his one-time manager, disagrees. 'He was always about musicians being comfortable and doing their best. I didn't find him to be a dictator at all. On [the Lovesexy tour], I remember there were some hitches. That day of rehearsals, he would say "How do we smooth that out?" He was always about making the musician centred and whole.'

Robyn Riggs remembers that in the court of the Prince, 'there was some in-fighting, people were starting to get their own careers and people had to walk on carefully constructed eggshells'. The word 'eggshells' recurs among employees of the late '80s.

If you made a promise, better know he would be keeping the same attention to time with the same precision as he programmed his beats. 'One time,' remembers Sal Greco, 'he calls me and shows me the video and says "I don't like that. I want the other one." The only one we have is the 12" studio dance mix.

"Could you cut that down?"'

Greco immediately surmised how long the job would take.

"That's going to take eight hours."

"Fine."

'Eight hours later, the phone rings. Guess who?

'If he had confidence in you, if you say it's going to take two hours, you'd better make sure you were printing it when the phone rang.'

Susan Hale, who often had to transcribe his lyrics for the music publishers ASCAP, made errors which amused rather than infuriated him. 'I think Prince as a boss was just really looking for loyalty and people who worked really hard on his behalf,' she says. 'He did not suffer fools lightly. Like if you were only around to "party", you were O-U-T. He was a massive perfectionist and I witnessed how demanding he could be with his band. But speaking for me personally – he was just lovely.'

Susan Rogers was struck by one of his mottoes which he would tell his staff loud and proud: there is only one asshole around and that is me.

'As the only one who gets to be rude and dismissive, he is the only one that gets to be on a power trip. This is a guy who's got employees in his early twenties, not all of whom are older than he is. When there were only two of us, he was a really good boss, he was a really good leader.'

By the twenty-first century, there was a calmness around Prince's inner circle. Country singer Toby Lightman spoke to him before they shared a game of pool in Portland in 2004. Prince advised her to 'put people around you who are like you. I never curse, I don't raise my voice and nobody around me curses or raises their voice.'

Lightman says 'I just started to think about how everybody thinks he's so crazy.

'If everyone is looking to one leader for direction, things were not necessarily easier as he was pretty demanding, but you knew where you stood.'

Lightman was only an acquaintance. Some of the ex-exployees do not share such warm and fluffy memories. Jellybean Johnson, for one. 'One employee told me "There's a whole bunch of different Princes and you have to figure out which Prince you're dealing with that day." That's hard as a human being to deal with that every day.'

While working simultaneously on Vanity 6, The Time and Prince records, Peggy McCreary would become used to the compliments he would offer. At least, compliments that came in the form of keeping her job. 'He called me in for another record. I said "Do you like my work?" "You're here, aren't you?" He never said "good job" or "thank you for the work", but there were appreciative gestures, like sending me to go on tour.'

Sometimes Prince would pay the wardrobe department a different compliment. 'He had Therese [Stoulil, head of wardrobe] give us thank-you notes,' sighs Helen Hiatt, 'and I can't remember if it was $50 or $100, and we had just worked 80 hours. I just made sure I thanked him. I realise he was making an effort.'

Staff who overstepped their mark would find out the hard way where the exit door was. Production manager Jeff Mason got excited in an encore break of the Lovesexy tour at Madison Square Garden and excitedly gushed to his boss, 'I'll pay for the overtime and what they wanna hear is a ten-minute version of "Purple Rain". From then on, I was a persona non grata. I was correct, but I shouldn't have told him what to do.'

Accountant Donnie Graves had a few drinks with Prince at the end of the Purple Rain tour and told him: 'Dude, you have got to get over the short guy thing.'

Friendships would be curtailed too. Les Garland and Prince were pals in the '90s when the then head of music video station The Box was often invited to hang out at Paisley Park or in Miami, where he helped Prince with a branch of his Glam

Slam nightclub. Around the middle of the decade, Prince asked Garland to be his manager.

Garland tried to laugh it off, responding 'I hear you're unmanageable' and then asked him to define what he thought a manager would do for him. He mentioned Jack Douglas. "Well, you know what a manager does – watches over everything. When Jimi Hendrix died, he had Jack Douglas to watch over his music."'

It's interesting that even Prince saw that as a responsibility of his manager – to protect his music catalogue if something should happen – two decades before there were wrangles about ownership of his music after his sudden passing and no will had been written. Back then, Garland quickly tried to let him down gently, arguing it might hurt the friendship. Saying 'no' hurt the friendship. 'I don't think the relationship was ever the same after that. The friendship cooled.'

If Prince was having a bad day, or you were having a bad day and he sacked you, sometimes you were fired in style. Take Chris James, the engineer who was Grammy-nominated for his work on Prince's final album, *HITnRUN Phase Two*. One day, he affronted his highness by neglecting to attend to the fader volume at Paisley Park.

'He yanked his guitar out the speaker and stormed out.'

Minutes later, James was called with the message 'Your car is in the driveway'. The driver tells him to grab his things. 'He takes me to the airport and there's a ticket for my ass to LA and I'm just devastated. I'm crushed. He [Prince] knows professionally and personally this is my world. He could have said "This is the last time I'm going to tell you". It would have taken a move of my arm by an inch to solve the problem. Instead, I'm being shuttled off on a first-class flight and a limo to LA. He wanted to prove a point.'

The next day James's telephone rang again. On the other end was a deep, soft voice he instantly recognised. 'Did you learn your lesson?'

James, who was reinstated and flown back a couple of days later, can laugh about it now. 'He was in a mood that day. To me, it's funny in retrospect. "I'm going to kick you to the kerb, but I'm going to do it in first class."'

Even if you got fired by Prince, it could on occasion involve an upgrade.

CHAPTER 10

U GOT THE LOOK

*When ordering a double did not meet with Prince's approval
... Prince and David Bowie are both Cat people ... Crystal
baller ... 'U Got the Look' ... Prince's purple reign had its
interregna ... Everything in Prince's world was by design –
even the designers ... before Black Sweat, there was perfume.*

When ordering a double did not meet
with Prince's approval

*S*ign o' the Times was envisaged by Prince as a triple album. His
record company never saw it that way.

Prince's relationship with his album releases had always been
something of a conveyor belt. When they were ready, he wanted
them in stores. And if he had extra songs, he'd give those away
to his other acts or stick them in his vault of unreleased music.

Between 1978 and 1996, the only two years when Prince didn't
put out a single or double album were 1983 (the year between
the double *1999* and the *Purple Rain* movie and soundtrack, to
which, by his standards, he gave extra aforethought) and 1993.
In 1996, he put out two. He didn't tour Europe until 1986 and
didn't tour the States between April 1985 and September 1988.

Putting out music seemed to be his main priority. Bob Dylan had his Never-Ending Tour. Prince had his Never-Ending Release Schedule.

Mo Ostin, the then head of Warners, was happy to have given him control. Ostin had been hired to run Reprise by Francis Albert Sinatra. 'The motto of Reprise Records was always about artistic self-determination,' says Bob Merlis, a former head of publicity for Warners.

Sinatra, hired Ostin and both felt strongly that each Reprise artist should be given as much creative freedom as possible, along with complete ownership of their work. By the mid-'80s, when Ostin was running Warners, of which Reprise was a subsidiary, not all of these principles remained intact. Prince was given latitude by a major label compared with other artists, but only so much.

Not owning his own masters would be a running sore for Prince throughout his career. The subject – not having proprietary rights of the material he, often alone, had created – would be one of the moments in the rare interviews he did give where you could 100 per cent guarantee he wasn't kidding or being flippant. 'If you don't own your masters, your masters own you' became a recurring mantra in rare interviews and less rare awards acceptance speeches.

For all that, in terms of artistic freedom, it's fair to say Warners gave Prince more rope than most. They let a teenager produce his first record and allowed him to push back against being marketed predominantly to an R&B audience, the obvious route for Warners to introduce him to the public. He wanted to make his fifth album, *1999*, a double. 'I didn't want to do a double record,' he told the *LA Times*' Robert Hilburn in 1983, 'but I just kept writing. I'm not one for editing.' Just when Warners wanted to bask in the commercial success of *Purple Rain*, Prince released *Around the World in a Day* against their wishes in the same month that the US tour ended. No European tour, no further *Purple Rain* momentum.

All his wishes, save for the then highly irregular wish of being given his own masters, would be granted. But every boss has a line in the sand and Prince's desire for *Sign o' the Times* to be released as a triple album seemed to be where Warner Brothers would draw theirs.

The stock market crash, better remembered as Black Monday, would happen on 19 October 1987, but the economy ahead of a March release was already looking dicey. Prince wasn't the kind of person to know the price of a pint of milk, but his record company knew close to $30 for a triple album would not help the momentum that had been slowed by the extremely commercial *Purple Rain* being followed by the left-of-mainstream *Around the World in a Day* and *Parade*, the soundtrack for a flop movie.

Prince finished 1985 and started 1986 in the studio. Recording sessions with Sheila, Levi Seacer and Eric Leeds on 28 December, followed by a 5 January session with Wendy, Lisa and Wendy's brother Jonathan produced a single track, 'Junk Music', that ran to sixty-three minutes. These would be known as The Flesh Sessions.

There was also ongoing work with the Revolution and new members Eric Leeds and Matt Blistan on the (ultimately unreleased) *Dream Factory* album, plus the main event, the designated triple album then known as *Crystal Ball*. There was *Camille*, an album under the guise of Prince's female alter ego of the same name. That was only the start of the experimentation: Prince with vocal modulators, Prince in his new guise as another female character, Prince finding his private place, carved away from five years with a full-time band.

Personal assistant Karen Krattinger only knew about the album when she helped coordinate the Sunday evening cover shoot with Jeff Katz. 'You never knew what he was doing. He was always recording.' Employees were not given advance notice on tours, when records would be released or even what they would be called.

Warners executives had expected one album. Prince was cooking up five. But he settled on a more conventional plan: presenting the triple album idea to Lenny Waronker at the label.

Carole Davis, the co-author of 'Slow Love', was signed to Warner Brothers at the time. 'I knew what was going on in that company.' They had been dealing with two commercially underperforming albums – compared with *Purple Rain* anyway – and underwriting the film which wags had renamed *Under the Cherry Bomb*. 'So it was obvious to me they didn't want a double album. They would rather he just put out an album.' Bob Merlis, the label's head of press at the time, felt that 'three is almost impossible, two is difficult'.

Warners were the bad guys, but Prince's managers could see the label's point, albeit not enough to find the courage to tell their client that. So, by and large, they left Prince and the label to have the awkward chat.

As Susan Hale, Steve Fargnoli's right-hand woman, says: 'One day it was a triple album, and the next it wasn't.' One day and the next is about right.

It all fell not to Mo Ostin, nor [Bob] Cavallo, [Joe] Ruffalo and Fargnoli, but to Lenny Waronker to force himself against his will into Henry Kissinger mode. Just as hair and make-up and wardrobe and bandmates could tiptoe around Prince, it wasn't easy for Waronker and the management team, who huddled among themselves to decide how to make the triple album a single.

Prince sat down with Waronker at a listening party at his managers' office and gave him the hard sell. 'He made it interesting. "Can you imagine driving down the coast with the top down?" He didn't play every song all the way through. He was smart. He understood attention span.' Waronker had 'listened to the triple album and tried really hard. I must have listened to it three times. I always got hung up at the same place, so I had my issues with it. Everybody was concerned from a business standpoint. I was more concerned from a creative standpoint.

'It became more difficult as time went by. I heard these guys trying to figure out how to talk to him into making it a single album. Everybody was intimidated by him. He was manipulative but funny too.'

Waronker knew a triple couldn't work for the label for financial reasons and took Cavallo and Fargnoli aside, steering them towards the idea of a double. 'To ask him to take twenty-eight tracks and squash it down to eleven or twelve... There was just no way, knowing the amount of time he'd put into it. I couldn't even pick out a rationalisation for starting a conversation with him. There were certainly enough tracks for a double album, and a double album would be a major statement. You can't ask him to do what you want because what you're talking about is marketing and he's not about that. You're not going to win that conversation, but if you could get it down to two albums, it wasn't difficult for a record company. The album would be better. I went through it step by step where it would make sense for a double album and I did a good job and they looked at me and said:

"You're right, you're absolutely right... You've got to tell him, we can't talk that way to him."

"I do not want to do this, all right. I will do it, but I will do it on my own time. I don't want to go to the studio because if I go down to the studio, he will kill me. It's his home turf.'"

Waronker then went out for dinner with his wife, had some wine and figured out how and when he was going to broach the subject. 'My head is telling me at some point, "I'm going to have to go to war."'

At least that could wait another day. Well, it could have if Steve Fargnoli hadn't had a conversation with Prince that evening. At 11 p.m., Waronker's phone rang.

"'Steve, did you tell him about the conversation we had?"

"I had to."'

Waronker was told to call Prince at the (his) office.

'I call Sunset Sound and as soon as I said my name, they put me right through. He had obviously talked to the woman at the front desk. He picks up the phone.

"I hear you don't like my album."

"Where did you hear that from because it's not true?"'

Just as the wine was about to chill in Waronker's bloodstream, his recent bedtime reading – *Editor of Genius*, Scott Berg's biography of the legendary book editor Maxwell Perkins (Ernest Hemingway, F. Scott Fitzgerald) – popped into his head. Perkins had to wrestle with an epic tome from his discovery Thomas Wolfe. 'As an A&R person, it was very similar to what I've gone through.'

Waronker pivots what he has read to this awkward conversation with Prince.

'I tell him how important editing is, as he knows. I was trying to talk to him on that level. He never lifted his voice, but I could feel his intensity.'

Waronker had got to know Prince pretty well in nine years working together. He was the man for whom he played all the instruments on his debut and who had been personally told not to market him solely to a black audience. Prince had sought Waronker's counsel ahead of completing 'When Doves Cry', his make-or-break lead single for *Purple Rain*.

Someone had to broach the conversation Prince's management team was unwilling to have. Waronker took a deep breath and told his charge that 'the difficulty in this situation is that nobody is going to edit this for you. You are going to edit it and my sense is that you're going to have an unbelievably tight record. It's expansive and creative to patch this album [together] and you should at least try.'

Waronker knew that 'a triple album equalled self-conscious'. He could also fall back not just on the memory of *1999* from five years previous, but mentioned classics like The Rolling Stones' *Exile on Main Street* and Stevie Wonder's *Songs in the Key of Life*. 'I may have [also] thrown in *The* [Beatles'] *White Album*. Ultimately, he knew that there were records that were tight. His instincts were open to some extent. When I said to him, "Nobody is going to do this for you, you have got to do it", I was saying "I trust you" but also "I challenge you".

'There was a pause, as there usually was, and he said "I'm going to Minneapolis" and hung up. That was the end of the phone call. It might have been childlike but it scared the hell out of me.'

Waronker immediately called key aides to shortlist and assemble some tracks to present to Prince. '"Be in my office at ten in the morning, and we're going to put this album together." We sequenced it. If we were right, and we did it properly, he would hear it. By about noon, I called Bob Cavallo.

'"I've got it down to two albums."

'"What do you mean? He's been in the studio all night editing his record. We're at twenty songs."

'We had twenty-one. There are three songs that we expected

that he had. There was one little pop song that was making fun of Michael Jackson that he knew I liked. It was gone.'

The thirteen hours since 11 p.m. the previous night had frightened the life out of Waronker – mainly because an unhappy Prince was bad news for everyone. 'I was way more concerned with him. The one thing I didn't want him to feel was that he was being forced into doing something.'

Waronker was right. Prince was angry. Unlike other rock stars, he didn't throw TVs out of windows, declare impromptu press conferences or rant and rave. He seethed, before taking control and sequencing the newly double album himself.

Susan Rogers was with him in Sunset that night. 'I remember him steaming. I remember him talking about it in the control room. I can't quite recall things he said, but I do remember him being angry. It was rare that he came up against a wall with Warner Brothers, but the Revolution weren't with him. I remember him saying "They won't let us do this". He would always use "us" and "we". He was a man of few words.'

Alan Leeds had been contacted by Bob Cavallo, who told him 'Fasten your seatbelts. It's going to be a double album, not three.'

'Prince called me a couple of hours later and he was livid and asked what I thought. I just tried to calm him down and tell him I agree with him so it is what it is. All I remember about the conversation was how angry he was. It wasn't his style to get too loud, but the tone of voice was enough. It spoke volumes. He would get this bitterly sarcastic twang to his voice and just say extreme things like "I think I'm through with Warner Brothers, the hell with them. Why don't they understand artists?"'

The relationship with the label would not improve over the next twelve months. Prince went on to demand the release of an album he would then cancel at the last minute, pull *Sign...*'s

US tour and, the following year, release an album with a nude cover and no gap between its tracks. These decisions, all Prince's, would exasperate Warners.

'I knew as time went on, there would be issues,' admits Waronker. But his conversation had lodged in Prince's brain, who would go into Maxwell Perkins mode and lop another four tracks off *Sign...*'s running order. So began an uneasy truce between Prince, his management and his record company.

Nonetheless, the making of *Sign...* had not been the joyride that Prince had enjoyed with previous records. 'The mood was unique on that record,' explains Susan Rogers. 'It was not the same mood that I saw on *Purple Rain* or *Around the World in a Day* or *Parade*.

'The making of *Sign o' the Times* wasn't an easy incubation period. It wasn't an easy birth.'

Prince and David Bowie are both Cat people

One principal cast member of the Sign tour and movie did not feature in the making of the record. She came into Prince's life at a dinner cooked by a former *Playboy* model at a home which would become the location of one of America's most notorious murders.

As he and Susannah were on the outs at the end of 1986, he reconnected with an old flame, model Devin DeVasquez, tipped off by their joint manager Steve Fargnoli that he was in town. Prince had a habit of keeping in touch with exes. 'He would call me and talk on the phone a lot,' she recalls. At the start of the year, DeVasquez featured on a US talent search with a cast list that included presenter (and Pierce Brosnan's future wife) Keely Shaye Smith and dance duo Pat & Cat.

'I wanted to use "Baby I'm a Star" in *Star Search*,' recalls the Cat in the duo, Chicago dancer Cathy 'Cat' Glover. 'We ended up getting beaten by an act called Christopher & Snowy. They were allowed to use Prince's song but I wasn't – which, as it turned out, was "Baby I'm A Star". Devin [then living in the same apartment block] said she felt bad and asked me to go to Prince's house in Beverly Hills at a dinner for his dad.'

The dinner party took place at 722 North Elm Drive, which would go down in history – but not for Prince-related reasons. It was where Lyle and Erik Menendez shot their parents on 20 August 1989. 'Steve told me he had broken up with Susannah,' explains DeVasquez. 'I wasn't in a relationship at that time. I cooked gumbo for twelve people in that kitchen. His dad was in town and Prince wanted us to hear his new album. I would love to cook gumbo. I cooked all day and, as it was a dinner party, I invited Cat. She had been trying to get Prince's attention from way back when.'

There were a few blooms in early *Sign…* folklore. Glover appeared dressed in purple and black, wearing a chauffeur's cap, which would end up on Prince's head during the Sign and Lovesexy tours, as well as the *Sign…* film. That night, Prince walked in with a DAT tape which Glover thinks ended up as 'Housequake'.

Glover modelled Seneca's maxim that luck is what happens when preparation meets opportunity by wearing flat pumps. These would come in handy after dinner when the party headed to celeb hangout Voila nightclub.

'She didn't tell me it was her dream to work with Prince.' DeVasquez adds. 'Sure enough, he finally paid attention to her, he asked her to dance.' Glover had already slipped the DJ the house music she was used to dancing to and did an audition more important than any talent show, jumping on and off tables in the process. She had asked Prince, 'When a good song comes on, will you dance with me?' Six, seven, eight songs passed when the DJ dropped Robert Palmer's 'Simply Irresistible'. Prince joined Cat, who mimicked his steps. 'He noticed I was keeping up with him.'

She debuted the famous 'Cat scat' twerk for Prince (*Star Search* viewers had already seen it) *et voila* … She overheard him say to Steve Fargnoli, 'I want her in my band.'

Another of Prince's on-off girlfriends, Maneca Lightner, was with Glover in LA. 'The night we were hanging out was the night he announced she was going to be his dancer. It was some old theatre and she ran down and said "I made it!"'

That was Friday of a pretty interesting weekend as, on the Saturday, David Bowie asked Glover to dance on his Glass Spider tour. The ever-competitive Prince would have relished the win.

Crystal baller

Prince was competitive way before he entered Battle of the Bands contests, at home in Minneapolis or on screen in *Purple Rain*.

There was a point when sport, not music, ruled his world. 'Most of our passions were sport,' reflects Paul Mitchell who, with Prince's half-brother Duane Nelson, spent pretty much every day with Prince from the age of twelve until seventeen. 'To be honest, we didn't have much to do with music. We never focused on that. Sports and girls.'

The three played basketball and US football together and, as there was sporting rivalry between the two sides of the city (Prince had just moved from the north side), Mitchell says 'he had to navigate that. That was a big deal moving from north Minneapolis to south Minneapolis. He didn't know anybody until we were around him and we would pick on each other about our issues.' Prince teased Mitchell about his mother having been in prison.

The other two teased him about his height. His stature would be the sticking point for a sporting career and Mitchell believes this would be what made him pivot towards music. 'It wasn't like he was talking to us about music. He was talking to us about basketball or wrestling. It comes back to what was important for the girls. He had girlfriends, he always did.

Mitchell, the quarterback for the football team who was dating the lead cheerleader, was six foot one. Half brother Duane was two inches taller. Prince was five foot two. Mitchell recollects their height and their success respectively in basketball and American football. 'He had great hand-eye coordination where he could play, but you have got to have some size. As he got older, I knew it drove him to say, "Look at me now." That's all he talked about – girls and sport.'

On 'U Got the Look', only Prince could whisper at the start of a duet, about the dream we all dream of, The World Series of Love and make you, and possibly her, forget that she was actually his ex.

In 1987, the Minnesota Twins beat the St Louis Cardinals 4–3 to win the actual World Series in Minneapolis, the first year in history that the home team won all their games. Prince wrote 'Purple and Gold', not his finest song, for the Minnesota Vikings and invited the team round for pancakes one morning. Bill Reeves has memories of a tough football game in which Prince participated in his heels.

'If there was a fight on pay per view, he would invite the band round to watch it,' says *HITnRUN Phase Two* engineer Chris James. 'During football season, he would have the games on in his kitchen. And he was a basketball fan.'

In 2015, the same year that album was released, after the

Minnesota Lynx won the WNBA championship, Prince invited the entire team round to Paisley Park, where he played a three-hour show starting at half past midnight.

Despite writing 2010's anthem 'Purple and Gold' (the Minnesota Vikings colours), Prince wasn't particularly into NFL, but the arrival of a legendary quarterback the previous year would change that. 'He, Shelby and I went to a Vikings game,' remembers engineer Jason Agel, who worked on *Welcome 2 America*. 'He told me, "I was never into football. When Brett Favre came to play in Minneapolis, I could see how uplifting it was for the community and I really wanted to be a part of that."'

There were two sports Prince loved to play.

Basketball, where he did sometimes change into sports shoes (and sometimes didn't), and ping pong – no shoe change necessary.

Ping pong would occasionally be played at his house parties where music was playing, and often at studios. Editor Éva Gárdos witnessed Prince beating Michael Jackson 'solidly' at Tedeo in LA when the sound for *Under the Cherry Moon* was being mixed. A 2014 episode of the Zooey Deschanel-fronted sitcom *New Girl* was built around Prince advising titular character Jess on her love life. The most unrealistic part of the episode is that he would lose so heavily at table tennis as he appears to against Jess's friend Cece.

Mark Webster, a friend from 1978, was hanging out at Paisley Park one day where George Clinton was playing pool and describes Prince checking him out from the ping pong table with 'that "Can I beat him? Is he good?" look about him.'

In Paris in the '90s, Eric 'Statik' Anest took on Prince at the studio table tennis table. 'I'm pretty good, because I had a table when I was a kid. He was being sneaky. He would pretend he wasn't going to serve, and then serve. I beat him [21–19] and I think our relationship did go down after that. I couldn't say for sure that it was because I beat him at ping pong, but it didn't help.' The producer-engineer pauses and considers his working relationship with Prince, which ended not too long after that game. 'I shouldn't have beaten him at ping pong.'

'If he put his mind to anything, he could have done it,' says his bodyguard from 1984–91, Harlan 'Hucky' Austin. After a gig one night, Prince watched the bodyguards playing the John Madden Football video game. 'I said, "Do you wanna play?" He says no. The very next day, he starts playing and beating the heck out of us.'

The sport Prince really hated to lose was playing basketball.

He would take on Terry Jackson and his cousin Charles 'Chazz' Smith, both over six foot tall, with Terry's five-foot-two dad. A home game in LA would be the courtyard between Studios 2 & 3 at Sunset.

His front desk soundman Rob 'Cubby' Colby describes him as 'a vicious basketball player. He would punch and push you, do whatever he had to do. He was a dirty player. That brought you a little closer to him as a man, but the minute he got back in his heels, you knew he meant business.'

Paul Camarata's dad Tutti was running Sunset Sound at the time and would regularly see Prince fraternising between Studios 2 & 3. 'A lot of people met a lot of people out on the basketball court.' There were also games of H.O.R.S.E. (a version of basketball, spelling out the letters every time there was a score) with Kenny Rogers and others including Richard Marx and James Ingram. Paul Camarata also remembers Prince fraternising in the court with Elton, Cher 'and one of those he met was Sheena Easton. He ended up doing "Sugar Walls" with her and they even dated.'

'U Got the Look'

Prince had been asked to find a song for Sheena Easton by producer and engineer David Leonard (whose credits include Paul McCartney, Rush and Toto) via his then wife Peggy McCreary.

He had written 'Emotional Pump' for Joni Mitchell (she passed on singing it) and 'God is Alive' for Mavis Staples, who balked at the lyric 'God is coming like a dog in heat', but didn't pass and sang it anyway.

After her breakthrough on a UK talent show fronted by British consumer TV presenter Esther Rantzen, and subsequent top ten hits 'Modern Girl' and '9 to 5', Sheena had no qualms about spicing up her image with a song like 'Sugar Walls'. She had been dating a record exec when she started working with Prince who, a source told the *New York Post*, 'drove Sheena to the recording and wasn't allowed to go upstairs, even though he was the head of a department at a major label. 'He looked at it like, "Well, that's it between [me] and Sheena."'

So it proved.

By the time 'U Got the Look' was recorded, just before the Christmas of 1986, that had been it between Prince and Sheena. Susan Rogers observes that, by the end of the year, Prince and Sheena had settled into comfortable non-silences. 'She was not shy or reticent but she was not blatantly flirtatious. I got the sense that they respected each other as peers. She wasn't a girlfriend type. He regarded her the same way as Sheila and Wendy & Lisa and considered her a peer. Prince was pretty good at hanging with the girls.'

'They dated for a while,' reflects Peggy McCreary, Susan's predecessor. 'It was obvious for a while.' But Simon Fields, who produced videos for both, says of the platonic status during recording: 'that helped.'

In a 2012 interview for the *Windy City Times*, Easton noted that "'U Got the Look" was a track he'd basically finished for himself. It was just a Prince track. He said, "Do you want to just come in and sing some back-up vocals on the choruses?" So I went into the studio and because I didn't know I was singing against him – I was all over the place – he said he kind of liked that, so he expanded it into a duet.'

In another interview for the BBC, Easton explained that they 'never performed together ever. We've never performed onstage. We did a video for "U Got the Look", set up like a live performance. We really got along very well. Our musical tastes came together and made an interesting sound, although he's different from me musically.' They kept in touch and she wrote lyrics for 'The Arms of Orion', a duet on 1989's *Batman* album, and faxed them over when she was in Rome. They recorded it in LA.

On 21 December 1986, Prince started recording 'The Look' (as it was originally known) and two days later – a lifetime by his standards – he was ready to let go.

Prince played 'a Tele knock-off' (in the words of keyboard tech and engineer Todd Herreman) on the rhythm track which was initially, says Rogers, 'a downtempo funk groove. He was dissatisfied with it and when we had six hours to go, he wiped out the top line and chord changes to make it a higher tempo and that took at least two days. He took extra time and care with that song. He knew that could work for him, like "Kiss" did, or "Raspberry Beret" did, or function in the way "1999" did, and be a crossover single.'

Laura LiPuma Nash, who designed the single and album sleeves, describes his mood as light. 'He was ready to get away from the darkness and the shadows and that photography.' Sheila E. even sneaked in some of her local lingo. When Sheena Easton from Bellshill near Glasgow sings that Prince's body is 'heck-a-slammin', the phrase emanates from Oakland, California and Sheila E. 'He was heavy on the Oaklandisms,' laughs Susan Rogers. David Garibaldi, also from Oakland, says it's 'just part of the language. I say something is Hella-good, [meaning] the same thing.'

Prince's purple reign had its interregna

The 'U Got the Look' lyrics extol the virtues of peach and black, the colours Prince asked those going to the *Sign o' the Times* tour to wear.

As the Purple One, His Royal Purpleness and the 'Purple Yoda' as he referred to himself in song ('Laydown' from *20Ten* – he rhymes it with Minnesota), he was definitely intrinsically linked with the shade given its own Pantone name: Love Symbol #2. This was inspired by the colour on the jacket when he sat on the motorbike for his era-defining biggest hit named after the Minneapolis skyline. A hue associated with royalty, alliterative with and perfect for his Christian name.

Bret Thoeny, the architect he hired for Paisley Park, explains that he designed 'a white building so he could light it in any colour, especially purple'.

Of all the myths around Prince, the issue of purple could be the most widespread. His sister Tyka caused a near-international incident the year after his death saying his favourite colour was orange. Elizabeth Dorr from his wardrobe team during the *Sign...* era, agrees. 'I am on Team Orange when it comes to his favorite colour.' One of the first things he said to Bruce Huisinga, his merchandise boss in the '90s, was: 'Not everything has to be purple.'

Prince loved using colour and wasn't tied to any – even purple

– in the way Johnny Cash was to black. As with other areas of his life, he made bold choices. He would order suit fabrics in every shade from his wardrobe team and his shoemakers. 'People are afraid to wear colours and he just does,' reflects Gary Kazanchyan of Andre 1 Shoes, of whom Prince was a client in the '00s. 'To be honest, I did all the colours on the colour wheel. It was just a matter of season. He would choose colours and have wardrobe people hunt fabrics that wouldn't dye real quick.'

That went for his home too, especially when Paisley Park was being built around the time of *Sign...*'s release. Buzz Goodchild, who worked on maintenance, saw his car preferences go 'from beige to cobalt blue to yellow. I was waiting for an order from him to paint the house gold. His guitars went gold.'

'[With] every album that came out,' adds Danny Soltys, who also worked at Paisley Park, 'we painted it [a different colour]. *Lovesexy* – blue and fuchsia. *Sign o' the Times* – peach.' Prince got a particular kick out of Soltys shining a 2K bat symbol at night, which he had cut out of sheet metal, around the time of *Batman*. 'That was a feather in my cap.'

Prince's colour schemes are just one of the obvious differences between him and the previous holder of the Hardest Working Man in Showbusiness title. 'When James Brown stopped, he was a regular guy,' says Alan Leeds, who, to Prince's delight, worked with both men. 'He had a life and the life wasn't an extension of his career. It wasn't like he painted his house a certain colour because it's the new colour of the album project. Nobody was as ensconced in his music career as Prince. Those guys had lives. Prince didn't.'

'When he would think of a new project and a new album,' remembers Laura LiPuma Nash of Warners' art department, 'he would think of the colour schemes and the whole vibe.'

If you want to know why he drives a yellow BMW in the 'Sexy MF' video, wears pastel blue in the 2007 Super Bowl performance, or is dressed in black with a white guitar on the sleeve of *Welcome 2 America*, these decisions weren't as random as they first appeared.

A clue to why he thought visually could be seen in other artists' methodology. One of his influences, Joni Mitchell (of 'Blue', 'Big Yellow Taxi', 'Shades of Scarlet Conquering' and 'Little Green' fame) thought visually as well as musically. 'That's where she is,' agrees her long-term bandmate Brian Blade. 'She's a painter. That's her world. She's got a vision.' In terms of Blade and Mitchell's conversations over tea or coffee, 'what I recall is so clear and so razor-sharp because there's images connected. She has that word gift – in terms of colour and the music and different periods. You hope that the visual aspect of it will pop. Even to write with that sensibility is a deep gift, talking about opening all the senses.'

Prince had that too, as far as Susan Rogers was concerned.

'Records had no identifiable start date. It was a continuum of songs. The way albums emerged from his methodology is that he would come up with a vision that would include a colour scheme. *Dirty Mind* was monochrome, punk meets soul, literally abandoning his R&B soul for something the critics would go crazy for. It seems to me he returned to that on the *Parade* album. *Around the World in a Day* is a rainbows record.'

Rashida (Robinson), Prince's resident DJ during the '00s, remembers a conversation about his drummer John Blackwell. 'He told me John saw music in colour and I think Prince did too. The way he sees colour, he sees music. It's more than just a music and more than just a sound.' Another drummer Michael Bland reflects that 'colour meant a great deal to him'. And another of Prince's favourite guitarists felt the same way.

'George Benson's perfect pitch is in colour,' explains guitarist and producer Jay Graydon, who wrote for Benson. 'He sees colours when he hears notes. Each note is a different colour.'

'It's such a beautiful thing what Prince gave us in colours,' reflects film-maker and musician Jeymes Samuel. 'Artists don't release a colour with an album. Two colours with *Sign o' the Times*. Music is colour and Prince gave us the colours.'

As a testimony to how deeply Prince felt visual tone was, the credits on *Parade* picked out collaborator Clare Fischer, who had contributed strings: 'With special thanks 2 Clare Fischer 4 Making Brighter the Colours Black and White.'

The handwritten instructions Dave Henders was given before creating the multi-coloured *Around the World in a Day* sleeve were suitably visual, and left the artist 'gobsmacked'. The brief from Prince included allusions to silent-movie actor Clara Bow (namechecked in the ballad, 'The Condition of the Heart'), a ladder and a raspberry beret (referencing two other song titles from the album), a clown and depictions of the Revolution.

'Although Prince's instructions were numerous and specific,' adds Henders, 'I knew there was latitude for me to create and interpret, as Prince empowered artists whom he trusted to employ their creativity. Being a practitioner of surrealism and psychedelia, I channeled Dali and Magritte to make the composition. I used people around Prince as models for many of the characters, including myself. That's me in the Cloud Suit.'

Everything in Prince's world was by design – even the designers

The Cloud Suit, sported in the 'Raspberry Beret' video, was just one snappy set of threads Prince was happy to wear.

It's one thing for your commitment to fashion to mean that

you buy the best clothes, your team calls up the world's hottest designers, or the world's hottest designers call you. It's another level for your commitment to lead to your own wardrobe department – a team of six – on the premises of your business headquarters and, subsequently, your house.

Prince didn't hire the stylist as much as he could *be* the stylist, with designers often working to his specifications – for instance the Hot Thing outfit on the *Sign o' the Times* movie to match LeRoy Bennett's Go-Blo lights.

His outfits on the first three record sleeves were as follows: naked, naked, bikini bottoms with thigh-length boots and trench coat. Around the *1999/Purple Rain* breakthrough, it wasn't just the music that got bigger and louder. *Purple Rain* changed so much for Prince, not least in helping establish a signature look. A key piece of the film's look was that purple knee-length coat with a metallic sheen.

Marie France was a costumier for TV and movies when, after a recommendation to Prince from Steve Fargnoli, she was hired for that movie. France maintains that a lighter lilac version 'was already established from the '1999' video. I did change the fabric as it unravelled at the seam. It was very effective for stage as it was shiny, but it wasn't good for films as you have close-ups. When you work for the stage, it has to be seen from very far away.' The result was arguably Prince's most recognisable look, the metallic purple coat sitting astride the motorbike.

The concept of living up to his regal name was not lost on France.

'I designed the ruffle shirt with the lace. The ruffle shirt was originally in white cotton. For the tour, it was made in other fabrics including lace. I'm kind of proud of that shirt. Lace is another thing that I am proud to have introduced to him. I knew he wore those cheap tuxedo shirts and that's one of the things

I told him. "You have to get rid of that. You need something much more Prince-like. I'm thinking eighteenth century, I'm thinking romantic." And that's what grabbed him. I was seeing him as a mixture of punk, hippy and romantic. I made a quick sketch of the shirt right there at that meeting to explain what I was thinking.'

The New Romantic movement happening in London could well have influenced him and, when he played the Lyceum in 1981, he was said to have popped into Steve Strange's Blitz club, frequented by Boy George, Spandau Ballet and other New Romantics. Sadly, no photographic evidence exists of his supposed visit. Maneca Lightner remembers a 'huge masquerade party' during the *Purple Rain* era where the host attended, dressed as Prince Charming, a few years after the 1981 Adam and the Ants single of that name.

The film and its subsequent success meant that Prince was able to work on and build his signature look with the help of France and others. 'For *Purple Rain*, I had boxes and boxes of lace gloves that I would give to the extras to create a style. When you see the hands in the air at the concert, you would see them.'

The coat would be replaced by a whole new wardrobe. In fact, a whole new wardrobe department. Prince was assembling in-house musical talent like the Time, Sheila E. and the Family. The next step was for his own in-house wardrobe team to dress them all.

At first, there were the tailors: Louis Wells and Vaughan Terry in Minneapolis. Then Jim Shearon – who had worked for Parsons-Meares who produced costumes for the Metropolitan Opera in New York before moving to the Guthrie Theatre in Minneapolis – was hired as a cutter, and was proclaimed to be 'a genius' by several members of Prince's new wardrobe team who, by 1987, would be assembled on the premises of Paisley Park.

From *Purple Rain* onwards, Prince would find France indispensable, which was not to her tastes because she was not accustomed to the rigours of tour travelling. Touring wasn't just hard on the team but on the clothes too. The four-ply silks (thick and durable to withstand the wear and tear of tour life) and wool he insisted on were not designed for two hours of splits and jumping from the top of stacked speakers. Prince would also throw jackets into the crowd until one of the wardrobe team or his assistant Karen Krattinger quietly pointed out how much they cost to make.

'We kept producing more clothes,' recalls France, 'and I would have to get fabrics [often at $300 a yard] and we were somewhere in the middle of nowhere.' That meant trips back to New York to procure more fabrics. France remembers Prince being 'upset that I would leave. I had an assistant in those days and so I don't know why he was upset like that.' To stop Prince getting upset, his team moved in-house and the budgets became more generous between *Purple Rain* and *Under the Cherry Moon*.

The heels he wore in the former were relatively cheap Di Fabrizio boots with three and a half inch heels before France upscaled. 'We copied that pair of cheap shoes at the beginning and, from then on, they were custom-made. As a fabric, they are leather, but the top of the shoes matched his pants.'

Working with Prince, she says, was quicker than the usual movie set-up. 'When you work in films, you have a meeting and you talk about it. With Prince, there was not time for an existential conversation. Very organically, I fell on to the same page as him. There was not a long conversation. He had a sense of style, but even then he needed help. Sometimes I saw him later on [in his career] and thought, *I would have said no to that*.'

For *Under the Cherry Moon*, Marie France got to stay in one place: the south of the country that shares her name. 'We did a black-and-white film, and we did choose fabric which would work with black and white to start with. I would say that I chose the fabrics and then I would run by him the ones for his costumes. We did camera test to see what worked best for black and white.' The old-school glamour Prince craved – represented in beaded and jewelled outfits, some of which wouldn't look out of place in a Regency drama or certainly not in the 1930s movies which inspired them – helped her with her fabric choices. 'At that time for people working in films, TV and videos, you could access the Paramount lot. There would be some of the fabrics we used for him [Prince] and Kristin and Jerome, and would date from the '30s and '40s, which would correspond to the feeling of that film there. We wanted to do a black-and-white film and we wanted it to be reminiscent of the great days and glamour of Hollywood. That's what inspired me. We never did have a formal discussion. We were on the same page somehow.'

France, the full-time stylist (and part-time rapper on 'Girls & Boys' from *Parade*), feels 'really privileged to be in the era of Prince that I was' and that she could stand up to Prince. But the style advice turned into a production line. Lisa Jordan, Elizabeth Dorr and Helen Hiatt would go on to look after his wardrobe needs as part of an in-house team and certain standards were set from the *Purple Rain* days. 'The shop was generally three cutters and three stitchers, depending on the project,' explains Dorr.

Firstly, no expense was spared, including fabric that stretched to $300 a yard, such as that used on the hooded cape France suggested Prince wore to the 1985 Academy Awards, at which he won for Best Original Song Score.

Elizabeth Dorr started as France's assistant on *Purple Rain* and remained with the wardrobe department until 1991. She insists the shop (main client: Prince Rogers Nelson; other clients: his band, for whom clothes were hand-picked by the former) made him relax. 'He seemed comfortable there, even in public. The shop later made lots of silk charmeuse pyjamas for private. I would get swatches and he would choose colours. He liked big comfy sweaters like the one in the dressing room scenes [of the 'U Got the Look' video]. If you're wearing silk and high heels, all you need is a big coat and you can go anywhere. It made flying easy and comfortable. In public, offstage, he had a rainbow of double-breasted silk suits with matching shirts, ties and shoes. It was a professional look, but not mainstream due to the bright colours, huge shoulder pads and matching high heels. I was well-trained to maintain a clean look – always camera-ready, thread-perfect and sharp. My mantra was: touch it once, do it right the first time and move on.

'My goal was always to permit extreme dancing. Having designed and constructed for many dance companies in Minneapolis for years, I was well-prepared to achieve that goal. With Cat in the mix, the level of choreography was advanced. After years of revising crotch seams with stretch fabric gussets, and repairing cut velvet tight pants, the move to four-ply silk crepe pleated trousers made my repair time much easier. Strong fabric made so much sense and it moved beautifully under the lights. Even though four-ply silk crepe is very difficult to cut, stitch and paint, the results were beautiful.'

Dorr recalls 'fewer costume changes and fewer dates and cities' on the *Sign* tour, which only made Europe. 'Marie France didn't do the tour so Prince asked me to submit sketches of "something new". I had about twelve hours to get that down on paper and to him. He knew that I could draw because he summoned me to the dressing room – "bring a pencil and paper" – to sketch a turtleneck tunic for him earlier at some point. He chose colours and styles for himself and each person in the band from sheets of thumbnail sketches.'

(Elizabeth Dorr is unlikely to forget the tour, as she married Prince's rigger, David Dorr, on 9 May 1987 at St Clara's in Stockholm. They remain married. Other couples who would be together on Prince tours included lighting director LeRoy Bennett and his then wife Brenda, a member of Vanity 6, on the Triple Threat tour.)

The *Sign o' the Times* and *Lovesexy* eras saw Prince arguably at his most confident in terms of determining his own looks. He was keen to move away from the monochrome of *Under the Cherry Moon* to peaches, yellows and turquoise.

'The evolution was determined by the movies,' adds Dorr. 'The *Cherry Moon* wardrobe was black and white so he could leave purple behind and wear the colours he liked. The peach and black line of the "U Got the Look" video cemented that palette. I have to add that the appreciation that Sheena [Easton] showed to Helen [Hiatt] and myself, when we made her look fit just right, was gratifying.'

Prince, Dorr says, 'had the ability to wring us out with his constant electric charge. He didn't waste words, but trusted us to execute his vision. Most of our exchanges took place looking at each other in the mirror with minimal verbiage and some sort of telepathy and assurance that his vision was reflected by me.'

For himself, the turtleneck tunic Dorr had sketched was selected in yellow with a matching coat and black hat inspired by Cat Glover, who had turned up wearing a police cap at Devin DeVasquez's dinner party in LA. It turned into one of the *Sign...* signature looks. 'In true Prince fashion, the shop made several of them in many colours – peach, pale turquoise, and so on. The hat was Cat-inspired, but he had a long history of using police type hats before this. [He wears another for his drum solo in the *Sign* movie.] The wide cuffs that he wore for the photoshoot are mine. I was wearing them that day and he asked to wear them for the shoot.'

Helen Hiatt recalls the wardrobe department moving into Paisley Park while she was on the road for the Sign tour. The jeans Prince wore were based on denim she bought in Sweden; 'the fabric was too thick for our little sewing machine.' She also recalls the team shopping for peach socks in a rare moment of downtime. Another challenge for his jackets was 'that the buttons would have to snap not unbutton. He would rip them off and the buttons would fly off.'

Cat's peach dress, for the sleeve of the 'Sign o' the Times' single, was, says Dorr, 'made of this bubble stretch fabric that worked well for all of that motion. The peach outfit was a *Parade*-like style and I made the wide garter to match.' Heart-shaped mirrors would be sewn onto the coats by 'the crew working at Paisley Park and then what we needed to contract out. We would adjust and change it and Prince would say, "I want another one of those tonight."'

While the four-ply silk peach outfit on the cover of the album sleeve was knocked up by the wardrobe team, the black leather jacket was Prince's. 'The wardrobe was a combination of clothes made in the shop and off-the-rack pieces that we customised according to each personality. Everyone spent so much time onstage [that] there was little room for changing clothes. He chose the jumpsuit with the side cutouts, tunics, trousers and matching big coats. The big chunky jewellery, mirrored hearts, peace signs with the buttons and fringe, finished out the look. More fun less flash. The music was the focus.'

Lisa Jordan helped on the tour and movie with Sheila and Cat's outfits. 'Cat just wore what we put on her,' she says, before observing of Prince: 'He wasn't money-minded. He wasn't doing it [touring] to make money. He was doing it to put his best art onstage. The jumpsuits were from my sheet of sketches.' Jordan was also responsible for Sheila's asymmetric white trouser suit from the movie and admits 'that wasn't her favourite look'.

The wardrobe team had a scary moment during 'Hot Thing' with Cat's yellow skirt. In the movie, filmed in less enlightened times, Prince would slide under her legs taking off the skirt with his teeth. 'The net skirt was torn during pick-up shots and we didn't have another. Helen and I were the dynamic duo and made another in five minutes, but he wasn't happy that we didn't have a duplicate. At this time, there was little to no communication with wardrobe, so it caught me off guard, but we rose to the task.'

He would, of course, choose the colours too, hence the black capes Madhouse and the band's saxophonist Eric Leeds would wear on stage with Prince.

The group were instructed to make their TV debut in capes. 'Somebody thought it would be a good idea to appear on *Video Soul* with Donnie Simpson,' recalls Madhouse's bassist Levi Seacer on his own Facebook page. 'My thinking was, we would wear regular clothing to do the interview. Somebody said "How boring would that be?"

'It's not an average day to see a black man in a cape and polka-dot shoes, on a major Black TV network, promoting new directions in garage jazz funk. Well, that "somebody" in this story is Prince, and, like always, he was right.'

Prince's style evolution was more organic than the common industry styling favoured by some, including David Bowie and Madonna, where a look would go with the designated album or single campaign. By the *Lovesexy* era, the polka dots, a feature of Maneca Lightner's dress on the sleeve of the first Madhouse album, would become a fashion template for Prince and Cat.

But they would appear in other eras, as would other colours like the familiar purple, yellow or turquoise.

In the early '90s, his look became a little flashier. 'It was basically nine to five,' says the head of his wardrobe team at the time, Heidi Clemence, 'but if there was a video shoot, sometimes I would go to New York or LA. There were times I was a little frustrated trying to read what he was trying to convey, but for the most part, we always figured it out. We had amazing patterners and stretchers so that everything fitted him. Fashion sophistication came in. We did a lot of silk. Silk, chiffon, all the suits were four-ply silk. We would have a dyer who would have to match the colour he was looking for.'

Prince would go out of house on occasion, more often after the '90s when the in-house wardrobe team at Paisley Park, alongside much of the staff, was stripped back.

Marilyn Monroe once said, 'Give a girl the right shoes and she can conquer the world.' Prince's focus was similarly minded in terms of his feet (which were women's size six). In the *Purple Rain* era, he used Hollywood shoemaker Willie Rivera, the man who made Charlton Heston's sandals in *The Ten Commandments*, before Helen Hiatt got in touch with British cobbler Cos Kyriacou in 1988.

Kyriacou's spell with Prince in the '90s involved next-day Fed Ex deliveries from his store in Shepherd's Bush in west London to Paisley Park. 'We never used leather,' he recalls. 'It was always fabrics. They used to send me a design. We would get a box of between 10 and 15 pieces of fabric, all different, and they would want a pair in all these different fabrics by a certain day. Once we made the first pair, it was pretty straightforward.'

Well, not always.

Prince once wanted shoes with a face on them. 'It's a face but, because of the way the pattern was made, it's in two places and somehow I had to cut it in a way where, when the two pieces joined, I could see the face on the front of the shoe. I remember how much time we had to spend on it.'

Kyriacou had questions about Prince's album project *The Versace Experience*, and so the singer suggested direct contact:

'"Why don't you just talk to Donatella?"'

'[With] every word that was uttered about making his shoes and outfits, there was joy in her and she was very excited about the whole project. I assumed that was because she was a fan.'

'She was definitely eager to please him,' remembers Prince's merchandise chief Bruce Huisinga, who also spoke to her on the phone. 'It was a feather in her cap to have him wearing their stuff.'

The shoes, according to Stacia Lang, another wardrobe director during the '90s, were important to Prince, recalls Kyriacou. 'Stacia told me every time he would get a package with a pair of shoes from me, he would put on one and dance around the studio. That gave me a good feeling.'

Prince decided to do his homework on his twenty-first-century shoemaker of choice, LA-based Gary Kazanchyan. 'He would study you before he would come into your shop,' says Kazanchyan of Andre 1 Shoes in Hollywood. 'He would do a lot of homework. He didn't want to waste one second. He had everything drawn out before he would even talk to you.'

Soon after their first meeting, the company was 'averaging thirty or forty pairs a month and that was still not enough'. Those pairs would cost between $850 and $12,500, with boots sometimes going up to $6,000. 'You might have a hard time finding photos of him in them. Thigh-high, furry, all white, or purple, white, black ...' Prince would order 'eight-to-ten pairs of those, four in white, two or three black and all the rest were purple. He orders a pair in that style and if he likes it, he orders multiple materials of different colours.' With white shoes, the neat freak in Prince emerged, and he would order 'a minimum of ten pairs because he didn't like to be shown with dirty shoes.'

Kyriacou recalls certain themes. 'Obviously, purple was a popular one. We did a hell of a lot of black and white. Paisley design was popular. Polka dots and pin stripes were quite popular. I'm a big fan of polka dots myself.'

The wear and tear, though, was quite pronounced. 'I think that's why we did so many of the black and white, because they would get damaged. With the kind of treatment he gave them onstage, we would need new ones.'

Not trainers, though.

'Never! I didn't think he wore them. I think he wore heels all the time.'

This isn't quite true. Prince would use sports shoes for his games of basketball. Elfar Sigmundsson, a Stockholm-based fan who got to know him on occasions when his tour came to Sweden, recalls he 'changed to white Nike Air basketball shoes to play the game. Straight out of a new box.'

Many interviewees talk of Prince's dancing in the '80s and the damage it would have done to his feet. Cos Kyriacou and Gary Kazanchyan, who made his shoes in the '90s and '00s, had tried to mitigate this. 'Our boots were made with heavy padding on the inside and a bit of bounce in the back part of the heel so that protected his feet,' says Kazanchyan. 'If you're always jumping in the air and doing the splits, eventually you're going to break down. How I know that is I deal with a lot of people onstage who do the same thing and they pretty much [all] have the same issues later on. It's not unusual for people. If you ask ballet dancers and people who do incredible moves, eventually they are all in pain.'

Helen Hiatt remembers, after hiring one shoemaker, getting

'to trace [Prince's] feet and it broke my heart. When you wear a shoe like that, you get bunions. These feet took a beating.' Many with subsequent knowledge of the cause of the pain mitigation which led to Prince's death trace it back to the intensity of his dancing in the '80s – plus those heels.

Part of what kept Prince ahead of the trends was that nobody knew what he would be dressed in until he was wearing it. 'He didn't like to announce he's coming,' remembers Kazanchyan. 'He will call if he's a block away from the shop. "Do you have time for me?" If you said yes, [it was] "Clear out your showrooms. I will be there in less than thirty seconds." He was always private. With new styles, I would always work with him on the first couple of pairs.'

Kazanchyan also worked with Lady Gaga and Bruno Mars, both of whom asked for Prince themes, and rock band KISS, whose boots he made from the '70s onwards. The shoe designer – Kazanchyan not Prince, although the client fed in on the detail – would be spirited to Paisley Park and, just as when it came to choosing musicians, Prince's preference would be female. 'When he used to fly me out to Minneapolis for four or five days, we would go over designs, the new designs, the new cutout, the new styles. Something like that we can't really explain over emails. He would do a lot of drawings. He would also cut out different shoes from a magazine and the heel from another one – a lot of cutouts from different shoe pictures from magazines. Probably no male.'

Two '90s outfits stand out for Heidi Clemence for different reasons. '[For] "The Most Beautiful Girl in the World", we had that wonderful Italian stretch black bodysuit – especially without underwear!'

There were repercussions for the outfit which stretched to the 1994 Winter Olympics in Lillehammer. 'We purchased the end of the fabric roll and apparently Vera Wang had also purchased this fabric for Katarina Witt's performance costumes. Vera contacted me wanting me to sell back a quarter yard of the fabric. Needless to say, I could not as I had just shipped via FedEx to Costas [Kyriacou] to make another pair of shoes.'

The other stand-out outfit for Clemence was the semi-sheer bodysuit Prince wore for the 1991 MTV Video Music Awards performance of 'Gett Off'. MTV admin said they couldn't go on without something underneath and that had us sweating to find thongs and panties.' And, of course, skin-colour dye.

'He wanted a calligraphy feel [for MTV] so we had cans and cans of gold spray paint. I think it's the highest I've ever been. I remember it was this flurry of craziness. We had to spray paint it gold and find the undergarments.' Gold underpants were unavailable. 'Everything was happening in hyper speed time. We had to find anything that looked like a gold colour so it looked like he wasn't wearing anything.'

The colours mentioned in 'U Got the Look' can be attributed directly to Prince, according to Helen Hiatt. 'Peach and black. It's all him.' When they were making the single's video, she heard, 'I want peach clothes. Make it peach.'

Not just any peach. He got the one he wanted. 'I think we researched fabrics of what was out there and he picked the peach. He wanted mango and we asked him, "The outside of a mango or the inside of a mango?" So what we would do is send colour swatches to him. That was the colour from that one.'

'Once he'd done *Sign o' the Times*,' says Laura LiPuma Nash, the Warner Brothers' sleeve designer from *Purple Rain* to *Lovesexy*, 'he never went back to peach and black. This is a guy who moved on.'

Before *Black Sweat,* there was perfume

Not quite purple, but Madonna said it was always of lavender. One constant about Prince in the 1980s was how he smelled.

He may have released a 2006 single called 'Black Sweat', but his odour, like everything else, was always carefully controlled. 'He smelled really good' is one of the most frequent statements from ex-girlfriends and colleagues of both sexes.

Sal Greco offers a male perspective of a colleague who worked in dingy studios through anti-social hours. 'There would be many times for us when we would be in the control room and [you'd say], "Dude, you really smell," but he never did.' His was definitely an upscale aroma which didn't extend to the whole band.

Colleagues and ex-girlfriends agree that 'he always smelt incredible.' 'It was lovely,' recalls sleeve designer Laura LiPuma Nash. 'Lemony. It smelt natural, like a beautiful floral scent, never that strong.' Hairdresser Bevla Reeves says he smelled 'kind of spicy. Not floral.' Marylou Badeaux from Warners agrees with Madonna. She 'can't remember a time that it wasn't lavender. It just always smelled calm.'

Maneca Lightner, an ex-girlfriend, says 'he smelled the same all the times all the years I knew him. I never got the name. A woman's perfume.' Karen Krattinger, who was Prince's personal assistant, changed her own purchase habits. 'He turned me on to perfumes. Salvador Dali [by Yves Saint Laurent], Rive Gauche, the classic nose bottle.'

One trip to Rodeo Drive in the mid-'80s with bodyguard Chick Huntsberry and his daughter Tina saw a detour to shop for perfume. 'I picked out one of his favourites at the time – Pavlova,' she recalls. 'His whole house always smelled like that perfume! It always reminded me of him.'

Elisa Fiorillo was recording her solo album in Minneapolis in the late '80s when she stopped for lunch and joined Prince and his dad for some carrot and ginger soup. Being Italian and 19, the awkward silences were not for her. 'It was just quiet. All I could hear was little slurps. I'm Italian so I said to his dad, "You smell really good."' John Nelson's reply – 'I like it. I got it at Target for $10' – led to an epic eye-roll from his son. 'It just made him human for that moment,' Fiorillo laughs.

Prince may have partnered with Target and cut out a record company in 2009 to sell his triple-album set *LOtUSFLOW3R / MPLSoUND / Elixer* for $11.98, but he wasn't going to be buying fragrances from there, at that price.

Fiorillo, who dated Prince in 1990, feels the spray got out of hand that decade. 'In the '90s, that man wore way too much perfume – not cologne. That perfume he would put in the room. Carotene. Samsara. Smells really full.' Fiorillo once asked him why he smelt like her grandmother. She says the aroma was subtler when she returned to sing back-up for him in the 2010s alongside Liv Warfield and Shelby J. She has happy memories of Baies Candles 'all over the dressing rooms' but she would like to point out on behalf of the trio that 'we bought ours'.

Prince stayed immaculate in all areas of presentation – and expected others to do so, also. 'You could always tell he always was on,' recalls LiPuma Nash. When members of the Revolution were on duty and wanted to nip down to the hotel lobby, 'they had to get dressed. They could never look like normal people. You could never be seen in public unless you looked good.'

This fastidiousness started early, according to Prince's cousin Charles 'Chazz' Smith. 'When he first got his record deal, I looked in the trash can in his bathroom. "Hey, cuz, there's a bunch of underwear in your bathroom trash can." "I don't wear any underwear twice. I don't even wash them."'

'First record deal, he didn't have that much money. Someone was getting them for him. I've seen them in the trash can every day. "I'm not wearing those again."' Michelle Schwartzbauer, his housekeeper around the time of *Sign*, remembers washing his underwear, so this wasn't a habit continued throughout adult life.

Frank McComb, who played a load of private parties with him in LA in the mid-'00s, agrees he was always finely turned out – even for rehearsals. 'He would come down fully dressed like he was ready to play a gig. He did nothing small. Even the dress, clothes, make-up. He was clean as a whistle.' A phrase Prince used to describe his own attire to Shelby Johnson was 'cleaner din da Board of Health'.

Bassist Josh Dunham, who was 'fairly heavy on the jeans, coming from Texas', learned the hard way and soon squeezed into a suit coat. 'That's how he wanted us to come to rehearsals. He would say, "Dress like you own this house." I wanted to be in my pyjamas and flip-flops. That's not what he meant.' Morris Hayes, his keyboard player over the past 20 years, agrees. 'That's what he hated about modern groups. Seeing them in baseball cap and jeans. It's showbiz. When you're Superman, you put a Superman suit on. He liked Superman so much he never took the Superman suit off. He hated jeans and T-shirts. He always would tell me, "Morris you're a rock star, you should look like a rock star."'

According to former tour manager Craig Rice, even the bodyguards couldn't escape. 'He's got this thing, the look, you have got to look like a rock star. He instilled in everyone, you couldn't have any logo T-shirts – not even Prince T-shirts. On the Purple Rain tour, we decided the security couldn't wear black T-shirts. We wanted them to look like secret service agents – they had to wear suits, management had to wear suits. I took everyone in security to buy suits. They didn't like it. I wore a suit all the time. We had to represent a look, which was professional and sophisticated. I didn't even wear logos, even at Paisley.'

Prince's late-period lean towards decorum emerged during his 2014 *HITnRUN Phase Two* tour. 'He definitely had a dress code,' recalls Mari Maupin, who danced and then sang onstage with him and 3rdEyeGirl. 'No undergarments could be showing. I knew him the last couple of years of his life. He was a very spiritual person, a very reserved person … That included showing your undergarments. That's something he was very firm on. It's kind of expected for artists to be sexual. [He would say] "Adele doesn't have to do that. Let the music speak for itself."'

If you held the (very) unofficial title of Prince's girlfriend, this policy included you too, remembers his mid-'80s personal assistant Helen Hiatt. 'He's a controlling guy. If you're his girlfriend, you don't come around him without make-up on. He was sharp, [so] why weren't they?'

It certainly applied to employees, even the ones working anti-social hours. Engineer Jason Agel was told before coming to work on the *Welcome 2 America* album in 2010 to 'make sure you're dressed nicely'. This was because of 'an engineer who wore short shorts. Prince had apparently said, "Get the guy with the Daisy Dukes out of here." He didn't want to see anybody getting too comfortable.'

Everything onstage had to be just right – even the inanimate objects. 'I had a Rhodes piano,' laughs Frank McComb, 'and was in the process of rebuilding it.' This explains the instrument's slightly dowdy appearance, with an overhanging cloth on it. 'He called me [to play] for a party. He looked at me and just smiled and said, "No, Frank. Take that grandma cloth off. Let me see what it looks like." Even the piano had to look sharp.'

Peggy McCreary has a memory of him once entering Studio

3 'dressed in jeans, white T-shirt and high-heeled boots', but it wasn't like he was breaking character. He dressed for the part. 'He cut a rockabilly song.' (That was 'You're All I Want', parts of which would morph into 'Delirious' from the *1999* album.)

There was a period in the early '90s, as engineer Michael Koppelman recalls, where 'he would come in a sweater, not really dressed up. It seems like he was trying to find himself.' This didn't last long. There was normally a reason he dressed down, as Marie France explains. 'In *Under the Cherry Moon*, he had a leather jacket he purchased from somewhere in Paris which he wanted to use in the film. But the rest of the film, his suits were made by a tailor in Nice.'

This slickness would inform Prince's style for the rest of his life. Or if you want to know why he never dressed like Bruce Springsteen, his dancer from the *Diamonds and Pearls* era, Robia Scott (the 'Pearl' to Lori Werner's 'Diamond'), explains it like this: 'I did have a minute when he was vulnerable with me. He said that growing up poor with the struggles he had as a kid, somewhere inside he had made a vow then that when he became famous, he would never not dress as a celebrity because he had made the money. He didn't just want to be a vain superstar. *As soon as I can afford it, I will never be in rags.* He was never your common man. He was always a superstar.'

Scott knows this from experience, in particular from a dinner she and others enjoyed chez Prince. 'One night, the chef was cooking and Prince was in his whole outfit with the suit, gold buttons, jacket with the shoulder pads, the matching four-inch heels and stirrups. It's all red. He says "I'm going to change into something more comfortable." I gave him the look – "Am I going to see you in jeans?" And he walks back in – you could just sense him, he never needed to say anything – and he's in the exact same outfit in blue.'

CHAPTER 11

IF I WAS YOUR GIRLFRIEND

The Voice, for Prince, was ideally female ... Peggy, Susan,
Sylvia and Lisa ... The two Eves ... The new 'woman' in
Prince's life: Camille ... 'If I Was Your Girlfriend' ...
If I actually was your girlfriend ... 'Don't fly her in' ...
Prince and Kim ... his two wives ... Relationship
status: it's complicated

The Voice, for Prince, was ideally female

The *Sign o' the Times* tour represented a breakthrough for Prince when keyboardist and vocalist Boni Boyer came to the fore. Subsequently, his touring band was rarely without a female powerhouse. Rosie Gaines joined him in the early '90s, while one band had three: Elisa Fiorillo, Liv Warfield and Shelby Johnson. British singer Beverley Knight was a popular guest star on gigs, while LA singer Judith Hill played with him publicly and privately at Paisley.

When Shelby Johnson joined Prince's band, he gave her either some gifts – or homework, depending on your perspective. 'He had bought me every album by Joni Mitchell ever made.

He really loved the female voice. I thought it was going to be his songs to learn. It was the songs he liked to hear the female voice sing. Aretha Franklin, "I Never Loved a Man". Amy Winehouse, "Love is a Losing Game". Dorothy Moore's "Misty Blue". "Sweet Thing" [by Chaka Khan]. "Baby Love" (by Diana Ross & the Supremes). He had a lot of respect for real singers.'

Just as Italian (*la voce*), Spanish (*la voz*) and French (*la voix*) all place 'voice' with a feminine definite article, Prince's preference would be towards female vocals. It would not be a stretch to say that his mother's singing influenced this decision. Or it could be that as his former manager Ruth Arzate notes 'the female voice characteristically has more nuance and more range'.

Vocalists he admired were those with a work ethic. He also set great store by those, from Joni Mitchell to Amy Winehouse, who formed their own particular sound. 'He asked me if I have ever heard "Coat of Many Colours" by Dolly Parton,' recalls Fiorillo. '"You need to hear that song." He was a fan of Patti Labelle, Lalah Hathaway and Mavis Staples.'

'We talked a good ten minutes about Dolly Parton one day,' adds his drummer in the '90s Michael Bland. 'Her name came up. "I *love* Dolly Parton and I love her voice and I love her sound." He really respected Chrissie Hynde. We talked about the first couple of Pretenders records.'

'He loved, loved, loved Mavis Staples,' remembers his keyboard player of two decades, Morris Hayes. 'She was a singer's singer. He gravitated to the feeling.' He appreciated singers who could do it without electronic help, so men like Al Green and Luther Vandross and Vintage Trouble's Ty Taylor would be respected too, according to Hayes. 'He appreciated Luther's voice. Luther always singing on pitch. They just did it. It wasn't about autotune. They had to go out on the stage.'

Ruth Arzate intimates he was a Radiohead fan. 'It was the whole package, but he did love Thom Yorke's voice.'

His competitive instincts would maybe kick in with men, although he also admired Maxwell, Anthony Hamilton, Cee Lo Green and D'Angelo. This meant when he did work with another man he thought could sing, like Frank McComb who played many of his parties around the *3121* era, he showed off. McComb remembers, 'There were male R&B singers come up [to the party] and they didn't come up [onstage]. Man, Prince was funny. He used me as a weapon.'

Chaka Khan was a touchstone for Prince. He was a fan of her work with Rufus, she had a UK number one with his song 'I Feel For You', and he often played live with her, as well as recording an album with her and Larry Graham. Rhonda Smith, who played bass with both, said he rated 'her voice, her persona, her personality, the space that she takes and the space in what she represented to music for her catalogue during that time she grew up. Somebody who has contributed a major point of music.'

In 2004, the same year Prince was inducted into the Rock & Roll Hall of Fame, he chose the emerging solo talent that was Beyoncé Knowles to duet with him at the Grammys. Patrice Rushen, another voice Prince respected (and a three-time Grammys musical director, including that year) explains that the duet from that ceremony was destined to work, because they both put the effort in. 'She's a hard worker and wants things just right and so was he. She was willing to do what it took to make sure it [worked]. He respected people who were willing to do the work.'

Prince loved the female voices he grew up listening to – from Betty Davis to Chaka, Joni, Mavis and Dolly – and those who harked back to a golden age before autotune – Mary J Blige, Amy and Beyoncé. He would also while away evenings with friends at Paisley Park by looking up old clips on YouTube and enjoying music documentaries, such as Morgan Neville's *20 Feet From Stardom*, which showcased Judith Hill, a trusted collaborator.

In the latter stages of his career, his mentoring and admiration for talent often gravitated towards those who could be called the Female Prince by music writers. 'He was always looking for other people who were like him,' laughs Fiorillo. 'He was very much interested in [fusion bassist] Esperanza Spalding. Andy Allo looked just like him. She was around for a while and joined the band and I thought *Oh shoot, I think I lost my job*.' (Other female singer-songwriters Prince supported, promoted and advised during the 2010s included Janelle Monáe, Laura Mvula, Lianne La Havas and Alicia Keys.)

His final main touring band was comprised solely of women until he dispensed with 3rdEyeGirl and played solo on piano. Morris Hayes chuckles at the memory of his final two touring incarnations. 'Prince wants an all-girl band. Prince wants a clone band all of him. Just him as clone. He did two. 3rdEyeGirl and instead of many Princes, it's just one.'

Peggy, Susan, Sylvia and Lisa

Of course, Prince didn't just love women, but hired them, promoted them, sang about them endlessly, borrowed their clothes and, on occasion, their perfume. In terms of girlfriends, when he was getting serious about a woman, sometimes there was a determining factor… whether they could sing. The only way he could get closer to them is through music.

Susannah, his long-term girlfriend from 1982–87, sang; Sheila, his on/off long-term musical collaborator and girlfriend, sang and kept rhythm; Jill Jones, another on/off romance from the earlier '80s, sang; mid-'80s ex Sheena Easton sang; first wife Mayte sang and danced. He asked Kim Basinger, who studied ballet from the age of three, to audition dancers for him.

The legion of women for whom he wrote songs is many: from Madonna to Mavis Staples, Bonnie Raitt to Stevie Nicks, Martika to the Bangles' Susanna Hoffs. He may have had romantic designs on some – various interviewees confirm a crush on Hoffs – but not all. He was cagey about that sort of thing. He wouldn't confirm, he wouldn't deny.

If you worked with Prince, and you sang or danced with him, being romantically linked with your boss seemed something of an occupational hazard. Like almost everything else in Princeworld, that was not accidental.

Some who did work at close quarters with him, such as his four female engineers – an unusually high number for artists of that era – were very keen to keep it professional, but as Lisa Chamblee, who worked with him in the '00s, says, so was he.

'He was the most masculine man with feminine energy, but I was very fortunate I didn't have that type of relationship with him. He showed me the respect of an engineer. That's why I had a deeper level [of relationship]. I could tell that he respected me for my passion and I could tell he didn't want to mess that up. He wanted me around because I could help him record and he didn't give that energy.

'The studio is the most intimate place as an artist. They need to feel comfortable. They need to feel protected. They need to feel vulnerable. That's why he liked female energy. We were facilitating music. We weren't in competition with him. We didn't want to be him.'

'He loved what a woman represented,' explains another, Susan Rogers. 'He loved women and he loved them even more with music in them. It's a piece of comfort for him. It really resonated with him. It was probably deeper than music, even spiritually. He definitely connected with the women more so.'

As well as Rogers (1983–87) and Chamblee (2004–06), Peggy McCreary (1982–86) and Sylvia Massy (1990–1993) engineered for Prince. With male colleagues, engineers, producers, guitarists and vocalists, there was always the danger they wanted to be him. 'With women,' says Morris Hayes, who worked with Prince for two decades and even lived across from him, 'it was always another thing. Prince always related well to female energy.' Scottie Baldwin (with two decades service on Prince's sound) points out, not inaccurately, that he produced his biggest hits working with those four female engineers.

The two Eves

Anthony Hamilton, a Grammy-winning soul singer, puts Prince's appeal down to 'just him being a mystery and women are into the mystery of trying to solve things and figure out a man. What puzzle had so many pieces other than Prince? They wanted to understand how this man, who was not so tall and not so big, was so manly? You could tell in his music and in his lyrics, he knew how to treat a woman. He knew how to make an "I love you" sound like you have never heard it before.'

Bevla Reeves, his hair stylist around the *Sign...* era, agrees: 'He was unique that way. He could do anything. There was a part of him that really understood women. He wore women's perfume. He wore the high heels. He was very much in touch with his feminine side and women could relate to that. Women were really attracted to him.'

Morris Hayes, in Prince's band on-and-off for two decades until his death, once house-sat his boss's Beverly Hills pad for a few months. 'In his house, he had this painting called *The Two*

Eves and it was Eve twice and no Adam. That painting was in his house in three different places.'

Mari Maupin, who, as The Golden Hippie, recorded at Paisley Park and went on tour with Prince in 2014, recalls him telling other female staff that 'I never make a decision unless a woman is present.'

Country singer Rissi Palmer was working in retail when she was introduced to Prince, who very quickly found out about her music and asked to hear some of her songs.

'I had been shopping for a record deal for the past five years. I was mostly just writing at the time, and I didn't feel wanted,' Palmer says. Her greatest appreciation was that after five years in an industry where she had felt undervalued, Prince refused to categorise Palmer, telling her: 'For someone like you, don't worry about your country bona fides, worry about the undeniability of the song.' Palmer expands on this, saying 'he really was encouraging about me working out my own voice. He was very interested in "Who is Rissi Palmer? And what does Rissi Palmer have to say?" And that was very important to me. He never told me to worry about "Rissi the *Country* Artist" and to worry more about "Rissi the Artist."

'He was one of the few people who saw me really clearly at that time. He respected female energy, female intuition, female intelligence, and musicality and creativity. I never felt stifled, I never felt objectified – none of that.'

Nandy McClean, a dancer in his mid-'00s troupe, once asked Prince why he surrounded himself with so many female employees, to which he replied 'Because they get me.' Hayes says he was 'tuned to female energy. "If I Was Your Girlfriend" was the perfect example.'

The new 'woman' in Prince's life: Camille

Back in the second half of 1986, the ever-competitive Prince wasn't just having musical differences with his band. He was having musical differences with himself.

Fed up with chasing the shadow of his own stardom and looking to branch out into different areas, he hit upon the wheeze of a new album without the Revolution, under the title and artist name of Camille, a female alter ego. 'He was experimenting,' remembers Susan Rogers. He had previously shocked audiences when wearing women's pants and suspenders onstage for the Dirty Mind tour, but this time he was going to put that same femininity on record.

'With the *Camille* stuff,' recalls engineer Coke Johnson, 'harmonisers were getting really big and he would sing into that in real time and I would split it out in a different octave or different key. He could sing in four or five different octaves so he could reach up there. There wasn't autotune or pitch change back then.'

They would work on the Publison IM90 Infernal Machine together and a set of songs would take shape: 'Rebirth of the Flesh', 'Housequake', 'Strange Relationship', 'Feel U Up', 'Shockadelica', 'Good Love', 'If I Was Your Girlfriend', 'Rock Hard in a Funky Place'...

That closing track would end up on *The Black Album*. 'Feel U Up' and 'Shockadelica' would become B-sides (respectively of 'Partyman' from the *Batman* soundtrack and 'If I Was Your Girlfriend') and 'Good Love' would be given to the *Bright Lights, Big City* soundtrack. Apart from track one, which eventually surfaced on the 2020 super deluxe edition, the rest would surface on the original *Sign...* double album.

In the May 2022 edition of *Mojo*, Jack White suggested that his label Third Man Records would issue a vinyl pressing of *Camille*. The Prince estate has not, at time of writing, backed him up. As with *The Black Album*, bootlegs were common, but physical pressings were rarer. 'Karen [Krattinger] had a copy which she sold for a lot of money,' reveals her friend Robyn Riggs. 'She had the one vinyl copy.'

'Shockadelica' was written from personal animus, at Jesse Johnson's expense, displaying Prince's competitive spirit once more. The previous year, he had been appalled when Minneapolis contemporary Johnson, immortalised on 'Raspberry Beret' as 'Ol' Man Johnson' popped round to discuss his new album.

'When Jesse Johnson came by the house,' laughs Susan Rogers, 'we were working in the studio and he had finished [Johnson's] album *Shockadelica*. We listened to some of it, and Prince said "Where's the song 'Shockadelica'?" He said there's no song [with that name] and Prince laid into him. "What are you doing? All the great albums have a song with the title name." I didn't point out *Rubber Soul* at that point. We took the multi-track tape we had been working on and Prince had me put on fresh tape and he immediately went to work recording a song called "Shockadelica".'

He sent Johnson the cassette a couple of days later, and the song was premiered on Minneapolis station KMOJ. It was a few weeks before Johnson's record, which reached 70 in the charts but sold one million copies, would be released. 'He did the "Camille voice" and he sent me over to Jesse's house with a tape and said, "This is how it's done." This sounds kinda mean-spirited, but competition made him laugh with joy.'

The creativity pouring out of Prince was so strong that he was working at Paisley Park with Mavis Staples, George Clinton and Bonnie Raitt on albums, *Dream Factory* with the Revolution and Eric Leeds and Matt Blistan and, to get past

Warner Brothers, his female alter ego Camille. 'They only wanted one album a year' explains Sunset engineer Coke Johnson, 'and so he was looking to create another artist where he could put his stuff out there under a pseudonym. The grooves were definitely Prince.'

Springing from the rich vein of that creativity was 'If I Was Your Girlfriend'.

'If I Was Your Girlfriend'

On 1981's *Controversy*, Prince didn't just address the rumours swirling around him, but manifested them by putting them to music. Black/white? Gay/straight? Does he believe in God or think he's God? Whether or not a conversation about him was taking place, he would sing about it and kick-start, well, a controversy – a typically Prince-style self-fulfilling prophecy.

On 'If I Was Your Girlfriend', Prince was doing something different, and in an emotionally more mature way than *Dirty Mind's* 'Head' or 'Sister' seven years previously, albeit no less startling. In 1980, he was looking to shock. By 1987, he wanted to share.

He was putting his private conversations with Susannah, or even deeper private thoughts about Susannah, to music. Their relationship was at a crossroads. The song tells us he wants to be able to talk to her with the kind of intimacy she does with her closest female companion – to dress her, to take a bubble bath with her, to go to a movie and cry with her, or to run to her if someone hurt her, even if that someone happened to be him. That kind of closeness. If he was her girlfriend, he asks her to remember to tell her all the things she forgets when she was with him romantically.

Who would enjoy that kind of intimacy and closeness with Susannah Melvoin?

Sometimes Prince's songs are as mysterious as he was. But sometimes figuring out what was on his mind wasn't hard. 'If you want to know me,' he would regularly say in the rare interviews he agreed to, 'listen to my music.'

In October 1986, the man who had grown up with a complicated relationship with his mum (a woman with her own complicated relationship with a twin) had fired the Revolution, featuring Susannah's twin sister and one of his key musical foils Wendy. Susan Rogers, often his only companion in the studio, had said he was missing Wendy & Lisa.

He recorded the song in Sunset's Studio 3 on 2 November 1986.

The song starts unusually, with the sound of the wedding march. Engineer Todd Herreman traces it from a vinyl copy of the BBC Sounds Effects library, while the Prince Vault website claims it as belonging to an album of sound effects by Jac Holzman (the former head of Elektra Records who signed the Doors).

Herreman isn't sure whether 'that kind of sample was an afterthought', but the wedding march sample was recorded in November after Prince's hymn to commitment, 'Forever in My Life', in August.

'If I Was Your Girlfriend', like 'The Ballad of Dorothy Parker', is regarded as a song that is sui generis to Prince. The dark brooding soundscape with the playful lyrics. A song freighted with mystery but letting daylight into Prince's most innermost thoughts. His instinctive understanding of gender and blurring of genre. A vulnerable lead vocal, female conversational skits, deep male background vocals, all from the same person.

The tone of the later song is brooding, dark, melancholy.

Patrice Rushen calls it 'multi-layered. That's the best way to describe his music.' To different ears, the song means different things. To Hayes, a keyboard player, the Fairlight with 'all of those sounds … made that song so funky'.

The R&B girl group TLC took the song somewhere else with their version on their 1993 album, *Crazy Sexy Cool*. Eric 'Vietnam' Sadler, of Public Enemy's producers The Bomb Squad, is another admirer because of the way Prince sequenced it. '"If I Was Your Girlfriend" reminded me of earlier stuff he had done. I liked a lot of stuff on it [*Sign…*] for different reasons. We were making albums. Side A, Side B, what's going to flow to it. That's what interested me, especially having four sides. You don't just listen, you're looking, as a teacher.'

This deeply unusual recording would lead to a commercial misstep, one of many around that era. Black radio, already playing 'Housequake' ahead of release, had been pushing for it to be a single. Others favoured the ballad 'Adore'. 'U Got the Look', which would be the third single, was the double album's most obviously commercial track.

Prince, his label and his closest confidants all decided to follow the title track with 'If I Was Your Girlfriend' as a second single when Warners, unusually, came to Sunset to hear the album. 'I affirmed the choice,' admits Susan Rogers. 'He asked me in front of these record executives and I said "Oh yeah! I have never heard a man say that to a woman" and I was wrong. It shouldn't have been a single.'

Alan Leeds was less committed to the choice. 'In retrospect, I suppose it was a mistake and I knew it was a mistake at the time.' For him, the struggle was in 'getting pop radio to figure it out'. 'I think we liked it somehow,' adds Warners representative Lenny Waronker. 'If there was something we respected, we stood up for it. Now it's much more difficult to go against the grain.'

The single only reached number 67 on the Billboard Hot 100. The first single (the title track) and third single 'U Got the Look' reached 3 and 2 respectively. Prince would perform 'If I Was Your Girlfriend' intermittently over the years, although it was played at his final full show in Atlanta on 14 April 2016.

In retrospect, for those who wanted to know what was going on in Prince's heart and brain four months before *Sign...* was released, this piece of music is as good as it gets.

If I actually was your girlfriend

This song might offer clues, but what was it like being Prince's girlfriend?

Just as with musicians, when it came to love interests, Prince always seemed to have a Plan B. It's fair to say that if his life was made into a future movie (beyond the narratives he controlled like *Purple Rain*), then there would be more than one female romantic lead. Detailing the start and end of each of Prince's relationships will always be a little fuzzy. He preferred things that way.

Alan Leeds, who knew Prince better than most, describes him as 'a man who enjoyed the idea of having options. The sense of entitlement of a rock star provides options. My girlfriends wouldn't have tolerated it. He [often] had two [concurrent] girlfriends, and relationships with him were very, very similar. He cared about them equally and each of them had an influence on them. Each of them played a role in his life that was unique.'

Professionally, Prince loved and promoted women. For instance, early appearances on the cover of *Rolling Stone* magazine saw Prince joined by his then girlfriend Vanity in 1983 and, three years later, bandmates Wendy & Lisa. Personally, it was the same. 'Always liked the ladies,' laughs his cousin, Charles 'Chazz' Smith, who recalls Loretta Pruitt, a girlfriend from Century High School, and Kim Upsher.

Tonjia Lowe was a friend from Bryant Junior High who remembers Prince in his early teens writing letters to his eighth-grade girlfriend, Marcie Dixon. 'He always dressed nice, even in high school. He seemed the same to me even after fame – always quiet, always focused. I can't say that he changed.' Mi-Ling Stone Poole, who dated Prince in the early '80s, recalls that 'in his early days, he liked curvy girls, black girls, then Kim Upsher'. Kim Upsher, followed by Susan Moonsie, were early but, by common consent, reasonably serious girlfriends.

The quiet man wearing women's suspenders on the cover of his 1980 record *Dirty Mind* would arouse curiosity from the opposite sex in all forms.

Prince loved women and the feeling was mutual. 'He was always obsessed with females,' reflects Alan Leeds. 'And the whole androgynous thing writing songs about wanting to pick out their clothes, there was a feminine side of him that was very profound.'

Romantically, there were many reasons why Prince appealed to women. Being a millionaire rock star who could fly them first class halfway across the world to join him backstage for dinner whipped up by his private chef or knock up a song about them in a few hours probably didn't hurt. Neither did 10,000 voices screaming along to his music in a stadium, as band and staff cater to his every whim. Scratch the surface, though, and there was something deeper.

The low voice. The big brown eyes. The reluctance to make eye contact drawing them in. The comfort around them, drawn from a mother with a twin sister, from sisters, from female bandmates and from girlfriends from the age of fourteen.

He also had the ability to go right to the heart of emotion in song.

The softly spoken voice cultivated a mystery, says his assistant in the late '80s, Therese Stoulil. 'I can't tell you how much that helped Prince. I could get anybody in the world except the Pope on the phone for him because everybody – everybody! – thought he was so mysterious.'

Prince was often inscrutable, a puzzle that his nearest and dearest couldn't solve. Tonjia Lowe was in the same Bryant Junior High class as Prince. 'He was always private, even in school. People have asked me if he had a girlfriend and, even then, I didn't know.'

'Most women weren't sure [whether] he was gay,' says an ex from 1979-80, Mi-Long Stone Poole. 'There was this feminine character. He was pretty. He had this different, other-worldly energy. He was just mysterious. You could tell that he was deeper than what he was. He was definitely awkward. The positive side was that he listened and was interested in women. He drew from them – their energy, their attitudes. He was a great talker, especially on the phone.'

As his career blossomed, it was perhaps inevitable that Prince would blur the personal and professional. Vanity 6 was not his first attempt to do so. An early attempt to form a girl band, says Stone Poole, 'didn't work out because the girls didn't have the dedication'.

By the time the Time were in full swing and Prince felt it was time for another attempt at a girl band, with Moonsie aged sixteen and Brenda Bennett carrying out Prince's orders, a new member was not auditioned so much as folded into the group by Prince: his new girlfriend, Denise Matthews, whom he would name Vanity, as well as rebadging the group in her name.

Allen Beaulieu, Prince's friend and the man who shot the *Dirty Mind* and *Controversy* sleeves, describes Prince's relationship status with the group as 'Susan at the beginning and Denise at the end'. Denise was one of Prince's most intense relationships to that point. 'They were really close,' says Beaulieu of her appeal. 'She had this thing that Marilyn Monroe must have had – animal magnetism. I took her to lunch one time and, every corner, the guys would just whistle, left and right, at her. She was supposed to be in *Purple Rain* and he wouldn't pay any money. Prince didn't know how it was going to do. If Prince had told her "I am going to be No 1 for ten weeks", she would have done it. Vanity had other opportunities.' She would be replaced by Patricia 'Apollonia' Kotero, with the band, who never released subsequent records, renamed as Apollonia 6.

Vanity and Prince, continues the photographer, 'had something together that I can't even explain. I don't think they could live without each other to tell you the truth, but they ended up having to do that because of life and what goes on. If she'd been a regular girl and him a regular guy, they'd have been together now.'

'Susan remained very good friends with him,' remembers Muriel Hodler-Hamilton, who worked on the Triple Threat tour with Vanity 6 and the Time. 'She's a lovely person. Very private. Prince seemed to be pretty active in terms of dating. I don't know how Susan felt about it. She had more of a business head.'

Bill Reeves, the tour manager for the second part of Triple Threat, shrugged it off. 'It's the road. In terms of romantic entanglements, all sorts of crazy stuff happens. Who's creeping around hotel rooms after midnight – that's just life on the road. In those days, the average tour was three months and you just live in this little bubble. As will happen with anything, alliances and romantic entanglements ensue and blossom and fade away. You just roll with it. That's the life.'

Prince had two girlfriends in Vanity 6, but this was often a default setting. By the time of the *Sign...* era, his relationships with Susannah Melvoin and Sheila Escovedo were not as exclusive as either of them might have liked. This pattern continued throughout his career with Carmen Electra and Mayte Garcia in the '90s and a series of more casual relationships. 'There was a lot of wannabe Fela in Prince,' adds former manager Alan Leeds (referencing the legendary Afrobeat musician Fela Kuti who married 27 women) 'in the sense that he had [the] vision and idea where he had this harem of girlfriends. This week it would be Susannah, this week it would be Sheila. He was hoping that they would both accept and tolerate each other. He was doing that on the *1999* tour with Susan Moonsie and Vanity and Jill Jones. He had a history of doing the same thing. "Who the hell cares?" That's my opinion.'

Another mid-'80s girlfriend, Maneca Lightner, would see Vanity 'in passing' and was familiar with the rumour that 'she broke his heart but that's not something he told me. No. He would not discuss.' They split before Prince worked with Susan Rogers, but that rumour reached the engineer too. 'It's said by many Vanity was the love of his life.'

Purple Rain director Albert Magnoli sensed a reluctance from her to accept what would have been her biggest role to date. 'When Vanity was first attached to the project, she said she had been offered to play Mary Magdalene for [Martin Scorsese's] *The Last Temptation of Christ*. [The part would ultimately go to Barbara Hershey.] She already had one foot out the door. She was in a dispute with Prince about almost everything.'

Although the split was said to hurt Prince, Vanity did not disappear from his life. Like Prince, in later life she became outspoken about faith – in her case, evangelical Christian.

'Don't fly her in'

While Prince was respectful when it came to courtship, when it came to being a one-woman man, forget it. If you dated Prince and felt he was disrespectful to you, your only coping strategy was one involving exit.

By the mid-'80s, Susannah was established as Prince's live-in girlfriend, but others were on the scene such as *Playboy* model Devin DeVasquez and Lightner, another model from the cover of the Madhouse records. 'He had a lot of people around him who were "yes people",' reflects Lightner, 'and I'm amazed that outside of the women he dated – Vanity, Jill Jones – the other women were at his beck and call. I was definitely not a "yes person". [Nor, by all accounts, were Matthews or Jones.] The only thing I will say is when he did call, I would make that time for him. I would do my own thing when he wasn't around. He had a bad habit of calling me in the wee hours – it could be one, or two, or three in the morning. It was usually because he wanted to call me. It was always loose, never consistent. I saw him every week or every month.'

Just as Sheila (and others) were on the scene when he was living with Susannah around the *Sign...* era, and Susan and Denise Matthews overlapped as girlfriends, there was something of a pattern. Kara Young, the model in the 'Kiss' video, dated him casually between 1986 and 1987. 'Of course I was inspired. He was really fun. I had never met anybody like that, I still haven't. He would act really shy, but he isn't like that. I liked the way he acted towards me. We never ever talked about other people. He never said "Do you have a boyfriend?" and I never said "Do you have a girlfriend?".'

'For him to be in the position that he was, this man who could have any women that he wanted, he still treated me as special,' adds Lightner. 'I hear different stories from different women but it wasn't what I experienced.' He definitely compartmentalised. 'When I was dating Prince, I didn't get to hang out with anybody. He always kept me separated from everyone. I know why now! I didn't really care at the time.'

This was also the case in the early '90s with both his protege, Carmen Electra, and the dancer who would become his first wife, Mayte Garcia. As production manager at Paisley Park, Skip Johnson worked with Prince in the mid-'90s, when he was two-timing Electra and Garcia. 'One of the European tours we did, Carmen opened the show and Mayte was a dancer in Prince's band and those of us on the side would see who's going to go home [with him]. One of them would get in the car and the other would look devastated.'

Prince would also use distraction, according to his assistant at the time, Therese Stoulil. 'I remember little Carmen coming into the office and she was going to go to the state fair with Michelle [Schwartzbauer, his then housekeeper]. Prince [had told us] some other girl is flying in. Prince told her "I think you would have fun at the state fair".'

When asked if he saw Prince marrying Mayte, Johnson is unequivocal. 'Never. Carmen was model-esque. I didn't see that in Mayte. She was like the girl next door. But maybe that's what he saw in her.'

One of those on security, Harlan 'Hucky' Austin, summarises Prince's success with the opposite sex beyond his rock star status. 'Talented. Would draw you in. Comfortable around them [women]. Prince treated women very well. I know there are stories which say something different. Prince was fair. He wasn't selfish, he would just be focussed on his music. He treated women nicely. Many others make the same claim.' Others, particularly those who value exclusive relationships, disagree. One of those was a girlfriend from the early '90s, model Robin Power Royal. 'I don't see myself as one of the many Prince has dated. I think of myself as one of the few, because if you think of the women in the world who wanted to be with Prince...' She remains upset about his lack of faithfulness. 'Prince was a child of God, but still a man – and a man who had a lot of power over women and frequently wielded that power for his own pleasures.'

'I think he did realise his own power with women,' says personal assistant (but not ex) Karen Krattinger. 'He was the furthest thing from gay and he was the most beautiful man I have ever seen.'

Sometimes, if you worked for Prince, detective work was required. As another colleague, assistant Therese Stoulil, recalls, Prince might show her a picture of a model in a magazine.

'I would have all the model agencies on speed dial. "This is a beautiful blonde. She's on the cover with a tiger. It's for *La Paris*." And they would say "That's so and so" and I would always put the phone call through. The next thing I knew [it was] "Can you get her on the next flight here?"'

Stoulil ascribes to him the 'you will never guess who I talked to' factor. 'Everybody wanted to speak with him. Nobody would not take a phone call from Prince. He was always charming. Everybody was blown away by him. I don't remember anybody saying no.'

Stoulil nearly gave him a final no herself in the run-up to his 1996 wedding with Mayte Garcia.

'It got crazy. I was trying to deal with his needs and Mayte is calling me every ten minutes. "I just got pulled over by the Chanhassen police [because] my windows are too dark." Her mother started calling me every ten minutes.'

After suggesting a wedding coordinator to Mayte, she also had to field phone calls from the groom, who of course was also her boss.

"'Can you call my mom and tell her she's not invited to the wedding?"

'I made every excuse and apologised. "It's such a small affair."

'Ten days later, he called me and asked me now to invite her.

"'Call your own mom. I'm done!"'

Sometimes, says Sal Greco, who worked in the early days setting up Paisley Park in 1987, it was knowing what not to do. 'I learned from the women flying from Minneapolis. Don't fly her *in*.' In other words, if he had made plans to spend the weekend in his hometown with one girlfriend, staff would be tasked to dissuade another who had made plans to see him.

Sotera Tschetter worked through a few drafts with Prince before alighting on his distinctive logo. 'In Prince's life, he always had a back-up person. If you don't succeed, there's always someone to clean up. And you see that with his girlfriends and his wives.' Sylvia Massy, the engineer on *Diamonds and Pearls*, found girlfriends could be a distraction. 'He *loved* women. He loved to be around women. He might even feel it was easier to work with a woman for many reasons. Guys or girls … we were all terrified.

'He would disappear. He had two limos outside. There might be girls waiting in those limos and [they would] leave the country and go to France. Management would call me every once in a while and say "Prince is in London. You can go home now." It was very difficult working for him.' The trick for staff, says Michelle Schwartzbauer, his housekeeper in the late '80s, was keeping schtum. 'The security guys knew when the social stuff happened. [Prince] was discreet when he wanted to be.' And so was she – 'which is why I was there eight years'.

The cliche about him being married to his music persisted because of his schedule. 'He wasn't this playboy,' argues his keyboard tech in the '80s, David Rule. 'He's all about the work. That guy worked twenty-six hours a day. He would do a show, [then] watch videos of the show to go through, and soundchecks for two and a half hours a day.' Others disagree, saying he *was* a playboy. 'It was *a lot*,' recalls publicist Robyn Riggs. 'People [meaning media] are always going to keep an eye on that. Sometimes it was just a friendship or a musical collaboration and they would make a conclusion.' He would enjoy that, as it was based on his public persona. 'People never got that close to him unless he wanted them to. He had a lot of security.'

For male colleagues, Prince's love life presented other challenges. Sal Greco suggests there should have been a plaque on the studio wall: Thou Shalt Not Check Out Thy Boss's Girlfriends.

'There was one woman he was dating who had one outfit on that was completely see-through. It was very hard to look at without staring. I had to send her home. How long can you look at the floor?'

'For years,' adds Danny Soltys, there in the early days of Paisley Park, '[us] young guys had to be careful where our eyes went.'

The overlap for Prince's serious girlfriends got a little too blurred for the staff's liking. It seems that – as well as Susan and Denise in the same band, and Susannah and Sheila around the *Sign* era, and singer/poet Ingrid Chavez, actors Troy Byer and Sherilyn Fenn shortly after that, and Carmen Electra and Mayte in the early-to-mid-'90s, at the same time as those women, there were others. Plenty of others.

'He would fly Carmen to shoot a video and have some other girl come in,' Soltys remembers. 'He was just doing what he was, being a rock star.'

Not all staff appreciated the revolving door of love interests. Bevla Reeves, who was on hair and make-up duty during the *Sign* era, says 'I could talk about what I saw … I feel he was a womaniser. I was not his type so I didn't have to worry.' On the *Lovesexy* tour, 'he would preach each night about his religion and that would drag out the shows. It was always bizarre. We were asking "What is happening to him?" He was exploring Jehovah's Witnesses, and that was in conflict with what we knew him to be with all the women around.'

'He definitely had a type,' says Mi-Long Stone Poole, 'dark hair, light skin.' When Prince married Mayte on Valentine's Day 1996, one of Stone Poole's girlfriends told her that he'd 'married a girl that looks just like you'.

Another model brunette girlfriend, Maneca Lightner, says this evolved. 'At first I thought he had a type which was dark hair and dark eyes, but he dated women who didn't fit that look as well.' 'The Beautiful Ones', where he namechecks Kim Upsher and references a Serena Williams lookalike he dated in his teens, suggests the myth around only having white girlfriends was just that – a myth.

Taking Prince to a place he called home was also attractive to him, as Playboy model Devin DeVasquez remembers. 'I told him I was from [Baton Rouge] Louisiana. All of a sudden, his whole demeanour changed. "My father is from Louisiana. Do you know where Cotton Port is?"'

Many figures from show business are attracted to one another, but Prince's shyness seemed to inform the way he approached women, as DeVasquez recalls. 'Playboy thought it would be nice if I got a photo of us and he said "I'm sorry, I don't like to take photos". He invited me to Sheila E's birthday party and I responded: "I'm sorry, I have to go to a party to meet Hugh Hefner." What a week I was having! Very politely, I said sorry. He says "Oh." Before I left, he got Wally [Safford, bodyguard] to tell me "Prince would like to see you alone, would you mind?" I went to see him. He was like a different person. He was waiting for me at the door with a chocolate chip cookie.'

The wooing accelerated late 1984 via telephone. 'Back in Chicago, the day after Christmas, Prince called me at two in the morning and that's when we began our relationship. I think what bonded us was his father being from Louisiana. I wasn't looking for anything from him except a photo which I never got.'

Prince and Kim

One relationship at the turn of the '90s was less publicised, but, say several close to Prince at the time, a serious one. It started, like many, at work. He had been on the set of Tim Burton's Warner Brothers 1989 big budget imagining of DC Comics' *Batman* and met the cast before completing an album of music for the film. Back home, he asked Therese Stoulil to send the fruits of his labours to the movie's Batman, Joker and Vicki Vale.

'I FedExed cassettes to Jack Nicholson, Michael Keaton and Kim Basinger. Michael didn't get back, Jack asked for money because we sampled him and Kim called the office to thank him. I put her through to his office. They had a very short conversation.'

On hanging up, Prince told his assistant, 'she's coming to Minneapolis for a visit – get a really nice hotel room'. Stoulil booked the best suite at the city's Sofitel, and she and his valet

Robbie Paster 'pfouffed it', adding flowers, candles and cushions for maximum fanciness. It wasn't necessary.

'She goes home with him that night and never set foot in the hotel. Next thing I know, I remember coming in of a morning, she had her car, a peach Mercedes, parked on the drive. All of a sudden, all her stuff arrived.'

Basinger soon became part of the furniture – to the extent she thought about choosing it. She made Minneapolis her base. She called Prince's housekeeper Michelle Schwartzbauer 'sweetie', had her assistant flown over to field calls from the likes of Hollywood studio head Jeffrey Katzenberg and, as engineer Tom Garneau recalls, 'drank rum and coke [and] made us popcorn and sweet potato pie'.

Before too long, the actress was also joining Prince in another of his love languages: pranking staff.

Prince had previously arranged a *Batman* screening for his team. 'The next day,' Garneau remembers, 'he asked me if I'd gone to the movie and what did I think. "The second Kim Basinger walked on the screen, the movie worked for me." "Oh, really!" Little did I know he was dating her already. Fast forward... Kim had been in town a while hanging out. Shortly after, Prince pages "Tom, Studio A". I walk in the control room and Kim is ripping 12" pieces of gaffer tape off the roll and sticking them to the SSL console. I say:

"What's up?"

"Tom, Kim wants you to tape her."

'I say "Up!?" quizzically. Kim smirks, all coy, and nods in the affirmative. I knew then they were winding me up. I said "Oh! You guys" and spun on my heels and left to them laughing.'

Therese Stoulil was also teased, because of a 15–20-minute film called *Hard Life* that Kim, Prince and Therese all appeared in together.

'He called me in the studio one day. He and Kim are sitting so close together it's become one person. "Have a seat."

Uh-oh... what's up?

Soon she knew, when the film on screen displayed her hair in less than flattering condition.

'Up on the TV screen, I can tell it's *Hard Life*. They both started laughing.'

Her hair had been caught in the rain and Kim exclaimed: 'Oh honey, your hair...'

'I looked like I was in Poison. They looked like two kids. "Can I go now?"'

There were light-hearted moments but anyone who wanted to be with Prince had to manage his main focus: work. Stoulil, who joined Prince's payroll just as he and Susannah were breaking up, was a fan of Kim's. 'She was the nicest person on the planet. Everybody loved her. She went out that Christmas [1989] and bought us all presents [Stoulil received a perfume decanter]. Very beautiful, very sweet. I don't think, in ten years, I had ever seen Prince happier. They would go shopping together. Prince never went out shopping. They would stop in all the little shops. It was actually very adorable. It looked like a couple of teenagers in love. They were just taken with each other. It was fabulous.'

Prince's then make-up artist Terra Hinrichs agrees that Kim 'was madly in love with him. I couldn't figure it out. She is stunning.'

Kim and Prince's most notorious collaboration was a remix of the ballad from the Batman soundtrack, 'Scandalous'. Sal Greco walked into the Paisley Park's Studio B a few days later and had to clean up the mixing desk as the feeds weren't working. 'We were trying to guess what it was. It might be, like, Jägermeister.' Then it occurred to them. 'Honey. Squirt bottle. Prince had blown one of the speakers.' The honey bottle was not credited on the 19-minute late-night remix 'The Scandalous Sex Suite', but the pair had worked together, leaving a trail of sticky destruction on the mixing desk.

Because Kim wanted to be with Prince, and he wanted to be working, he got one of Hollywood's then most in-demand actresses working too – and not just on remixes of his songs. 'He had put her in charge of recording sexy women singers,' recalls Hinrichs. 'Being out of *9½ Weeks*, I'm looking at her thinking, *You're insanely gorgeous*. She seemed almost trying too hard. She's telling these girls to "be nasty" and it seemed out of character for her. She was crazy about him. I loved Kim.'

The relationship was intense. 'I think she got serious with him,' says Danny Soltys, who helped build up Paisley Park in its early days. 'She was looking at a property.'

'Back in the late '80s and early '90s, Chanhassen was still a little small town,' adds Therese Stoulil. 'I remember having a long conversation with her [where she said] "I just want this beautiful farmhouse". She just loved the whole landscape.'

But while Basinger may have envisaged a life with Prince, he was making other plans. Not for the first time, work seems to have got in the way. 'We had a photoshoot,' says Soltys, 'and she was directing it. I could tell it was not rubbing him right.'

Stoulil says they split up because 'things were promised. Things didn't happen. I remember it.' The farmhouse and domesticity Basinger had envisaged in Minneapolis was not that espoused by Prince. 'We didn't see Kim around anymore much after that,' adds Soltys.

'Everybody wants to be closer to the sun,' says Craig Rice, one of Prince's key lieutenants in the early '90s. 'Kim is one of the few people that doesn't talk about him. The females have a different relationship with him, and he with them.' Because of the need of both for privacy, and how much of it took place in Minneapolis, the beginning and end of a relationship between two of the most famous people in entertainment passed without too much comment in the press.

Elisa Fiorillo had her second album produced at Paisley in 1990 by Ricky Peterson when Prince took a professional and then romantic interest. 'We were very good friends and it turned into something else which was funny for me.' Her understanding of Prince's split with Kim Basinger 'was that he didn't like that she drank'.

Fiorillo listened with interest to a podcast interview on Podcastjuice.net with Prince protégé, singer and rapper Robin Power Royal, where she discussed an affair while Prince was supposedly with Kim.

'Listening to Robin Power,' Fiorillo says, 'I was cracking up because I didn't think there was anything between them. I was so gullible and now I know she was with him. That man got around, didn't he?'

Fiorillo dated Prince between 1989 and 1991, but the lack of exclusivity eventually wore her down. 'I felt very loved, but I felt I wasn't the only one and I couldn't do that. I grew up in an Italian family and my brothers and my dad were very much ladies' men and that's the first thing I'm not attracted to in a man.'

Prince, not yet 31, would confuse her with strange statements. 'At this point, he felt like this old wise man. I was scared of some of the things he would say to me. "You wanna move to Japan and get out of music and be the mother to my son and make my son an emperor?" I'm like "What?!" I'm hearing this at two-thirty in the morning.

'Every time I would say "I want you to meet my mum or brothers", he would say "I don't meet family".'

Prince also famously didn't celebrate birthdays as he didn't believe in time. He would call time 'a trick' on the Rave Un2 the Year 2000 DVD and claimed he only had one birthday (the one on the day he was born), explaining to Dutch interviewer Ivo Niehe in 1999 that the refusal to recognise time was why he looks so young.

When asked if he was a considerate boyfriend, Fiorillo notes that everything 'was always on his time – the time that he didn't believe in! He was very gentle, he was very sweet, [but] it took a good solid year before he would call me his girlfriend. "I liked the fact that nobody would know that you would be my girlfriend." That's how he [dated] all the people.'

Fiorillo recalls the 'one arriving in Minneapolis as another leaves' principle of girlfriends all too well. 'I remember leaving and I saw Susannah Hoffs coming in. One time I was in LA and I was hiding and Sheena Easton came in. I saw those two – I'm sure there were others. Coming back [in the 2010s] being his bandmate, I got to see all the girls coming in and out. I got to see it at rehearsals ... I was right!'

While working, Prince was discreet. 'He never let on to anyone in the band there was more than a friendship. He enjoyed beautiful people and talented people and he loved young energy. We met Ana Moura and she came around, as well as Misty Copeland. There was another girl that had a deal, Bria [Valente]. She disappeared.'

Robin Power Royal dated Prince for three years in the early '90s and regards him as 'disrespectful to a lot of women. When I met Prince, he was with Kim Basinger, he was with Anna Fantastic [real name Garcia; the surname 'Fantastic' was a choice of Prince's]. He was buying her a pink cashmere coat, there's her thinking she's his girlfriend [but] he's with me, and Kim Basinger is also his girlfriend. Anna didn't know about me, Kim didn't know about me, but I knew about them.

'It was exciting and it was amazing because Prince was the most intimate romantic man I have ever met. Inside the bedroom and outside the bedroom, Prince loved to kiss. Most women who want an intimate connection with another human being love to kiss. Not only does it release endorphins, it feels like they're touching my spirit. Prince liked to kiss romantically anywhere. He would leave messages and kisses and run baths. Because of Prince's size and stature, it wasn't very animalistic. It was more feminine-based. The female essence of Prince was more present.

'Prince was very masculine outside the bedroom, more feminine inside but Prince was competitive with women. His feminine essence was more competitive to be honest.'

Robin Power cut ties 'when he started to step over boundaries with women that I had introduced him to. That was a borderline that I couldn't cross.'

Kara Young, the model he kisses in the 'Kiss' video and who had a less serious relationship with Prince, details his courtship routine. 'He was mysterious. He sent my agent a letter and, of course, she opened it. A proper piece of paper with a PRN heading. [Just] "2", "U" and "eye". Brevity. He signed off "PRN" [Prince Rogers Nelson].' He would send her messages like 'I'm pining for you, my stomach hurts', which she calls 'the cutest.'

Post-it notes in the shape of love hearts were not unusual.

He would also tweak his girlfriends' taste in music. Young told him she loved Heatwave's ballad 'Always and Forever'. She soon regretted the conversation.

'Do you hear that they're off-key?'

'I love this song.'

'It's so bad. They're so off-key. How can you not hear it?'

'Now it's all I can hear! He ruined that song for me.'

Prince would often, but not always, stay on good terms

with his exes. As well as attending Vanity's funeral shortly before his death, he also hired Fiorillo as a backing singer with Shelby J and Liv Warfield. 'I had a beautiful experience,' says Fiorillo now, 'but the best experience of it all was that, after twenty years, [it was] as if nothing ever happened and we never left each other and he felt so comfortable with me and I felt comfortable with him.'

Fiorillo echoes Maneca Lightner's sentiments, perhaps another reason both stayed in his life for years rather than months. 'I was around him enough to see all the "yes people". I remember saying to him "Why does everybody kiss your butt?". Later in his life, I think he asked me to sing not just because he liked my voice but because I could be trusted.'

His two wives

Prince married twice – to dancer Mayte Garcia, and Manuela Testolini in 2001.

He did not broadcast personal details, even to his inner circle. Mayte was a dancer with Puerto Rican parents. In 1990, her mother persuaded Prince to watch a video tape of her dancing. Ten minutes later, she was invited backstage and they kept in touch. Robin Power Royal claims she advised Prince to hire her based on watching the tape together while in Spain during 1990's Nude tour. 'Mayte's mother gave Prince a VHS tape and Prince put the tape in and said "Look at this girl. What should I do?" "Put her in your band."'

Two years later, Mayte was invited to become part of his 1992 Diamonds and Pearls tour. They did not become intimate until she was nineteen. They married in 1996 and split in 2000. Prince bought her and her family a house in Spain while staying in Minneapolis.

In 2001, Prince married Manuela Testolini but their relationship was pretty private. She would go on to work for his charity, Love 4 One Another.

Nandy McClean, who danced with her sister Maya as part of the Twinz in Prince's '00s entourage, once saw Manuela backstage in Minneapolis. 'I didn't know who she was and I didn't know anything about Prince's personal life. She said to Maya "I'm the wife" and Maya goes "Whose wife?".'

Sam Jennings who ran Prince's online business around that time would see how music would often take first place in Prince's life. Music, Jennings argues, is 'what he wanted to do all the time. As a partner, you'd have to be comfortable with coming second. It was a challenge for a lot of people.'

Morris Hayes, Prince's musical consiglierie of two decades, was introduced to Manuela by Prince before the boss started dating her. 'Manuela was much more reserved. Prince was trying to set me up with her. He brought her on stage which she reluctantly did and then he said, "What's your name? When I give you your cue, I want you to do your thing, you ready?"... "Everybody, Mr. Hayes' new wife!" It was like a joke. Literally a lot of people thought I had married this girl. She wanted to be behind the scenes.'

Like keyboard player Hayes, front of house sound engineer Scottie Baldwin worked with Prince for two decades. 'Any woman in his life was only a mistress to music. Music was his real partner. Manuela ended up being a brain and someone who could be a business partner in a lot of ways. They all had their roles. She was a real partner and challenged him on things.'

They split in 2007.

Matt Fink calls Manuela and Mayte 'both very kind women, generous people. Like Susannah. He always picked good women but for whatever reason he couldn't commit. I'm not sure what that was, or why. Maybe due to not having the best example set for him by his parents and their relationships.'

Relationship status: it's complicated

Such was his devotion to his art, Prince had two dancers he called Diamond and Pearl. One of those, Lori Werner, dated Prince through the period of the 1991 album and world tour of that name – before, and then during, the time he and Mayte became an item. Pearl – aka Robia Scott – had a platonic relationship with her boss. The audience didn't know this and nor would they. 'He liked that,' Scott says of the uncertainty. 'He loved in interviews when we were coy. He didn't want us to say "That's not happening". He wanted to play that cat-and-mouse game. He's all about mystery … He had this mysterious way about him, a flirty way.'

Scott says there was never any romantic developments with her, unlike the relationships he had with Lori and Mayte. 'With him? Never. He had some things going on with some of the other girls. I think that was why we got on. There was always flirtation and that was always his persona and you always feel like that, but that was one of the reasons we had such a cool thing. I never got into a situation.'

Although he was respectful of the talents of many women, Scott adds that he did not always show the same consideration to their emotions. 'He wanted the women around him to look like superstars. I have always been more kind of a jeans girl and he didn't like that. I got sent back to the hotel because I was dressed too casually. He doesn't tell you. The band manager tells you. I'm not the kind of girl who will go on a 13-hour plane ride in full make-up. I never saw him in something other than his finest.'

Nandy McClean remembers attending the premiere of *The Bourne Ultimatum* in London with her sister Maya. 'When he got out the limo, he grabbed me and Maya's hands.' As there had been no romantic intimations with either sister, her first instinct on Prince holding each of them by the hand was '"What are you doing? This is new." I didn't pull away – there was a "what's going on?" moment. He took the reins and did what he wanted.' This led not to any kind of a relationship, but more headlines about Prince dating his two dancers in the London press – just the attention he'd had in mind.

If this sounds disturbing, or a MeToo moment, McClean is very quick to dispel this. 'He was definitely like a host and gracious and making sure you're eating and getting a ride home. He was always hosting people like he does on stage.' He seems to have seen the opposite ladykiller perception of him as part of how the press depicted him.

Raised by parents originally from Louisiana, his inclination towards old-fashioned courtship is often referenced. None of his female engineers – Peggy McCreary, Susan Rogers, Sylvia Massy and Lisa Chamblee, those who spent the most time with him outside of his wives and girlfriends, in some cases probably more time – reported an issue. 'He was very respectful,' recalls Chamblee. 'That's why I am so happy that we had a working relationship. He was my client.'

Bassist Nik West, with whom Prince had informal discussions about being part of 3rdEyeGirl before Ida Nielsen was hired, details a flirtation that didn't turn into dating but reflects how Prince could talk to women. 'I never felt uncomfortable, some sort of thing brewing in the air … It wasn't like this brother-sister [thing]. It was flirtatious in 2016. Prior to that [when she jammed for him, it was] "Let's get this going", but when I started being myself, I think he felt comfortable doing the flirting.

It wasn't anything like "Will you be my girlfriend?" [It was more] "Oh, we have got to look good together." Nothing happened. He was very respectful. Playful. Nonchalant.

'I feel like he wanted people to feel comfortable around him. It seemed like that's what he was trying to do. If someone was nervous, he would say "Let's play ping pong". I feel like he would purposefully try to make people feel comfortable, make sure their guard was down.'

What he wasn't, says almost every interviewee, was inappropriate.

'What I thought about,' says Lisa Janzen who worked for his management in the *Sign...* era, 'is how he never managed to get any of the girls pregnant. It still stuns me that there aren't extra babies out there. He pretty much held the line about being a decent person through his whole career. I never heard any bad Prince stories.'

In the '90s, Prince became friendly with Les Garland (head of MTV and then The Box) and they would party in Miami together. 'I remember four lovely women leaving a nightclub at two in the morning and he couldn't have been nicer. I think we gave them a ride to whatever club they were going to. He would do things like that, which was nothing other than him enjoying his life and being Prince. There was nothing skulduggerous about it.'

'Many women that dated him were protective of him,' agrees Terra Hinrichs. 'I never heard a horror story apart from Sinead.' Sinead was Sinead O'Connor who accused Prince in her memoirs of having been physically abusive to her at his house. Terra Hinrichs did hair and make-up for both. 'Sinead didn't want anything to do with him romantically. She called me that night and that's the first time I heard of him doing drugs. She was really scared. That's a real story.'

They didn't get on. Sinead was managed by Steve Fargnoli, who had been let go by Prince. The singer for whom Prince wrote 'Nothing Compares 2 U', Paul Peterson, recalls how unhappy this version made him. 'Prince couldn't be happy about Sinead O'Connor making it a global hit.

"'It should have been me. It could have been me."

'I said, "She made it such an international smash and I'm happy for you. You must like that cheque."

"It's not about the money."'

'We had a disagreement and it got a bit physical between the two of us,' O'Connor detailed in her book, *Rememberings*. She claims Prince suggested a pillow fight where a hard object was hidden in his pillow. 'And it was quite scary for me 'cause I was young ['Nothing Compares 2 U' was released in January 1990, the month after her twenty-fourth birthday] and I didn't really know where I was.' O'Connor, who called Prince 'a violent abuser of women', added in a 2021 *New York Times* interview: 'He took me to the house and he started telling me that I mustn't swear in my interviews and I must talk like this and talk like that. Of course, being Irish, I told him how he could take a long walk down a short pier. And that didn't go down very well, and it all descended from there.' In the *Daily Mirror* in 2007, she said: 'He can pack a punch. A few blows were exchanged. All I could do was spit. I spat on him quite a bit.'

Hinrichs, who worked with both, was shocked to read of prescription drugs on his passing and O'Connor's allegations around his drug use. 'That blew my mind because that wasn't the man I knew.' Hinrichs calls him 'very proper'.

'I got stuck with Sinead O'Connor,' remembers Therese Stoulil. 'She used to call my home and scream at me and demand that I put Prince on the phone. This is my private residence. "Prince isn't here right now." I have a very vivid memory of standing in my kitchen, trying to convince her that he wasn't there. I almost had to hang up on her. Out of ten years of working with Prince and the hundreds of women that came and went, I never heard anyone even hint that Prince would be physical. Prince was very respectful of us women that worked for him. Prince always held the doors for me, always said please and thank you, even in his notes. I would have to agree it's out of his character. Prince never even raised his voice. Prince never swore in front of us.'

Other complaints about Prince centred around his controlling nature. Women whose boyfriends became knowledge to Prince were quickly despatched. Maneca Lightner discusses how he cooled after she found out that she was expecting another man's child.

Robin Power Royal and he were discussing a girl band they both wanted her to lead. 'It was the things Prince was doing behind my back. With Carmen Electra, I wanted her to be in my band and Prince told her not to and then he signed her to a record deal.' She retaliated by aiming for his most vulnerable area. 'Prince and I were talking and then Sheila E walked in, and I chose the tallest guy in the room to dance with. He didn't like basketball players. I ended up dating him [future husband Donald Royal of the Minnesota Timberwolves] for five years and we had a daughter together.'

On the whole, women seemed to have adored Prince, particularly in the mid-'80s. The world premiere of *Under the Cherry Moon* was attended by Susannah, Sheila E and Maneca Lightner, who were all known to have dated Prince. MTV's Martha Quinn interviewed him, asking if he was a good kisser. 'I was thinking about that later,' the VJ adds. 'Every female in the country especially at that time had a definite case of the "Princes".'

CHAPTER 12

STRANGE RELATIONSHIP

Sign o' the Times goes on the road with a new band ... back to Minneapolis for a home movie ... Lights, camera, outfit ... 'Strange Relationship' ... Prince and Miles – watch this space ... Welcome to the Madhouse ... Prince's mood turns Black – and so does his record company's

Sign o' the Times goes on the road with a new band

With an album packed with potential hits, there was a sense that, with the Revolution gone, Prince was wading through a period of change. There was one way to increase momentum – new band, new live dates.

Prince had not suggested this was in the plans. 'There was a time that Prince wanted to go to Paris to take ballet lessons before *Sign o' the Times* came out [on 31 March],' recalls Todd Herreman who was heading to his girlfriend's place in Evanston, Illinois. 'Alan [Leeds, tour manager] would say "You might have a bit of time off." I got to Chicago and checked my voicemail. "Prince changed his mind. He wants to record at Sunset." When you think you have a day off, Prince changes his mind.' Herreman was summoned back to help Prince with his Fairlight synthesizer.

World tours are months, sometimes even years, in the planning – certainly those that visit arenas and sports stadia. Prince didn't roll that way.

Shortly before the 31 March release of *Sign o' the Times*, Prince wanted to reconnect with live audiences – but not back home.

Jeff Mason, who'd been working on tours with Prince since the Dirty Mind concerts, was called into Cavallo, Ruffalo and Fargnoli's LA office. Prince's spell making *Under the Cherry Moon* had led to a continued interest in Europe and his preference was to launch the tour there.

'Prince handed me an 8½-inch by 11-inch piece of paper with some doodles on it. He was detailing a set.' The stage, set up high like a cycling arena, had the band playing at an angle. 'He just tore it out from a notebook and said to me, "Make this."'

There followed what Mason calls 'some logistical headaches'. The first piece of advice he imparted was to have the set built in Europe. The sets would be transported on dollies on top of casters. It was assumed, as much as assumptions could be made around how Prince worked, that the tour would hit the States after Europe.

The boss would not want to be bothered with the detail that the casters originated in the US and dollies in Europe, but Mason had to be, signing travel carnets for both. 'It would be expensive on the back end because of [both] the carnets and when you want to bring it back where the cranes originate, it will have to be stored. They say that's OK, right there and then. The next thing I say is that you will have a rough design in a week, a rough estimate in another week and that would give you six weeks to build because we only had eight weeks, and we book out a week for rehearsal and delivery, which only leaves five weeks.

'That is going to be one big mess to clean up for the freight agents and the insurance people at the end of this. The dollies can't move without the casters and the two have to get to their originating places. Nobody cared about this.'

What Prince did care about was a two-metre corrugated-fibre ramp to the stage which he'd seen used on a previous Hollywood awards show. Mason had misgivings.

"This is not going to work. We're playing velodromes and that means there's tracks for the bike and that angle will be too high for the band to come in."

"You're fired."

'Fargnoli comes in the room. "No, no, no. Come back again next week."'

Next week, another meeting, Mason presents plans, still no ramp.

'He fires me again, just like before. We did this a couple more times and Fargnoli comes running in. "No, no, no, it's OK."

[Prince] "I want this ramp. How does it work?"

[Mason] "If you understand that 80, 85 per cent [of venues] are not going to be able to put it up, there are some buildings it will work in. You're going to have to trust me and I will decide how logistically I can build it for the bandmates to the entrance to the ramp."'

It was at this point Mason mentioned another problem with Prince's ramp proposals.

"'You're going to have people looking up Sheila's skirt."

"No, no, no, we can't have that."

'It wasn't until we were doing dates that he figured it out.'

The ramp was used, says Mason, for '10 per cent of the dates – maybe three dates. Berlin [six shows into the tour] was probably the first date we used it in.'

At the outset, Prince had already shown lighting director

LeRoy Bennett photos from Jeff Katz's album cover shoot. 'He showed me pictures from the shoot and said "I want the stage to look like that". It was my interpretation of the cover. I understood the premise about bringing that backdrop to life. I wanted to incorporate lights into the set.'

This presented another logistical wrinkle for Mason. 'All the neon was really neon, which was painful. Truckloads of spare parts. This was before LED [which wasn't commonplace in stadium concerts until this century]. There were certain sequences where specific neon signs would come on as a precursor to what the song was. It was a musical as much as it was an abstract storyline.'

'All we had to go on was the album sleeve,' recalls Simon Austin, the head of LSD, the firm used for the tour. 'We recreated the album sleeve. We worked morning, noon and night. The company that we brought in to do it were based in Redditch [15 miles south of Birmingham, England] and thought we were mad. We wanted another one that says "LOVE", another one that says "SEX" and another one that says "GIRLS". And we wanted them all to be delivered on the same day.'

But there was method in Prince's madness, the kind of method which would become standard on world tours.

Mason recalls the semi-circular stage with a ramp at the front which was 'the beginning of the whole barricade system in world tours. This is where Prince was really on top of it because he really influenced the barricade system and we had trucks, worth of this crap. But it's now the state-of-the-art stuff that you send on to every show. This is the stuff they didn't have enough of when people died in Texas [at the Astroworld Festival in Houston in November 2021, when there was a crush during rapper Travis Scott's set, resulting in ten deaths]. It's the same barricade that has been in use ever since *Sign o' the Times*. Its business operation is still based in Holland.'

Musically Prince was used to working at warp speed and he felt confident that, with Sheila E.'s help, he could get his brand new group ready in that time.

This was a tour built in the US, with the usual rigorous soundcheck in Minneapolis before a rehearsal period where the sets were at Birmingham's NEC Arena. Matt Fink – who, along with Prince was the connective tissue between the Revolution and Sheila's Oakland-based musicians – says the band didn't take much time to get ready. 'They were all very professional and experienced players, and good at what they did, so it really didn't take too long for them to step up to the plate.'

Bill Reeves worked as production coordinator on various Prince tours and says that Prince 'didn't stumble or stutter' over personnel changes. 'It never really dimmed his particular genius because musicians in his band were just that – like tools to achieve his current vision. If you're a carpenter and you get a new hammer, it doesn't make you a different carpenter.'

By the time they arrived in Birmingham, they had 'a day or so, two days at most' in England before they were ready. Tour accountant Spencer Churchill recalls 'about two weeks' of rehearsals ahead of the first night of the tour on 8 May in Stockholm. 'As far as I was concerned, he was ready to go when I walked in the door. They knew what they were doing. You really see that in the film.'

Three or four weeks were slated for rehearsals, but Simon Austin recalls a happy Prince. 'We arranged all the rehearsals at the NEC Birmingham for three and a half, four weeks. When he arrived on the first day, he loved it. That's unheard of. There wasn't any "Yeah, but…"'

Sheila knowing Levi, Miko and Boni from Oakland couldn't have hurt. Bevla Reeves, a friend of Sheila's, was Prince's hairstylist around that time. 'It wasn't the same energy, it wasn't the same vibe; he wasn't doing the same kind of music. There was something really special about that band – Levi and Miko and Sheila. That was the best band he ever had. Nobody puts together bands like her. She finds the right musicians and the right energy. He would often steal band members from her. He was in transition. He was trying to figure out who he was and what he believed in. It affected his moods and even his music.'

Susan Rogers sees more pragmatism, and the change of personnel, as 'the best option that was available for him at that time. It's clear Sheila was powerful and bringing her into the fold was going to bring an asset to his music.'

Austin, Bennett, set designer John McGraw and Mason sorted out the stage design in England, set it up in the NEC Arena and booked the venue, and Prince rehearsed there. Soundman Rob 'Cubby' Colby remembers a week and a half of rehearsals before the boss arrived, with Sheila as 'the team leader when he wasn't there. She would take charge.

'He sent a load of instruments to Paris and he comes back to Minneapolis and the next thing I know we're off to Sweden doing production rehearsals. I know how quickly things could change on a dime. It's not my business to figure out why.'

The mood was good with occasional flashes from Prince. 'He was a moody guy,' admits McGraw. 'He was into surprising people all the time. You never knew what he was going to come up with. He was so focused and so talented to a point of … maybe too much.'

Nick Atkins, who worked on the *Sign o' the Times* tour's sound with Colby, noticed a more relaxed Prince. 'When we started, we did three weeks in Birmingham. Prince by then had started to become quite relaxed, I think because he was shot of the Revolution. It was in one of the NEC halls and they had basketball courts and they would put teams together and he would play with them. Cubby would say, "He's so relaxed."'

It led to what Mason calls 'one of the best tours in the world hardly anyone in the world ended up seeing'. The reason it was barely seen remains a point of conjecture.

There were dates at predominantly sports stadia in Sweden, Italy, Austria, Switzerland, West Germany and four nights at Paris' Bercy – the same venue where 'It's Gonna Be a Beautiful Night' was recorded in 1986 – before the band reached Belgium and the Netherlands. Next stop: two nights at Wembley Stadium.

Except Prince abruptly changed his mind.

One theory, says Austin, may be the ruination of many a cricket game: rain stopped play in Utrecht. 'The whole point was we were supposed to play Wembley and Prince turned around and said "It's raining. I'm not going to do it." Instead, all the equipment went back to Minneapolis.'

'He was pissed,' adds Mason. 'That was one of the velodromes in the Netherlands where it rained.' His team were trying to calm him down. 'We were going, "We know it rains." We had this runway he could walk in front of the PA and overnight I built covers on them.'

LeRoy Bennett remembers it well. 'What started sending the tour south was that we played outside for the first time and Prince got rained on for the first time. There was an overhang that was sized to cloak him and the piano from rain and it just fell down on top of him. It was a deluge.'

Did the band laugh?

'Inside.'

He finished his contractually obliged dates and, after a failed attempt where Kensington & Chelsea Council refused to let him play two dates at Earls Court, the tour staff were told that the Wembley dates were abruptly cancelled. So was the US tour.

Because Prince tours were not booked way in advance, like those of many music superstars, it would not be uncommon for dates to be cancelled at short notice. Prince was not one to sweat over financial details and would often make spur-of-the-moment decisions. (Interviewees confirm him turning down lucrative gig offers and saying yes to others which were unpaid.)

Helen Hiatt, from the wardrobe department, thinks the rain and the stage sloping may have been a factor. 'He got mad and there was a slope that went down the stage. You're on the stage, it's raining, it's muddy, people are rushing the stage and they had to go and pull them out. Prince had to stop the show to tell people to move back. It was frightening. After that,' she speculates', he thought, *'I'm not going to do that.'*'

Rob 'Cubby' Colby felt the European weather detracted from the American's showmanship. 'He would come in and it was very windy and he would say "Can you make the wind stop?". He knew the answer to that, obviously. He's a really smart individual. He was so into that production. I think he saw the rain and the outdoor element as taking away from the lighting and smoke, those bits of the show he relied on.'

Cat Glover refers to a storm one night. 'Me and Prince were on wireless mics and this rain was coming down, then this bolt of thunder came and hit one of the signs on the stage right above Boni's keys and it fell. That was what made Prince decide to put *Sign...* on to film instead. Prince was worried for the band [and] the fans' safety with the storm and I think it kinda shook him up too. Combined with the whole stage set-up and electrics, he pulled it.' Prince's childhood epileptic seizures could have been a factor in how much an electric shock might have spooked him, but make-up stylist Terra Hinrichs thinks it might be something more mundane related to the rain. 'He did love his hair. If he shut [Wembley] down, it was probably because of his hair.'

Film director, musician and Prince fan Jeymes Samuel, who used an Allen key to prise out a poster for the aborted 25 and 26 June shows which he still has framed at home, is in no doubt about the cancellation. 'We all knew Prince couldn't sell out two nights at Wembley Stadium. Michael Jackson could do Wembley Stadium. Prince couldn't. He was cool. He wasn't popular like that. My brother [the singer Seal] told me "We will believe it when we see it". He cancelled both shows. I think he had his non-rain-related reasons – the only person who's cancelled Wembley Stadium. He wasn't selling out those tickets.'

Erik Stroeve, a fan who was thirteen when he saw the Parade tour in Rotterdam and fourteen when he attended the following year's concert in Utrecht, claims Prince's fan base had grown – and grown up. 'The *Parade* tour audience was much more pop. The *Sign...* audience was wilder, much more like a rock concert, almost like Queen. I hardly knew anyone who saw all the dates of the Parade tour in the Netherlands, but I do know many who saw all the dates of the *Sign o' the Times* tour. It was the first tour where the real fans came together, much more than *Parade.*'

The light and shade of *Sign...*'s songs, which go from dark and brooding to playful and childlike, sexy to romantic, was reflected in the concerts. The intensity and freshness of the album was also reflected in the setlists, as Erik Stroeve says. 'I think he realised with the *Parade* tour that he has to catch up with Europe and he was playing all the old songs, and with *Sign...*, he basically played the album.'

Back to Minneapolis for a home movie

The expense and profit tied into a world tour did not inform Prince as it would have other rock stars. He often acted on instinct, the instinct being whatever the next thing was. And the next thing was another movie.

At his four Paris dates in June 1987, Albert Magnoli and Prince talked. The director recalls them being close at this time and Prince saying, 'We should do something together again. Let's continue this wonderful relationship.'

Magnoli returned to Los Angeles for other work when a panicked Bob Cavallo, one of Prince's three managers, called. 'What conversation did you have with The Kid? [Management and record company execs would occasionally call Prince this.] He doesn't want to do the *Sign o' the Times* tour any more. He wants to start doing the music for *The Dawn*.'

Magnoli maintained his innocence as he thought, like everyone else, Prince would be following up the successful *Sign…* European tour with dates in the States. He knew too that things changed quickly in Prince's world. So did Cavallo.

Prince asked at the end of *Sign…*'s title track if anybody would see the dawn. They wouldn't.

The Dawn was his planned movie that, it is believed, would go on to become re-versioned as *Graffiti Bridge*, Prince's fourth, final and arguably least successful cinematic enterprise. There may well be a version of what Prince conceived as *The Dawn* in his vault, just as there is a *3121* movie, and a *3 Chains o' Gold* movie.

Back in 1987, after the summer in Europe, Team Prince was focused on the road. The US leg of the *Sign…* tour would, his management, crew and record believed, have established Prince's new band to his home audience and help drive album sales. 'He was in all-out revolt with his record company,' says Bill Reeves, 'and that had some impact on his thinking. He was very Eurocentric at that point.'

Prince nixed it in favour of a movie.

As it would be shot in his new entertainment complex of Paisley Park, that meant bringing it all back home – particularly the sets inspired by the film, which would need to head to Chanhassen. This impacted on Jeff Mason worse than other employees. 'There was so much going on for me that Wembley being cancelled was only part of it. I was told that was happening and to ship the stuff home.' The carnets for the dollies for the sets in Europe and the casters in the US had to be negotiated. The six weeks required to take the set back home was six weeks that Mason's team didn't have.

'That is challenging in itself, but [we needed to] get it there quickly because we're going to shoot a movie. We had to go to Luxembourg and get a DC10 and a 747 to fly to Minneapolis', which costs, he recalls, 'probably half a million dollars between the two of them at short notice. I took a company to Luxembourg with extremely valuable items. Almost all the crew was Europe-based but had to be trained [in the US]. To be able to set the stuff up, visas would take weeks and by the time they got there, the European portion of the crew had set the stuff up. Some of it had to be taken down and set back up again and there were only nine or ten of us. Sixty or seventy people [were] doing it while we were on tour.'

LeRoy Bennett remembers the schedule being torn up as a regular occurrence. 'At that point, he was moving a zillion miles an hour. He was on to that next thing so it was faster and faster.' Make-up artist Robyn Lynch references the precedent of the *Purple Rain* tour, which was also abruptly pulled by Prince, this time before it left the States. 'We didn't do the European leg and, as a sorry, he did a telecast for Europe out of Syracuse. He was done and he wanted to move on. He wanted to get to the next thing. He wanted to start shooting.'

Because Prince wanted to make another film, there was

another snafu. 'When you pull yourself off a tour,' recalls Magnoli, 'you have made contracts to a lot of people, and to break those contracts, there's liability.' Not for the first time, the Cavallo, Ruffalo and Fargnoli heads had to be banged together to avoid a financial black hole.

The answer wasn't *The Dawn*, which, despite being a reality in Prince's head after a conversation with Albert Magnoli, wasn't a reality in terms of script or scheduling. The *Sign o' the Times* film was intended as a precursor to *The Dawn*, a quick fix before Prince's latest entree into movies as an actor (the *Controversy* tour had been filmed for a cinematic release before that idea was shelved for the scripted *Purple Rain* film).

Unlike *Under the Cherry Moon*, no one would be confusing this for a sequel to *Purple Rain*. Prince decided he wanted to spend more time at his new HQ back home so decided to shoot a live concert film, in the vein of Talking Heads' *Stop Making Sense* or Led Zeppelin's *The Song Remains the Same*, to showcase the chemistry of the new band.

Confusingly for all parties, it was made in Minneapolis, Los Angeles and Rotterdam, with a wee bit of Antwerp (the intros for 'Housequake' and 'Forever in My Life' were snipped from Belgian shows). Rob 'Cubby' Colby recalls shows filmed in Antwerp, Paris and Rotterdam, and a light in Prince going on when the camera light did the same. 'It just seemed like a whole other gear when the camera was on.'

In late June, Tim Clawson, who worked on Prince's videos, was in Portland, Maine, producing a music video for Heart, when producer Simon Fields rang: 'Do you have your passport? I need you to get on a plane to Amsterdam.'

Prince had been playing three nights and on the first night at 9 p.m., Michiel Hoogenboezem of Wisseloord Studios, an hour away in Hilversum, got a call with a simple brief: 'Nothing more

STRANGE RELATIONSHIP | 333

than "Get the audio on tape". The recording itself was a piece of cake. Susan Rogers was engineering and mixing. A complete film crew was also flown in from all over the world that day. Their preparation time was even shorter than ours. On Saturday, two trailers with additional lights were brought in to get the job done. During the very last songs of the Saturday show, Prince decided to also film the Antwerp show the next day. All three shows were recorded without any problems or issues from an audio point of view.'

So the audio, done. The video? Needed redoing. 'When we got everything home,' says Rogers, 'the problem was the film. We had too many distant shots [and] we didn't have enough audience shots. Prince was unhappy with the look of it. It was grainy. The crew just didn't have enough time to get it together.'

Prince was very particular about how things were shot, which was unusual for a musician. 'He had high standards,' recalls Clawson. 'It was very common to shoot 16mm film rather than 35mm.' Prince insisted on the best film stock and would tell his video producer 'I want the sauce'. 'That's his way of saying he doesn't want to cut corners.'

Because the light show couldn't be shot on 35mm, according to Hoogenboezem, 'all the footage of the Friday show disappeared in the trash can.' Luckily, there was an answer to the problem back home. Clawson remembers that 'it might have been Prince, it might have been Bob Cavallo who said, "Let's just shoot what we shoot today and we will bring the whole set back to Paisley Park."'

Paisley Park, with its sound stage and 55-foot ceiling, had just opened. It had been purpose-built for records and films to be made, so why not Prince's? 'He wrote some of these pick-up scenes that would involve Wally and Sheila,' recalls Rogers, 'and we did those pick-up scenes with audio we had recorded in the

Netherlands, and they would play along. They were such a good band that was easy for them.'

At Paisley Park, the new staff had work to do. Danny Soltys, the venue's facility director, went to the local union for fifteen stage hands and the sound stage intended for concerts was turned into a movie set. Simon Austin sent two or three staff and Albert Magnoli was also dragooned to brainstorm with Prince.

Relocating the European crowds of between 7,500 and 9,000 was more of a challenge for Magnoli. Some crowd shots worked, but the movie also displayed the sparser crowd of around 100 at Paisley Park. Although Prince is credited as director, it appears the duo huddled together to form a brains trust. 'They called me when they had already made a decision and built Paisley Park the studio site where they would shoot. The organisation was constantly moving forward on a short-term plan. They had one day of shooting, possibly two and I sat with Prince to see what he was trying to do. "I will come in and talk. I don't want credit for it." I just wanted to help him get to that place he needed to get to. At the time, it was just "let's fix this".

'He wanted to drop the video ['U Got the Look', shot in Paris where Prince and Magnoli had talked] right in the middle of it. It was a hodge-podge. The idea was just to shoot the musical numbers extremely well and lay in these vignettes and then start building the additional sets necessary to build in the vignettes we were trying to do.

'I had [between] six and eight cameras. I was able to move very quickly. When I was finished, I brought in an editor, Steve Purcell. He was on the set maybe a day.' Magnoli shot every number twice to give the impression of sixteen cameras. I had got cameramen, I had the cranes and we were able to fit in original tour footage. Some of it [the film] is on tour. You can get the shots in that are more tour-oriented.

'I had a crane and a camera with an arm, which can swing and swoop in, a snorkel camera. That's how I shot Sheila E. doing her drums. That camera you can turn down and around. The concert stage was in a wide shot. That's where he said, "Not bad for a girl [during 'Play in the Sunshine']." We're going to rebuild the entire solo and I'm going to shoot Sheila and then, when Prince says, "Not bad for a girl," I'm going to have a shot of Sheila E. with a little smirk. That's how you build the intimacy.'

Susan Rogers' challenge, which she describes as 'so damned hard', was to replicate the sound of thousands of people in an arena from the acoustics of a couple of hundred people on a sound stage. 'We were working in Ocean Way studios [in Los Angeles], but the only thing that worked was a Quantec room simulator. It did exactly what it said it did – it simulated rooms. It would be no big deal today, but in 1987, it was a huge deal and I was able to simulate the Ahoy Arena audio and the Paisley Park footage into the film.'

'For about ten days,' adds saxophonist Eric Leeds, 'we filmed the show to get enough variety of footage for Prince to assemble the concert film. In reality, most of what is seen in the film was shot at Paisley and not from an actual concert. We also rerecorded most of the music because Prince was unhappy with the recording quality of the original live concert. The process was rather tedious. On the set at Paisley, we were just stopping and starting so that the film crew could get various shots to edit into the live footage. While the film was generally well regarded, I don't think it fully captured the nature of the live show. Pretty much everyone involved with the show regretted his decision to produce the film instead of touring the States with the *Sign o' the Times* concert.'

Most of the music would be rerecorded in the studio. 'Very little of the film, audio or video, was from the actual live footage shot in Europe,' Leeds adds. This isn't quite true. The audio from the concerts in Rotterdam and Antwerp has been matched to the movie, but Prince would record audio as well as video, apart from Dave Hogan's 'U Got the Look' video filmed in Paris, which was plonked into the middle of the film.

Prince, already used to having all his shows shot and watching footage the same evening, knew what he wanted. So the consultations between Prince and staff were to the point. He also wanted an audience, but no more than 1,000 crammed into Paisley. Tour manager Jeff Mason arranged 'an occupancy permit for the parking garage and that's how they could get all the extras. The extras were funny because they got fed McDonald's one day and there was a huge downpour and the basement gallery all flooded because the French fries clogged up the drain and the water kept coming. They had worked out a flood system for the drain, but they hadn't planned on 500 bags of French fries.'

'They might have got paid twenty-five bucks a day,' adds Danny Soltys.

The storyline? This was pretty much an afterthought for Magnoli and Prince, who gathered in impromptu huddles to shoot what needed to be filmed. 'Prince wanted this whole story of me and Brooks,' remembers Cat Glover, 'and this Brooks-wants-me-but-Prince-does-too kinda thing, but then, of course, I'm distracted by Prince because Brooks had this other girl. It played out more in the movie.'

Bodyguard-turned-dancer Greg Brooks points out that at the time, he had two young daughters, aged one and four. Prince created a love triangle from his own imagination – 'it was all him', says Brooks – but a script wasn't part of that plan. Simon Fields, who says he had two weeks' notice to help pull the movie together, admires the fact that 'it's intentionally unpolished and rough, and you have to respect him for that'.

Lights, camera, outfit

One song which brought pictures, sound and something else together was 'Hot Thing'.

Prince's outfit for this was inspired by Roy Bennett's Go-Blo lights which the singer's wardrobe team knocked up with matching shoes. The other impressive logistic is more questionable – at least as viewed in the twenty-first century: the routine where Prince slides through Cat's legs and pulls off her skirt with his teeth. 'There was a misogyny that was more accepted then, which was not accepted even five years later,' argues Albert Magnoli. 'At the time, that was seen as spectacular – and obviously rehearsed many times.'

The trick provoked positives and negatives for Cat. Two weeks before the tour's first night, in rehearsal, 'he grabbed my skirt with his teeth and the floor linoleum had this bump-like ripple in it. As I run from Prince, I tripped and tore a ligament real bad. I was in agony, but we had doctors all through the tour looking after me.'

The positive came from one of Prince's signature outfits in the movie, where he plays his drum solo. As with her peak cap from the dinner, Prince saw Cat's embroidered denim jacket and incorporated it into his look. 'I started working on it when I was laid up with my torn ligament.'

'Hot Thing' was, however, says Magnoli, 'only performed twice. One take and then shot again from a different angle so it looks like we have sixteen cameras. There was no fooling around.'

Those rehearsals were important for Lisa Jordan, who was in charge of Sheila and Cat's outfits. 'We were down to our last yard of material for that skirt and he kept ripping that off. Then there was no more and that was a little bit of a nail-biter – him getting it right. Prince and I had little discussions about that. I told him it was the end of the material and he doesn't like to be told something can't happen, and he ignored me. Luckily he pulled it off.'

The movie was best known for a drum solo – not Prince's, but Sheila's, which she rerecorded to sync with the images – which closes the jazz instrumental, 'Now's the Time'. The filming took, says Magnoli, around 'five to eight days' of 'twelve-to-fourteen-hour days' after a fortnight of rehearsals with the band.

Six days in, Mason hoped he might get a break, as the crew had a day off 'so I thought I was getting a day off'. While having brunch at his hotel, however, Prince called.

'I'd like to shoot a music video in the corner. I have called a TV station, they're bringing a truck.'

Mason had already been called halfway through filming with another of Prince's demands, one related to a neon sign based around the furry hat worn by dancer Greg Brooks. 'Where is the Squirrel Meat sign? Build me another sign.' As Mason explains, 'Nobody wanted to be around him because they are going to be told to do more.'

Once filming wrapped, Steve Purcell really went to work in an edit suite in North Cahuenga Boulevard in Hollywood, less than a mile from Sunset Sound, with only the film's director and star for company. He recalls a 'small 15-foot by 15-foot room, coffee table, size of a bedroom'.

Purcell had edited the videos for 'Kiss' and a *Parade*-era concert, but this was a whole other kettle of fish, matching video to audio. 'Albert's role was to give it a storyline,' he explains. 'In a situation like this, Prince would take the track from Rotterdam, and there would be times he would be lip syncing as there were vocals he wanted to put to the track and so he would lip sync it and go back to the studio. I didn't understand it at the time.'

Danny Soltys corrects this, saying that the lip syncing was actually Prince playing live. 'I have never known him to lip sync.'

Prince prepped for this concert movie while moving ahead with *The Black Album*, building up Paisley Park and, on occasion, driving. 'Sometimes I would send off a song,' continues Purcell, 'and didn't hear back and the next day I would be editing and he would be in his car and he knew the shots based on hearing [them] over the phone and would give me notes on what needed changing.'

Prince and Purcell kept each other company, but Purcell remembers his boss's sweet tooth. Prince's then security guard Gilbert Davison was despatched to the sweet shop for two pounds of candy and assorted nuts. 'There was one kind that he liked, and he would get this two-pound box of chocolates and break every one off and eat the one he liked and put the rest in the trash. He would go through this process. He never shared one with me. He would never offer me any. It was very strange. We were literally a foot from each other.

'He was very, very focused. This is not his background. He is a musician. Everyone was trying to figure out how to make a concert film work. They were all shot on film at the time. It was a tough process.'

That sense of collaboration with musicians and for the movie with Magnoli wouldn't work when it came to release. Tour movies were normally summer releases to act as an alternative to the action blockbusters, but Prince, as was his wont, wanted the movie out by the end of the year.

Live movies are also invariably a greatest hits set, but apart from 'Little Red Corvette' and Charlie Parker's 'Now's the Time' ahead of the 'U Got the Look' video, the set was culled from *Sign...* alone.

Warner Brothers, who hadn't requested the film in the first

place and whose movie division was separate from the music team, was still smarting from the reception to *Under the Cherry Moon* and were not exactly consulted heavily throughout by Prince. They passed.

'I remember hearing afterwards that nobody was really interested in it because it had been shot and cut and packaged and they hadn't been involved in the process,' recalls Mason, 'so they weren't invested in paying. He paid for the distribution in the end.'

Prince, with the kind of independent spirit he would show in later years when he bypassed the major labels, paid for Cineplex Odeon to take the film round the country after a bit of promo – not from him, of course, but Cat and Brooks were interviewed by *Video Soul*'s Donnie Simpson on BET. The first screening was held in New York in October, rather than as a premiere at Mann's Chinese Theatre (which *Purple Rain* enjoyed) or in Sheridan, Wyoming, where MTV unveiled *Under the Cherry Moon*. Because of its lack of (emotional *and* financial) investment from Warners, it was Prince's second consecutive underwhelming cinematic release. Some, including him, according to Simon Fields, were relaxed. 'Not everything has to be big.'

'Strange Relationship'

Prince and Cat and Brooks, Prince and Sheila and Susannah… Prince liked to keep the public guessing: in his movies, in the media coverage he could influence, in his music.

Given the caged-bird status of many of Prince's lovers, from whom he demanded exclusivity while he saw others, 'strange relationships' were more of a default setting. In what, on first listen, sounds like a chirpy pop-funk uptempo song but reads like a dark essay – Prince claims that, for someone who doesn't like winter, he gets a kick out of doing his lover cold – 'Strange Relationship' is the sound of a man unsure if he's been spurned or doing the spurning. He sings about someone he can't stand to see happy but, more than that, hates to see upset.

As the Revolution were first credited on a Prince record in 1984 and he broke up with them towards the end of 1986, and this song's lifespan was between '83 and '87, it's fair to say it's Revolution-flavoured. 'They worked initially on a number of the songs,' Matt Fink says of Wendy & Lisa. '"Strange Relationship" was a Revolution thing, "Starfish and Coffee" was Susannah's lyrics. "If I Was Your Girlfriend", "Strange Relationship", "Starfish and Coffee"… "It's Gonna Be a Beautiful Night" – they played on it, they didn't get writing credit. That was me, Eric, Mark Brown. "Adore" was one they also worked on, and "The Cross" maybe. "I Could Never Take the Place of Your Man" – that was with the Revolution.'

'The thing about those songs I know is that, after the fact, if they had participated in any degree, I believe Prince pulled their parts off those songs and redid them himself in order not to be attached to them.' He adds, not unreasonably as Prince recorded so much on his own, 'I don't know that for sure.'

Prince is indeed believed to have minimised their parts after saying goodbye to the Revolution. Eighteen songs on *Dream Factory* became eight songs on *Sign...* – 'Dorothy Parker', 'It', 'Strange Relationship', 'Slow Love', 'Starfish and Coffee', 'I Could Never Take...', the title track and 'The Cross'.

In between *Dream Factory* and *Sign*, there was *Camille*. No one apart from Prince knows for sure, but what is known is that 'Strange Relationship' first popped up in 1983 and was slated to appear on *Dream Factory* and then *Camille*. He invented Camille as a character and, when he gave the album to Warner Brothers, Prince's name was not intended to appear on the artwork. Aside from 'Strange Relationship', it has nothing in common with *Dream Factory*. *Sign…* contains ten songs from *Dream Factory*, seven from Camille, and fifteen from the 1986 twenty-two-song album Crystal Ball (not to be confused with the entirely different 1998 triple album of the same name). Once Lenny Waronker asked Prince to trim it down to a double album, he recorded 'U Got the Look' in December 1986 and *Sign o' the Times* was born. On 15 January 1987, he recorded the intro segment from 'Play in the Sunshine', completing the album.

In 2017, Wendy Melvoin told *Backspin* that for *Sign…*, 'Lisa and I were given a lot of tracks, he was busy doing a million things again, we were getting tapes of general ideas, go finish this, go finish that. "Sign o' the Times" the song, we had nothing to do with that, but we did a lot of work on that record.'

'…"Beautiful Night", "Strange Relationship",' adds drummer Bobby Z in the same interview. 'There was a lot on that record.' There was a version of 'Strange Relationship' which, like 'The Ballad of Dorothy Parker', had an Eric Leeds line but Prince took off the horns on both tracks.

The Prince Vault website recounts sixty-three tracks written for the *Dream Factory/Camille/Sign* sessions, a lot of it with input from Wendy & Lisa. The earliest recording of 'Strange Relationship' is dated to the year when a version appears on the acoustic *Piano and a Microphone* 1983 record. It resurfaces in the summer and autumn of 1985 on the *Purple Rain* tour and prior to production of *Under the Cherry Moon*. Another version of 'Strange Relationship', recorded at The Complex in Los Angeles on 1 July 1985, features Fairlight samples of a sitar.

In one version, Lisa is credited – in Dave Hill's book *Prince: A Pop Life* – as playing sitar and wooden flute, with Wendy on tambourine and congas. That summer, Prince was in *Around the World in a Day* mode, influenced by the oud and tabla of Lisa's brother David Coleman.

By 1987, Prince was reconnecting with his funk roots and black audience, and editing the Revolution's sound out of his recordings.

'With "Strange Relationship", that was an odd one,' marvels Susan Rogers, there for most of its incarnations. 'Man, did he love working that out in rehearsal and onstage and in soundcheck, but he kept wanting to put it on a record. There was clearly something holding him back. I always assumed it was about Jill Jones.' Jones, an on-off girlfriend since Prince met her singing back-up for Teena Marie on the *Dirty Mind* tour in 1980, had her solo record finally released on Paisley Park Records the same year as *Sign*.

Others think it could have been about Susannah, whom he couldn't help himself hurting in 1987; another theory is Denise 'Vanity' Matthews, who offended him by dating other men. Infidelity was something Prince felt strongly as a victim, but was seemingly less concerned when he was the perpetrator – although, in 'Strange Relationship', he does say sorry.

It is a hard song to categorise.

'Every now and then,' says Rogers, 'he would ask me to pull a tape and that's why it was necessary to start a tape [for songs which were unreleased – this would become known as The Vault] and gather them all in one spot. During the making of the *Sign o' the Times* album, he had me pull out "I Could Never Take the Place of Your Man" and we had to call it out and cargo it to the studio in LA. Same thing with "Slow Love". With "Strange Relationship", he was satisfied and we recorded it.'

Prince and Miles – watch this space

Another artist, with whom Prince was rumoured to be making a record and who shied away from genre categories was Miles Davis.

Davis had just returned to Warner Brothers with the 1986 album *Tutu*, on which its proficient producer Marcus Miller had played most of the instruments, with Davis blowing his horn on top of Miller's playing. He had expressed admiration for Prince and visited Edina Warehouse where Prince and the Revolution and his subsequent bands rehearsed.

Prince had a jazz sensibility, in terms of both his playing and his band-leading instincts. Miles had a pop sensibility. Davis's last album for Columbia before he moved to Warners, *You're Under Arrest*, features covers of Cyndi Lauper's 'Time After Time' and 'Human Nature' from *Thriller*.

'He referred to his music as social music,' explains Davis's nephew Vince Wilburn Jr. 'It was music for the world. I don't think Uncle Miles was too keen on categorising his music. I would imagine both Prince and Uncle Miles hated categorising their music.'

Collaboration could have been an option, says Alan Leeds, but not for Prince. 'Something that might be intimidating or challenging – it never struck him as something he might want to do. When he signed George Clinton to the [Paisley Park] label, the original point was for them to work together. It never happened. He gave George a couple of tracks, but he really wasn't interested in working with anybody. Miles was begging him to work in the studio. I had a conversation with him.

'"Dude, don't you understand? Miles wants to go in the studio."

'"I can't tell Miles Davis what to play."

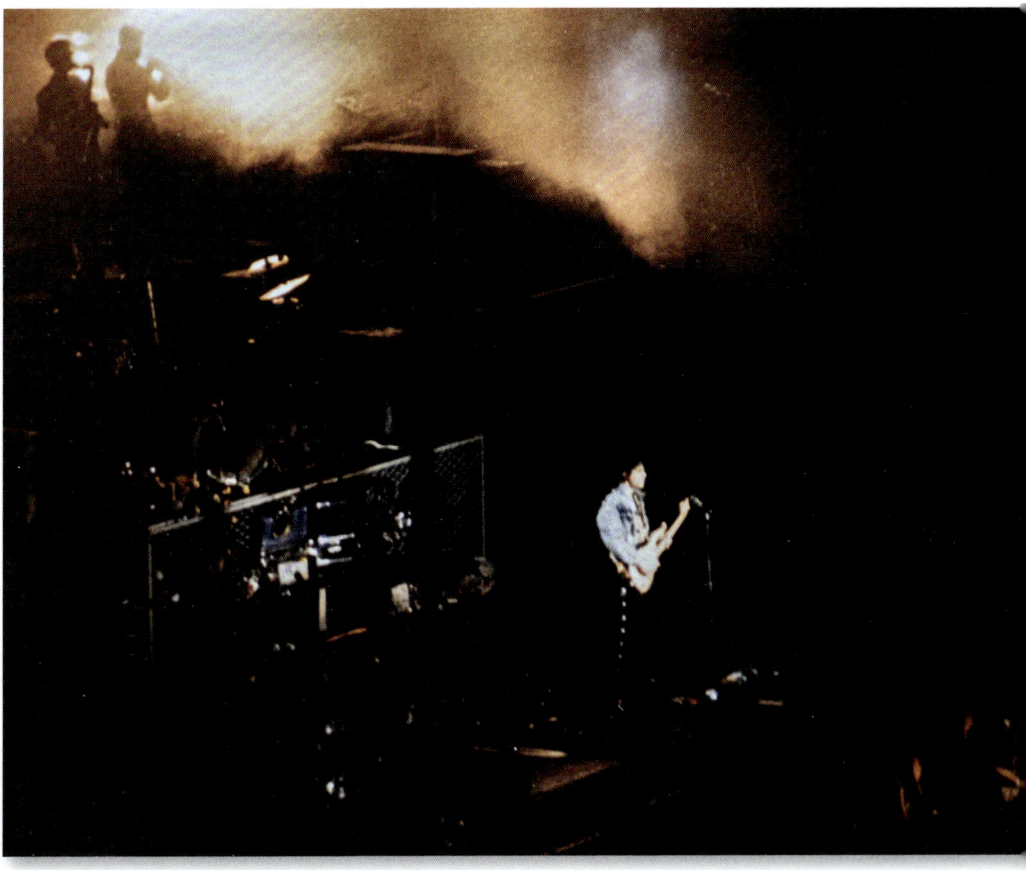

Prince on stage at the Ahoy, Rotterdam, where some of the *Sign o' the Times* movie was filmed, 27 June 1987.

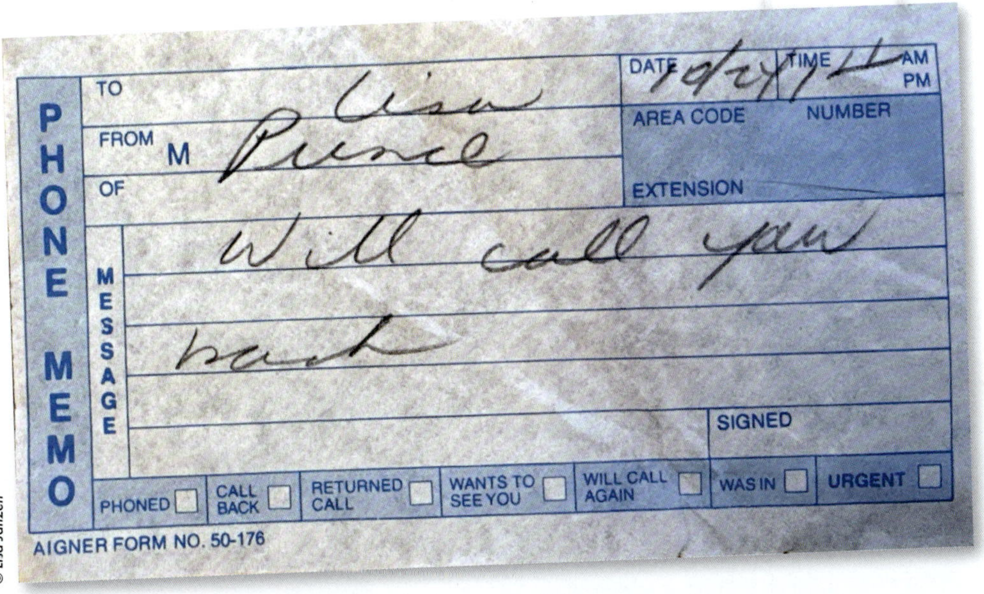

Prince's personal note to management.

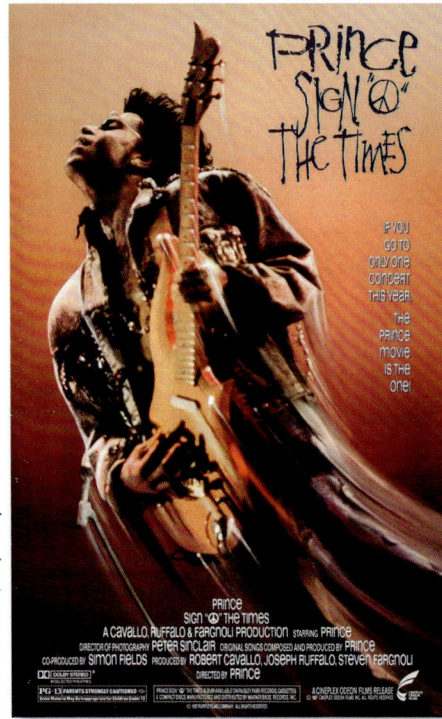

Above: Prince and Kim Bassinger.

Left: *Sign o' the Times* movie poster.

Below: Prince and Mayte Garcia at Wembley, London, 1995.

Designer Tom Butsch's sketches for the Chanhassen Dinner Theatre 1975 production of *Guys and Dolls*, which would form the backdrop for the *Sign o' the Times* cover.

More sketches of the *Guys and Dolls* production based on Jo Mielziner designs and the backdrop itself, which would be used 12 years later for the album cover.

Top left: Prince with his second wife, Manuela Testolini.

Top right: Prince at the Rock & Roll Hall of Fame ceremony in New York, 2004.

Below: A statue of Prince's love symbol outside of Paisley Park.

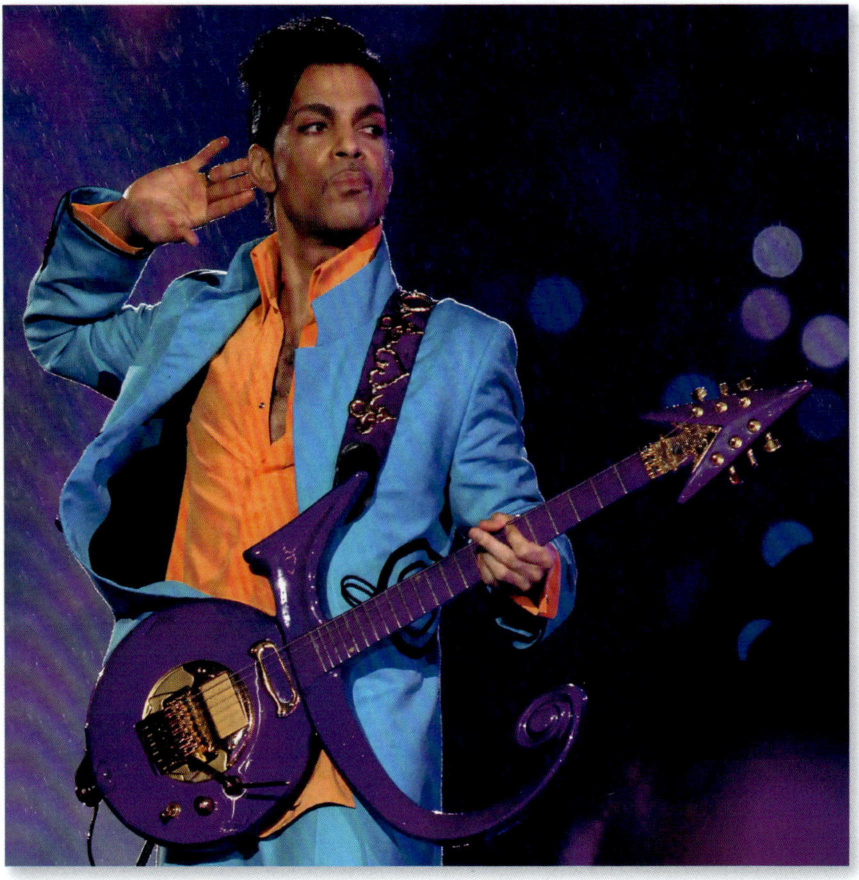

© Theo Wargo/WireImage

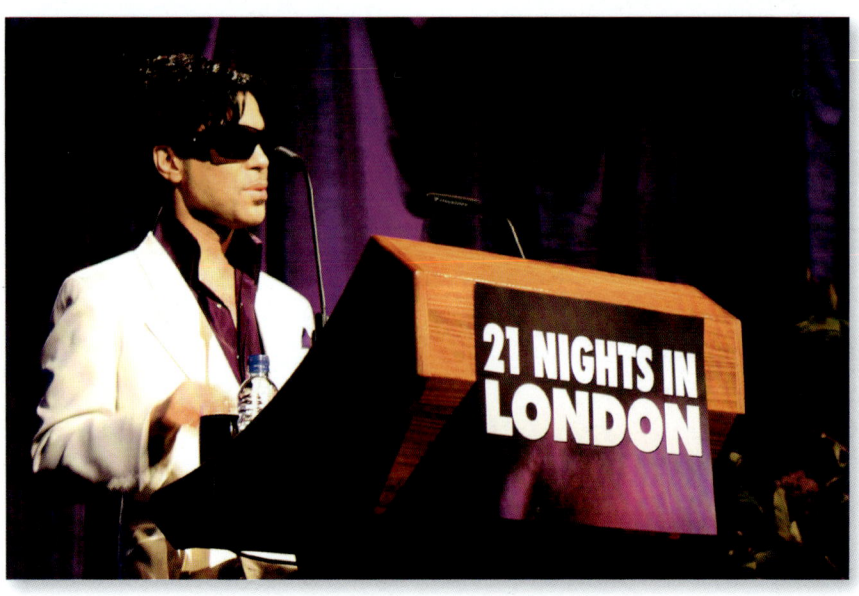

Prince performing at the half time show during Super Bowl XLI, 2007.

© Claire Greenway/Getty

Prince announces his record-breaking run of 21 sell-out shows at London's O2 in August–September 2007.

© Dave J Hogan / Getty

Prince and 3rd Eye Girl onstage at The BRIT Awards 2014.

© Mark Ralston / AFP / Getty

Messages left by Prince fans as they pay their respects outside
Paisley Park following Prince's death

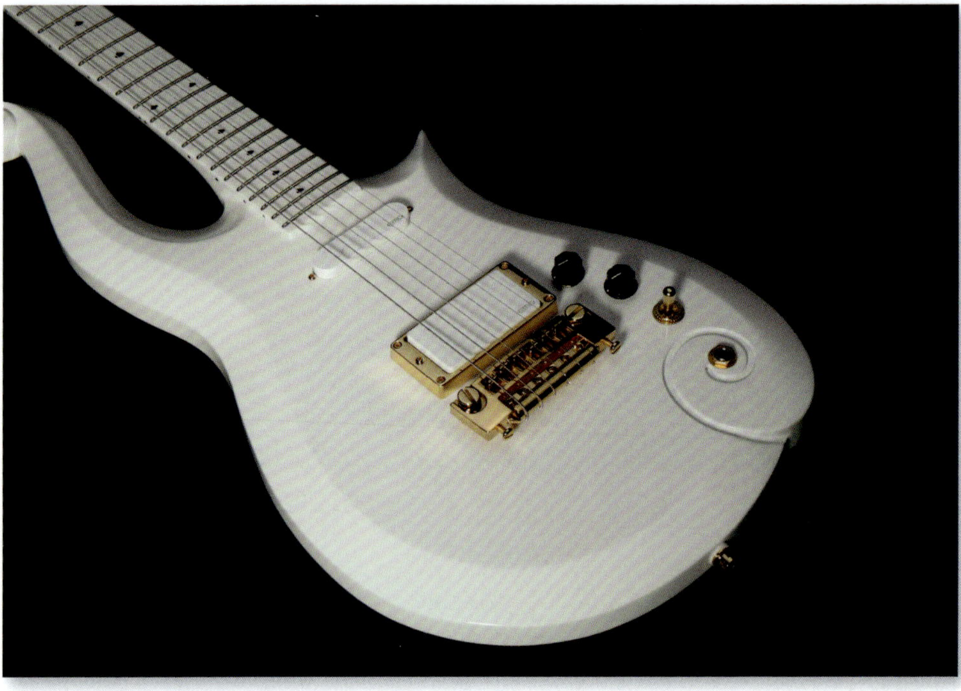

© Bob Cole

Prince's Cloud guitar, which he asked Dave Rusan to design for him. A peach version is on the cover of *Sign o' the Times*.

© Paul Camarata

© Dave Rusan

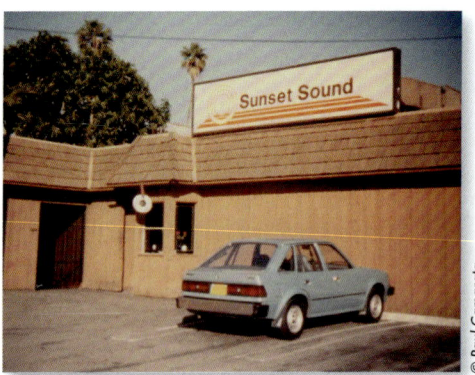

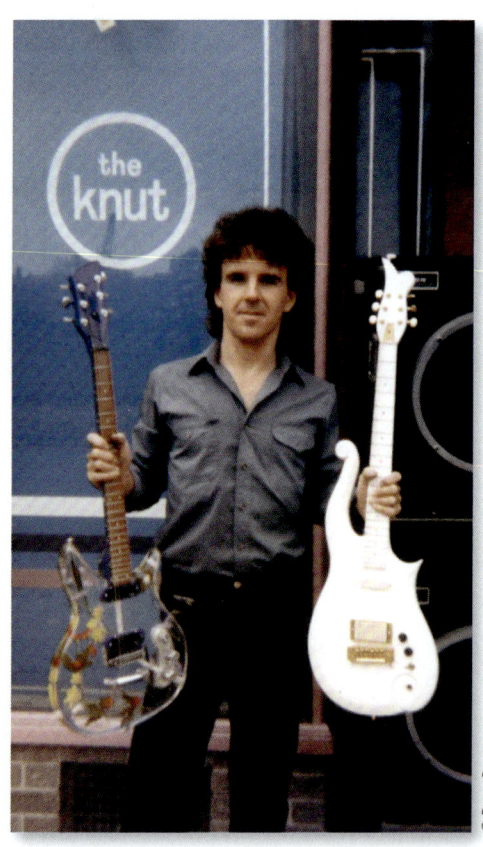

Above: Sunset Sound Recorders, Prince's home from home in Los Angeles, where he recorded much of *Sign o' the Times* outside Minneapolis.Cat Glover in Utrecht, Netherlands, 1987.

Right: Dave Rusan, the designer of Prince's Cloud guitar (right) and a clear-bodied guitar with silk flowers commissioned by Wendy Melvoin outside his guitar store of choice in Minneapolis, Knut-Koupee music.

'I can only conclude that he was scared.'

A recurring theme of Miles' autobiography isn't just the notes, but what is allowed to exist between them. For someone known for the sweet sound he could elicit from his trumpet, he often references 'the space between the notes'. It's all over Prince's work too and can be heard throughout *Sign o' the Times*: when the title track pauses between the blues guitar and the drum machine; the echoes around the guitar solo in 'I Could Never Take the Place of Your Man'; and 'If I Was Your Girlfriend', which doesn't just use silences, but whose final lines extol the ultimate relationship goal as Prince and his girlfriend figuring out what authentic, comfortable silences look like.

Morris Hayes remembers one particular Miles gig which had an effect on Prince, where 'it was grooving' until one of his band contributed and things fell apart. Hayes recalls Prince hearing the bandleader say 'The reason it sounds good is because you're not playing!'

'Miles was trying to tell him that "the space was what you were appreciating and you ruined it". It was a great lesson Prince tried to teach his band.' Prince grew to love those silences, what late-period collaborator and bassist Dwayne 'MonoNeon' Thomas Jr calls 'a fancy for minimalistic funky thangs'.

Dave Hampton worked with Prince between 2004 and 2010, and, after that, as production manager for Miles Davis' Electric Band, which consisted of Miles' former band members. Space was vital. 'That's the reason I came to understand Miles after I did Prince and it taught me what I was there for.'

The influence Prince had picked up from Miles expanded into other music. As Prince's soundman for two decades, Scottie Baldwin was acutely aware of the space between the notes. 'Prince was a master at note value – when to play, when not to play. It's call ... pause ... call. Not call and response. He created his whole style.' Baldwin offers 'How Come U Don't Call Me Anymore?' as a classic 'Prince-between-the-notes' example. One regular phrase still rattles around his head. 'He said it fifty times. "C'mon, y'all. Let's respect our two extra band members – Scottie and silence." Silence was a band member.'

Bassist Rhonda Smith agrees. 'If there were five members in the band, he would say that the band had a sixth and that was silence. There was space, which was the engineering of funk and duplicating it properly. It has to have air. That to me is the epitome of great pop music. You can't fill everything with notes. Space is a big deal, especially to the listener. People need time to digest things. You have to start to build on what you have done and Prince is a great builder.'

Matt Blistan felt that the space was a frontier to experiment with and that this fitted into how both Prince and Miles Davis worked. 'When you're composing, you're thinking way ahead of where you are. You don't have to think what you're going to play all the way through things. It's going to let the song breathe a little bit. That's what the space is. You have to back off sometimes and let the song breathe. Both of them did that. It wasn't intentional on either part. That's just the way they thought of the music. It's the ups and the downs. You have to make some space to make the other parts of the music be exemplified.'

Public Enemy producer Eric 'Vietnam' Sadler was taking notes when the band made their debut album. 'When we were making *Yo! Bum Rush the Show*, one engineer said "You can't put too much reverb on it" and all I could think of was Prince: "There's no rules." Sonically, you can do anything as long as you are not tearing up equipment and I would always argue with engineers. Eventually we got rid of him.

'I always had that in the back of my head. "There doesn't

have to be any rules to this." We don't have to follow any kind of format.'

There were other, less musically profound, similarities between Prince and Miles. Both men were sharp dressers, for one. Miles had been told he needed to 'dress more hip' by saxophonist Dexter Gordon when he was in Charlie Parker's band. Charlie Watts, a pretty snappy dresser himself, was quoted in the Darryl Jones documentary *In the Blood* saying that the green buttoned shirt Miles wore on the cover of *Milestones* was coveted by 'everyone in London'.

His style evolved from suits – with encouragement from his second wife, funk singer Betty Davis – to, like James Brown in the '70s, something less formal. By the '80s, Miles would wear, according to his son Erin, 'a lot of shoulder pads… stuff that would look good onstage'. 'Whenever we were in Europe,' recalls his nephew Vince Wilburn, 'we would grab a fashion magazine. He designed the stage sets.'

World tours had made him cosmopolitan and Erin Davis would be told "'this is a good place to get leather. A lot of good leather here in Barcelona." He had an Italian shoemaker. He had his own way of style – a little bit of Italian, a little bit of Japanese stuff. Issey Miyake, Kohshin Satoh, Armani, Gaultier. He had these two twins in Paris making him stage clothes. His fashion was very forward.'

One of the things Wilburn recalls is how often Miles would change clothes; 'sometimes five or six times a day. I don't know anybody who would do that.'

Well…

Keyboard player Frank McComb played with Prince at several private engagements in the mid-'00s. 'I remember one time he wanted a party at his house. Prince changed his clothes three times. Every time he did, I picked on him.'

Another thing Miles and Prince did in that period was to work quickly and spontaneously – with both specifically asking someone to speak French on their records. Sting, an admirer of Miles's, popped into the studio at the invitation of his bassist Darryl Jones and was asked if he could speak French. That's the former Police singer you hear shouting the Miranda warning in French on the opening track of the 1985 album, *You're Under Arrest.*

It's an album featured at the bedside of Christopher, Prince's character in *Under the Cherry Moon.* The recording of that soundtrack also led to an unexpected call for Prince's head of wardrobe Marie France (unlike Sting, actually French) around eight in the evening from his bodyguard.

'"Would you be OK to come? Prince wants you to translate something in French."

'He gave me a paragraph to translate into French. I said, "You could say it this way or that."

'"Here's a microphone. When I lift my hand, the music will stop."

'I thought that I would get a feeling for it by the second take, but there was never a second take. He applauded and Wendy & Lisa applauded.'

Thus, the rap in the second single from the *Parade* album, 'Girls and Boys', was created.

Welcome to the Madhouse

Prince's deepest excursion into jazz was probably the Madhouse project.

Jellybean Johnson, who was in the Time, the Family and nearly the Revolution, was once told by Prince, 'Bean, I change bands like suits'. As well as the Revolution and the Sign touring band, which were one of the few of his bands that didn't have a name, there was Madhouse.

The press release in January 1987 announced Madhouse, serving up instrumental jazz-funk (or 'faux-jazz' as Eric Leeds calls it), as the brainchild of a keyboard player from Atlanta called Austra Chanel. He was joined by drummer John Lewis, bassist Bill Lewis and saxophonist Leeds. The eponymously titled album credits the studio location as 'Madhouse studios, Pittsburgh, PA'.

The only true part of the above is that Eric Leeds played on Madhouse's three records: *8*, *16* and the unreleased *24*. Leeds (not the Madhouse Studios) was from Pittsburgh, John and Bill Lewis didn't exist and Austra Chanel was the same as Joey Coco, Alexander Nevermind and all the other noms de tune Prince invented. Outside of actors and Laura Albert's writer J.T. LeRoy, Prince is one of the few figures in entertainment who built his own myth by pretending to be other people.

Madhouse were slotted in as the support act on the *Sign o' the Times* tour with Matt Fink, Leeds, Levi Seacer Jr and drummer Dale Alexander onstage, but no Prince. That was the only part of the Madhouse story where he wasn't centre stage. They released two albums (*8* and *16*) and recorded a third (*24*, which was shelved in 1988; another version was planned but also jettisoned in 1994 when Madhouse were joined by drummer Michael Bland and guitarist Sonny Thompson, both of whom *did* exist).

Madhouse is a footnote in Prince history because an avant-garde instrumental album was unlikely to sell (it didn't), but he didn't let the grass grow under his feet as he made it. Todd Herreman regards working on the recording of the first album as one of the most trying weekends of his life. 'They went to rehearsals on a Friday and delivered a song in one sitting. He had a light purple Yamaha grand and said, "Just mic up the piano, set up the piano track, one take, set up the drums, give me the bass. At one in the morning, he called Eric Leeds and you think at two in the morning, he's done with the track.'

Herreman's dread – and, he claims, his first grey hairs – emerged in the early hours when hearing Prince shout out 'fresh tape'.

Eric Leeds remembers the sessions – over a weekend in the autumn of 1986 – as 'pretty much a blur. I do recall that we finished the second or third night about two or three in the morning and I went home, only to be called by Prince just as I was getting into bed. He needed me to come back for another track. I threw on some clothes and was back at the basement studio of his home about 5 a.m.'

Finally, by the Monday morning after the Friday rehearsals, the album was done.

The music of Madhouse did have an afterlife, as Leeds remembers. 'Years later, Prince sent some finished tracks from an unreleased Madhouse album to Miles. Miles would play several of these songs with his own band in the last year or so before he died.'

If you think you haven't heard any of the Madhouse album, you may be mistaken. Prince could recycle, as Todd Herreman remembers. 'Madhouse used the same pitch sample that was on the beginning of "U Got the Look". We used it a couple of times, [including at] the end of *Madhouse 8*.

At the age of sixteen, Maneca Lightner had nabbed Prince's autograph at a record signing her friend had dragged her along to at Colfax, Aurora, Colorado. 'We're talking about the guy who wears underwear and high-heeled boots. I was so not into him.' She saw him again at nineteen. By twenty-one, when she saw him backstage when the *Triple Threat* tour with the Time and Vanity 6 rolled into town, she was a convert. 'I had on a black-and-white vintage polka-dot dress. We finally made eye contact. I got to know Jerome and Jesse Johnson. I knew there was something there between us.'

They stayed in touch and, in 1986, started dating.

One chilly autumn day that year, she was working as an assistant at Denver International Airport answering phone calls. One call stands out. Prince told her he was working on a jazz album and wondered if she would like to be the cover star. Lightner was flown to LA where she was met by Laura LiPuma Nash, who was nominally in charge of record sleeves.

The concept, where the model feeds a hot dog to a smaller actual dog, was not without logistical headaches. Prince inquired after her dress from the Triple Threat tour. She had altered it and 'messed it up', but his wardrobe team patched it back together. A rescue dog was found, whose owner was on set, several hot dogs were bought and an image of Lightner feeding a small dog a hot dog was created at Prince's behest. 'Everything was his idea. They told me to hold it with my fingers and he'd be sniffing and that's how he was able to get the picture. That was my first professional assignment.'

Lightner was trying to make a name for herself as a model but was slightly hamstrung by Prince, as was his wont, refusing to let her work for other clients, apart from City Buses and a commercial for training schools for computers. 'I'm trying to build the Madhouse brand' was the excuse he gave her.

Madhouse's debut *8* (followed ten months later in November by the equally commercially underwhelming *16*) had some visual resonance. Just as Prince's purple jacket on *1999* was a precursor to the famous *Purple Rain* look on the motorcycle, the polka dots seen in Denver in April 1983 and on Madhouse in January 1987 were resplendently displayed on

Prince outfits on the Lovesexy tour throughout 1988 and on the 'Alphabet Street' and 'Glam Slam' videos from that album. They themselves were predated by one Mattie Shaw. Prince's mother loved polka dots. Hayley Drinkall, Cat Glover's friend and manager, says 'that [Lovesexy live] costume to me was an homage to what Mattie used to wear'.

The flavours of the project had stayed with Prince, says MonoNeon, who played bass on his final musical project, 2016's *Black Is the New Black*. 'The tracks I do remember from the *Black Is the New Black* session were in the vein of Madhouse stuff … structured improvisational jams.'

Prince's mood turns Black – and so does his record company's

Fast forward to autumn of 1987, after the release of *Sign o' the Times*, and Prince was flying – and not just to Europe, where the March–June tour of stadia and sports arenas had, rain aside, been a huge hit. By October, only 'Lost in Emotion' by Lisa Lisa and Cult Jam had kept 'U Got the Look' off the top of the Billboard Top 100, his biggest hit since 'Kiss' in April 1986.

How could he go from this to two furious and bitter fights with his record company within a month?

Having delivered and toured *Sign o' the Times* around Europe, it had been ten long years since he had told Warner Brothers A&R executive Lenny Waronker on the floor of the Record Plant in Sausalito not to 'make me black'. He was clearly restless, fed up with the accusation that he had neglected his black audience. He recorded songs like 'Adore' for black radio, but that hadn't sated him.

Levi Seacer Jr detailed his grumble in 1987 on the Blu Ray

version of the *Sign* movie. 'They said Prince has lost the funk. That's why I'm going to make the funkiest album anyone's ever heard.'

Prince informed Waronker of his plans. And they would not be pleasing to his ears, or those of the label. 'I got a call from Prince. *Sign o' the Times* was doing great, he was feeling really good about it. My concern was that things had been moving down instead of up. Great artists go up and down, everybody has their moments. *Sign o' the Times* was a lifeboat in my mind. It solidified where he was. It was growth. I got a call from him. This is the most conciliatory Prince, very sweet. He was being totally honest. "I go to clubs and they don't play my music. They play dance music."

"On the QT, below the radar, I want to put this thing out and call it *The Black Album*, and nobody will know it's me." He's saying this and I'm thinking, *No, no, no, not in the middle of this record. Sign o' the Times*, it just started to breathe, it's got months. If you put something out, there's no way it's going to be under the radar.'

Susan Rogers, who left around this time (like many Prince employees, she just wanted her life back), recalls her boss being 'accused of not being black enough and that's why *The Black Album* was the one that followed this'.

For those who think Warner Brothers were tough on Prince, he could be tough on them too.

Even after Waronker's 'No, no, no', Prince went over him to label boss Mo Ostin, who had the same reaction. But Prince had developed a way of manipulating Waronker and Ostin. His management would agree with him privately, but let Warners take the fight to him. Sometimes, more often than not, it was easier to let him have his way.

In between trips to nightclubs in LA like Voila and Vertigo, he kept working, mainly at Sunset, with Susan Rogers, Todd Herreman, Coke Johnson and Sheila for company, with occasional drop-ins from Eric Leeds and Matt Blistan. Johnson was told to compress the low end to make things funkier for vinyl. A ballad, 'When 2 R in Love', would end up on *Lovesexy*, but the rest was hard-sounding funk (such as 'Le Grind' and 'Cindy C', the latter about the supermodel Cindy Crawford) or entrees into hip hop like '2 Nigs United 4 West Compton', 'Dead On It' and, with Prince's voice manipulated on a Publison pitch-changing device to sound even deeper than his speaking voice, 'Bob George'. This was a diss track about one of his managers Bob Cavallo and the writer Nelson George, who had criticised Prince in an opinion piece.

Johnson remembers 'an experimental time. [The songs] were all written, performed, composed and produced by Prince, so anything was viable to be on any Prince record. Or he could give them to anyone he wanted.'

The UK charts were also reflecting the passion for acid house music and the illegal raves near motorway service stations which would usher in the Second Summer of Love in 1988, which would bleed into a third such summer in '89. In that same era, British chart-toppers included sample-heavy dance hits like M/A/R/R/S's 'Pump up the Volume', Bomb The Bass's 'Beat Dis' (recorded in '87 but a number-one hit the following February) and Chicago house DJ Steve 'Silk' Hurley's 'Jack Your Body'. Prince was listening and sampled 'Music is the Key' by J.M. Silk (who was actually Hurley; it wasn't just Prince who used alter egos) on 'Cindy C'.

It wasn't just the funk that was hard-edged, according to Coke Johnson. 'The fairly funkier stuff had some controversial lyrics. It had a lot of animosity and anger in it. The rough edges were smoothed out on what most people heard. Anything that could be misconstrued as slander was taken out. The blacker side, the nastier side, was taken out.

'I thought we were making music for Sheila E.'s birthday. We recorded them all on 24-track and he could take them to the nightclub. We would do a test pressing and cut it on a lacquered disc. We had a turntable in there because it was in the other room. We had the whole A-side of an album and I would take that down to Bernie Grundman [who ran a mastering studio in Hollywood]. It would take several hours and I would pick up the tapes and then we would play it.'

'Prince would record the masters,' says Todd Herreman, 'and take them to the club, play them to see how they went down and then chuck them away.' Those searching rubbish bins in the vicinity of West Hollywood nightclubs at the time would have discovered rare Prince masters, much to the consternation of Alan Leeds who had begged him not to dump his records. The fact many would end up in the dumpsters suggests Prince wasn't serious about releasing it as music.

'It was just music that Eric and I had played on for months at a time and it never came out,' Matt Blistan theorises. 'I don't remember any specific time [Prince said] this is coming out or this is not coming out. You just roll with it. We really never knew.'

At one point, Prince knew, having beaten Ostin and Waronker down and got his way.

Everyone at Warners was mobilised.

While most of the record was in the can by March (the month *Sign...* was released), the final track, *When 2 R in Love*, was recorded in October and the album was scheduled for release in December.

Depending on whom you ask, there were between 100,000 and 400,000 copies pressed, along with a load more sleeves.

Bob Merlis, then working Warners' publicity, points out that 'to release an album by a major artist, you always overproduce the sleeves and leave them in reserve so the records can fit into the sleeves thereafter. In [*This Is*] *Spinal Tap*, they have an album that is mainly black. This was life imitating art. An amazingly self-indulgent person was imitating an amazingly self-indulgent band.'

Laura LiPuma Nash, whose department looked after sleeves, knew that 'everyone was walking on egg shells' for Prince. Confidence gained by leading on the design on *Parade* and feeding in heavily on the *Sign...* sleeves meant another important decision was her responsibility – although, with an all-black sleeve, this should have been easy. She visited the printers in Seattle.

'They wanted to know if I should do a warm black or a cool black. Bob [Merlis] said 'just do a rich black'. That one I found I could answer without checking with him.'

Marylou Badeaux was ready to market the album too. 'I had twenty-five cassettes and twenty-five albums getting ready to go out the next day and we got an urgent memo saying we were to "return everything and further information will follow". This goes to show how artist-friendly Warner Brothers were. My understanding was that Prince called Mo directly. If it had been at CBS or A&M, at the very least they would have argued profusely or released it in spite of him. Few copies got leaked.'

Sometime in the late autumn of 1987, Susan Hale's phone rang at 3 a.m. As point person for Prince's day-to-day manager Steve Fargnoli, she instantly knew who was calling.

It was the day before *The Black Album* was to be distributed to radio ahead of its scheduled release on 8 December and all the trucks were loaded with the product.

'To be clear, we all got phone calls from him at all hours, with every sort of weird request. But this was different. He sounded scared and panicky. He said that everyone was right and that *The Black Album* was a mistake and he never should have fought everyone and I had to get the records recalled from the trucks before distribution began. I kept saying I didn't know how to do this and to please call Steve [Fargnoli], call Bob [Cavallo]. He kept saying no, I had to do it. He was begging me to help him and I remember I was pacing and shaking talking to him. So when I got off with him, I gathered my thoughts and then called Bob at home, 4.30 a.m. and he took it from there. I had no choice.'

After Prince had the release shelved, *The Black Album* would become the most bootlegged album of all time.

But why did he have it shelved? Again, this is open to interpretation.

Eddie Miller, one of the first engineers at Paisley Park, shares a memory of Prince 'in a different frame of mind and the sense I got was to do with Ingrid Chavez. On a spiritual level, they probably had some private discussions and they were talking some spiritual ideas and that had a lot to do with him wanting to change direction and the message in him putting out a new record.'

Ingrid Chavez was 'a little hippy spirit', according to engineer Michael Koppelman. Prince had spotted her performing in a Minneapolis nightclub and, says Karen Krattinger, 'was very impressed by her'. Most of the aspiring talent Prince spotted were singers, musicians or dancers. Chavez styled herself as a poet. His driver Robbie Paster spotted that soon they were 'spiritually connected'. Romantically too, say many in his then circle.

Chemically? The urban myth is that Prince killed *The Black Album* because of a bad ecstasy trip. Susan Rogers admits 'the stories were that Ingrid entered his life, and he did experiment with ecstasy. There are plenty of hints that that was the case on the *Lovesexy* album. Some of his idols did drugs and [I believe] there were a couple of times he experimented with drugs. The song 'Moonbeam Levels' [a song slated originally for *Purple Rain*, which dates back to 1982] reflects on it.'

Eddie Miller 'got the sense that he probably went through a cocaine phase because when I worked at Paisley Park, the studio manager, whose nickname was Hotguy, kind of laid down the law. No cocaine in the studio. I feel that was to keep it away from Prince.'

That may be unfair as another interviewer remembers George Clinton doing cocaine in Studio A. Clinton, who wrote about his own drug use in his memoir, told *Rolling Stone* on Prince's death that Prince 'didn't do no drugs'.

'Prince and drugs? At the time, it didn't even cross my mind,' adds Miller. 'I didn't know how he could be as focused and do the kind of hours he worked for at least ten or fifteen years. I don't think that would have happened if he was a heavy drug user. He was probably using some to get inspiration. Some of the ideas for *Lovesexy* might have emanated from that, but it was probably a more fleshed-out series of themes.'

Susan Hale takes a different view, referencing that 3 a.m. call. 'It was scary and I was scared for him. He was really freaking out and I've heard many say in retrospect it was a bad drug trip. I just find that so hard to believe unless I was completely naive. You see, Prince was the most anti-drug person I knew. If you dared show up inebriated in any way, you were O-U-T. Even if we were on tour, you would basically be thrown off and replaced the next. He wasn't kidding. Prince demanded a drug-free zone or you didn't have a job. I actually credit my time with him for keeping me *off* drugs, so the whole *Black Album* thing – not to mention the way he passed on – are just not the boy I knew, or at all representative of my time with him.'

Whether or not drugs were in his system, a few colleagues say Ingrid Chavez influenced his decision-making on killing *The Black Album*.

'I think it was all part of this epiphany,' suggests Marylou Badeaux. 'He had been driving around with Ingrid Chavez and he felt he had to stop it. Mo honoured that wish. I don't see that Mo would have got into a big argument with him. Prince was very passionate about stopping it and Mo would have picked up on that. That's the kind of company it was.'

His then publicist Robyn Riggs ascribes a higher power. 'He kind of wasn't sure about *The Black Album*. He landed at LAX and, at that time, there had been an earthquake [most likely the 1 October tremor in Whittier Narrows] and he took that as a sign from God.'

An earthquake on the West Coast had inspired 'Housequake', but *The Black Album* was a different kind of earthquake.

'*The Black Album* crushed the promotion of *Sign o' the Times*,' argues Lisa Janzen of Cavallo, Ruffalo & Fargnoli. 'At that time, we were so linear in promoting records. One single, four months later, then another single comes out. That was the soft spot for Prince. Most artists – as long as they have creative control of their record – then they turn it over to the business people who sell it as they see fit. Prince was the opposite of that. That's why he ended up with "SLAVE" painted on his face.'

Randy Newman, a friend of Waronker's, feels Prince 'almost produced too much. There was so much stuff and it's astonishing, but it might have been counterproductive for him. He could have had an album out every six months.'

'He was very future-facing,' offers Sam Jennings, who worked with Prince in the noughties. 'It was all about the next thing.

Even when a record would be done and hadn't been out yet, he was already on to the next thing and over it.'

Prince had turned a collection of songs to replay in clubs for Sheila E.'s birthday party into an album called *The Funk Bible*, and then named *The Black Album*. His record company begged him not to. Then he begged them not to release it at the eleventh hour.

'We destroyed all but 100 of them, which we kept,' remembers Waronker. 'We caved, and then he caved. It ended up being OK for the relationship because he decided it. I could feel a sense of too much power and some of the decisions started not to make any sense. *The Black Album* wasn't a smart move and it ended up being an expensive mistake. He paid for some of that. I can't remember how.'

Prince skipped Europe and Asia after the *Purple Rain* North American tour to release *Around the World in a Day*, he directed *Under the Cherry Moon* himself, and chose not to tour *Sign...* in the US. So, by late 1987, Prince's spur-of-the-moment decisions were not a surprise to Warners.

Around half a million records, and even more sleeves (to cover spares), were pulled a week before they were due for release. The album would finally be released in November 1994 for a short time, just as Warners and Prince were about to part company.

Randy Newman chuckles when he remembers the aftermath when Prince was paranoid about it being bootlegged. 'He went up to Lenny's house. Prince saw a copy of the record on Lenny's desk and Lenny had to say "I'm innocent!"'

'I got a phone call,' recalls publicist Robyn Riggs, who kept her own cassette copy. 'Scrap it.'

Video Soul presenter Donnie Simpson had heard the music played at an October 1987 party Prince would throw for David

Bowie at Paisley Park. 'We knew about *The Black Album*, and we knew it was a mysterious thing. Two or three years later, I ran into Prince and he said "you're the reason I didn't release *The Black Album*. You said 'this is such a groove' and I'm so much more than that." I wish I had thought to tell him that he shouldn't have listened to me.'

Simpson had an unlikely guest on *Video Soul*, Donny Osmond. After their chat, the clean-living brother of Marie couriered his copy of the record to Simpson.

'It was the funniest thing that the coolest record was sent to me by this white Mormon. How would he have one?

'That's how I got my copy of it.'

Returning to a lighter mood with more wholesome messages would be important to Prince, even though he performed some tracks from the album on the *Lovesexy* tour. Three days after *The Black Album* had been due for release, on 11 December, Prince recorded 'Positivity' at Paisley Park. The same day, he recorded the first track for the next album *Lovesexy*, 'Eye No', which starts with a voiceover from Ingrid Chavez. On the first video from that record, for 'Alphabet Street', letters floated behind Prince: 'Don't buy *The Black Album* – I'm sorry.'

Prince was sorry, Warner Brothers were sorry, but the record added to his mythology, in the way that the unreleased *Smile* from 1967 had for the Beach Boys. And, as one of Prince's wisest counsels, Dave Hampton, points out: 'When you have money, you can recover from bad decisions.'

Relations between Prince and Warners would stabilise, but *The Black Album*'s release/non-release hardly helped smooth relations between him and the record company. Twelve months prior, he was mad at them for not releasing his triple album. By December 1987, the tables were turned. The record he wanted released and then unreleased had his bosses in full eye-roll mode.

Momentum for *Sign o' the Times*, hot on the heels of the decision not to tour the US, was killed stone dead.

Tour manager Alan Leeds is more hard-headed in his appraisal of *The Black Album*'s merits. 'As I look back, I don't regard it as important. Because it was illicit, it acquired a cachet it probably didn't deserve.'

CHAPTER 13

I COULD NEVER TAKE THE PLACE OF YOUR MAN

*The man who came with strings attached ... Somewhere
in the Cloud, there's a guitar ... Prince enjoyed guitarists.
Sort of ... When his guitar gently – and not so gently – wept
... 'This music is for my kids' ... 'I Could Never Take the
Place of Your Man' ... Eine kleine Princemusik ...
His environmentally friendly side*

The man who came with strings attached

Songs that Prince recorded after the '80s were generally performed live sparingly. 'Guitar' from his thirty-second album *Planet Earth* (released in 2007) was a song with a theme of Prince loving the person on his arm but preferring the object around his neck. It was a number he would play again and again. From 2007 through to 2016, whenever he had his trusted Hohner HS Mad Cat Telecaster draped around him, there was a chance it would slip into the set.

He had an intense relationship with his guitars.

Perhaps because he started on piano like his father, who would consider his son's keyboard skills not up to the required standard, or because he was the bassist in his first band Grand Central, it's possible Prince considered playing electric guitar an escape either from living up to his father or from the piano he would play at Bryant Junior High talent shows.

He was in a school piano class with Jimmy Jam when they were discussing who'd play where in the band. 'He said guitar and I said drums.'

Across his life, his closeness to his guitar is a recurring theme.

When he moved in with the Jackson Family at 1248 Russell Avenue, because he didn't get on with mother Mattie's second husband Hayward Baker, his second mother figure Glenda Jackson (two doors down from his third mum figure, Bernadette) died in 1976. 'The day of my mum's service,' reflects her son Terry, 'he was in the basement playing the guitar like crazy. Seven people in the house had to go and get him to stop. That was his way of coping.'

As well as an escape, it was a release right up to his passing.

Chris James, the engineer who worked on his final released album, 2016's *HITnRUN Phase Two*, has an enduring memory. 'I would look at him playing guitar at four in the morning and he was so geeked out making music, still like a little kid.'

David Rule, his guitar and keyboard tech from *Purple Rain* to *Sign o' the Times*, considers it the instrument on which Prince felt most at one with self-expression. 'When he was playing guitar, that's where he got more into himself.'

The guitarist most often mentioned in association with Prince was obvious.

When Knut-Koupee guitar shop employee Dave Rusan tried out playing guitar for Prince's band at Del's Tire Mart on 2nd Street South in Minneapolis, where Prince hired out a rehearsal space, he noted that 'the only thing Prince had put up on the wall was a picture of Jimi Hendrix'.

No pressure.

Saxophonist Adrian Crutchfield – who, with Prince, bassist Mono Neon and drummer Kirk Johnson, recorded the unreleased and unfinished album *Black Is the New Black* in the early months of 2016 – recalls echoes of Prince's hero. 'When we were playing with Mono, I saw a lot of Jimi in him in that element. There was a freedom, living in the moment, not worried about the crowd, not worried about how many verses are in the song. Jimi never worried about any of that.'

Around the time that *Sign o' the Times* was recorded, keyboard technician Todd Herreman recalls a rare moment of Princely demureness when he turned down a guitar gifted to him by Hendrix's father, who had attended a concert on the Purple Rain tour. 'Prince felt like he didn't deserve it. Prince could be very humble at times. Not often.'

That gig in Tacoma in February 1985 inspired a performance that David Rule says was on a par with Prince's 2004 Rock & Roll Hall of Fame tribute to George Harrison, arguably the most celebrated guitar solo in his career, even eclipsing the one on *Purple Rain*'s title track. 'Jimi Hendrix's father came to the [1985] gig. I'd seen Jimi a couple of times and I saw him again that night.'

Prince and Hendrix was the obvious comparison for joining-the-dots music writers who saw a black musician playing rock guitar. But Jimi wasn't his favourite. The same year as the Tacoma gig, Prince told *Rolling Stone* that the comparison was 'only because he's black. Hendrix played more blues, but Santana played prettier.'

Carlos Santana, the Mexican-born bandleader of the band which took his surname and a guitarist who incorporated a spread from Latin rock to jazz fusion, comes up in Prince conversations again and again.

'When you listen to him,' says Alan Leeds, 'if he sounds like anybody else, it would be Santana.'

Susan Rogers agrees. 'He said the person he patented himself on as a guitar player is Carlos Santana.'

Terry Jackson posted online a setlist from an early Grand Central concert (the band ran from 1971–74) that featured Santana songs 'Shades of Time', 'Jungle Strut' and 'Black Magic Woman'.

Prince gazed up at Sheila E.'s reflection in his dressing-room mirror at the Circle Star Theatre in 1979 when she first introduced herself to him. His first words were 'I know who you are'. He would have. She'd been in Carlos Santana's band (as well as his girlfriend), which made her someone Prince would go on to covet both professionally and personally.

There are Santana echoes on the 1987 version of 'I Could Never Take the Place of Your Man', but the song predates that version by a full eight years, from the time he was working on his second album, *Prince*. The solo from the later version, and that use of space, is reminiscent of Santana, but Prince enthused about other guitarists.

'Prince loved the hell out of Jeff Beck,' says his cousin Chazz Smith. 'He loved him. He thought he was a monster.' Beck was a guest at Paisley Park, which brought out the owner's rare fanboy side. George Benson, another one he admired, came to Paisley to play as well. Prince also told Ricky Peterson that 'Sonny Thompson [an under-the-radar contemporary from Minneapolis who played with Prince on several tours and still gigs in the city] is my favourite guitar player.'

Was Prince just being nice about one of his childhood mentors? 'That doesn't surprise me or anyone [around at the time] at all,' says Margie Cox, who still sings with Thompson at Bunkers in Minneapolis most Sunday nights. 'Sonny is from another planet.

Sonny probably taught Prince half or more of what he knew. He really had a great effect on Prince.'

Most axe gods are known for their long solos, but throughout his career, Prince played both lead and rhythm. As well as soloists like Hendrix, Santana and Clapton (with whom he would jam onstage in London afterparties around the time of the Parade tour), Prince also admired players like Tony Maiden from Rufus & Chaka Khan ('That's Tony Maiden,' he told Dan Piepenbring, the co-author of his memoir, at a Paisley Park gig. 'I learned how to play rhythm guitar from him'), Jeff Beck and George Benson.

Benson discussed his Jehovah's Witness faith with Prince when recording at Paisley, as well as gifting him an Ibanez signature series guitar.

Producer and friend Jimmy Jam sums up Prince's guitar influences as follows: 'For me, it was Freddie Stone as a rhythm guitarist, James Brown's guitarist [Jimmy Nolen] but it is also Carlos Santana. The intricacy of the way he plays is Lindsey Buckingham. He was a huge Fleetwood Mac fan. Obviously it was a combination of those players that made him the guitarist he was.'

The relationship with Prince and other musicians could get tricky.

'He had a funny relationship with Prince,' says Greg Errico, who drummed with Santana at Woodstock. 'He had asked [Carlos] to come to Paisley. Carlos found out he was there for an audition [which Prince hadn't specified] and he didn't like that. If you hear Carlos, you really hear him, you can hear two seconds of one note and you know it's Carlos. How do you audition that?!? You can ask him to come down, but it's not an audition!' The Santana reaction was more polite than you imagine Prince's might have been: 'He pulled his lead out of his amp and said, "You don't need me here."'

By 1999, the relationship was more on an even keel. Santana's Grammy-winning album *Supernatural* had inspired the collaboration-heavy *Rave Un2 the Joy Fantastic* the same year. 'That was conscious,' confesses Jacqui Thompson, then working at Paisley Park. 'He was really good friends with Carlos, and Carlos had done a record like that and he dug that.'

Another unusual aspect to Prince was that although he loved to shred on lead, his rhythm guitar playing was a huge part of his songwriting. Ray Parker Jr, one of the most successful rhythm guitarists of all time thanks to his work with Stevie Wonder and Michael Jackson among others, says that 'rhythm guitar is definitely more difficult. You're playing six strings at once instead of one string. More people get excited when they see someone playing a guitar solo, but that's a lot easier to do than six strings. Most people who write the songs are rhythm guitarists. Look at Keith Richards.'

Parker, the studio musician who hit big with Raydio's 'Jack and Jill' and then 'Ghostbusters' feels that Prince 'had a great groove. He's more of a guitarist that plays a style to his own music. His talent isn't playing his songs. He never intended to be a studio musician.'

'Prince was all James Brown,' adds Alexander O'Neal, who had JB's guitarist Jimmy Nolen, the innovator of the 'chicken scratch' style, in mind. 'Even his guitar rhythmic choices, the way he stroked his guitar. Some guitar players play with a strum. He kept his guitar air tight.'

As Jimmy Nolen influenced Prince, so his own guitar playing was influencing others – Miles Davis, for one.

'He would always refer to Prince and James Brown,' recalls Adam Holzman who played keyboards in Miles' band around the time of 1986's *Tutu*. 'He was particularly fascinated by the horn riffs and rhythm guitar, and how they functioned and fit together like a big clock. He would talk about Bud Powell, he would talk about Bird, he would talk about Coltrane. He would definitely refer to Prince often and to Jimi Hendrix.'

When asked if he was a lead or rhythm guitar player, Tony Maiden – one of Prince's favourite guitarists who came to prominence playing on the Rufus and Chaka Khan records – says, 'He's both. He could do both. He took from Miles Davis and Santana and Larry Graham and he just took everybody into that melting pot and made it his. I hear everybody in Prince. He was a great listener. He studied everybody like Coltrane, and Bach and Beethoven.'

Mono Neon, no slouch on the six strings himself, played bass with Prince on *Black Is the New Black* and notes that Prince's 'rhythm guitar stuff was definitely enough for me to realise I need to work on my guitar playing'.

Guitarist Steve Vai (Frank Zappa, Whitesnake) adds that Prince 'was totally locked and his playing was completely appropriate for his songs and his persona. I always felt Prince was a dynamic and colourful rock and blues soloist that could also throw down bulletproof funky rhythm shapes.'

Vai has discussed Prince with other musicians, all of whom say the same thing. 'How can one person be so talented at so many things?'

Somewhere in the Cloud, there's a guitar

Prince being Prince, he had to be different.

That meant his own guitar.

Dave Rusan didn't make Prince's first solo band, but he made something longer-lasting: the Cloud guitar, shaped with the ornate squiggle, a peach-coloured version of which adorns the cover of *Sign o' the Times*.

As with his Telecaster, his Rickenbacker ('his baby in the recording studio,' recalls Peggy McCreary) and the guitar he'd play in the '90s and '00s in the shape of his logo, the cloud guitar would be produced in various colours. No surprise; Prince would do this with outfits and shoes.

He came into Rusan's South Minneapolis workplace, Knut-Koupee Music, just after *Dirty Mind*. Rusan was commissioned to construct a guitar for $2,000 each ('a lot of money in the '80s') from 'hard maple, the same wood they make Fender in. It's very hard to carry, but I figured it had to be rugged as a movie prop as these things can get banged around. It weighed the same as a Gibson Les Paul. He was very fit and he worked out, so he had no trouble playing the guitar in that hard wood. They all got broken as he would throw them to the guitar tech. I built three.'

Rusan wasn't the only one who would make him a guitar.

In his more emotionally immature days during the Purple Rain tour, another guitar was commissioned from New York luthier Roger Sadowsky, who also made guitars for Keith Richards, Pat Metheny and Steely Dan's Walter Becker. Sadowsky was flown first class to Minneapolis. 'Prince and his giant bodyguard [Chick Huntsberry] would stand fifteen feet away from us. Prince would whisper what he wanted to say to the bodyguard and the bodyguard would walk over to me to say what Prince wanted.'

What Prince wanted this time was a guitar that appears to ejaculate. This would be for the *Purple Rain* film and subsequent tour.

'That was a prop guitar linked up to an ivory liquid. We built the neck of copper tubing and it went through the body into a cavity and into a valve which they had for this prop guitar. They were going to connect it to a tank of ivory liquid offstage.'

David Rule has a memory of installing the plumbing on what he calls 'the jizz guitar. He was insistent that I do it one night so, to do it, we had to change the parts in the tank and we didn't have time to test it and it dribbled out the top and leaked out the back. We said, "Dude, you didn't give us time to check it."'

Of Prince's guitars over many campaigns, the two that most frequently recur are the maple and leopard-print Hohner HS Mad Cat Telecaster and the Cloud.

The Hohner was the leitmotif you would see around Prince's shoulders at the 2004 George Harrison tribute, the 2007 Super Bowl half-time show and the Santana medley at the 2008 Coachella festival. Rumours vary on where it was bought: one says at an LA gas station for $30; Rule thinks it was from Knut-Koupee. 'That was like his shop of choice – and Pete's Guitars [also in Minneapolis].'

The Hohner was durable, and not just in terms of Prince's career. 'There were times he would get so into it,' recalls Rule, 'he would take the guitar off and just drop it. If it was the Cloud guitar, it would break. He would throw the Hohner across the room and nothing would happen to it.'

'He called me at the beginning of the *Purple Rain* tour because Hohner had stopped making the Mad Cat guitar,' says Roger Sadowsky. 'So they originally called me in to make two reproductions.'

There were other guitars memorable over the years, such as the white angular one that adorns the back sleeve of *Welcome 2 America*. This one, designed by Jerry Auerswald, was given to him by Princess Gloria von Thurn of the Bulgarian royal family.

'She would throw parties when he was there,' remembers his make-up artist Robyn Lynch.

'That guitar was from her. She was a big fan and would fly around to see him and she presented him with that guitar.'

For her part, Princess Gloria reveals that 'he loved the guitar so much, he rerecorded the guitar part of an entire album [she does not specify which but *Welcome 2 America* is a reasonable guess] with it.'

Everything about and around guitars appealed to Prince. He had plectrums that featured the words 'Love God' in purple writing. 'I have a bunch of them,' laughs Dave Rusan, 'because when he ordered them, they came in the wrong thickness and the owner of the store gave everyone some.'

'Even though he was quite rough on equipment,' adds his soundman Rob 'Cubby' Colby, 'he was very attached to his guitar, to his pedalboard, his mic, his stand. We would clean them for him without asking. He would catch the scent of fresh Lysol that I used to brush the mic stand.'

Although he had guitars custom-made, he borrowed engineer Sylvia Massy's Fender Gemini 2 acoustic ('a cheapie I bought for $100,' she says) when they were working on *Diamonds and Pearls* together. It's the Gemini 2 you hear on 'Walk Don't Walk'.

Being Prince's guitar tech should have come with danger money or some form of music industry pre-nup. Morris Hayes singles out Takumi Suetsugu, in post most of the twenty-first century, for praise. 'He dealt with Prince on many harsh days. He's the Yoda of guitar techs because he had a trial by fire. He had Prince's respect because he was just a good guitar tech. I have seen Takumi save an entire production singlehandedly because the sound system wasn't there. He just got on the phone and did what he needed to do.'

'I was originally hired as Prince's guitar tech,' admits Rule. 'There was a problem with his effects. They couldn't fix it so it was "Gimme another guy". Three guys got on the phone and tried to talk me out of it. He's difficult to work for. There's very little direct communication – it goes through three different people before it goes back to him.

'Two days from the end of production rehearsals, he decided he didn't want me doing his guitars because I smoked. Technically I got fired, but I got a bunch of knuckleheads to get me a new job. I used to set up the grand piano in his dressing room. Dressing rooms are usually big enough to hold it. I had five or six guys with me and set up a grand piano. It's not rocket science.'

Rule, whose two weeks in Prince's service were worthy of a gold clock compared to some guitar techs, admits the role 'was a revolving door. It's a personality thing. If he didn't like the guy, that was it. It was very little communication with him. Working out details of how you want things done with him is difficult. He was looking for someone who could watch him and pick it up.

'I just looked after the dressing-room piano. The guy who was looking after Wendy went to work for Billy Idol. The guy who replaced him didn't last more than a week.'

After that, Rule helped out Wendy and stayed with Prince until the *Sign* movie.

Prince's relationship with guitars wasn't entirely dissimilar to the one he had with his girlfriends. He wasn't entirely faithful, but if he wanted one, he liked a level of exclusivity – as ever, it was all on his terms.

An example is the 1961 custom Epiphone Crestwood owned by the guitarist Kirk Douglas of *The Tonight Show*'s house band the Roots. Prince turned up for a 2013 episode of Jimmy Fallon's show without a guitar. He asked the show's musical director Jonathan Cohen if he could use one of Douglas's, who wasn't around. The white Crestwood caught his eye. Prince wanted to play it on the show – and to buy it.

Douglas's sense of ownership of his guitar kicked in. 'He can totally use the guitar,' he recalls, explaining his mindset at the time, 'and totally not buy it from me. It's one of my favourite guitars and it had a very distinct sound. It was not for sale. I thought, *Maybe he doesn't want to use it.*'

After playing 'Screwdriver' with 3rdEyeGirl, 'in between songs, he says, "Let me see that other guitar," and then proceeds to do the song "Bambi" on it. He does an amazing version and the feeling I had was excitement. At the end, I thought he was going to play behind his head, but instead of doing that, he tossed it in the air and it came crashing down to the ground. I remember the feeling – such a shift of emotions.'

The side of the headstock had broken off and the fret board had separated completely.

After the performance had been mixed and it was time to leave, Douglas had one last way to retrieve his memory of the situation and asked Prince:

'You broke it. Can you at least sign it?'

'I haven't signed anything since the '70s.'

Andrew Watt, who interned for the Roots before becoming one of the world's most in-demand record producers, laughs. 'Kirk is on TV and watching his idol play his favourite guitar and break his favourite guitar.' The inference is that Prince's perspective was, 'If I can't own this guitar, no one can own this guitar.'

Douglas can now see the positives from his favourite guitar being (temporarily) wrecked.

'I got the guitar fixed. It got so many cool conversations. We are talking about somebody that is not used to hearing the word "no". His perception of reality by this point was different from most humans. For all I know, who knows if his genius is "I'm going to help this guy out by giving him something to talk about by breaking his guitar"? I'm giving him the benefit of the doubt, but I will say this: hurt people hurt people.'

Prince's team arranged to pay for the repairs by electronic transfer the next day.

And there were some other fun by-products for the guitarist

known as Captain Kirk. Jackson Browne, a user of the Crestwood (Jimi Hendrix, Elliott Smith and the MC5's Wayne Kramer were others), emailed Elvis Costello, who had recorded an album with the Roots, with suggestions of where the Crestwood could be repaired.

As comedian Chris Rock told Douglas, 'Now you have a "Prince Was an Asshole to Me" story.'

James Poyser, who plays keys for the Roots, says he will never forget 'the look on his face when that guitar landed. He was so crestfallen. The band just started laughing. Everybody was laughing apart from Kirk.'

While Poyser admits it was 'a bit of a jerk move', he adds that 'in my mind, Prince knows the effect on the story that would come out of it. This instrument will never be the same. This guitar will now be legendary.'

And for those asking why Captain Kirk's protective instincts towards the Crestwood didn't extend to it being stored safely at home and not at the famous NBC Building, Douglas offers an explanation. 'It was in the 30 Rock because the Roots had to play a tribute concert within seven days at Carnegie Hall.

'For Prince.

'The reason that guitar was in the building broke the guitar.'

Prince enjoyed guitarists. Sort of.

Randy Newman also believes Prince's prowess on other instruments informed his playing with an understanding outside of other maestros' realms. 'He's got some ideas that a drummer wouldn't have and they're good. They're great as a matter of fact. His guitar ideas aren't the kind of ideas that a guitar player would have necessarily. He will do different things on an instrument from what they will.'

An example of this would be how he recorded his music.

'A lot of times,' Prince told *Guitar Player* magazine in 2004, 'I'll sample a guitar that I've recorded, and then overdub the same part with a keyboard. The attack of the keyboard gives guitar lines more impact and punch.'

Hans-Martin Buff, an engineer for Prince in the '90s, notes that this was 'one of the things that really set apart Prince from many other great musicians – he didn't write for his instrument. A lot of people are really great guitarists and write for their guitar. He would play a really great solo and chuck it out.'

Prince enjoyed guitarists. Sort of.

Ricky Peterson has an indelible memory of his boss's reaction to Minneapolis guitarist Jimi Behringer, with whom Prince would occasionally sit at clubs in town, when he heard his playing on 'The Most Beautiful Girl in the World'.

'It's really good, but I hate other guitar players.'

As Peterson notes, Prince's pragmatic instincts kicked in and Behringer's work was used: 'He didn't cut off his nose to spite his face.' The finished product trumped jealousy. It would be Prince's only UK number one.

Both his hiring process and ears were instinctive. When Dez Dickerson tired of Prince's out-there expressions of sexuality ahead of the 1999 tour and skipped a soundcheck, Prince heard bandmate Lisa Coleman's then girlfriend Wendy Melvoin strumming in the next bedroom.

'I was totally influenced by Joni Mitchell and auto-tunings,' she recounted to *MOJO* magazine. 'I played this big, fat progression. And his eyes were like pinwheels.'

'It was pretty impulsive,' argues Susan Rogers. 'Here's this eighteen-year-old kid, she's sitting on the bed playing, and he hired her on the spot. When he encountered someone who he thought was ahead of the game, he wanted them.

'He put Wendy in his band because he really believed she could do it. Because he was such an extraordinary teen and such an extraordinary learner, I think he believed that people closest to him were capable of the same.'

As talented as Wendy Melvoin was, she could possibly not emulate one particular solo from 2004. This would reframe the way Prince was considered as a guitarist for the rest of his career and reverberates long after his passing.

When his guitar gently – and not so gently – wept

Growing up listening to Santana and Hendrix and the rhythm of James Brown's band meant Prince played both rhythm and lead. This duality often meant his guitar-playing was overlooked and not regarded as highly as that of other players. This led to perhaps the most remarkable thing he ever did. Or, as his friend and long-time front of house engineer Scottie Baldwin put it, 'just a day in a life ... a very normal performance'.

In 2004, with twenty-five years having passed since his debut album, Prince was inducted into the Rock & Roll Hall of Fame at New York's Waldorf Astoria. The same night, George Harrison would be honoured posthumously.

Prince's band would open the show with a ten-minute set of his songs while Outkast paid tribute. Everyone was talking about how it should end. Joel Gallen, the producer and director of the whole ceremony, had thoughts.

'As well as helping shape their own sets, I'm also trying to think about how to end the night. "Wouldn't it be great if 'While My Guitar Gently Weeps' was the last song and out comes Prince who had opened the show?"'

He put the idea to Prince's lawyer and Prince asked to meet in north Hollywood. 'I was in there for a good ninety minutes, two hours. We talked about the Rock & Roll Hall of Fame. He had seen a lot of my work, which was a shock, and was very complimentary.'

Prince admitted to Gallen he didn't 'normally participate in group finales or songs [but] this is something he'd consider. He would listen, think about it, listen to the song and he also wanted to know who would own the material. I am sure the Rock & Roll Hall of Fame would want to own it, but I said I could put the Rock & Roll Hall of Fame in touch with his lawyer, but it was never brought up again.'

Prince also had an idea he put to Gallen for his own tribute: adding Alicia Keys to the Outkast section.

'We did reach out to her, but she has a gig in New Orleans.'

'Yeah, but she needs to be there.'

'Perhaps you would like to reach out to her.'

Alicia Keys attended.

'He was looking for someone who could speak about him better than anybody. When we look back on that, most people remember Alicia Keys's poem. Nobody remembers what Outkast said or what Prince said. Even a short speech would have more impact. Everybody was talking about Alicia Keys's speech, so he was right.'

The speech *was* memorable – to the extent Prince screened it for months before his subsequent shows that year. But it took one more meeting before Prince signed off on the idea of an arguably more enduring snapshot from the same evening: playing on the Beatles song.

'Once I knew 100 per cent,' recalls Gallen, 'that's when I reached out to Tom Petty and Jeff Lynne's camp. To my surprise, they thought "Taxman" would be the better song. Nothing against "Taxman", but it's not as legendary. After a few back and forths, they finally agreed.'

On YouTube, Prince's guitar solo lives on as part of an all-star band (Jeff Lynne, Tom Petty, Steve Winwood, George Harrison's son Dhani …) on 'While My Guitar Gently Weeps' on a night Prince and Harrison were both being honoured.

Prince, dressed in a dark suit and red shirt, with matching handkerchief and hat, pops in and plays a solo that is, depending on your perspective, an incendiary, out-of-body experience peacocking other world-class musicians onstage into mere shadows – or, if you're one of the musicians adept enough to play their own guitar solos, an attention-hogging hijack of a small group of men who for decades had been on close, Wilbury terms with a quarter of the Beatles.

Petty and Lynne had assembled a band featuring Dhani, Lynne's guitarist Marc Mann, and drummer Steve Ferrone and bassist Scott Thurston from Petty's band the Heartbreakers. They were joined at rehearsals by Traffic's Jim Capaldi on percussion, along with keys from Steve Winwood and Jeff Young, who played for another honouree, Jackson Browne. Young was there as insurance as they weren't sure Winwood could make it. In the end, both played.

Gallen had spoken with Prince about the solo. He admits on the night before he was asking himself, *Would he really come back and if he doesn't come to rehearsals, is he going to do it? Will this dream performance that I have envisaged in my head actually happen?*

At ten on the dot, Prince returned.

Ferrone remembers the special guest's arrival. 'We ran down the song a couple of times and we look across the stage and somebody was setting up Prince. That was run past Olivia [Harrison, George's widow] and she was a bit resistant to it. There was a little bit of "What's he going to do?" and he sort of arrived and got plugged in.'

Young was talking to Winwood 'about Hammond organ stuff, then I noticed a guy plugging in his guitar between where Scott and Tom were standing stage left. He was dressed in a suit and red shirt and was about the same size as Dhani Harrison who was standing behind him onstage.'

Ferrone admits that 'there was a tension on the stage about "What's this guy doing here?". I said to Winwood, "I think I'm going to go and say hello" and Winwood said, "You're not!" Prince had this reputation that he didn't want anybody to talk to him. I ran round the back of the amps and said:

'Nice to meet you. I'm Steve Ferrone.'

'I know who you are.'

For all Prince's swagger, he was walking onto a stage with a tight-knit group made up of musicians who had worked with Tom Petty and Jeff Lynne, both close friends of George and bandmates in the Travelling Wilburys. Olivia had personally said she wanted the band to be comprised of people that knew and loved George. Prince was the interloper.

'It's always difficult to walk into a situation like that,' argues Ferrone. 'Prince didn't know anybody on that stage. He was put into that by the powers-that-be. When I walked up to him and said hello, he seemed very happy that somebody had done that.

'When I walked back and was talking to Winwood, Prince is looking right at me and playing 'Schoolboy Crush' [from Ferrone's previous group Average White Band's 1975 album, *Cut the Cake*]. He does know who I am!'

Then it was time to tackle 'While My Guitar Gently Weeps'. 'We ran down the song and Tom went "Just make the second solo and go for it and I will tell the band when to finish."'

Gallen recalls the plan to navigate the two guitar solos being that Marc Mann would play the first solo and Prince would join in and play another solo at the end. 'Marc starts playing the guitar solo and Prince stands down strumming the rhythm and I huddle up with Tom and Jeff.'

'Tom wanted Marc to do the first solo and for Prince to take it out,' adds Scott Thurston. 'He had been through all of the rehearsals for *A Concert for George*. Tom is the sweetest. He was afraid to take that away from Marc because he had worked it out.' Gallen, the Hall of Fame showrunner, had worked out a future where Prince was front and centre.

At this point, Gallen was concerned. As the show's director and producer, he was aware that Lynne's guitarist playing lead while the man who opened the show strummed away on rhythm might not emit the star wattage desired by the producers.

'So I talked to Prince about it. I pulled him aside and had a private conversation with him, and he was like: "Look, let this guy do what he does, and I'll just step in at the end – for the end solo, forget the middle solo." And he goes, "Don't worry about it." And then he leaves.'

Those closest to Prince, like his then photographer Afshin Shahidi, noticed 'a quiet energy throughout the day. Even in the day's rehearsals, it was a very subdued Prince. He wasn't happy with the sound, which is paramount for him and that often sets his mood.'

By the time the show started, the stars were in the room as well as on the stage.

The opening performance with Prince and his band, featuring 'Sign o' the Times' and 'Kiss', had gone well. The sound issues of the previous day, where Prince had gone through three sound engineers, were a past-tense problem.

Jeff Young notes the tables of eight dotted around: 'The Mick and Keith table, Yoko and son [Sean] table, [David Letterman bandleader] Paul Shaffer's band's table, Jimmy Page and Robert Plant, Prince, Larry Graham, Anita Baker ... Others were seated together. And *The Sopranos* were at a table – all except [James] Gandolfini, but I swear Edie Falco was the best-dressed woman in the room.'

Ferrone feels Prince's intended audience were not those at the tables with the *Sopranos* actors, nor the TV viewers at home, but his fellow players onstage. 'He put on a show but it wasn't for the audience. It was a show for us.' This was, after all, a man who had moaned to his engineer Susan Rogers in the mid-'80s in a control room at Sunset about a magazine's description of him as a diminutive singer. 'I was there and Wendy and Lisa were there and he's reading the article out loud and said, "Why do they always call me diminutive? They never write about my guitar playing."'

This would be where he would show some of the most celebrated musicians in rock history, to use one of his own phrases, 'what time it is'.

Scottie Baldwin, who was helping with sound for the show after the other front-of-house technicians were replaced, admits he 'didn't know what to expect'. He was, however, given a hint. 'He just said, "Turn my solo way up." I was mixing his guitar and the [show's production] guy just said "Just do what you want with his guitar" … You could tell it was going to take more than sixty-four bars to get done.

'What happened there is that no one in the band was going to tell him when to stop his solo. He knew what he wanted to say in a solo. Prince knew they were all in awe of him so he took as much time as he needed to say what he wanted to do.'

Scott Thurston, who also played with Iggy Pop and the Stooges, was standing next to Prince and could see his competitive instincts kick in. In a room of world-class musicians, Prince was a panther about to devour his prey. 'I got that sense. "This is my meat." It was just very exciting standing right there – a pinch-yourself moment. You feel charisma. It was undeniable. You feel it. That's a thing Iggy had too. Can't take your eyes off him.'

'It took off like a rocket,' admits Jeff Young. 'The story I heard was that, next to all the other famous rock star guitarists, he wasn't regarded as being in their class, so maybe he had something to prove. Everybody was surprised I think, because his R&B pedigree was so strong. He proved that night that he could play guitar with the best rock guys in the room.'

Prince was already motivated after a recent edition of a certain magazine. 'From what I hear from Quest', says the Roots' Kirk Douglas, referencing a chat with bandmate and Princeologist Ahmir 'Questlove' Thompson, 'that was borne out of *Rolling Stone* not mentioning him in their Top 60 Guitarists of All Time.'

'He stood over there [stage left, in the shadows] in the run-through [playing a shorter, simpler solo],' recalls Ferrone, 'and when we did the show, he moved centre stage. He had his gigantic bouncer guy in the audience who caught him and we had no idea he was going to do that. Then he played his blistering solo and I got the cue from Tom to finish and he tossed the guitar up in the air.

'I saw him walk away and thought "Where did the guitar go?"'

Prince cultivated mystery, but one mystery even he couldn't control was that airbound guitar. It wasn't seen again, like the ball after Chris Waddle's sky-high penalty kick at the 1990 World Cup semi-final (ask an English, or German, football fan).

Speculation surrounds what happened to the guitar. The romantics' theory is that the Telecaster was mystically transported up to George Harrison himself. Prince told Morris Hayes to spread the word, to 'tell 'em God caught it'.

The more mundane answer is that guitar tech Takumi Suetsugu, familiar with Prince's guitar-throwing antics, caught it off camera. 'Takumi was going to catch it at all costs,' chuckles Hayes. In fact, Baldwin believes Suetsugu's pal and unofficial second-in-command Vince Dennis picked it up from the floor. 'That's the show where it broke the neck.'

The *New York Times* headline, on an article about the solo, was: 'The day Prince's guitar wept the loudest.' There are, at the time of writing, more than 130 million views on YouTube of the solo. And the guitar has still not been sighted.

The solo redefined the Rock & Roll Hall of Fame's sense of moment, just as the Super Bowl half-time show would three years later. Petty, who died a year after Prince, recalled in that article, 'You see me nodding at him, to say, "Go on, go on." I remember I leaned out at him at one point and gave him a "This is going great!" kind of look. He just burned it up. You could feel the electricity of "something really big's going down here."'

Steve Lukather, a close friend of George's, was impressed by Prince's showmanship. 'He comes in with the swagger and the look and the clothes. The playing was great, it was amplified [by his presence]. He's a showman and he's a natural-born performer.' Steve Vai agrees. 'He was so very Prince, confident, visceral, bluesy and nicely suited for it.'

Morris Hayes was the only one who had an inkling of how special it might be. Prince told him afterwards: 'I just went half-gas on them at the rehearsals and then on the show, I turned up the gas.'

'He said Tom Petty was a little hot. It was so funny. He was like a girl at the prom. It was one of the greatest moments on TV and he murderised that solo.'

Prince, for once, was mistaken. Gallen disputes any irritation on Petty's part – 'very much not annoyed' – and he released a 2021 cut of the performance where Petty, Lynne and Dhani

Harrison grin like Cheshire cats while Prince tears through the solo. 'We went to Tom's suite afterwards and everyone was pleased as punch,' adds Scott Thurston. Spencer Churchill, the Sign tour's accountant, says he 'travelled with Tom and his core entourage [subsequently]. I never heard a bad word about Prince, and I was close to those guys.'

With a storied career working with Jackson Browne, Sting, Tracy Chapman, Steely Dan, Bonnie Raitt and Bruce Springsteen, Jeff Young says he is asked about the solo 'too many times – as if nothing else I've ever done as a working musician mattered as much.'

Producer Andrew Watt has watched it 'way more than a hundred times' and transcribed the solo so he can play it 'note for note'. He has a tattoo of the Prince symbol on his pinky. 'Every time I play the guitar, I look at my right hand and I say "This is what you're striving for. You are striving for Prince at the Rock & Roll Hall of Fame."

'It's all the things you want. He's not onstage until his guitar solo. The best band ever, all these amazing, amazing people and Prince is not even onstage with them. I talked to Dhani about that. They hadn't heard if he was coming or not. All of a sudden, the show is starting. None of them knew what is happening and you can see it, and my favourite thing, Tom is so cool and he's singing the song as good as George, even Tom Petty breaks at the end of his solo, you see Prince and he's having so much fun doing it. He's holding back as much as he's not holding back.

'It's another level and then he falls back into the [security] guy's arms. He is so good at [knowing] where the camera would be. "How are you thinking of all these things at the same time?!" The single greatest guitar solo.'

Gallen has overseen nineteen Rock & Roll Hall of Fame shows and a couple of all-star charity concerts. He thinks this solo 'might rank as number one, when I think of the impact and the lasting memory that's created. There might have been performances that in the moment felt more special but for lasting memory ...'

Scottie Baldwin summarises the solo in a more run-of-the-mill way. 'For other people, it's a life-defining moment and for Prince, it was Tuesday [Monday, actually]. It's just work.'

Another lasting memory was a personal note Gallen received thanking him for a great night:

'Tom Petty and Jeff Lynne did a solid job and Prince was the rocket that blasted it off. There aren't too many surprises these days, but "While My Guitar Gently Weeps" was one of them. It was a fantastic moment and I was personally thrilled to hear George's song played with respect and maximum tilt.'

The letter writer, Olivia Harrison, felt her husband had been honoured with maximum tilt.

'This music is for my kids'

Prince was across all aspects of that solo: how it sounded, how it looked on TV, how long it lasted. He liked to be responsible for everything. Well, nearly everything. It was Susan Rogers who invented The Vault.

She started work with Prince in August 1983 while he was writing songs for *Purple Rain* and, soon after that, one day at the height of his productivity, he was at his Kiowa Trail home studio. 'He's working at a pretty feverish pace. He would say to me at two or three in the morning "Get me that tape" and I had to know where everything was.

'That home studio opened up to the garage and in the garage there were metal shelves with tapes, but by no means was that all. Some of them were in the bedroom, so I could root around in there, but I had to know where all of it was. So I started to call Sunset Sound. "Please send all the tapes in your Prince vault to Minnesota." Then I started getting bold and calling earlier studios where he had worked, just reading the credits of his early albums, and asking them, "What Prince tapes have you got in your vault?" Then I got even bolder and did something you're not meant to do. I started calling Warner Brothers in Burbank, saying, "I'm Prince's engineer. I'm calling from Minnesota. Prince has asked for the masters of those tapes."'

As anyone with a working knowledge of Prince history knows, the battle to own his own masters would be a constant irritant (which was settled just before his passing), but his engineer just wanted to help her new boss when he asked for his old recordings. He taped everything: soundchecks, live shows and recording sessions, keeping them for posterity.

Sometimes though, even in rock 'n' roll, creative visionaries have to rely on a spreadsheet.

Rogers assembled one detailing the two- and four-inch tapes which she took to the office before storing the tapes in his garage. That would work, right?

Not where Prince lived.

'So we got to the point that a garage in Minnesota is not a safe place because of the extreme temperature changes – hot in the summer, freezing in the winter. There was a warehouse up the road – storage for highly sensitive documents – and they agreed to start doing storage for all our tapes. They had these grey plastic tapes and, in each bin, you could put six or eight two-inch tapes, so our office staff started putting all these tapes into bins, tagging all these. You could call the storage centre. They had a twenty-four-hour line.

'Prince was so happy that, when a reporter from *Rolling Stone* came to do a cover story, we took him to The Vault. As we were planning Paisley Park studios, we put a vault in the blueprints because he had to have somewhere to file his tapes. We filled that pretty fast – or he did. By the '90s, it got so full that you couldn't close the door.'

The Vault soon became Prince's pride and joy, as much as his Hohner Telecaster or LM-1 drum machine. 'He was excited about The Vault, but he was always changing the combination and he would forget what it was. The door would either have to remain open or he would have to find somewhere else to store his stuff.'

Mercifully, Prince had shared the combination with other engineers. He *had to* share the combination. 'I have heard there was a point,' laughs Rogers, 'when he was the only one who had the combination.

'That did not work out too well.'

The Vault's initials are capitalised because Prince fans speak of it in the same awestruck manner that Alec Guinness addresses the cello case full of money in *The Ladykillers*.

What's inside? Pretty much everything you haven't heard or seen.

It is where his unreleased material lives. As his forty studio albums reflect only a fraction of Prince's recorded output, there are thousands of songs and live performances, recorded in a pre-digital era before leakers were more common. (He is believed to have taped and filmed every live show and a fair few aftershows. Morris Day of the Time and then Brenda Bennett of Vanity 6 were tasked with videoing the early '80s tours, many rehearsals and all the music which he didn't release, including collaborations with the likes of Chaka Khan, Bonnie Raitt, George Clinton and others. Some of the outtakes of his work on Madonna's *Like a Prayer* album are also believed to be there.)

Who has seen and heard them? Hardly anyone.

The award-winning photographer Mathieu Bitton, who has chronicled tour life for Lenny Kravitz and comedian Dave Chappelle, got to know Prince towards the end of his life. He witnessed his determination to chronicle his own work. 'Part of it is just having the knowledge that you have so much in you and you know that you're not going to be able to put too much stuff out in your lifetime. You're archiving your own legacy for later on. One of the things that is very misrepresentative is the position that Prince wouldn't want any of the new stuff out. That's completely false.' Prince saw Bitton's work on remastered Miles Davis records and told him: 'You need to do this with all my albums.'

Lisa Chamblee says: 'He told me, "I never give the labels my best songs." I'm not computing what that means right now. Where are these other songs that you think are better?'

In 2020, when Warner Brothers raided The Vault for the *Sign o' the Times: Super Deluxe Edition*, it came with sixty-three previously unreleased songs. The deluxe edition of *1999*, another double album, came in at five CDs; in 2023, *Diamonds and Pearls* managed seven.

Whether Prince was best placed to separate his own wheat from his chaff is open to debate. Randy Newman, although a big fan, admits to 'one caveat. I wasn't sure he knew his good stuff from his less than good stuff.'

Getting rid of material could depend on Prince's mood or what he was willing to share of himself to his audience. Susan Rogers was ordered to erase an entire recording of Prince's song 'Wally', a post-Susannah break-up confessional, in front of him. (He did make another recording, though, which would surface on the 2020 Deluxe issues.)

Prince didn't linger in the past.

But Sal Greco, who worked at Galpin Boulevard home studio and the early years of Paisley, recalls Prince accessing his old recordings frequently. 'Sometimes he would listen to all of them. He would decide there was nothing he wanted to release. He was always three albums ahead.'

He would tell his friend Les Garland there was 'at least ten years' worth' of material, which Garland took to mean there was 'enough for at least ten albums'. As this conversation was in the '90s, and Prince never stopped recording until he died, there would be significantly more now.

Engineer Eddie Miller explains that 'at one point, he had this list of songs and we would wheel out a card of tapes from The Vault. He tried to document the best stuff that was in his head. Some of the stuff he would come up with really wouldn't be for that record and he would have to figure out in retrospect where to put the song.'

'He would go and study them,' recalls another engineer, Chuck Zwicky, of the tapes. 'Other people would say he's looking for inspiration, but he wants to know what questions he left unanswered. He moves on from things when they didn't work. He goes back to them with new knowledge of where they don't work and maybe does them with a whole new direction.'

'I have to approach it like Picasso,' adds Miller. 'That was the approach he took to releasing his paintings. He had to be judicious in what he released. I'd think generally the better stuff got released.'

From 1987, the year *Sign...* was released, The Vault would move about a little from the warehouse to its new HQ at Paisley Park in Chanhassen and then in later years to LA where most of the content was digitised. Its contents remain a source of feverish debate among fans. Like Moses, Susan Rogers did the groundwork, but would never see The Vault in its promised land of Paisley Park, Chanhassen. She left Prince's employment before a designated space, around 40 feet long and another 20 feet wide, would be left for it. Even that wouldn't be big enough.

Sal Greco seems to agree that Prince kept extra albums in reserve. 'In Paisley Park, there were four already completed in the Vault.'

Craig Rice, like many employees at Paisley, valued job security by not knowing the combination. 'That's how you protect yourself.' There were two decades of pretty constant recording and taped live shows after Greco left, but he estimates there were 'two and a half thousand unreleased masters.' Some things were wiped, but unlike the BBC's 1960s episodes of *Top of the Pops*, this was deliberate, according to Rice. 'When he got into Jehovah's Witnesses [estimated to be sometime around the mid-'90s], he did decide to eliminate some things that were against the religion.'

The Vault was proof that Prince would go back in time, if it helped move things forward – as he did when he used the kick drum sample from 'Housequake' for Scottie Baldwin.

Ruth Arzate, Prince's manager in the '00s, remembers a conversation at Paisley's Studio A.

'He had just recorded some song. "Are you going to put that on the album? Why not? It's a really amazing song."

"I have lots of amazing songs. The world is not ready for this song yet."'

The unreleased material would occasionally, but not often, be time-lined to his commercial peak – and that included 'five albums that the Revolution made' contained in The Vault, according to Arzate. She was told '"They're in The Vault and when they're ready to come out, I will put them out." It was all of its time. He would reminisce a little bit. He was wistful. He was more focused on moving forward. He wasn't nostalgic in that way. This was my heyday. It was like more factual or current to whatever the conversation was.'

'That's what they expect from me' was another stock Prince response when quizzed about why another great song remained unreleased.

For those who think Prince was wise enough to release his best material, a conversation in the '90's he had with his friend and keyboard player Morris Hayes may cause them to reconsider. 'Prince told me years later that he had material better than *Purple Rain*. He played me four or five songs, *Purple Rain*'s B-Roll, that's what he told me. It was the time he was fighting with Warner Brothers.'

Hayes reacted as many of us might. 'Whatever, dude ...' before listening to them and reconsidering. His boss's comment may have had validity.

"Prince, you have got to put these out! This is crazy."

"No. This music is for my kids."

"You don't even have any kids."

"This is for legacy. This is for them."

'I'm sitting here dying. I didn't believe him and then I thought maybe I did, maybe this is for your kids. I didn't doubt him any more. *This dude is severe. This is bananas.* I wish I'd been more present of mind. Maybe I'd have listened again and remembered the name of the songs. I only heard them once.'

"I Could Never Take the Place of Your Man'

'I Could Never Take the Place of Your Man' predates the Revolution, Sunset Sound and the building of The Vault itself.

'Prince rarely adopted the mindset of demoing,' argues Susan Rogers. 'If he put that on tape, it was going to be the canonical version of that song. Unless the song didn't turn out in a way that met his expectations, it would go into The Vault and he would revisit it later. We didn't demo the way most people do.'

'"I Could Never Take the Place of Your Man" is the perfect example. The artist that made it in 1979 was probably happy with it but it ultimately didn't make the cut for his album, he shelved it.'

This old-school rock 'n' roll song about a man spurning the advances of an interested party was first recorded at Hollywood Sound Recorders on 23 May 1979. By the summer of 1986, Prince was looking for tracks for the triple album *Dream Factory* he was recording with the Revolution. The Prince Vault website records him dusting it down and rerecording it on 3 June with the Revolution and then again from scratch on 16 July for the version of *Dream Factory* that was ready to go two days later.

But then *Dream Factory* was gone and soon were the Revolution, so Prince played everything himself.

The song is about Prince styling himself as a gentleman turning down the chance to sleep with his friend's now ex. On the first version, he isn't quite so chivalrous, expressing dissatisfaction with a one-night stand. Perhaps the later version from the perspective of having a live-in girlfriend was softer.

Prince tears through the song with a virtuosic guitar solo, although the drums and bass are his too. All traces of the Revolution had been excised.

The guitar solo, redolent of his idol Carlos Santana, while also using the space between the notes value practised by Miles Davis, was typical Prince: some ideas borrowed from others filtered into his own style.

The song sees Prince in storyteller mode and, as befits a man behind four cinema releases (1984's *Purple Rain*, *Under The Cherry Moon* two years later, *Sign o' the Times* in '87,

Graffiti Bridge in 1990), he told stories on the big screen differently from how he would in song.

For someone who was credited as director or co-director for all three films after *Purple Rain* (those were the ones released, there are others in The Vault), it feels a bit of a stretch to call Prince a cinematic auteur. He did, nonetheless, enjoy going to the movies.

A Prince cinema visit would not be as you or I go. He would hire out the whole picture house, for starters, often for midnight screenings. His staff would accompany him. 'It was ten or eleven o'clock,' recalls Todd Herreman, the man who installed Prince's Fairlight synthesiser, of one 1986 trip, 'and Prince wanted to go see a movie and chose *Ferris Bueller's Day Off*. Alan [Leeds] called the local movie theatre to get it closed and open it up for their private security. Ferris Bueller had an emulator which is a keyboard and he calls up the headmaster and uses a cheap Fairlight as a sample machine and Prince hits me in the back of the head at that point.'

Movies are a bittersweet experience for Prince's team. Those touring with him in December 1984 still remember the time he announced they should go en masse to the cinema after a long show that night. Cue a few musicians dozing through a midnight screening of David Lynch's 137-minute epic *Dune*.

Going to the movies with Prince on a date could lead to irritation – or even a teachable moment.

One visit to see *Home Alone* in 1990 was with an aspiring singer who had been recording her debut album at Paisley Park. Elisa Fiorillo was dating Prince at the time and the trip helped her realise she maybe wasn't cut out for her then boyfriend's level of fame. She would go on to sing back-up for Prince in the last decade of his career.

Fiorillo had gone back to LA and was called back to

Minneapolis. 'Duane [Nelson, Prince's half-brother and then head of security] picked me up in the car that's in *Graffiti Bridge*. In my hotel, there are scarves, perfumes, candles. What the hell is going on?

"You ready to go to a movie?"

'We had to enter after the movie started and leave before it ended.

"This sucks! How do you deal with it?"'

It was, Fiorillo says, the point that she realised 'maybe I don't want to be a star'.

Rose Ann Dimalanta, who played keys in the New Power Generation in the mid-'00s, recalls 'a camaraderie. It was demanding and it was circus-like. There were calls in the middle of the night. "Let's go to the movies."'

She says now, she had to ask herself: 'This is my job? Is this fun?'

Prince couldn't just watch a movie without analysing it. 'We'd watch a flick, talk about the director or the storyline,' Brenda Bennett, one third of Vanity 6, recalls. The films he favoured were 'mostly past films… with a leading female. Marlene Dietrich, Marilyn Monroe, Katherine Hepburn, Rita Hayworth.' *Bringing Up Baby* was said to be a key influence for *Under the Cherry Moon*.

A clue to the movies Prince was watching at that time is the 'kissing Valentino' line he wrote for the Bangles in 'Manic Monday' or the reference to silent movie actress Clara Bow in 'Condition of the Heart' from *Around the World in a Day*.

There were movies he adored. David Lynch's *Eraserhead* was one. He and LeRoy Bennett would watch the 1977 experimental horror classic over and over at his house. 'He knew I would be the only person who would sit there and watch it numerous times. It wasn't a story. It was an emotion.'

It makes sense that when Prince collaborated on the *Sign*

movie, the tone and look were as important as the storyline. 'He was absorbing. He was studying what it was. Why was it messing with his head and why was it drawing him in? It was the abstractness of it all that fascinated him.'

Another favourite was Marcel Camus's 1959 Brazilian film *Black Orpheus* of which, according to Ahmir 'Questlove' Thompson in a short film for Criterion Collection, Prince owned ten copies.

He and Bennett enjoyed watching the first two *Godfather* movies, whose character Apollonia inspired the lead female in *Purple Rain*. Snippets of dialogue from both *Godfather* films, rather than singing, would be the vocals breaking the instrumentals of the first two Madhouse albums.

Prince's taste in films was, like his taste in music, pretty Catholic. He was gripped by *Goldfinger* and *Thunderball* as a youngster. 'His hero was James Bond as 007,' laughs childhood friend Terry Jackson. 'We saw all the movies. Sean Connery was his favourite Bond.' Peggy McCreary remembers him taking her to a late-night screening of Jean-Jacques Beineix's *Diva*. (Craig Rice would contact Beineix about directing *Graffiti Bridge*. He passed.) In his own memoir *The Beautiful Ones*, he references Richard Curtis's 2013 rom-com *About Time*.

Prince also liked children's movies. When Thompson was DJing for Prince at a party in 2004, a Prince staffer interrupted a Fela Kuti track with a DVD saying 'Play this'. Thus *Finding Nemo* was screened during his set.

He hired out a cinema in 2016 for *Kung Fu Panda 3* and, when in 2006 the producers of *Happy Feet* asked for the use of *Kiss*, he gave them a new song, 'The Song of the Heart', leading to a Golden Globe win the following year. Prince must have had a soft spot for penguins; the stuffed penguin kept in the crew's flight case ended up being given a credit for 'Housequake'.

Eine kleine Princemusik

Around the mid-'80s, it's fair to say that Milos Forman's *Amadeus* also had an impact on him: the musical wunderkind with the brattitude he could back up with music; the battle-of-the-band themes; the clothes ... Even after his own ruffle-shirt period between *1999* to *Around the World in a Day,* the fashion template for Sheila E.'s 1985 album *Romance 1600* was clearly inspired by Theodor Pištěk's work on Forman's film from the previous year.

In 1987, Prince bought the rights to Forman's 1965 film *Loves of a Blonde.* Co-producer Craig Rice notes that Forman and Bernardo Bertolucci were two other directors he tried and failed to persuade to direct *Graffiti Bridge* before they plumped for ... Prince.

'I liken him to a Mozart figure,' says Matt Fink, referencing Tom Hulce's performance in the movie. 'He's writing a symphony one day and walking around his billiard table and he's hearing the parts in his head, and writing them down for each instrument as he goes and smiling, giggling and really getting off on that. It was flowing from his brain to his head and he could write the parts down. When Prince was in the studio, he could do the same thing, usually in one take. He could hear it and make it.'

Prince didn't write musical notation but his vision was clear, says Matt Blistan. 'He has got these notes in his head of what his music should sound like. He would just sing them to us. Some of the songs we did with him might be ten minutes long and on that he doesn't do the regular A-A-B-A scenario for writing music. He composes as he goes and he can remember it. He does the drum track and he already hears what he's going to be playing on bass, what he's going to be playing on guitar, what he's going to be playing on keyboards. He doesn't write it out like Mozart but he has it in his head.'

Blistan calls him a 'Mozart of our time – one of the most, if not the most, creative musicians I ever worked with. Personally, I don't have to hear the other stories of other people to let me know how creative he was.' Engineer Mike Koppelman agrees. 'I think he would hang with Mozart, with any living or dead musician, and keep up with them. Besides being a great pop star, he was a phenomenal musician.'

Brent Fischer, with his father Clare, took charge of the string arrangements on Prince's records. 'He listens to the cassette tape while he is at the piano and figures out what is going on. He works out the chord progression and he needs to put the notes down so that he can figure out the orchestral score.'

Some collaborators see Prince's greatest musical attribute as an arranger. Matt Blistan mentions Duquesne University's celebrated arranger, Dr John Wilson. 'He was an amazing arranger – twenty or twenty-five instruments in his head. Prince's thinking was even beyond that. He was composing and arranging at the same time. He's composing a new song, on-the-spot composing. That's what he would do with the band. He would start the tune and say "Let's not do that. Let's try this." He would remember something we did ten minutes ago that we forgot and he would sing it back.'

Prince didn't work with classical musicians in quite the intentional way other pop musicians such as Rufus Wainwright, Elvis Costello and Paul McCartney had with operas, symphonies and concertos, although he did write a ballet for Misty Copeland.

Scottie Baldwin feels the Mozart comparison is 'a little generous. Prince had his things. It was rock and it was pop. Quincy Jones would be a more apt heir to Mozart. Someone who read music and knew about composition, and who worked with Miles Davis, Frank Sinatra and Michael Jackson.'

Mozart played nine instruments (piano, violin, horn, flute, harp, bassoon, oboe, clarinet and trumpet) and would become famous for writing concertos for instruments, such as bassoon and oboe, for which other composers hadn't catered. But 800 compositions of symphonies, concertos and operas rocketed his estimation to a master of many forms. Prince would write for the instruments in front of him which he played himself, originally using his Oberheim synthesiser for the horn parts before finding Eric Leeds and other horn players, and singing their parts for them.

Prince was also in charge of his own wardrobe department, drew covers for some of his sleeves and oversaw the creation of his own logo. Rose Ann Dimalanta identifies this criss-crossing in his music.

'There are jazz musicians who love Prince. There are punk musicians who love Prince. There are country musicians who love Prince. I don't even categorise it. I just felt like in many ways he was all people in terms of having no boundaries.'

Dylan Dresdow – who worked with all the 1958-born Midwest Comets (Madonna, Michael Jackson and Prince) – says of Mozart and Picasso: 'I compare those guys to Prince, I don't compare Prince to those guys.'

The Mozart comparison was not that frequent. But it might have been had one TV episode been different. Hans Martin-Buff recalls an early draft for the September 1997 episode of *The Muppet Show* reboot on which Prince was to appear. 'I remember he got a script and we did basic tracks ['She Gave Her Angels' and 'Starfish and Coffee'). Then we went out to LA and he had a read-through. It was just one day. Everything else was suggested to him.'

One idea was partying like it's 1799, with Prince and the Muppets dressed in the Viennese splendour of the late eighteenth century, skipping over the inconvenient detail that Mozart died in 1791. 'The set was there, the outfit was there and the song was recorded – "1999", Muppeted up.'

Plenty of spun gold remains in The Vault, but sadly this nugget was shelved before it got filmed.

His environmentally friendly side

The music industry doesn't stretch back to the eighteenth century, but when it realised it could monetise heritage and nostalgia, things changed. Bands honed residencies where their classic albums were played in full, and record companies commissioned cover versions of the entire album, along with anniversary reissues, documentaries and feature films about the making of said album. If the stars could make a documentary or commission a musical about their warts 'n' all personal lives, even better. Prince didn't do any of that. By and large, his small rear-view mirror kept in proportion with his larger windscreen focus ahead.

While other stars with similarly strong forward momentum – like Madonna, the Beatles and David Bowie – would create looks to go with their new albums before leaving them behind forever, Prince's process was slightly more evolutionary.

He wore a long trench coat for *Dirty Mind* and a slightly smarter one for *Controversy*. The coat was purple by the time of the *1999* video before a new, flashier version covered his shoulders astride the motorbike for *Purple Rain*.

Lyrically, he sang about the sky turning purple in '1999' and the following album, the purple clouds opened. He ushered in 1988's *Lovesexy* album with the words 'Welcome to the New Power Generation'. From 1992, his band took that name.

Sometimes, there was 'Joy in Repetition', a song which was taken from 1987 and the *Sign...* sessions and transplanted on to the *Graffiti Bridge* soundtrack. Whatever worked.

There were countless examples of sneak peeks into the future if you squinted far enough into the past. It helps to have a vault full of every song you've ever written – and every concert and aftershow you ever did – recorded starting from the early 1980s.

On the *Sign...* album itself, 'I Could Never Take the Place of Your Man' first dates from 1979 and 'Strange Relationship' from 1983. The *Sign* sessions saw 'Eye No' recorded, which ended up on *Lovesexy*. There are others. 'The title song from [1999's] *Rave Un2 The Joy Fantastic* is from '87 or '88,' reveals that album's engineer, Hans-Martin Buff. Prince also used the title *Crystal Ball* for a 1998 compilation unrelated to the aborted *Crystal Ball* triple album.

Prince would often try for the right sound but if it was taking too long, he'd use The Vault and an engineer for company. Michael Koppelman remembers the night in Studio A at Paisley Park when Prince recorded 'Love, Thy Will Be Done', the 1991 hit he wrote for Martika. 'He came in and sampled someone. He'd kick us out when he did the vocals and one night he had everything down. He sang all the background, all the leads had been done and then he gave it to her.'

When he did have guests, as with the series of stars on his *Rave Un2 The Joy Fantastic* album (a reaction to Santana's all-star *Supernatural* and a formula Tom Jones and others would follow), there was little that was organic about the duets. 'All of the songs that had collaborators on it were finished songs with spots for them,' admits Buff.

He interspersed snippets from '1999' and 'Let's Go Crazy' into 'Million $ Show' from 2015's *HITnRUN Phase One*, just because he could – or maybe because Warner Brothers who put the record out had just given him his masters back.

Prince had a disagreement with Scottie Baldwin in Japan over a kick drum sound before he suggested the original from 'Housequake'. There are samples on 'If I Was Your Girlfriend'. 'The first part is an orchestra that came out,' explains Prince's friend on the Fairlight, Todd Herreman. 'The BBC Sound Effects Library on vinyl.' The Beatles used the same source for 'Blackbird', which birders gleefully pointed out later was actually a thrush.

'I don't look back,' he told Arsenio Hall in 2014. 'There are a lot of bootlegs out there that are unfinished.' What's more remarkable is how many songs he recorded, awaiting release. He said in the same interview that 'if I want to hear new music, I make it'.

CHAPTER 14

THE CROSS

My Name is Prince ... or was ... Prince gets in shape –
a specific one ... A rebel with several causes ... Faith, Prince
and charity ... 'Ahead of his time' ... Party Like It's 2006 ...
The whistle blows for half-time ...

My Name is Prince ... or was

His name is Prince. That's what he told listeners in a September 1992 single before adding the perhaps unnecessary detail that he is funky.

The complicated relationship with his own name took a decidedly left turn on 7 June 1993 barely eight months after 'My Name is Prince' was released.

His name would not be Prince, in a move designed to block out his record company who insisted they had ownership of every record with his name. With colleagues, he would no longer answer to the name Prince and was referred to as The Artist Formerly Known as Prince (TAFKAP) or his new symbol reflecting the male and female sexes, which reduced some outlets to refer to him as O(+>.

In some respects, it was a pivotal moment in his career and in other regards, a footnote.

By 2000 when he went back to being called 'Prince', it was like it had never happened. The no-name era does not include his most fondly regarded music.

It will, however, go down as a mark of his fearlessness and demarcation from the way other entertainers sold themselves. When his engineer on 1992's *Symbol* album, Michael Koppelman, is asked how he will be remembered, he says, 'The guy who made *Purple Rain*, and the guy that had a symbol for his name.'

Koppelman noticed it happened as he was leaving Prince's service, when he saw contracts referencing 'anything Prince does for Warner Brothers' and calls it 'a very shrewd, weird thing to do'.

'He was getting to the place that he wanted to resist that he had become a commodity,' reflects Zaheer Ali, an academic who curates a Prince syllabus at Hutchins Institute. Ali, borrowing Professor Robin Kelley's expression, calls Prince 'a freedom dreamer'.

The freedom Prince often craved extended to freedom from his own name.

For those dealing with him back in the summer of '93, it was challenging.

Everyone at Paisley Park was tasked with banning the P-word from earshot of Paisley's CEO.

Staff like Danny Soltys (Facilities Director at Paisley Park from 1987–1999) would adapt by just calling him 'boss'. Girlfriends would favour 'hey' or 'hey you'.

'I think Prince was sort of playing with us. He was seeing what he could get away with,' says Koppelman.

Some regard it as a declaration of commercial suicide. Cos Kyriacou, who made his shoes that decade, calls it 'a difficult time. He was having all these issues where he became a little paranoid. There was a big change in his life.'

While talk show hosts lampooned him, and Prince planned a break from his record company, the 'TAFKAP' period from 1993 to 16 May 2000, when he held a press conference taking back his own name, could be seen as yet another of his resets.

He started turning up to the shows of singer-songwriter Ani DiFranco, who formed her own label, Righteous Babe, and played with James Brown's saxophonist Maceo Parker, who would go on to play with Prince.

'I see Prince as someone who was born freer in his mind and heart than almost any of us. I feel like he resisted falling into those hierarchies and a cage in this machine. He was one of the strongest resisters.'

Lenka Paris, who DJ'ed for Prince at the end of his career after growing up in communist Czechoslovakia, felt kinship in that yearning for freedom. 'I felt like an outsider most of my childhood and teenage years. I didn't want a pre-mapped life. Prince told me his story. I connected to it hard. I didn't feel alone any more. He told me to fight for my freedom. To block the noise, to block negativity. He told me he was determined to make it because he didn't want to have a boss. He told me not to tone myself down. And to keep playing no matter what. Get better and better at my craft. He also said he records every day, and will never stop playing, because he can't.'

Like an actor going method by adopting the traits of a character in their downtime, Prince went all-in. The Artist Formerly Known as Prince wasn't a stage name as much as a lifestyle choice.

'My mother died on 6 June 1993,' recalls Therese Stoulil, who worked with him from 1988 to 1996. 'Prince changed his name on 7 June 1993 (his thirty-fifth birthday, although in later years he would not mark these, refusing to acknowledge the concept of time). I was out. I got home from the hospital and my mom had literally just died and I was sitting on the couch and the phone rang. It was Prince and I remember calling Karen [Krattinger, Prince's assistant].'

Two or three weeks later, she returned to work. 'I remember the day I came back. He comes by my office and does the "Oh, you're back" face.

"Prince, I have some messages for you."

'He literally doesn't turn around, sticks his head in the door and says, "Don't call me that," and keeps on walking.

'I had no clue until I came back to work a couple of weeks later.'

Stoulil figured out a work-around. 'Do you call your wife by her name every ten minutes? We didn't need to [with him]. Internally we just said:

"Is he up yet?"

"Have you heard from him?"'

That didn't mean work got easy. 'I remember no conversations, no inkling that he was thinking about changing his name. We never knew. I remember going in the office one day and I had a mile-long list of things to do. Alan [Leeds] would come up and have a cigarette. I just remember going on and on to get stuff done and one smoking break he said, "This isn't a cure for cancer. Do the best you can. You can probably change his mind in three days anyway."'

'We were confused,' adds tour manager Skip Johnson, 'and said, "What should we write in a memo?" I was sending him memos, I would just write down and preface the memos "Prince" but I would slip it under his door and every once in a while, shortly after the name thing he said, "Stop with all the memos and don't call me Prince!" That was the extent of the conversation. I didn't use any name at all. If it was a memo, I wouldn't use any. Maybe just "Salutations" on it.'

Bandmates faced the same dilemma.

Drummer Michael Bland once started – and abruptly ended – a sentence with 'So, Prince …'

'He ice-grilled me.

"When you call me Prince, it's like calling me a cuss word. Don't call me that."

'I had decided it was a publicity stunt to stop them holding him to certain terms in his contract but he was visibly upset.'

Other bandmates like Tommy Barbarella, Sonny Thompson and Morris Hayes, Bland says, 'learned from my mistake' and never started a sentence the same way.

'I think the idea of giving up the name Prince grew in time,' continues then tour manager Skip Johnson. 'When he first did it, it was a shtick and then he grew into it. He liked the idea of not having a name but he was serious about it because he called me into the office and he had his passport there and said, "Can you see if they can get my symbol on it instead of my name?" I knew there was no way. But I didn't tell him that immediately. I always tried to follow through and ask.

'He's Prince, maybe I can go to the US customs and there's a Prince fan and he calls someone in Washington DC and he's a Prince fan and maybe they'll make an exception. He had that kind of power. I didn't get further than the local post office.'

Prince's merchandise man in the '90s Bruce Huisinga had an envelope left on his desk to give his half-brother and security guard Duane an item of his jewellery, a silver ring bearing the legend 'Prince'. 'I remember I told him, "I don't think you should give this away; you might wanna have this someday." And he said, "No, it's not me." It ended up sitting in my office for a couple of years. He asked me for it back when I left.'

Stoulil admits it created a challenging work environment. 'I heard every single day for a year, "Why is Billboard still using my old name? Why is *USA Today* still using my old name?" That's when we came up with the shape with the font on it.'

Singer Lizz Wright, the last act Prince saw live, sees a fearlessness in the decision. 'It makes sense to have some way to describe things, to share them, to sell them, but yeah, he really resisted that. I appreciate him being himself. He pushed to open up that layer of the conversation about how black people are seen and perceived and the hierarchy of how we see each other and he was very actively resisting. He initiated a battle with the label which was symbolic for resisting an entire system. I appreciate he was such an authentically strong spirit that he could go nameless; we would know who he was. "I don't need the name to be who I am." That's freaking crazy. That's the God move.'

In November 1999, just before he reverted back to Prince, music executive Nick Raphael was introduced and after conversation, couldn't resist asking what he would say if a heavy object was hurtling towards the man with no name's head.

Prince reflected before answering: 'That's a me problem. Not a you problem.'

Prince had experienced a complex relationship with his name long before he fell out with Warner Brothers.

From 1958 on, his mother didn't like the name, presumably because his father John was often away from home with gigs with his own band The Prince Rogers Trio. She called her son Skipper.

He also told girlfriends Anna Garcia (Fantastic) and Apollonia [as recounted on the latter's podcast] he had a dog called Prince.

When dating, Elisa Fiorillo would call him 'hey' or 'hey you' and first wife Mayte referred to him at the time in interviews as 'honey'. When they first met, he tried to call her 'Arabia' until she quickly nixed the idea. But he also (according to Apollonia's podcast) chastised girlfriend Anna Garcia, whom he dated around the turn of '89/'90 and who addressed him with 'hey', for *not* calling him Prince.

Then again, he called her 'Joy Fantastic' before settling on 'Anna Fantastic'.

He was one for picking names even before he junked his own. As the mystery producer and songwriter of works by the Time, Sheila E. and Sheena Easton, he was billed as Joey Coco, Jamie Starr (or The Starr Company) and Alexander Nevermind – and he even used 'ecnirp', Paisley Park and The Phantom. In later years, he called from hotels as Mr Peter Bravestrong, which was also on his luggage. He recycled too. 'Christopher' wrote 'Manic Monday' in 1984 and two years later, he played Christopher Tracy in *Under the Cherry Moon*.

Matt Blistan, the trumpeter from Pittsburgh suggested by Eric Leeds and a key part of his sound around *Parade* and *Sign o' the Times*, didn't have a choice in the matter on his second day at work in Eden Prairie. 'The next day we have all got together and Prince isn't there yet and we have all warmed up and Prince comes dancing into the warehouse and he's playing air trumpet and that's when he said, "Atlanta Bliss plays like this," and I thought, "I guess that's me." There was another Matt in the band. I was living in Atlanta. Bliss comes from Blistan.'

The other Matt in the band had also been given a name by the boss without huge consultation. After a fair amount of costume workshopping, they decided during the *Dirty Mind* tour on the very early 2020s image of a surgical mask and medical scrubs.

'One was a gold satin tux and tails which was very Elton John. I think I wore it once on the *Midnight Special* TV show. I got an idea. Khaki green army issue like test pilots wear. He liked that but thought it was too drab. Then I came up with a guy in a black-and-white-striped jail suit which was worn on *American Bandstand*. It harkens back to *Jailhouse Rock* by Elvis and the black and white stripes match the black and white stripes on a keyboard. It really stood out, the zebra look. That worked out for a year, then we're on tour with Rick James and he does an album *Bustin' Out of L Seven* and we couldn't have any crossover so he ditched that. "You're going to have to switch. What was your other idea?"

"How about we go back to the paratrooper's jumpsuit?" I did consider a surgeon's scrub suit. He went, "Mmm." The cogs are moving, and he says, "Let's try that tonight." Our wardrobe girl went out and got me a powder-blue authentic scrub suit, the surgeon cap, gloves, masks and then they even got the leather strap with the reflector mirror, the whole shebang.

"I want you to wear the mask when you go onstage."

"But nobody will see my face."

"That's the point. You're mystery keyboard dude. Trust me. It's going to be great. People are going to point at you."

'So that was it. People in the audience were pointing at me. Prince being Prince, the next night he had me painting at a painter's easel. I don't know if he started calling me Dr. Fink. How about if I take out my 110 camera and take a picture of the audience? They went wild. I have pictures of that tour. That was Chicago.'

Dr. Fink had a more collaborative experience than most of Prince's female employees.

Prince selected the girl bands' names. Denise Matthews drew the line at 'Vagina' so she became Vanity and Patricia Kotero was Apollonia, inspired by Prince's love of *The Godfather* movies. (His favourite character, claims childhood friend Terry Jackson, was Luca Brasi.)

His dancers for the Diamonds and Pearls tour, Lori Elle Werner and Robia LaMorte, were renamed Diamond and Pearl.

He tried to rename Nandy and Maya McClean, who danced as The Twinz, as Incense and Candles.

When country singer Toby Lightman supported Prince in Portland in 2004, her band, by then appraised of his modus operandi, teased her that he was going to give her a new name.

The names he gave his bandmates, dancers and protégées – Atlanta Bliss, BrownMark, Dr. Fink, Carmen Electra, Diamond and Pearl, Tommy Barbarella – would stick. He informally called make-up artist Terra Hinrichs 'Miracle Whip' after the US brand of mayonnaise on account of her Californian whiteness.

Prince insisted on a name for Jimmy 'Jam' Harris, the keyboard player in the Time who would go on to become one of the most successful producers of the past half-century with Terry Lewis. He was always called 'Jimmy Jam' – not even Jimmy.

Even his girlfriends were stuck with the names he would pick for them. 'I think because the only other women I had around were Vanity and Apollonia, he gets a new girlfriend and calls them a name,' says model Maneca Lightner. Except he didn't call her Maneca. 'He told me my name should be Samantha so he wanted to call me Sam.'

She was baffled, telling him: 'What? That's not even sexy. You just don't know how to pronounce my name.'

'He had his whole crew of people calling me Sam. [Bodyguard] Hucky [Austin] calls me Sam.' She soon gave in, calling him and announcing, 'This is Sam.'

Such is Prince's power that decades after they dated, and years after his death, Maneca Lightner still calls up restaurants and books reservations under the name Sam. 'It's easier to say than Maneca.'

Prince gets in shape – a specific one

When most pop stars, from Cat Stevens to Terence Trent D'Arby, change their names, they don't go for a shape.

Prince may have had a bad experience opening for the Stones in October 1981, but he must have appreciated their branding. That red-lipped logo, unlike the devil Mick Jagger sang about, needed no introduction.

When, in the mid-'90s, he was not selling what he was in the 1980s, Warner Brothers told him records with his name on it represented a breach of his contract. Prince, wrestling for as much control as he could, started putting out records – just not with his name on them.

In the TAFKAP era, a visual identity beyond his wardrobe, videos and record sleeves would be required.

The idea of a logo, crucially his own logo, started germinating at the start of the '90s when Prince was recording 'Gett Off'.

Sotera Tschetter grew up the daughter of a dairy farmer in Dakota. Working for Prince as his art director in 1991, she was assigned a new task: find a new logo, and unlike his recorded masters, he would need to own it.

The symbol, a circle on top of an arrow with something akin to a trumpet across it reflected both sexes as well as Prince's asymmetrical style. He didn't follow clean lines.

'You see him using references of it,' remembers Tschetter, 'and he's getting ready to launch a tour and he says, "Can you do a new symbol?" [The video for 1991's] "Gett Off" was based on *Caligula* and *Barbarella*; he would watch them a lot. We just carved it [a prototype logo] and painted it on the floor. He was excited about it. He loved it.

'The merchandise sales were equal to the ticket sales. A lot of people would be able to counterfeit it. He didn't have an icon that he owned so the "Gett Off" one he owned. He was ecstatic. "This is what I wanna do." He had the original love symbol. That was 60 feet long styled with the lights on it. "I want the new symbol for the tour." Everything is already done. He has the old design on the floor. He's pushing for that identity.'

Tschetter went down a rabbit hole of 'hundreds of hours' of research on 'alchemy, colours, astrology, astronomy'. She started digging into the symbolism of gold and circles and visited Egypt with Prince's first wife Mayte, during the shooting of Spike Lee's *Malcolm X*. There was also the idea that 'there are no more kings in the world, only princes – a slam on [self-styled King of Pop] Michael Jackson.'

Tschetter worked with graphic designers Liz Luce and Mitch Monson to emerge with a logo ready for Prince's 1992 tour to Japan and Australia.

'He's the only artist who has a graphic symbol which represents who he is. Parts of it are unique. It's not symmetrical. It's not the same on both sides. It's mismatched in a way. It represents his character very well. To each person it means something different when they look at it.

'The only thing he could do was to change his name in the middle of that contract fight. It evolved into something that represented him.'

The creation of the logo, or 'the love symbol', took 'three to probably seven' iterations. It criss-crosses in and out of male/female branding, tapping into thoughts Prince had expressed before from the fashion template of *Dirty Mind* to the lyrics of 'If I Was Your Girlfriend' and the concept of *Camille*. They also wanted to avoid pitfalls like not making it too similar to a cross to observe religious sensibilities, and avoid existing logos such as the Nabisco one.

Animator and graphic designer Dale Hughes was tweaking a

final draft which Prince supervised. 'I was in the room with him. You had to be in his inner circle. He would come in with his entourage and the whole room would be on high alert and tense.

'It was just another job coming through and I don't even remember what we got paid. It wouldn't have been anything big. We certainly had no claim to it.'

Prince's understanding of branding meant the glyph symbol would become ubiquitous, first in his own orbit. It would be built on to head cushions on his guitar, pianos, light display and the shape of his stage. He even played a guitar in the shape of it.

Once he saw the logo everywhere from fans, Hughes wished that 'I'd have kept better notes of the files I deleted. Second [thought] was, 'Oh. He must really like it then.'

Tschetter and the designers' success mainly depends on her following his lead and giving Prince something he designed and guided.

And of course it lives on not just as a statue outside Paisley Park but in fans' tattoos, key rings, earrings and jewellery. (Chris Rock wore a logo necklace for his 2022 Netflix special.) As Tschetter says of the fans – 'it means something to them.'

A rebel with several causes

Prince always liked the idea of cool. He wrote a song of that name for the Time and at least two others with 'cool' in the title for others – one for Sheena Easton, another for Mavis Staples, both of whom he helped back into fashionability.

If coolness is to be ascribed to him, one factor could be his clothes, or his stubborn resistance to music industry interference or expectation, his desire to be the boss as opposed to having a boss, the ability to live in the present in the face of all pressure not to, the way he avoided selfies, autographs and cultivated mystery, and his concerts and small club after-hours shows where he could dance on a sixpence in heels while spinning his guitar around before launching into a solo.

If you wanted to offer your own authentic analysis, you could suggest what made him cool was his music.

Or all of the above.

Here is a counter-argument about the coolest thing about Prince. In an era known for the dawning of big charitable and very public statements – Live Aid, *We Are the World*, Amnesty International and Nelson Mandela concerts, Prince's charitable acts were often on one condition: that no one knew.

He was once quoted as saying: 'Any charitable act is love in motion, and love needs no publicity because love just is.'

In an age when philanthropy was being shouted from the rooftops, Prince whispered his.

Dave Hampton, who ran Paisley Park in the early '00s, said: 'If he wanted to help somebody, we were in charge of making people know that he wasn't in charge of helping them.'

Jacqui Thompson, who ran Paisley Park in the late '90s, is now on the board of PRN Alumni, an umbrella organisation where good causes considered to be representative of him are chosen. She acknowledges that 'the music side of him is going to be what it is forever' but wants to stress the importance of his philanthropic instincts.

David Z Rivkin, who helped mould Prince's production room instincts and produced the Fine Young Cannibals' *The Raw & the Cooked* album at Paisley Park, says, 'He was very kind and gave money and nobody even knew. He supported people he believed in and people who were down on their luck. He gave a lot of money to the black community. He gave to schools. He didn't tell anybody. I don't think he ever mentioned it to anyone. He gave with the right attitude.'

'He was clear about not promoting too many different things,' observes his dancer Nandy McClean.

Prince viewed charity as intrinsically linked to his already blurred personal and professional lives, as a key part of his work and person. Sam Jennings, who would do more than most to help Prince's online retail presence with his NPG Music Club, was originally asked to help build a website for his Love 4 One Another charity. 'I was the only one building websites professionally and so when he wanted it to be a business, slowly we started working together.

Love 4 One Another, or In a Perfect World, was a charity set up by Prince where he put second wife Manuela Testolini in charge.

'It was a lot of advocacy for community, building and sustainability and education for sure. Those things,' adds Jennings.

'He really felt that was part of his responsibility,' explains Craig Rice, who worked with him between *Purple Rain* and *Diamonds and Pearls*, 'and that's why he continued the PRN Alumni Foundation. Mayte has her non-profit. Manuela has one.'

The causes he espoused were disparate but often recurring – urban regeneration, help for musicians down on their luck, autism (perhaps inspired by Cynthia Rose, the subject of 'Starfish and Coffee', or his own childhood struggles with epilepsy), emerging black businesses and education for disadvantaged children.

'He gave $100,000 to the Rhythm and Blues foundation with the caveat to make sure the older artists were taken care of [with health insurance],' recalls Thompson. Like another Prince (now King), Charles, son of HRH Queen Elizabeth, 'he was into organic food and sustainability. He had a greenhouse with his property.'

Diet from sustainable agriculture was important to him, especially since he turned vegetarian and then vegan in the '90s.

'When he first started,' adds Rice, 'he was eating Doritos and Reese's Pieces for dinner before ultimately he went nice and healthy.'

'I know he believed in what you feed yourself with,' agrees Thompson. 'There are many urban places in America where these kids do not even know what a vegetable is.

'There were many farms and co-ops. The family of my girlfriend back in the day were vegetarian and I found out there was damage to her garden and he donated ten grand.'

One recipient of his charitable giving was singer Taja Sevelle, whose 1987 debut album was released on Paisley Park Records. She founded an organisation called Urban Farming where green projects were planted in inner city areas. 'We had numerous conversations – hours and hours and hours – over the course of a decade about Urban Farming and all of the ways we would and could collaborate to help our world as much as possible,' she recalls. 'Prince really, really loved Urban Farming. He even wanted to come out and plant some vegetable plants in the community garden that he had funded us to create at a beautiful but abandoned church that he had purchased on the north side of Minneapolis.'

Prince didn't just stick to his home state. Whether it was music therapy in Ohio, or urban farming in Detroit, if he believed in the cause and he could keep his donation private, he would give to it.

Another favoured cause was struggling musicians or their families – he is understood to have given privately to, among others, the families of Rosie Gaines, Chance Howard and former bodyguard Chick Huntsberry (even after Huntsberry had participated in a tell-all *National Enquirer* story in 1985). Melissa Huntsberry Kahn remembers Prince paying for his funeral expenses after her father passed aged forty-nine, and sister Tina remembers his support for Chick's widow Linda. 'Prince wrote her a beautiful letter and also did a benefit concert to help her with mounds of hospital bills.'

There was also the failed attempt to help Sly Stone, then living in a trailer home. He also wrote off the medical bills of Clyde Stubblefield, one of James Brown's drummers and the man understood to have originated the sound of the funky drummer. 'This human never knew he was the most sampled drummer in the history of music,' laughs Prince's cousin Chazz Smith. 'Prince paid for his hospital bill. I never heard of James Brown doing that.'

Stubblefield's widow and partner for twenty-five years Jody Hannon adds: 'In 2000, when Clyde was fifty-seven, he was diagnosed with bladder cancer. Through surgeries, chemotherapy and hospital stays, Clyde's medical bills were mounting and mounting. I organised benefit after benefit to try and stay ahead of the bills. Clyde didn't have health insurance and I was so afraid he wouldn't get the medical treatment he deserved if we weren't sending in some amount of payments. At the end of the day his bills totalled over $90,000. We were able to raise $30,000. One day, Clyde's manager Kathie Bowman called me at work and told me Prince's people will be calling me. The call came in and I was star-struck. She asked how much we needed to clear Clyde's medical bills. I wasn't sure what to say and the woman assured me that Prince himself had given the order. So I said it, "$60,000." Without hesitation she said, "Does Clyde need any more for anything else?" and Clyde said no. Clyde was a humble and proud man. It was difficult for Clyde to accept help. At the end of our conversation they told me that Prince was starting a fund called Love 4 One Another. It was designed to help musicians like Clyde who need help with medical care. Since the money came from

Prince personally and not the fund, we were asked to keep it to ourselves. After Prince passed away in 2016 and before Clyde passed away in 2017, he told this story. He wanted people to know what a wonderful man Prince was.'

His gigs may be legendary among his fans but among his employees and musicians, his charity gigs had real cachet – often because Prince refused to publicise them.

'People don't know about the philanthropy he did,' argues his former guitar tech, Mike Soltys. 'We did a lot of these benefit shows for disabled people which we kept secret. He loved doing that stuff.

'That's the way he was. He would donate a lot of money to inner city organisations. Multiple black youth organisations. Basketball camps. No record of it.'

David Tickle, who worked on Prince's sound in the studio and live between 1984 and 1986, is unlikely to forget one 2 a.m. call in Dallas:

'"Prince wants to do a show at six in the morning. You've got to be there at five to prepare."

'He rented some hall for about 500 kids, and all these kids were deaf, dumb and blind. With that, we doubled up on all the low end for the sub-woofers [speakers]. We went in and did the sound check and he did a full-blown show for all the kids who went absolutely nuts.

'One kid about twelve years old came up to the console and had a big grin on his face and said, "Can you turn it up? I'm deaf." They were making fun of the predicament they were in.'

When Prince admired someone, be that a musician like Larry Graham, for whom he bought a house, or a dancer like Misty Copeland, for whom he constructed a show around his music, he went all-in.

Former substitute teacher Marva Collins was famously

dissatisfied with the opportunities granted to children from the inner cities so founded her own preparatory school, Westside Preparatory in Chicago. Prince and the Revolution spent the best part of a day there in 1985 at the heart of his *Purple Rain* fame on condition of no press. 'That was one of the stipulations,' remembers Collins' son Patrick. 'He didn't want the media there as he said that he didn't want to disrupt the flow of lessons.

'He gave $350,000 then sent more money because he wanted the children to have instruments, and he wanted the children to start a music department. He really seemed to be a proponent of education. He stood up and told the students, "What you are receiving here is a gift, and Mrs Collins is the giver of that gift. Use the gift for the betterment of yourself and your future children."'

When he found out Patrick's father was driving a 1975 Buick LeSabre, he bought the family a 1984 Lincoln Continental. Every 31 August her son would hear the phone ring. 'He would call her for her birthday. He had called and my mom was out and he says, "This is Prince and I called to wish you the happiest birthday." [This was before Prince stopped celebrating birthdays.] My mom was really sad she was out, but my sister used it at the beginning of her voice recorder.'

Prince rarely gave autographs – Mike Soltys (Prince's bass tech from 1984–1987) has a memory of Prince asking him for a Sharpie at one charity show precisely because it was so rare – and even fewer selfies. The Academy Award-winning actor and Prince fan Jamie Foxx recalled to Howard Stern in 2017 having a disposable camera when he first met Prince on the key date of 31 December 1998 and being refused.

But if he could help privately, he would.

Marylou Badeaux, who worked with him for decades at Warner Brothers, reveals, 'If I asked him for something quietly, he never turned me down. Part of the reason why is that he knew I would never tell a bloody soul. He did a lot more for the black cause than people were aware.

'Make A Wish contacted me about a girl in hospital who was dying. She couldn't speak. I contacted him privately about asking for his autograph – he normally didn't sign them – and he wrote a confidential four- or five-page letter which her mother read out to her. Tears start coming out of the girl's eyes, she opens them and then she dies. He made her last moments the best. But I could never tell anybody because of his need for privacy.'

Prince's cousin Charles 'Chazz' Smith feels his instinct for giving was one aspect of his personality that never changed. 'People change, but Prince was always sweet, always cared about everything, every little animal, the air, the moon, the stars, the earth; he didn't just develop that. He was always like that. Always wanted to help people.'

He would often make thoughtful gestures like flying in singer Ashley Tamar's father to his LA rental in 1235 Sierra Alta Way (once home to Elizabeth Taylor) and performing a pre-tour warm-up soundcheck just for him. 'My dad is from Mississippi. When he flew to LA, to Prince's amazing house, he's in the audience. It's just my dad and me. Prince had two boxes with bows on them. It was the framed pictures from that show.'

Part of his contradictory nature was his determination not to be fleeced by the music industry, while some of his closest musical lieutenants considered him less than generous in payment for their services – it was a source of friction with many in the Revolution and other bands – and yet the money he did make he often let flow like water.

Terry Jackson grew up in Russell Avenue with Prince when they were in and out of the Anderson family's home. Bernadette

Anderson's son André Cymone would become Prince's best friend and bandmate.

'When the [i-35W Mississippi River] Highway Bridge collapsed [in 2007], Prince gave a lot of money to total strangers. He's helped a lot of other artists. André Cymone listened to all the accolades.

"He never gave nobody in my family any money." Even though Prince bought her [Bernadette] a car, he didn't give her it outright. She was still making payments when she died.'

Jackson says his father, a lawyer, 'restructured his contract for him at Warner Brothers. My dad saw his rise in power. I never saw Prince reach out to my dad and say thank you. From Bernadette to his sister, he never reached out to anyone financially.'

Although some close to him felt short-changed, there are other strangers and acquaintances for whom credit on many outweighs the debit. Kathleen Johnson sang in his band, her sister Mocha was his personal assistant for five years, and brother Kirk drummed for him. 'I will never forget him for taking good care of my mother when she was at the end stages of her life,' she says. Prince paid for home care for their mother for five years. 'People don't really talk about how kind-hearted he really was. He's done a whole lot of things. I could tell you what he did for me and for my family. He paid for home care as she refused to go into any type of home, and I was able to keep the family together instead of putting her in a nursing home.'

Patrick Collins compares the private individual to another huge corporation. 'Philip Morris spent $1 million feeding the homeless but they spent $10 million telling everyone about it. He would rather spend the $10 million on the homeless. The reward for a job well done is to have done it.'

Former Paisley Park records president Craig Rice even maintains there was another cause beyond individuals Prince initially propelled forward before his death. 'He was the original finance for Black Lives Matter. He would just say, "Send this." He felt it needed to get started. Prince was a black man in America and he grew up with all the stuff that happens in this country. He just wanted things to get off the ground.'

Ex-manager Ruth Arzate adds that 'he wanted to support black business. He was BLM before BLM was BLM. The tone he set was that he was going to give it where he could. He was going to put everybody that spoke for him in their proper place.'

Faith, Prince and charity

What drove this kindness?

When somebody worked with Prince, there were various stages. It might be getting a pass to work behind the scenes at Paisley Park, or on tour. Then there was Prince asking a trusted lieutenant such as Alan Leeds, Dave Hampton, Jacqui Thompson, Craig Rice, Ruth Arzate, 'Who is that? And what do they do for me?'

He could then watch them for about six weeks. And when he felt comfortable, he would on occasion initiate a conversation. He would look them straight in the eyes – he was allowed to do that being the boss – and ask, 'Do you believe in God?' For him, this was one of the most important questions he could ask.

Alan Leeds says he brought up the subject 'as if we were talking about football. And I learned that he asked that question to everybody.'

Unlike other black musicians like Sam Cooke, Aretha Franklin and Whitney Houston, Prince's music didn't grow up in the church tradition – his parents honed their musical chops in jazz clubs.

To those who knew him when younger, however, he always

found comfort in his faith. According to engineer Peggy McCreary, 'He was epileptic as a child and he prayed and an angel came to him and said, "You won't be sick any more," and he became religious after that.'

'Since we were little kids,' adds his cousin Chazz Smith, referencing one of his most overtly religious songs from *Around the World in a Day*, 'we were looking for "The Ladder". He wanted to know that he was doing the right thing. He knew that God had ordained him and he wanted to please him in that way.'

He wouldn't put a name to it – religion, spirituality, faith – but belief in a guiding light was a thread throughout his career. His bodyguard from 1984 to 1991, Harlan 'Hucky' Austin, has a memory of 'talking about religion more than politics or music. Prince always felt the need for spirituality and you can hear that even from the early singles. It was an inner battle between being this bad guy and doing these bad things and being on the straight and narrow.'

Minneapolis pastor and musician Spencer Bernard, who has a co-writing credit on Janet Jackson's *Control*, noted his 'internal tug of war between his faith and the temptations of the world. He even did a bit during an earlier tour when a huge booming voice comes out of the PA. It tells him to be good. Prince responds, "But they (meaning the audience) like it when I'm bad." The only other artist I've seen having that kind of internal wrestling match was Johnny Cash.'

That earlier tour was *Purple Rain*. The booming voice of 'God', who spoke to him from a distorted speaker (as in the start of the '1999' single) morphed into Prince's more proselytising tone to audiences by 1988's *Lovesexy tour*. This was, it's fair to note, the same tour where he performed a mash-up of 'Erotic City' and 'Sex Shooter'.

In 1987, *Sign* had its share of songs about sexuality but

the anthem ballad 'The Cross' wasn't just religious, it was explicitly Christian.

He would sing about not dying without knowing the sacrifice made on the cross, presumably the sacrifice of Jesus Christ. It is the central tenet of evangelical Christians. It has the same intensity as 'Purple Rain' but where that song could be seen as about everything and nothing, the subject matter of 'The Cross' is specific.

'I think it's a very distinct statement as to where he was,' adds Marylou Badeaux. 'He was starting to show his Christianity which may have been hidden. It's incredibly moving, almost more than "Purple Rain".

"The Cross" is just as powerful as "Purple Rain" if not more so. I remember the conversation we had around '79, '80 where he told me, "If they listen to my music, they know me; they don't need to interview me." When I heard "The Cross" for the first time, that conversation popped up into my head. This is who I am proclaiming.'

Robyn Riggs, his publicist at the time, remembers attending a 1987 gig in Berlin with MTV presenter Kurt Loder, where 'The Cross' was part of his encore and hearing the song connect with the audience. 'The Wall was still up. I'd never seen anything like that in my life.'

The through line of Prince's faith over most of his career was as a Jehovah's Witness, certainly from sometime from the mid-'90s to around the turn of the century, after his childhood where he was raised as a Seventh Day Adventist. At the peak of his fame, Hucky Austin, late hair stylist Earl Jones and bassist Mark Brown also professed the JW faith. 'He was around that but he wasn't into it,' says Craig Rice of the '82 to '89 era. 'He was still searching.' The conversion to his Jehovah's Witness faith is most commonly believed to be associated with his friendship with and admiration for Larry and Tina Graham. He would even pull Sly Stone's bassist Larry into interviews when he wanted back-up to talk more to journalists about his faith.

Ricky Peterson, an employee of Paisley Park, believes that George Benson, an early client of the studio, was more responsible for his conversion. This would see Prince as a regular attendee at JW services at The Kingdom Hall for two decades from the '90s. 'Prince loved Larry,' reflects Peterson, 'but George was the advocate for that. He said, "It's my duty to come to you and invite you to the Kingdom Hall." I always turned him down. George was the one who took it over the line.'

This belief system would mean 'The Cross' was in the '90s rewritten as 'The Christ', as the JW belief system is that Jesus wasn't crucified but impaled on an upright stake.

'Jehovah's Witnesses are very anti-symbol and anti-worshipping [objects],' says Sam Jennings. 'It shouldn't be a cross any more so we talked about that. This relationship changed a lot from 1987 to the 2000s.'

Prince's faith, which started with childhood adherence to Seventh Day Adventism, strayed into more explicit content in the '80s. 1980's 'Dirty Mind' was still raunchy but in 1987, 'The Cross' offers an interesting counterbalance.

Unlike Aretha Franklin and others, Prince's love of music and his place of worship were not explicitly intertwined. 'He had an idea to record some music to give them (the Kingdom Hall) to play,' adds Jennings, 'but I don't know if that actually happened.'

His religion would change but the intensity of his conversation would not. 'Sometimes he would force this stuff down you,' says producer Dylan Dresdow, who worked with him in late 2015 on *HITnRUN Phase Two*. 'He would keep a pocket Bible with him. "What do you believe? This is my owner's manual."

It's one of the things if you're going to work with him, you will talk about it, but I'm not going to look to talk about it.'

Early '90s girlfriend Robin Power Royal says they 'talked about God and angels and love a lot. Any conversations, God is a part. Prince believed in God but he was not a faithful Christian. A faithful Christian would not have been doing what he did with women. Prince was a faithful soul until he wasn't.'

The conversion to Jehovah's Witness changed some aspects of Prince's lifestyle. Larry and Tina Graham moved to Minneapolis to live at a house owned by Prince for many years.

Josh Dunham, a bassist in his band in the 2000s, remembers other changes: 'He didn't curse. He even started changing some of the lyrics in his music. That song "Sexuality" he changed to "Spirituality". He tried to do things a little differently. Whatever he wanted to do, I would roll with it.'

DJ Rashida found out in the mid-noughties about Prince's cleaned-up vocabulary. 'In our very first conversation I cursed. He said, "Do you talk to your parents like that?" I said yeah. But I felt like I had offended him. I learned very early that I couldn't play records with cursing including his. If someone played "Darling Nikki", he would go and tell them to switch it off. I would sneak in intros, like "Erotic City". Later on, I could get away with it.'

At the time of 'The Cross', where Craig Rice feels he was more in tune with Seventh Day Adventism, Susan Rogers was with him for most of the making of the record. But she never saw a Bible, as Dylan Dresdow had in 2015. 'He didn't quote Scripture at me. The guy that I worked with was not an overtly religious person. There were those songs such as "God" (B-side of "Purple Rain"), (*Around the World in a Day*'s) "The Ladder", and "The Cross" where I felt he wanted to pay something back, and he wrote some of those songs when he was feeling especially grateful, so when he needed an emotional touchstone or he needed to ground himself, he would write about something that was bigger than himself.'

Shelby Johnson, a Baptist who accompanied Prince to the Kingdom Hall (the place of JW worship in Minneapolis), says she 'needed to understand what that meant to him.' His faith would inform his setlists. 'The fans would be calling out all sorts of songs but he would perform and do the songs where he was. He was very true to that.' That didn't stop moments of mischief, such as playing the first couple of chords of 'Darling Nikki' in concert, to whip audiences into a frenzy. But if he liked the song but not the sentiment, she says he just changed the words. 'All of the songs were pieces and parts of him. He could do what he wanted.'

Sam Jennings likens the song changes to 'how George Lucas changed the *Star Wars* movies; it was up to him to change how it is depending on the time.'

'Ahead of his time'

Like his relationships, his philanthropy and to some extent his records (he would work on them, often on his own and then they were done and released), Prince practised his activism quietly.

As with all of the above, that didn't mean it wasn't powerful when he did.

Some interviewees say that the subject of politics came up rarely, others suggest he loved to while away the small hours talking affairs of state. He and Stevie Wonder played Obama's White House but he didn't endorse him. 'It wasn't to do with the politics of it,' argues DJ Rashida. 'He didn't vote for Obama. He really did care about uplifting his people.'

Rashida adds 'we were always talking about what are we

reading, and movies. He was just informed.' This didn't extend to a Blue State-Red State argument from the man most associated with purple. 'I knew he didn't believe in it – one side is better than the other. He was very clear about where we stood as black folks. He was not disconnected from that, the true history.'

Marylou Badeaux, who worked at Warner Brothers with Prince for two decades, calls him 'very cluey. He was very switched on to what was happening in the world.

'I can remember a big deep and meaningful conversation he and I had in Nice during the first Iraq war. He was sitting outside his dressing room an hour before the show and he really got into it.

'I know from a third party that he made some very strong comments about the Make America Great Again slogan. These comments were much in disdain.' Badeaux contends he would have got 'involved in the 2016 election if he hadn't died'.

Engineer Hans-Martin Buff likens Prince to Chuck D as 'a great missionary. He was a great preacher. There were a lot of discussions or questions on ethics, morality, politics, religion, and the black experience is certainly high up on that list.'

Former manager Ruth Arzate maintains that the concept of the hardships placed on black musicians from their white employers would have come from his parents, both of whom had to work day jobs after music could not sustain them. 'Much of the downloaded information mostly likely came from his parents as they were musicians doing the club gigs and attempting to reap a career from it. John probably talked about how he wanted a record deal and they were not paying him enough at the club. I feel that may have lent itself to how Prince saw things.'

When in 1995, Prince painted 'SLAVE' on his face at the BRIT Awards, he was ridiculed (Dave Rowntree, the drummer from Blur who won four awards that night, painted 'DAVE' on his), but the fight for artists' rights, to own your own masters, would be a preoccupation of many other artists from Anita Baker to Taylor Swift well into the twenty-first century. Rapper and activist Talib Kweli calls him 'ahead of his time' with the campaign and admires his commitment to activism at the expense of not doing what his fans expected of him. Kweli argues that not being a people-pleaser is 'vital. I think that's what we look to artists for. Once the fans know what to expect, you're no longer challenging them as an artist and they move on to something more dangerous. It's vital for artists to change.'

Heidi Clemence, who was based at Paisley Park as his wardrobe director for five years, says 'I think that (the SLAVE message) was something he did for the public. I don't recall him having his face painted.'

Growing up in the black community of one of America's most predominantly white states may have contributed to his mindset.

'I liked that Prince gave money without fanfare to anti-apartheid and Black Lives Matter,' adds Kweli. 'I also love that he used every single public appearance whether it be at the Super Bowl or an awards show to make some sort of social justice statement. Sometimes it would be about the people, sometimes it would be about the art.'

Prince would often invite academics known for writing about historical civil rights like Dr. Cornel West and Michael Eric Dyson to dinners as well as his parties. His activism would be tied into his philanthropy.

The tour manager in the '80s, Bill Reeves, instituted a movement called Roadies of Colour for more diversity among crew in the music industry. He says that Prince 'was very aware of racial issues and certainly a supporter of diversity in his band, particularly when it comes to women. Over a thirty-year period, things evolved. When I was with him, I don't think there was any difference in the way he related to black and white crew members.'

Ian Boxill, one of a few black engineers Prince was able to hire in the mid-'00s (others included Femi Jiya, Lisa Chamblee and Chris James), recalls: 'He talked about racial issues a lot. He was definitely aware of it [racism] and it was important to him. He definitely wanted to work with black engineers.

'To me, it just seemed like he wanted to work with people who would understand the roots of his music more. Our appreciation for James Brown and Sly [Stone] came up a lot.'

'Being black in the entertainment business,' adds Chamblee, 'we're born black and we're going to die black. The thing is, you want to be known for what you're doing: "I'm an engineer", "I'm a black woman". For him, it was "I'm a rock star", "I'm a pop star". He was always a black man. He always cared about black people. It's not something we always want to talk about.'

She mentions Whitney Houston, who was criticised for her mainstream appeal to a white audience, as an example of 'how they categorise people' and argues Prince's focus precluded him from too many public statements to avoid categorisation. 'He was trying to be a frickin' rock star. He was who he was.

'He didn't want to be in a "black man box". What the world puts us in, he wasn't going to be in. If he'd said [more on] what he felt about black people, it would have put him in that box.

'He wanted to appeal to more people. It sounds like market research not that he wasn't into being pro-black. The world didn't want to categorise him as that.'

Prince announced he had started work on a memoir called *The Beautiful Ones*, in March 2016, the month before his death. So it only touches on a small corner of his career. In it, Prince mentions the 1921 Tulsan massacre when white residents killed many of the participants in the burgeoning phenomenon which became known as 'black Wall Street'. Jacqui Thompson, who worked with Prince in the '90s, argues that 'if he had finished that book, there would have been a lot more about that (BLM) in it.' Boxill also remembers Prince rushing to support Black Lives Matter after 2005's Hurricane Katrina. Others insist that he may well have had something to say about the May 2020 murder of George Floyd in Minneapolis.

Prince's final musical project, with drummer Kirk Johnson, bassist MonoNeon and saxophonist Adrian Crutchfield, was 2015's unfinished *Black Is the New Black*. 'Everything in pop culture was being derived from black culture,' reflects Crutchfield, 'and I think Prince wanted people to take more pride in that. In fashion, black is like the original statement, it goes with everything. I think the title was calling attention to that and saying the original popular colour is the new popular colour. Trying to bring back the heritage. I think he wanted to bring attention to it, bring pride to it.'

Party like it's 2006

If Prince's public utterances on political and social issues were idiosyncratic, his business models were even more of a one-off.

Take 3121 as an example.

He wore a jacket with the number on the back then made it the name of his 2006 album, with that jacket as the cover image from Sam Jennings. These in turn led to his Club 3121 residency at the Rio, as an early pop star adopter of the Las Vegas residency before Adele, Shania Twain and Celine Dion, where he would stay in a suite opposite Sir Elton John; a 3121 perfume (some proceeds went to old friend Taja Sevelle's sustainable farming initiative); and charging £31.21 for tickets to his record-breaking twenty-one concerts stint at London's O2. When he moved

LA rentals to 1235 Sierra Alta Way in Alta Vista and 77 Beverly Park, he was said to have changed the names on the door to 3121 which, chuckles Morris Hayes, 'led to some confusion with the post office. He didn't care about that kind of stuff. That was technicalities.' Ruth Arzate confirms he kept Beverly Park as 77 because he liked that number too. And he named a song on his 2009 album *LOtUSFLOW3R*, '77 Beverly Park'.

Arzate had been tasked to find him an LA rental while he was jamming and while searching online, she suggested 3121 Antelo Road. Before she had completed the transaction, he had turned it into a song. He then turned it into a business.

'3121 was supposed to be a brand – merchandise, perfume, we were looking at homeware, children's stuff, incense and candles, that kind of stuff,' recalls Arzate, his manager at the time. 'There were a lot of things we were going to do with the brand so 3121 could become its own thing, and as symbolic as the Prince symbol.'

Maybe he liked it because the numbers added up to seven, another of his songs (in December 2022, singer Lizzo told Howard Stern that Prince paid her for a collaboration in instalments of seven), and he was a fan of Egyptian imagery, where the number represented perfection or completeness. Or maybe he was thinking ahead as he had been with '1999' seventeen years prior to that.

'To take the number 3121 and make a jacket, make an album, make a residency. He was a marketing genius,' adds musician Frank McComb, who didn't mention the 3121 perfume. 'He took the colour purple and made it famous, and *1999* which was so far away when he released it. He was like Midas. Everything he touched turned to gold.'

The *3121* movie is a notable exception but, suggests Arzate, that could be for the best.

'It's about Coco, played by Lisa Hernandez, the ingénue, the hero. She makes Prince's acquaintance and becomes his muse, while his limo driver and assistant steal a million dollars from him.

'He asked me, "What do you think of the plot?" It felt like a test. The assistant character seemed based on me because I was his assistant at the time before I became his manager. This character throws Hollywood soirées, as did I. One of Prince's sayings was: "Everything you think is true." Was he forecasting that employees were going to steal all this money from him?!? Perhaps it wasn't a forecast because it seemed that indeed nearly everyone stole from him. It was a pattern. But honestly, the movie is terrible.'

Prince had enjoyed Los Angeles – and Sunset Sound – as a recording playground in the 1980s. The 3121 era, where studios could become more of a movable feast in the Pro Tools age, saw Prince building a new playground, this time live with his own house parties. As Shelby Johnson notes, Prince was 'the star of stars' so there was no one who didn't seem to defer to him, want to see him play or, on occasion, join him onstage.

On the *Parade*-era tour, Robyn Lynch remembers a party at Kensington Roof Gardens after a gig where Sting and Ronnie Wood had played with him. 'Everybody in British rock history was there. They all think he's amazing. Does that make me amazing? That was my boss. Robert Plant. Eric Clapton. The girls from Bananarama.' The sound of some of Britain's most venerated rock stars all whispering to one another like BTS fans, "Did you meet him yet?" has stuck with the make-up artist three and a half decades on.

Sam Jennings, who helped Prince with his website, had the same treatment two decades later in the 3121 era, having talked to the man in whose guest house he was staying. He heard a star say, 'You actually know him?!?'

Prince's parties with musicians started late and finished early, as Minneapolitan singer Cynthia Johnson remarks. 'He threw parties until morning. There were always great performances … a lot of musicians just sitting in jamming. It was a great time and everything was free.'

The 3121 parties in LA were another level, or as Morris Hayes puts it 'the nuttiest of all time. Alicia Keys, Herbie Hancock, Joni Mitchell's in there shooting pool. I met J J Abrams at Prince's house. It was the who's who of the A-list just hanging, having a great time. Oprah. Everybody's there. I remember seeing Frodo (Elijah Wood) and Jessica Simpson asleep on a stool. Prince was a great fan of *The Matrix* and Laurence [Fishburne] was sitting there like Morpheus all night.'

Prince would tell US talk show host Jay Leno in 2001 that he had asked Fishburne the plot line for *The Matrix* sequels and when the actor couldn't – or wouldn't – help, Prince gave him tickets for his next gig up in the nosebleed section.

Gabrielle Union told Trevor Noah on *The Daily Show* that Prince's parties represented an opportunity for many black artistic creatives to meet and make plans to work together, where other Hollywood parties didn't. Comedian Cedric the Entertainer insists they weren't 'rah-rah' as he puts it. 'They would be fun and vibrant but never would anybody be over the top.'

Portuguese singer Ana Moura remembers 'something that was always common at his parties was his particular humour, which led him to do things like playing hide and seek in the early hours of the morning. Everyone always knew where Prince was because he had sneakers with lights, and every time he took a step, they blinked.'

You wouldn't expect Prince on clipboard duties, and these parties hardly organised themselves. Those would fall to his long-suffering assistant turned manager, Ruth Arzate, to whom Prince would say, 'You do it.'

'There were parties where I was completely autonomous. The only thing that he would organise was the music.

'I gave a speech before every party.

"You don't approach these people."

"If I see you giving your phone number to anyone, that's grounds for you to leave."

"You are not to ask for autographs."

"You are not to ask for photos."

"If anyone yells at you, it should be me and only me."

'They were pretty legendary. The biggest lead time I had on a party was five to seven days. The shortest was six hours. That one was the party Cameron Diaz shouted at Justin Timberlake. That's when they broke up. He showed up with Jessica Biel. Tom Cruise and Katie (Holmes) were there, and Jamie Foxx. That was the one that had the least time. I was already ahead of them [the parties] … I'm almost certain that he tested me to see if I could do it. For him to decide to throw a party means he has the energy to perform and then he wants to know who's going to be in town. He makes the list. Sometimes I had the ability to create a list. Sometimes I couldn't invite anyone who wasn't on the list. I'd invite a friend who was a huge fan and he'd say, "Who is this?"'

Normally there would be around 500 attendees and if she had notice, there would be sponsors. 'I would organise travel and accommodation for the band and flowers. These were $250–300,000 parties that I would end up spending $30–50,000 on.'

As she suggests, they would be pretty hard work. 'When you're working twenty hours straight, you don't care who's in the room. Oprah is in the corner, Lena (Morgan) the chef is getting breakfast … I don't care.'

Musician Frank McComb, whom Prince singled out to play in his band for the parties but not his live band ('it was all behind closed doors') after a gig at LA's Level 1 nightclub, where Jeff Goldblum used to play piano, remembers him to be amped up as if he was playing Madison Square Garden rather than his back garden. 'He would come down fully dressed like it was a show and he was a member of the band. We would rehearse and rehearse. We would rehearse like it was a gig. He would come like he was ready to play a gig. Even the dress, clothes, make-up. He was clean as a whistle.

'I remember one night it was me, Questlove, Herbie, Stevie, Jill Scott, Maceo [Parker, saxophonist] and his guys. I had this arrangement of "Superwoman"; we played it that night and when we finished doing that, Stevie remembered the tune and he jumped in and joined with us.'

Another gig, McComb had a post-gig early morning breakfast with Prince's then protégée Ashley Tamar, Joni Mitchell, Herbie Hancock and Stevie Wonder.

'Lots of eggs. Coming out all of the time. He was asking questions. Herbie is a Buddhist, Joni is an atheist, Stevie is Christian ...' For those wondering about the breakfast pecking order ... 'Stevie was the first to get a lot of eggs. I think they were scrambled.'

Other times Jamie Foxx would be chilling in the kitchen with a drink, or Joni would be in the next room playing pool. Then there was the party Matthew McConaughey decided to perform. 'Matthew was playing bongos,' says Hayes. 'He had played to the point his hands were bleeding. I go into the kitchen and he wants to shake Prince's hand.'

'We could be blood brothers,' Hayes recalls the actor saying, which cut no ice with the host.

Ruth Arzate offered the barefoot actor a towel and asked him not to touch Prince's hands.

Prince prepped for his house parties as if they were stadia, but in the same year as much of the 3121 activity and his twenty-one sell-out London shows, there was another rather sizeable concert planned for 4 February 2007.

The whistle blows for half-time

The half-time show at the Super Bowl is where the biggest musical acts in the world come to play. It is for legends and superstars only – sometimes, they are only the guest stars to an equally stellar headlining act. It is where The Weeknd added $7 million of his own money to the $10 million production budget to beef up his 2021 show, Rihanna had the stage set up to levitate in 2023 even though she was four months pregnant, Coldplay asked Beyoncé and Bruno Mars to join them in 2016, and where, the previous year, Katy Perry danced onstage with sharks. In 2022, Dr. Dre didn't take any chances and brought Snoop Dogg, Mary J Blige, Eminem, 50 Cent and Anderson .Paak onstage with him.

For the 2007 show, Prince took some persuading to follow Paul McCartney and the Rolling Stones, the English rock legends both brought in to reassure Middle America in the years succeeding Janet Jackson and Justin Timberlake's infamous 2004 'wardrobe malfunction'.

'I think with Prince,' recalls Charles Coplin, the executive producer of the show and NFL's head of programming, 'why wouldn't we choose him? Jimi Hendrix and James Brown all rolled into one. It felt like the right guy for the stage. Those were British white acts so to have a black act from America was a really good fit.'

Prince turned down many big gigs (he never played the Glastonbury Festival for instance), but on this, once his mind was made up, he decided to do some persuading of his own.

The organisers of the show had approached Prince and, thinking it over, he invited them for dinner at his home.

There was a DVD player where he reviewed some previous shows – 'This was good but I wouldn't have done this,' he'd told tour promoter John Meglen, who reported this to The Ringer.

Then, the *coup de grâce*.

Prince tells the four execs from the NFL and TV to follow him. There they are faced with drummer Cora Coleman-Dunham, her then husband bassist Josh Dunham, and keyboard player Morris Hayes.

Prince introduces them with the words 'Can Paul McCartney do this?' and he and his band play a half-hour set.

Game, set and match, Prince.

'It's a wall of sound,' laughs Hayes. 'They get the shock and awe. That was really cool. We're going to blow 'em away. We killed it. Then he did that little pimp walk back to the table. They were looking like, "Where do we sign?"'

A follow-up meeting at the Beverly Wilshire saw Prince become more expansive to the execs. 'He tried to explain what we were about to hear but he was doing it in his esoteric way,' recalls Coplin. 'You're going to hear thunder and the first lines of "We Will Rock You".'

'It was more a mood, a tone. It became pretty obvious. He'd studied half-time shows.

'Springsteen may have done the same thing in his own way, but Prince seemed to do his homework more than the others. He had a competitive streak in him to be the best.'

Prince was told that the logistics around a Super Bowl half-time meant it couldn't all be about him.

Contractual obligations for one meant Prince would need to interrupt his 3121 shows in Vegas for a press conference.

He told them, 'I don't do interviews,' and then, when it came to the press conference in question, responded as he had to the NFL execs with a plan he cooked up with his band.

'That's what he said before we went onstage,' Josh Dunham remembers. '"As soon as the first person asks a question, I'm gonna cut it off." I guess he wanted to play a game with the press.'

Prince announced, 'Any questions?' and he interrupted the first softball about playing Miami with the intro for 'Johnny B. Goode' (a song recorded and released the year he was born) before launching into *Parade*'s 'Anotherloverholenyohead' and *3121*'s 'Get on the Boat'.

'That was another example,' says Coplin, 'of Prince saying, "I'm not being difficult; I'm just trying to do something that hasn't been done before."'

Further Super Bowl half-time show protocol was broken as everything is normally pre-recorded to the last second, often months in advance. On hearing this, Prince reminded the execs of one non-negotiable point – he always plays live.

Prince had decamped from his *3121* Las Vegas residency at the Rio Hotel to Paisley Park and then to Miami to make sure everything was just so. Super Bowl organisers shared his caution that nothing would be left to the day – except for two things.

'Everything was recorded at Paisley,' his engineer at the time Ian Boxill recalls. 'The whole medley and the only thing that was live was him and his guitar. You have fifteen minutes to get the show on time so they don't take chances setting up live instruments. We would mix and remix the whole medley again and again. I would say three or four times.

'I had tracked everything at Paisley but was mixing it at the Rio Hotel. He kept having me do it again and again. I wasn't working in the best of studios so there was only so much I could do. He was happy in the end.

'By the time I sent the tapes to the producers, it was a couple of days before the show. The producers of the shows were like, "Where's the tracks?" They kept calling me. They're on a deadline. They have got to figure out the choreography.'

Another aspect of the performance requiring attention, according to Gary Kazanchyan who custom-made Prince's shoes at the time, was his outfit. 'A shimmering, sequinned purple. I remember finishing the shoes months in advance.'

Until Prince changed his mind. Kazanchyan was told:

'We are not doing that colour any more; we're going a different route.'

'There was a limited amount of fabric, the points had to be made first and whatever was left over, that's what I got to make the shoes out of.'

With the day approaching and Prince setting up drill camp back at Paisley, Morris Hayes started getting calls. 'Why is he being so weird? He called me four or five days ahead of it. "What are you wearing?" He was trying to mitigate what we were going to do. My job was to make sure Prince didn't get electrocuted. I have had Prince get some pretty bad shocks because something wasn't grounded properly.'

On the morning of the show, everything was ready. Prince's medley was recorded, the band and dancers (Nandy and Maya McClean) were rehearsed, his purple symbol guitar – which matched the shape of the stage – peach shirt, pale blue suit and matching shoes were laid out. Prince, a seasoned live pro, just had to master the live vocals and guitar.

One more slight wrinkle.

It was raining.

Not drizzle, but a torrential downpour of almost biblical proportions.

The rain had been attributed, perhaps erroneously, in Prince's decision not to play Wembley Stadium in 1987. This was different – minutes away from the biggest live TV performance of his career, the weather presented major logistical challenges.

'It had been sunny all week and that morning it was literally like a monsoon,' remembers Shelby Johnson. 'It's never rained in the history of the NFL on a Super Bowl. We said a prayer.'

The execs working for the NFL and CBS network were doing more than praying. Now it wasn't just Prince who was worried about being electrocuted, which was a real concern. Dancers could slip, musical equipment could malfunction, cameras might miss key shots. The NFL's producer and director Don Mischer had to navigate something unprecedented in forty Super Bowls, and called Prince. He recounted the conversation to Rich Eisen in 2023.

'Now I want you to know that it's raining.'

'Yes, it's raining.'

'And are you OK?'

'Can you make it rain harder?'

Belying such bravado, according to those closest to him, Prince was as on edge as they were. 'I knew they kept the lights off the band,' argues Josh Dunham, 'because they were afraid that water was going to get in. I think Prince was nervous but he wasn't going to show it.'

He was terse in the car coming in with then manager Ruth Arzate until she mentioned his appearance on *Muppets Tonight* ten years prior to the Super Bowl to lighten his mood. She refers to his then mood as 'relaxed intensity'.

'We all knew it was a big deal, including him. I just didn't think he would be nervous. That threw me. I think he was a little concerned. There was a real risk of the dancers falling offstage or being electrocuted. I think from the night before, there was a moodiness he had; it wasn't until after someone sent me the [*Muppets*] DVD, and I felt like it gave me the opportunity to have this little pep talk. There is something when you are someone like Prince and you are not vocalising an insecurity, it does come across as something else because you're not allowing people to see your vulnerabilities; when I realised he was nervous it took me by surprise and it took him by surprise. The pep talk was stupid, but it was just the fact that someone said, "I get you." It could be a stranger on the street that gives you encouragement.'

'He had an attitude,' admits Nandy McClean. 'Me and Maya sat out on the stage and he said, "Don't hurt yourself. We don't have insurance." He wasn't being funny. He had his mic stand and at the end of the performance, the elevator drops and that's when he says goodbye. During rehearsals, the mic had hit him on the head. It also happened on the filmed performance. That mic film thing was him being nervous. He's in the middle of a performance.'

Morris Hayes claims his nerves were not for him. 'Prince was always nervous ahead of TV shows, but he wasn't nervous for the sake of being nervous. [He would say] "I'm not nervous about me; I'm nervous about all of y'all."'

Jitters were flying around in all quarters – particularly over the setlist.

The NFL had been hoping for Prince's Greatest Hits. He had other ideas. He had in mind what singer in his band Shelby Johnson calls A Show.

Dunham adds that the NFL execs were initially not keen on the lack of Prince material. 'I knew he mentioned they wanted him to do more of his hits.'

Not for the first time, Prince pleased himself.

That meant extrapolating Queen's 'We Will Rock You' – 'he loved, loved, loved Freddie Mercury,' says his former make-up artist Robyn Lynch – into 'Let's Go Crazy' and adding Creedence

Clearwater Revival's 'Proud Mary' (the first song he learned on the guitar) to his own 'Baby I'm a Star' and '1999'.

Arzate had been bringing him CDs of new and old music and so he added his own version of Jimi Hendrix's cover of Bob Dylan's 'All Along the Watchtower' and Foo Fighters' 2005 hit 'Best of You' before a 100-strong marching band joined him for the closer 'Purple Rain'.

'Foolishly,' says Coplin referencing his hotel meeting with Prince, 'I had said, "There's no 'Little Red Corvette'." The guy who worked with us says he's written a soundtrack for the show. He had designed something that was specific for the Super Bowl instead.

'He viewed it as a cohesive show rather than "I will take five pieces and just play". Rather than doing a mini-concert, he viewed it as a start to finish show.'

'We shot the full thing full regalia like it was the Super Bowl,' says Hayes of the rehearsal. 'If we have to we will run the footage and superimpose the crowd on the top. He said, no … rock 'n' roll. His whole thing was there's all walks of life and all sorts of people at the Super Bowl and he wanted something that would pull in everybody. The Creedence Clearwater was a crowd favourite and Prince played the Foo Fighters. He was more concerned with the flow of the show than the message of the show. He put more thought into the show than doing all of his own hits.'

Prince's own in-house DJ, Rashida, agrees: 'You're creating a story, a vibe, a shift. He could have done it with his own music, but he was totally playing DJ. There were great mixes he would put together onstage and have them [his band] do a live version.'

Every decision, including the last-minute do-rag to keep the rain from his hair, was his.

'Some artists want everybody else to do the thinking, but

he was involved in every aspect of what he wanted the finished product to be,' adds Shelby Johnson. 'He's got so much swag that he can wear a do-rag and make it look cool.'

The rain, says Boxill, 'worked in his favour because he had the purple lights on during "Purple Rain". I don't know how the dancers didn't slip wearing heels. He wasn't dancing as much as they were.'

'I was kind of shocked it was going to rain so steadily for so long,' says Coplin. 'We were told by certain people it was going to stop raining. About a year later we did the Tom Petty (half-time) show in Arizona and they had a retractable roof and they were so afraid it was going to rain they made us close the roof.'

Johnson's perspective is that 'the rain made it classic.'

Everyone was happy. Don Mischer was being hailed as a visionary after Super Bowl XLI's half-time show peaked at 140 million viewers. 'Right after the Super Bowl,' he told *The New York Times*, 'I flew into Beijing and at the airport I was met by reporters who were talking about the Prince half-time show. And the first question to me was, "How many water trucks did it take to create the rain effect that you achieved on TV?"'

Coplin reckons it also sated Prince's competitive instincts. 'I did six of them and across the board, Prince is always 1, 2, 3. He tends to be the one people choose as number one 75 per cent of the time. They mention U2, they mention Beyoncé. I think that will go down as the best. If anybody beats him, it's not going to be as an individual. I don't think one human will ever get better raves than that.'

Arzate adds: 'He's not a person who used the word "magical" but he used it in this instance.'

Prince was unusually content and called DJ Rashida. 'He basically said, "I did it, this is it." In terms of earthly goals, he was a spiritual man, he just knew that he had done it.

'There was nothing left to prove. He knew that. Just all he'd had to accomplish as an artist. Even we felt like we did something impactful.'

CHAPTER 15

IT'S GONNA BE A BEAUTIFUL NIGHT

'It's Gonna Be a Beautiful Night'... Hip hop: the music that doesn't stop – or start if you're Prince ... Follow the leader ... To play's the thing ... Pop's ultimate completer-finisher ... Mentor and tormentor ... 'I'm supposed to be a mysterious person but I'm not mysterious' ... Boys Keep Swinging in Minneapolis ... Prince. Funny how?

'It's Gonna Be a Beautiful Night'

Just as the *Sign o' the Times* movie was cooked up in Amsterdam and Rotterdam and made in Minneapolis, the record's penultimate track, 'It's Gonna Be a Beautiful Night', was made in Paris and reheated in Los Angeles.

Prince and the Revolution were playing Le Zenith on 25 August 1986 but it was two members of his future band who worked it up over a soundcheck. '"Beautiful Night" was rather spontaneously written at the soundcheck before a gig in Paris,' recalls Eric Leeds. 'It began with a basic groove to which Matt Fink added a keyboard line and I added a horn line. We recorded the song "live" during the concert that evening.'

'Matt Fink might have come up with the basis of the song,' explains trumpeter Matt Blistan. 'It might have been the same day Eric had come up with the horn part and he had the group together during the day and we recorded it live that night. It was that quick.'

He may have been sound checking with the Revolution – the band is namechecked in the song – but horn lines from Leeds and Blistan were recorded live that night by Susan Rogers. She would be ferrying from Sunset Sound to Galpin Boulevard in Minneapolis and was also despatched across the pond with equipment when the occasion arose, be that for the movie or recording a live track, as Prince fancied.

'I was the recording engineer. We would have mobile trucks [ready to capture on tape], whether it was New York, Los Angeles, Rotterdam or Paris, to record "It's Gonna Be a Beautiful Night". That was my role.'

Such was the way he worked, if Prince's musicians had given him the inspiration to write a song predicting a beautiful night, he would have it written and recorded before that night turned into dawn.

The 'twenty-four or forty-eight hours' maximum' notice that Prince would give his trusted engineer to get the sound on his movie or a live track like this right did not mean he gave her leeway or basic courtesy.

Prince did appreciate people who worked hard for him, even though he might wait until after the work was done to show it.

Todd Herreman, who recalls the track because of Susan Rogers' contribution to the sound, remembers that 'after that show, Prince gave her a big hug. It's not that he wasn't a nice guy, he was just focused.'

The timeline will notice that Wendy, Lisa, Mark and Bobby would all have played on the original record. By the time it appeared on the record, their contribution would have been written, or played, out of history.

'Weeks later, we added additional horn parts and lyrics in the studio, so it's kind of a live/studio mash-up,' adds Leeds. 'He overdubbed a lot of it afterwards,' recalls Matt Fink.

Eric Leeds remembers the version which ended up on the record as coming from the gig at Le Zenith, but then Prince went to work at Sunset in LA. 'He redid the vocals, added the rap by Sheila and a whole bunch of horn parts in the studio. So what remains of the original live recording is pretty much just the rhythm track, the original primary horn line and the sax solo. Everything else was studio post-production.'

Prince had a new band and even though Fink and Leeds – who were given writing credits – and Blistan were part of the new band, so was Sheila E. The others weren't. So Prince's tweaks reflected that, with Sheila's rap recorded in the early hours of 27 November.

One hitch. She was on the East Coast, having just played Riverfront Coliseum in Cincinnati, Ohio as part of Lionel Richie's band.

Susan Rogers laughs at the logistics involved in nailing what she calls 'the Trans Mississippi rap'.

'We were in the studio and the techs were on the telephone so they could patch in Sheila E.'s rap. They patched it over the phone. We could do that with some EQ filters but it was the sound of the telephone.'

Prince's child within reappears on the record. Sheila raps about the table and the chair, an Edward Lear nursery rhyme, after Dr. Seuss featured in the second track, 'Play in the Sunshine'.

Susan Rogers was grateful for the technology then available to her way before MP3s or mobiles which offered a split-second delay.

'She was somewhere on the East Coast and east of the Mississippi River and we were in LA and we had to record her over the phone. Over hundreds of miles, there is a delay, so we had to time the delay. Sunset had a transformer that worked.

'You unscrew the mouthpiece and you unscrew the earpiece and you have access to the rhythm. The problem we had to solve was the delay. She would rap and it was 500 milliseconds, half a second late and we had to make the difference on the tape and then we had to offset those two things. She's hearing it in real time and we recorded her recording it down the line.'

Giving an answer only a renowned puzzle solver – Rogers admits to starting each day with coffee and *The New York Times* crossword – could, she laughs: 'It was fun.'

Hip hop: the music that doesn't stop – or start if you're Prince

For all her many talents, and starring role in 1985's movie *Krush Groove* alongside LL Cool J, Kurtis Blow and Run-DMC, Sheila E. was not at the forefront of rap in 1987.

A month before *Sign o' the Times* was released on 31 March, Public Enemy released their first album, *Yo! Bum Rush the Show*.

It was the same year as Eric B & Rakim's *Paid in Full*, (N.W.A. and The Posse's *Straight Outta Compton* would follow in '88), Kool Moe Dee's *How Ya Like Me Now*, Whodini's *Open Sesame* and Ice-T's debut *Rhyme Pays*. Three of the aforementioned acts, and LL Cool J, would form the Def Jam Tour the same year, visiting USA and Europe.

Another seismic hip hop event occurred in 1987.

Kendrick Lamar, the first rap artist to win a Pulitzer Prize for music, was born in N.W.A.'s backyard of Compton on

Wednesday 17 June.

Prince was schooled in the history of black music and could master every instrument and access all the cutting-edge technology known to man. He was tailor-made to sweep in and take advantage of hip hop the way the Bee Gees jumped on the disco train and hit pay dirt with *Saturday Night Fever*.

The reasons he didn't are both geographical and generational.

The roots of music which emanated in pockets of New York were not reflected in Chanhassen.

'He couldn't relate to what was going on in the Bronx or big cities in the north east,' points out Alan Leeds. 'People have a tendency to assume that black people relate to the same things. His upbringing couldn't be more different. He didn't get it from the beginning. I actually felt bad for him because it was obvious that this was where the culture was going and his attempts to relate to it once he decided he had to seemed pathetic.

'The idea that someone like him was singing into a gun-shaped mic... as MCs they weren't nearly as good as the musicians that he would hire and that underscored that he didn't understand the culture because if he did, the quality of his MCs would have been higher... a Chuck D or a Q-Tip; he would have found that person.'

The generational impact can be traced to James Brown, the most sampled act in the burgeoning days of hip hop. Prince belonged to a generation with Cynthia Johnson, Jimmy Jam and Terry Lewis's Flyte Tyme and his own Grand Central band who would turn up to high-school parties and play JB's music.

Bill Stephney (born 1962), the president of Def Jam records, traces the divide back to those who were in high school when The Sugarhill Gang's 'Rapper's Delight' was released in 1979.

'There wasn't any indication that he had an affinity for it [hip hop],' argues Stephney. 'He looked at James Brown through the lens of a musician. That generation coming out of New York looked and listened to James Brown through the filter of a DJ which was completely different. You are focusing on the snare drums and the rhythms specifically and how they can be DJ'ed for an audience. If you are a great musician like Prince, you are looking at him as a musician – the bands and instruments.'

Stephney reckons Prince 'fell victim to a change in the times. It's a whole different era. Michael Jackson had to contend with it. Stevie Wonder had to contend with it. Whitney Houston had to contend with it when she was receiving an award and she got booed because she wasn't considered black enough.

'It's just this shift and it would have been difficult for someone like Prince given his own musical training, given his ear, his pedigree, his location; he's not in the clubs, he might visit now and then.

'You're not going to see Prince at The Tunnel with Funkmaster Flex. He was from a different era.'

'My own view is that when Prince did make a concerted effort to create hip hop, it sounded like someone from Minneapolis who had never been to the Bronx or Harlem, and you can understand why. Even from an age standpoint. If you graduated a year before, you probably hated hip hop. The line of demarcation between those who were into the music and those who weren't was really that stark around that era. He always wanted to be on the cutting edge, but to have a real ear and feel… even things like drum sounds, it didn't sound like what he would have heard from those making the music.'

Ceding control (rap's top tier would have insisted on writing or production credits on condition of participation) may have presented another issue.

The rise in hip hop for a young audience wasn't just cultural. It was financial, says Bill Stephney, born four years after Prince.

'For somebody like me there was a point where parties in our communities became bands. I'd be in a group of fifty or sixty young people and there would be a funk band playing covers. Like the dinosaurs disappearing because of nature, the same happened with us when the turntables and the MCs arrived. Why should you hire six or seven kids trying to mimic a band of the day when you could get turntables?'

As someone who sought out female bandmates, it's possible rap's testosterone heaviness didn't sit that easily with Prince either. The feeling from the hip hop community was mutual. 'In our crew,' adds Stephney, 'I would say that there was a youthful mocking of Prince stylistically that he represented what hip hop was trying to deviate from.' In 1984, Run-DMC had a motto – no curls, no fades. The same year, while they were in black leather and Adidas, Prince was wearing a light perm, lace gloves, high heels and frilly blouses. 'They were trying to move away from that new romantic era of Prince, Ready for the World, The Deal, even Duran Duran. There was an element of femininity that the machismo of hip hop wanted to reject.'

He knew the rap wave was crashing over the music industry as early as 1985, according to Susan Rogers. 'He was aware of it, and he was not pleased around the time of *Around the World in a Day*. I remember him saying, "The next wave of music coming will be bass and drums and vocals on top of it, and the emphasis that melody will be devalued in the coming years. When a woman comes along and does what I do, she will rule the world."'

In 1985, Aerosmith hired Van Halen's producer Ted Templeman for their comeback album with Joe Perry, *Done With Mirrors*. It reached an underwhelming 36 in the Billboard Hot 100.

The following year, Run-DMC asked Aerosmith's Perry and Steven Tyler to join them for a rap version of the rockers' 1975 track 'Walk This Way'. Supported by both white and black radio, it hit six in the Billboard Hot 100, four places higher than the previous version. It was, says Stephney, 'incredibly impactful' and gave rap a route into white radio few previous records had done.

Michael Jackson tried to get Run-DMC on *Bad* (a demo they wrote together, 'Crack Kills', was unfinished) and LL Cool J on 1992's *Dangerous*. He settled on Heavy D (on 'Jam') and engineer Bill Bottrell, under the pseudonym L.T.B., a tribute to *Leave It to Beaver* (on 'Black or White').

Even though there is rap on *Sign o' the Times* if you count Sheila E.'s through the phone delivery on 'It's Gonna Be a Beautiful Night', Prince was warier.

The Black Album from the same year as *Sign* attempted to reconnect with his black audience. He played with vocal distortion and experimentation, as well as the rap staple of a diss song. 'He did the song "Dead on It". It was awful,' Susan Rogers remembers. 'He knew it was. It didn't suit his methodology.'

Adam Holzman, who played with Miles Davis around the *Tutu* era, adds: 'I don't think Prince took the whole hip hop thing that seriously. He could sing in 20 different voices … why does he need to rap to a drum groove?'

By the time hip hop had got huge in the early '90s, Prince's appreciation for what he often called 'real music' kicked in, as manager Alan Leeds remembers. 'He wanted to be unique, so the very fact that he was beginning to accept something new was scary. Is this the end of his creativity? Is he ready to jump on a bandwagon or the wrong bandwagon? Later on, he got it.'

Prince, a James Brown fan and keen student of both musical proficiency and black ownership, wasn't crazy, says Leeds, about 'the fact that in early hip hop the sampling stuff was so blatant. There was a time he and I were in Paisley and we picked up

Billboard and the Hot 100 chart and he said to me, "Do you know how humiliating it is that my record is struggling to make the Top 40 and people like MC Hammer and Vanilla Ice are in the top five? You spent time trying to learn a craft and you're losing to people who can't play instruments? Do you know how frustrating that is?" He didn't accept making a record with loops and samples.'

Engineer and early Paisley Park employee Eddie Miller was having a social drink in Minneapolis when he believes his boss displayed his first appreciation of hip hop – and it was a Def Jam artist.

'We all went out and we were all just sitting at a table and they're playing LL Cool J's (1988) track about Kool Moe Dee ['Jack the Ripper']. They were having a feud. He'd sample a James Brown loop, and both our eyes popped open and our ears perked up.'

The groove was undeniable, as Prince knew at that moment, according to Miller. 'You can't argue with the funkiness of it. After a while you just kind of broke down and that was the funkiest parts of rap and I think I saw the moment that it happened. [His reaction said] "Oh, yeah, this is funky."'

By his thirteenth album, 1991's *Diamonds and Pearls*, Prince took the approach with most of his business, from his wardrobe to the way his music was produced, to keep things in house. While other mainstream artists like Janet Jackson were working with leading titans of rap like Busta Rhymes and Q-Tip, rapper Tony Moseley, aka Tony M, was part of his touring band with Kirk Johnson and Damon Dickson, known as Game Boyz (possibly a continuation of the comic foils such as Morris Day, Jerome Benton, Wally Safford and Greg Brooks). They had been dancers in *Purple Rain*.

Saxophonist Eric Leeds is not alone in arguing it was his

downfall. 'If Prince made any "mistake", it might have been to attempt, perhaps for the first time in his career, to "react" to that environment rather than "respond" by continuing to be himself.'

Scottie Baldwin is more sanguine. 'He still had something to prove. It just wasn't going to happen. He was trying to do his version of new jack [swing]. I just don't think it worked out.'

Michael Bland, who was in the D&P band when Prince was considered to have 'gone hip hop', disputes that it was a concerted decision. 'Prince knew what to do with every one of us. He had Tony Moseley in his band as one of the Game Boyz dancers. The fact that he was an aspiring rapper was unbeknown to us. People say it was something contrived but really it just went the way it did.

'We were playing [Digital Underground's] "The Humpty Dance" and he [Moseley] jumped up and started doing the rap from "Humpty Dance" and Prince said, "Woah! I didn't know you did that." He added some rap into the Nude tour (1990) and I think Tony would rap between "The Future" and "1999" a few bars here and there, a good solid sixteen. From there, they just kept working at it. Tony was hired to dance. It worked out for everybody. He tried to hear from the culture. We were playing more from samples and loops, that much is true, and now we are going to get Black Prince, but you get Mature Prince.'

Minneapolis singer Kathleen Johnson, who worked with him in the '90s, views his move into rap music as almost an existential set of questions. 'The tensions of him taking on hip hop – is this a standard business [move], working on trends? Is this a challenge? Or is this sampling that you can do easy?' And so, she says, he had a go.

Into the twenty-first century, with albums like *Musicology* and *3121*, Prince's own groove largely remained old school. 'He wasn't a big hip hop fan. He was a more traditional, old-school musician,' reckons Ian Boxill, his engineer around the *3121* period. 'He could appreciate a couple of artists here and there. Tupac might have been one of them. Definitely Neptunes.'

Without being entirely on board, he had come to love some of it in a club. 'They're sampling all his favourite records,' points out DJ Rashida, who started working with him in 2004. '[There were] even the ones that sampled him. There was a "Pop Life" remix [2Pac and Big Daddy Kane].' Rashida would drop A Tribe Called Quest, J Dilla, De La Soul into her set. 'I never got any complaints. "Vivrant Thing" [Q-Tip] was a song he really loved. I would play the instrumental, and he would play over the top of it.'

Another of Prince's resident DJs Lenka Paris (2000–16) says, 'He loved a lot of '90s hip hop. Just off the top of my head: Common, Lauryn Hill, Q-Tip, TLC, Mos Def, Eve, Arrested Development, and lots of R&B and neo-soul. Jill Scott, Erykah Badu, Musiq Soulchild, Alicia Keys, Beyoncé, D'Angelo, also some people from the UK – Ms Dynamite, FKA Twigs and Laura Mvula.'

The activism of hip hop would also be appealing to him. Jacqui Thompson remembers Prince joining her for a talk from Chuck D about the future of the music industry. 'He loved Chuck D because he was independent in his thoughts on the music industry. He really dug that.'

Prince would work with Chuck D as well as Eve on 1999's *Rave Un2 the Joy Fantastic*.

Craig Rice remembers the pair becoming 'really good friends'. Talib Kweli and James Poyser recall Common spending time with him and supporting him at his 2007 London O2 residency.

Soul singer Anthony Hamilton thinks he respected hip hop ultimately because it was 'a genre that started to outsell rock 'n' roll. That's part of his blackness. He knew what it was, and he knew what it represented.'

Jimmy Jam claims that hearing Freddie Stone's guitar from 'Thank You (Falettinme Be Mice Elf Agin)' turbocharged on Jam and Lewis's production of Janet Jackson's 1989 hit was transformational. 'The thing that changed his mind on sampling was "Rhythm Nation". If I remember correctly, he just ran out of the room. That really blew his mind about what he could do.'

Ruth Arzate, his manager in the mid-noughties, expands. 'He loved hip hop. He wasn't crazy about the sampling but he was behind the message and he loved the idea of beats, but he didn't like that the beats were sampled. On a certain level, he liked the idea of sampling. The black men taking over an industry – he was all for that. Hip hop and rap are now pop music. Black men built that, and he knew that.'

As for his own hip hop bona fides, The Roots' Ahmir 'Questlove' Thompson wrote a lengthy essay for *Wax Poetics* magazine about Prince being hip hop with a roll call of looking bling before bling was a thing, his own diss tracks, his own posse, style accessories and creating his own competition. Dave Hampton goes further than many are willing to. 'I like Prince's rapping. Because he produced a style that was in development. The rappers didn't have all the musical chops that he had. He listened to it and applied it in his own musical way. Was it as street as some of the others? No. It worked for the song [he was making].'

And in 2014, Prince and another rapper formed a mutual appreciation society when he (on keys, and his own freestyle verse) and 3rdEyeGirl joined forces at Paisley Park to perform 'What's My Name?' from 1998's *Crystal Ball* with Kendrick Lamar. Lamar had intended Prince to sing on 'Complexion' from Lamar's 2015 hit album *To Pimp a Butterfly*. The two men ran out of time. When they met in the studio, they had been in such deep conversation, the recording aspect was shelved. Once again, Prince – like Kendrick Lamar – didn't go for the obvious commercial opportunity. He was too busy having fun.

Follow the leader

If Prince was rare among stadium stars in the '90s for not having rap stars in his entourage, that doesn't mean he was any more relaxed with the musicians around him.

Prince didn't fine musicians as much as James Brown, who would charge his band for late attendance or lack of shine on their shoes.

Where Prince would demand payback was for what LeRoy Bennett would call 'a blatant mistake or they weren't paying attention to what he did. If you are a musician, you could never play as he did. He would fine them from time to time.'

Being any kind of guitarist, drummer, keyboard player in Prince's band was not for the faint-hearted. 'It was rough!' admits Matt Fink. 'There were times I would think, "He's as good a keyboard player as I am, technically better in some ways."'

Prince was in awe of certain bandmates – often those who could play, or blow, what he couldn't.

One of Prince's regular touring company escaped the wages dock through their time together. 'He never fined me,' Eric Leeds says before adding mischievously, 'not that I didn't give him good reason to from time to time.'

Eric Leeds, brother to his then tour manager Alan, remembers that 'his Number One lesson was to respect the music first. Learn the music and if the artist wants you to embellish it then you can, but that's the proper approach. It could be public humiliation.'

Prince would reserve fines for screw-ups onstage in front of a live audience. 'That's what rehearsals are for, but don't keep doing it. He didn't have a long attention span. If he told you how to do something, write it down because he was on to the next thing. You get used to it, but it's a tough environment.'

'I got fined once, maybe twice at most,' groans bassist Rhonda Smith. 'I don't remember the amount, but I do remember writing a cheque after the show. The bodyguard asked me to contribute to [Prince's charity] Love 4 One Another. It might have been a bum note. It might even have been not coming in on the one. I didn't like it but what am I going to do, quit?'

'If you love someone,' argued theological writer Tim Keller, referencing King James I's favoured poet George Herbert, 'you are "quick-eyed" with them. You watch intently for the merest facial expression or gesture, or tone of voice that hints at a need, so that you can meet it.'

Whether it was love, or fear, being in Prince's band demanded that speed with the eyes, and ears.

If you wanted to follow the leader, there was one main instruction.

'I think that's the James Brown school of music,' argues his keyboard player from 2003, Rose Ann Dimalanta. 'You are focused on the leader – what he's singing. That's also kind of jazz. You have to be listening constantly.'

If you could play, if you could keep up with him onstage in front of a stadium of fans or in the jazz club in the wee small hours, you had a ringside seat to the best of Prince.

You'd also have your work cut out for you.

'I have never been in the military,' admits bassist Rhonda Smith, but likens it to 'the difference between the army and the special forces. If you're not ready for it, you won't be around very long.'

His dancer Robia 'Pearl' Scott says, 'He wasn't a drill sergeant,' but as she admits, she wasn't a musician. 'He was really great to us. People say he was really difficult to work with but that's mainly the musicians. He was such a consummate professional that he could be playing with a ten-piece band and tell if someone hit a wrong note.'

His cousin Charles 'Chazz' Smith says that becoming a musical general was an inevitability.

'I don't think there was a person in the world who would have stopped him. The drive was there. He becomes a leader without being the leader. No one can even act like they said they want to be the leader because it's gonna be Prince. "I will do the punchlines for the horns on the keyboards." Prince said we need a keyboard player and I said, "Why don't we get Linda (Anderson, sister of André Cymone)?" And Prince said, "OK." Prince walked up behind her and put her fingers where they should be and she would do it. She just kept her eye on him and right away, that's leadership.'

But as Rhonda Smith says, recording became less acceptable 'because he works at a very fast pace and you're not allowed to record anything because it's been bootlegged so much.'

Only the boss could have these recorded, knowing that the tapes would not be sold on a market, but be kept safely in The Vault.

Prince was asked in 2014 by Arsenio Hall what job he would have done had he not gone into music. It's an interesting question when Prince put music above all other personal and professional priorities in his life.

The answer: teacher.

'He had a schoolteacher thing going on,' reflects Rose Ann Dimalanta. 'Not a nurturing one; he was more, "Come on now, you should know this."'

'There is a sense of where the teacher thing comes from,' she adds. She describes bandmates who 'come in shy and they come out and they are more confident and have more of an aura. I learned stuff from both those guys (Prince and Sheila) that I never learned from anyone else.'

Many musicians turned into pupils around him.

'Prince always knew the personalities of the people he worked with,' says Morris Hayes, who knew him better than most, and for whom Prince bought a house next door. 'Being a bandleader he was able to read where he needed to step in and where he needed to be the head coach. In order to work at this frequency, you have to be better than the average bear.'

Prince was all that … and jazz

To understand Prince as a bandleader, the greats of jazz provide a helpful route.

The obvious entry point is James Brown, whom he saw when he was ten and clearly studied, but The Godfather of Soul learned at the feet of the jazz greats.

Christian McBride, at time of writing in charge of the Newport Jazz Festival, had his career ambition come true when he got to play in JB's band at The Hollywood Bowl. 'One thing James Brown said at that show, I will never forget, was when the first song we played was the old blues song, "Kansas City". We did a jazz band version. Mr Brown got so reflective, he stopped singing. "Thank you for taking me back to my original bag. Jazz is where I wanted to go before I got sidetracked by the funk."

'When we had dinner together, our whole conversation was about jazz musicians. I feel he was both impressed and relieved he could have that conversation. Lee Morgan. John Coltrane. Art Blakey.'

'Mr Brown took a lot from the swing era. He was inspired by all the great bands like [those led by] Lionel Hampton, Duke

Ellington, Count Basie, Billy Epstein. All bands had dress codes. He brought a lot of those rules to a new era. The Stones understood how great his legacy was.'

That dress code, looking to the leader, fines for those who screwed up: there is a direct through line between the old jazz bandleaders, from Soul Brother No. 1 to Prince, bringing his own version of the stadium rock star into the twenty-first century. Hampton, Ellington, Basie, Miles Davis and more would bring in gifted musicians, sharpen their skills (often to the point of bluntness) and move them on to allow both for new recruits and for their sound to evolve.

Jack DeJohnette, who played drums for Miles in the '70s, Herbie Hancock in the '90s and Chick Corea in the '00s, hears a variety of influences. 'He's got a sax player playing avant-garde in solo sections and they're playing Duke Ellington as the blues and Prince plays the guitar with a jazz sound. It's fantastic. So all of those things are concentrated in a five-minute space. He was so eclectic. You can see Michael [Jackson], you can see James Brown, the way he plays the solo in "Kiss".'

Another jazz link was the improvisation with the band in rehearsal which could lead to pop radio hits.

'I thought there were parallels with Duke Ellington,' argues Rose Ann Dimalanta, who played keyboards for Prince in 2003, 'the way he would bring out our personalities in his band. "How can I put this character in the band? How can I work in what they do that's special to them?" In *Sign o' the Times*, everyone is a character in the band *and* in the movie.'

It also might explain Prince's love of another bandleader and jazz nut Joni Mitchell, who worked with Herbie Hancock, Wayne Shorter and Jaco Pastorius before recording and releasing an entire album with Charlie Mingus named after the bassist.

Matt Blistan explains another link to jazz. 'I think he had

in the back of his mind that his dad played jazz. Jazz is a more open type of music than rock is. That's the way he thought about his music. He was never one to play the same thing twice. Let's move on.'

'I think his dad was a really good jazz musician but his dad was more of an avant-garde musician – Sun Ra, Ornette Coleman. He was more that school of jazz,' suggests engineer Eddie Miller, who worked on *Lovesexy*. 'I think his dad had great ears and was a really good musician. Most jazz guys don't do a good job of playing funk.'

Prince, whose mother also sang jazz, embraced the genre's principle of experimentation. He formed bands, Madhouse (1987) and *Black Is the New Black* (2015/16), who would play an experimental, free-form, largely instrumental music.

Patrice Rushen is unusual in having worked at the top of both pop and jazz. 'Jazz includes being in the moment. Compositions include risk taking and a certain kind of improvisation. Pop music does not allow for that. Pop music is going to manipulate the audience to get across the reaction the artist wants to put across. Not to say those things are not beneficial in jazz. He took the best of both worlds and wasn't afraid to experiment in pushing and pulling from one side to the other. He really did appreciate jazz musicians. He dug it.'

The odyssey of jazz involved a certain free-form, which is why Prince loved the late-night aftershows in small venues.

Then again, so did the musicians, as he must have realised. Rose Ann Dimalanta got used to the 2 a.m. call to the lobby. 'People came. That's testament to the fandom that's behind him. After a rehearsed theatrical show in the arena, the aftershows were a moment for us to play the way musicians play. He would say, "Let's just jam on this one." That is the moment where, if you're a musician, after playing so much structure everybody could let out your ya-yas. I could play a cowbell!' Aftershows let the musicians breathe after rolling out the hits at the stadium or arena, Dimalanta notes. 'He was letting all of us do that, himself included.'

They could be a different musical version of themselves, just as he could.

The fact Prince could play a dingy club at 3 a.m. and rock a stadium at 8.30 p.m. shows him as a bandleader in a category of one – or two, if you include JB.

'We improvise or play in the moment; he had that all the time,' she adds. 'He wasn't necessarily playing swing but he had that stream of consciousness, although he also had that big stadium stage energy. Someone that can play the largesse of an arena and someone who can take you to the smallest club and still be funky. There are those elements of rock star versus serious jazz musician.'

The aftershows indicated Prince's relentless body clock.

'We walked outside after an aftershow in Europe once,' trombonist Greg Boyer recalls. 'The sun was up! I'm guessing around 7 a.m.'

The stamina-sapping schedule was not to everyone's tastes. Girlfriends, management, his lighting director LeRoy Bennett and others would excuse themselves from the early morning musical workouts.

Bandmates did not have that option.

For all that Miles Davis and other jazz bandleaders would embrace the mistake – 'If you play a bad note, do it again to make it seem like that's what you wanted to do,' Rhonda Smith, bassist, says, quoting the Miles ethos – her boss wouldn't always. 'I don't think Prince was like that. Prince wanted to control music and he wanted to control the notes around him. You couldn't go into his environment and learn halfway. He would chastise you and embarrass you and laugh you out of the room. He would really make you pay for it.'

To play's the thing

By the end of his touring life, as per the opening lines of 'Let's Go Crazy', he was often on his own. Just after he'd played two evening shows on 25 March 2016, Prince showed up at the Everleigh nightclub, Toronto at 12.30 a.m. in a velour robe. At 2 a.m., he thanked the crowd for coming and told them, 'If you all stick around, I'll come back and dance with all of you.' By 3.20 a.m., the club was about to close. At 4.15 a.m., Prince decided to play a forty-five-minute eight-song set to the two dozen hardy souls remaining. 'This one's for the lovers,' he announced, intro-ing one song. After two more Piano and a Microphone dates, and one more at Paisley Park, he would not play live again.

The fact that at fifty-seven he was willing to play to fewer than twenty-five people until five in the morning in a small Toronto nightclub illustrates Prince's passion for playing live. Prince *needed* to play live even more than people had a need to see him live, as much as that statement may confound his fans.

Before the first week of his Hawaiian honeymoon with Mayte in 1996 was through, he booked a gig in Honolulu. He would do gigs, sometimes twice in a day, on Christmas Eve, Boxing Day, New Year's Eve. He built a sound stage at Paisley Park so he could emerge from living quarters and play a gig at home. He followed live shows by relaxing… with aftershows which could last hours. He would find somewhere for a gig after the gig in the wee small hours, then stay up to watch the live performance with his band to see what cues were missed and, if necessary, fine them.

In 1979, he was in the early stages of a romance with early

girlfriend Mi-Long Stone Poole, seen in some quarters as the inspiration for 'Little Red Corvette'. She was at his house in France Avenue and he wanted to impress her. 'He was a challenge for me. I like challenges. We started to get together. One time we are at his house, he takes me by the hand and walks me down to the basement and he plays this two-hour concert. I was dancing. It was just him and me.'

He would occasionally play to a member of staff at Paisley, with a show or soundcheck or rehearsal which would stretch to as long as three hours. Producer Dylan Dresdow was just one recipient.

Sometimes, he would perform a shorter show to an audience of one without instruments, as his *Under the Cherry Moon* co-star Emmanuelle Sallet remembers. 'One day we were hanging out at his house and he had received a tape of the finished version of "Kiss". We went upstairs to his bedroom to listen to it on his equipment. As I sat on the edge of the bed, he lip-synced and danced the whole song just for me while being a bit silly … He had a great sense of humour about himself.'

His passion for playing live made him a performer who could work an after-hours jazz club or Madison Square Garden. His former valet and driver Robbie Paster explains: 'Put a guitar in his hand, and he's the guy. He can work any room.'

Saxophonist Adrian Crutchfield explains how his passion stopped him going through the motions as a live act. 'When he's onstage, he's having so much fun. You can't fool an audience. If you're not enjoying yourself onstage, they're not going to enjoy it either.' When asked if he ever got bored, Crutchfield added: 'Never. If he got bored, he'd either move on to something else or he'd actually find something else to do.'

Even without a crowd, he was always in pro mode. 'He pulled me to the side,' reveals Morris Hayes,' and said, "I don't care if it's ten people, you have got to do the best ever show. It doesn't bother me that there's ten people."

'Even when I jam with Prince, when I'm playing on drums and he's playing bass and nobody else is there, Prince would play for three hours. If I just get bored and I drop the tempo, he will be like, "Morris, why are you doing that?" That would just irritate the hell out of him. "Respect the music, respect the instrument."'

That respect extended to gruelling rehearsal periods with the setlist, which could be perceived as being tough on musicians. It also did them a favour. It stopped them – and his audience, many of them familiar with setlists dating back decades – getting complacent.

'We rehearsed an incredible amount for the tour we did,' recalls Rose Ann Dimalanta, who played keyboard for him in 2003, and would ask:

'We're good to go?'

'Not yet, not yet.'

'The challenge was, now you have got a seriously rehearsed show. We have cues. You [have to] keep a show that you have rehearsed so much feeling fresh every time you come to play it. That's where you have to pool and cull not just from your technical and musical ability, but still feel little surprises in the band because those little surprises make the audience feel like it's the first time they have seen the show.'

Aftershows also gave Prince the opportunity to show musicians who was boss – not only the band but bona fide stadium fillers too. 'A lot of those aftershows,' laughs Robbie Paster, 'a lot of people would get on the stage with him. He would beat these guys into submission. He would get Ron Wood and play circles around the guy. He did the same with Sting. That was his entertainment.' That was a 1986 aftershow in London. An LA gig in February the previous year saw him play 'Baby

I'm A Star' joined onstage by Bruce Springsteen and Madonna. It was a version onlookers quip could have been renamed 'Baby I'm *The* Star'. His guests were sometimes unprepared. He rarely was, especially if he knew they were due.

His album releases would represent the forward momentum he specialised in, no remixes or greatest hits short of the occasional sample of old tracks, but live, he could do what he fancied – deep cuts, anthems, cover versions, new material or just jam.

Prince liked to point out from the stage that 'I got more hits than Madonna's got kids', but he adapted to embrace his back catalogue and worked out what the space, be that a stadium or sweaty club, required. He once advised Outkast before a headlining slot at Coachella to 'play the hits' but he didn't always take his own advice.

That desire was honed from the greats including James Brown, the self-styled 'Hardest Working Man in Showbusiness', a title coined before Prince arguably usurped it. 'Mr Brown would rehearse after the show,' reflects Christian McBride, who played with him. 'A lot of fast and intense music. I can imagine you're so physically spent and James Brown decides he wants to stay for three hours and rehearse and you go on to the bus for the next concert. That could be considered cruel.'

Prince didn't rehearse afterwards but he did make them sit through videos.

Every day was a school day for him and his band.

'He studied the greats,' says Shelby Johnson, a singer for him from 2006 to 2014. 'You could see James Brown dance moves, you could hear the Smokey Robinson falsetto; that's where he wanted to be. The bar was Earth, Wind and Fire. You couldn't phone it in. That helped him cultivate his artistry to that level. That's why he could go out onstage and play for three hours.'

It was said for many years that the aftershow was where you

saw the real Prince. It might be more accurate to say that the soundcheck saw him at his best. 'The soundchecks were the most incredible thing on the planet,' argues his *Sign*-era make-up artist Terra Hinrichs, who was around for the gigs and aftershows too. 'When he would jam with his band, it was the most incredible thing I have ever heard. And it was so tight.'

Without a curfew time, or an audience demanding the hits, with his choice of musicians around him, it was where he honed his setlist and his band, and of course workshopped songs.

Sometimes these songs would be living in his head.

'The thing I used to marvel at particularly on *Purple Rain* and *1999*,' recalls Bill Reeves, the production coordinator and then manager on the tours from *Controversy* to *Purple Rain*, and then *Lovesexy*, 'was that he would come in for a soundcheck and have a song pretty much completely done in his head.' This could be based on what was in his head, or on what the band in question (the Time, the Revolution) had been playing in rehearsals. 'He would teach it to the band, they would work on it, and he would make little tweaks to the performance, maybe change the drums or a different bassline. He would come in with the song pretty much fully formed. It was a pretty much fully developed production when he introduced it at soundcheck.'

'He just had this passion when performing and playing music,' adds Hinrichs. 'It was sweet, it was so tight and it just sounded like they were having fun. He gave them that freedom.'

Soundcheck was the only place some huge songs were ever allowed to escape his Vault. One ex-publicist heard the comment, 'There's a Prince hit you will never hear.'

'He would play his private Vault stuff, then he would jam,' says Hinrichs.

Sometimes his band would help him.

'That (*1999*) tour eventually became tunes from *Purple Rain*,' explains Reeves. 'He would collaborate when he has a thought of a song and BrownMark might contribute a bassline or Lisa might contribute a keyboard part but I don't know if he was writing with a band. It was mainly coming out of his brain into the world.'

Even Prince needed some help with *Purple Rain*.

It was a rehearsal jam where Matt Fink's playing the high part on his keyboard led to Prince singing along.

Pop's ultimate completer-finisher

David Allen, the American productivity consultant and author of *Getting Things Done*, once wrote: 'Much of the stress that people feel doesn't come from having too much to do. It comes from not finishing what they've started.'

Prince did not tend to experience stress this way. There were frequent displays of frustration especially with colleagues, but when he walked into the studio with a song, his engineers say it was rare he left the studio without finishing it. It's easier when you can play all the instruments.

There are musicians (Michael Jackson, Beyoncé, Bruno Mars, Steely Dan's Walter Becker and Donald Fagen) known for sweating over every detail.

Michael Jackson is even said to have pushed to re-record a vocal which displeased him after the recording had been a big hit.

Not pop's ultimate completer-finisher.

Chuck Zwicky, an engineer in the early days of Paisley Park, said: 'Sometimes, he'd finish a song and I'd think, "Is it really done?" And if I didn't think it was done, I'd just leave it there.' Prince would sign off on it and put it out.

'That takes strength and a lot of courage.'

'What he was,' says Susan Rogers, 'was rarer than a perfectionist, he was a virtuoso performer. What sounds like perfectionism, we worked way too fast to consider ourselves perfectionists.'

It was a lesson he learned early in his career. 'The recording's becoming a little easier these days,' he told the *NME*'s Chris Salewicz in 1981 while promoting *Dirty Mind*. 'I used to be a perfectionist – too much of one. Those ragged edges tend to be a bit truer.'

Todd Herreman, who worked with Rogers on *Sign*, calls him 'astoundingly quick. That was just the way he worked.'

Chris James, Grammy-nominated for his engineering work on Prince's final released album, *HITnRUN Phase Two*, argues that 'he wanted to get an idea out. A lot of the records ended up sounding like demos because they were demos.'

Another engineer Eddie Miller has a vivid memory of how 'Pink Cashmere', which ended up on his 1993 Hits compilation, came to be.

'We were working on something else in (Paisley's) Studio B. It was probably midnight. I'd just got home and started to get some sleep and it was three in the morning. The beeper's going off. Prince wants you to get back to the studio. I think he was driving around town trying to work that song out.'

Another song Prince did in one session was also to order, except this time to complete a movie soundtrack.

Monique Mannen, the dancer from the 'Kiss' video, had a small role in *Graffiti Bridge*, and remembers: 'Long days; 6 a.m. call time. Then he would jam with the band.

'Next morning he would be there in the morning with a new song.'

Tom Garneau, another engineer at the time, clarifies the details of the song Monique Mannen remembers Prince writing overnight. 'Twenty to twenty-four hours was common. Though you could almost always sneak in a nap while he was doing vocals. Once set up for that, we knew we had a couple of hours' break. "Thieves in the Temple" was one thirty-hour session. Mike Koppelman did the first fifteen hours, I did the second. He needed just one more song for the movie. It was two-thirds done when I took over. He had me lift a harmonica part off a Chambers Brothers song with the Publison [keyboard sampler] for the solo. We did a few other parts and then we mixed.'

'He started it on the Friday night and by the Sunday they were shooting the video,' laughs Koppelman. 'He just loved to do things like that. He wanted to get one great thing on the record.'

Prince being his own producer lit a flame in director Jeymes Samuel. '*The Harder They Fall*: I wrote the film, I directed it, I wrote the film soundtrack, I produced it, I composed the score and wrote every song on the soundtrack. The reason I did that was because I grew up with *"Produced, Arranged, Composed and Performed by Prince"*.

'Where Prince excelled was being fearless and being himself, and it taught us all to be fearless. He could never have someone else produce a song he had written. With Prince, you just saw and smelled freedom. It's a big inspiration for me and a driver for what I do today.' Freedom, or at least the freedom to be his own boss, was everything to him.

Mentor and tormentor

The question of who's in charge was never a question when it was one of his projects.

From his managers being on notice unless they landed him a movie deal, to persuading his record company to put out an album every year as well as give him his own label (Paisley Park Records), and his most successful band suddenly becoming his most successful ex-band, the guy who stood five foot two inches didn't need his heels to give him stature.

Prince was actually quite clear on the parameters of leadership with those around him.

He would like to give positions of leadership on the understanding that he would be overseeing them.

He knew Sheila had assembled a crack unit of musicians to play for Lionel Richie so he took most of them lock, stock and barrel for the *Sign* tour. She had already done the corralling.

He hired Morris Day to replace his cousin Chazz Smith as drummer in the Time then moved him up front and left Morris with the decision on whether to fire Jimmy Jam and Terry Lewis when they missed a gig.

'We didn't do anything without full approval of him and the management anyway,' Vanity 6's Brenda Bennett says.

'To some people, he seemed dictatorial but he was also very open to other people's ideas. He would take them, shift them around, start going through them and then work through areas where he said, "I like that, I like this." He wouldn't say what he was looking for but he would tell you if he didn't like it.'

Nandy McClean was one of his dancers and ended up going from choreography to shooting videos for him. She is now directing and producing films.

'He would let you loose on something then go and edit.'

She recalls his advice for playing an area. 'We choreographed everyone facing this way. "You've got to give energy to all four corners. Come up with moments that you can face every direction."'

Sam Jennings started up his website and was given a camera and asked to be his in-house photographer. 'He could be professional and demanding but it never came off as impolite. It just came off as very direct which I can handle; I'm from Chicago.'

Mari Maupin was renamed The Golden Hippie and joined Prince and 3rdEyeGirl at Paisley, after she messaged the band on Twitter (as was). At first, he let her play drums. ('He never asked me to do it again.') Before long, she was invited to the *HITnRUN Phase Two* European tour. She was sitting backstage … until she wasn't.

'I had no idea I was going to perform out front in that tour. He very much liked to give chances to people to pull you out of your skin and just thrive.'

Soon she was singing 'U Got the Look' onstage, and getting used to Prince asking her to sing in a new key.

'He loved to play with my voice in that way. Every song I didn't find comfortable singing, he gave me his cane and said, "Just dance."'

DJ Rashida regards his tutelage as 'more than mentoring. It's giving you wings.' Scottie Baldwin, who worked with him for more than two decades, says that proactivity was key. 'Prince taught me how to be a fireman. How to light my own fires and put them out. Try not to come up with a problem until it's solved.'

Rhonda Smith adds: 'If you can work for him, you can work for anybody. It's the ultimate endurance test. It was actually very helpful.'

Other artists knew this too and hired ex-employees accordingly. Scottie Baldwin would go on to work with Madonna and Lady Gaga, Brad Marsh with Phil Collins and Genesis, LeRoy Bennett with Sir Paul McCartney, Lady Gaga and Bruno Mars. Sheila E.'s roll call of work outside of Prince, from Marvin Gaye to Beyoncé, Billy Cobham to Ringo Starr, Hans Zimmer to the Academy Awards is prodigious. Wendy Melvoin and Lisa Coleman worked on film and TV music, winning an Emmy and working on records by Neil Finn and

Grace Jones. Once he fired Jimmy Jam and Terry Lewis from the Time, they would go on to become one of the world's most successful pop production partnerships, behind more than 100 albums from gold to diamond. Prince had his own mentors – Sly Stone's bassist Larry Graham, guitarist Sonny Thompson, and his father. He appreciated musical leaders, telling Tavis Smiley in 2009 about Miles Davis: 'He was a wonderful mentor and really, really funny. He could critique something you'd done out of humour rather than being a punk. People [whom] he cared about he tried to help.'

'I'm supposed to be a mysterious person but I'm not mysterious'

Prince left the earth with unanswered questions about him – this was not accidental.

'I'm supposed to be a mysterious person but I'm not mysterious,' Prince told the *LA Times*' Dennis Hunt in 1980 when promoting *Dirty Mind*.

Well, you could have fooled everyone else.

Although Revolution bassist Mark Brown complained in his autobiography that Prince had the lights not shine on him throughout concerts, that didn't mean the spotlight would always shine on the boss.

'The only notes he would give me,' says his trusted lighting director and friend LeRoy Bennett, 'was what he was going to do during the show. Where he stood to be lit, where he wanted to be lit, where he wanted not to be lit. If he was not playing, there would be no spotlight on him. He felt the audience needed a break from him so that when he came back, there was excitement. He understood what it was like to be a rock star more than anybody else I have ever known.

'Human beings always want what they can't have. He under-stood to make yourself bigger than life, the only way you can do that is not to reveal too much of yourself. You have to let people know who you are by imagining.'

That sense of mystery extended to press interviews which puts his 1980 remark in context.

'In interviews, he would never answer a question with a straight answer,' argues Robia 'Pearl' Scott. 'He would always be poetic or use metaphors. He understood the value of mystery.'

She adds that 'Lori ("Diamond") and I were the spokespeople for the whole album (*Diamonds and Pearls*). We did all the interviews.'

As befits someone that controlling, whom he was dating would be kept as much of a mystery from his colleagues and the press as he could, as his dancer Nandy McClean recalls.

'We had our suspicions of whom he would be entertaining, but it was never like a group of people. It was more just a girl would walk in and they kinda hang out with us a little but he never held their hand, cuddled them or kissed them or anything.' McClean doesn't remember 'any romantic displays of affection in front of us. He compartmentalised. The mystery was more for business.'

If Prince wanted to be elusive to build the audience's anticipation of him, he wanted his girlfriends to fly under the radar. The supportive might say this was because of press interest. The cynical might say this was because of other girlfriends.

As one-time friend Alexander O' Neal notes, Prince's character 'was controlling and keeping everything secret. There's a difference between secrecy and privacy.'

Take the *Under the Cherry Moon* premiere. Devin DeVasquez, Prince's on-off girlfriend, was on Prince's jet. Sheila E., Prince's on-off girlfriend, was there too. Kristin Scott Thomas, Prince's on-screen romantic interest, also attended.

Lisa Janzen from his management firm chuckles at a memory ahead of the *Purple Rain* tour in LA. 'I was at The Forum one night and I remember Apollonia, Vanity, Sheila, Susannah and Jill Jones, all five were in the room, and Prince walked in and I thought, "This could go bad really fast."'

Another way he stayed mysterious was by not clearing things up. Dylan and Beatles fans love to speculate on the inspiration behind their idols' favourite songs, and Prince wasn't in a hurry to be specific about his.

'He liked it that way,' says Mi-Ling Stone Poole who only joined the dots about her dating period with Prince when she heard his breakthrough hit. 'Every girl thought she was the "Little Red Corvette".'

Prince had to get his music out and was never more prolific than he was during the *Sign* era. An album every twelve months if not sooner, leaving aside those not under his own name, was non-negotiable.

If it all got too much, it wouldn't hurt the elusive reputation to try another magic trick. Disappearing.

Cat Glover's account to *GQ* of her being formally hired at LA club Vertigo was not unusual. 'Prince saw me and he tapped me on the shoulder, and he says, "Hi ... I would like for you to be in my band." And I kind of blushed, and before I could pull my head up he disappeared. You know, he disappears really quickly. That happened to us a lot. The next week, he came back and asked me again, and this time I said, "Wait a minute – don't leave before I answer you." And I told him: "Yes." And then he walked away. That's how he is. He was always real slick with the mystery.'

At work, he enjoyed the secluded nature of Studio 3 which didn't back onto another studio like 1 and 2. Illustrious bassist for Eric Clapton and Stevie Wonder, Nathan East, recorded at

Sunset Sound in the '80s but never met Prince, describing him as 'very elusive'.

A-list megastars often hang out with other megastars, as it's an opportunity to relax. For these parties, some of which he threw, there was a calculation, according to Sam Jennings. 'The parties were amazing, unbelievable. For Oscars and other awards shows. At those parties, he wouldn't be very accessible. He wouldn't be mingling and he would be around a little bit but he was still this mysterious person. It created that allure and he had that other-worldly energy about him. Even when he was [just] in the room he stood out.'

And then just as quickly, as was his way, he was gone. That mystery extended to the way he communicated. But small talk? Not at work, and Prince was more often than not at work.

'When you talked to him on the phone about some technical detail, there wasn't any slang or innuendo,' recalls Brent Fischer, who with father Clare added strings to his records. 'It was very business-like.'

This didn't change too much throughout his career.

No one thought Prince was dull but there were certain topics he would hit hard – the music industry, for one, says engineer Chris James. 'Artists not owning their masters. He would go back to this topic on a regular basis.'

Singer Ashley Tamar remembers him as a man who 'asked you questions'.

He never missed a moment to educate artists. You were coming to his house to enjoy yourself and if you don't have conversations about life, what's the point in inviting someone over?'

Regular house guests would discuss race relations, politics, religion, music too.

From Nobel Prize for Literature winner Bob Dylan's

'prophesize' to The Spice Girls' 'zig-a-zig-ah', pop stars often have their own language.

Prince was no different.

When it came to talking to work colleagues, he could use jargon. It was only jargon he himself understood – others would have to figure him out. Alan Leeds talks of him discussing music somewhat poetically. 'Make the reverb on the strings more blue.'

For sound, Prince had another subset of his own language. If it was too muddy, he'd tell soundman Scottie Baldwin it was 'papery' or 'boxy'. When he was unimpressed, dancer Nandy McClean, whom Prince mentored and is now a film director, would hear the word 'pedestrian'. 'I use it a lot now.'

Chuck Zwicky has a memory of Prince instructing his engineer, as he moved the faders down on the drums: 'The bass has to make love to the drums and the drums have to make love to the bass.' Sam Jennings, who did more than most to help Prince understand the internet in the noughties by running the site where Prince first worked out how to sell his music, often heard the command 'Make it blue'. He would also ask him to 'Make It Like Jazz'.

Of course, his uses of 2 & 4 & U and the symbol 'eye' in songs weren't a passing phase. They would appear throughout his written correspondence on email and letters as well as in his songs, years before they became the accepted norms in text messages. He could use caps lock too.

Prince often thought and talked like a jazz musician. The late, great Wayne Shorter had a similarly elliptical way of referring to music.

Shorter often played with Joni Mitchell and just before he went onstage, the saxophonist would say the same thing to bandmates – 'See you at the movies.'

Drummer Brian Blade, who also played with Joni for many years, got to know what that meant. 'He always wanted to be making something; there's that pictorial thinker. He didn't say, "See you in chapter four of the book."'

For Joni, self-styled lonely artist who sang that she lived in a box of paints, musical expression would be right in front of her eyes.

'Great storytelling like great art can come in many forms,' says Blade. 'She embraced the dance of it, the musicality of it, the choreography of it, the painting of it.'

Prince tapped into that too. After Doug Henders, credited as a camera operator on the Purple Rain tour, had painted the mural for the 'When Doves Cry' video, Prince wrote him a note with instructions for the sleeve he wanted him to paint featuring 'a juggling clown', 'doves', 'an obese man hugging a tiger' and 'olive-skinned people wearing capes of purple'. Henders, referring to 'the *Sgt. Pepper's Lonely Hearts Club Band* fantasy of *Around the World in a Day*', presented the two by four feet canvas he had painted in hotel rooms over a six-week period.

'In the handwritten notes there was a reference to the clouds in blue sky. As the composition began to mirror itself in many places and faces, the clouds lent themselves to the characters' costumes. As I posed for this character I considered it my secret signature to the painting. When I saw Prince wearing an actual Cloud suit, I felt my creative spirit was embodied in the music.'

It also begat the video for 'Raspberry Beret', as Prince had a cloud suit and matching heels made in an attempt to recreate the album sleeve.

Joni used her paintings to inspire her lyrics and song titles. Prince went even further. For *Sign*, he didn't make it blue, but peach and black.

Boys Keep Swinging in Minneapolis

Joni Mitchell once said what she hated about critics is that 'they keep you in your decade'. That statement was possibly born from the commercial and critical hangover she suffered after a triumphant '70s. Joni was not the only artist perceived to have toiled throughout the 1980s. So did David Robert Jones.

Bowie in the '70s was weird and wonderful like no other solo artist before or since. It was the decade of skipping around gender and genre when Major Tom settled on 'Life On Mars', where Ziggy Stardust found his Spiders from the same planet, before Bowie promptly retired Ziggy and moved on to the angular rock of *Aladdin Sane*, the funky soul of *Young Americans*, and ice-cold heft of *Station to Station* within ten months of each other before finishing off the decade with the help of Brian Eno and Tony Visconti on his Berlin trilogy of *Low*, *Heroes* and *Lodger*. (These are the edited highlights.) Bowie produced a different musical and visual statement every year, many of which resonate for much younger artists half a century later.

The androgyny, image change with every album, a quality of music which defied categorisation, a daring and new visual aesthetic every year, moving on when lesser artists would stay in a sweet spot – Bowie's '70s and Prince's '80s had plenty in common (as perhaps did Bowie's '80s and Prince's overblown '90s).

Bowie in the '80s continued to experiment but those risks were often more miss than hit. The 1983 *Let's Dance* album was received warmly commercially but a positive critical evaluation took longer. The pink-haired role in *Labyrinth*, his hard rock band Tin Machine and two albums *Never Let Me Down* and *Tonight* rarely kick off most Bowie profiles.

Then there was the Glass Spider tour. Criss-crossing

arenas in the States and Europe, with dancers, two guitarists (Carlos Alomar and Peter Frampton) and spoken word introductions, it has subsequently been seen as epitomising the worst excesses of the '80s as Bowie wrestled between following an artistic path and packing out stadia with his hits.

Soon after, Bowie would admit to *Q* magazine: 'I overstretched.'

Cat Glover, who had been given a choice over one weekend between joining the Glass Spider circus or Prince's, was curious enough to check out Glass Spider on nights off with Susan Hale, Steve Fargnoli's then assistant.

'We attended many of the Glass Spider shows that year in Europe,' Hale recalls. 'Bowie came after us at almost every venue that summer so during load in and load out, our paths crossed a lot. I had a friend at Bowie's label and we swapped concert tickets all summer. I think I went six or seven times.'

Hale admits to a crush on Bowie which ended abruptly. 'My adulation for him went kaboom the moment I met him in Milan during *Sign*. One overlap time, we were all at a club and Bowie sent his people over to ask Sheila E. to come and talk to him and Sheila grabbed my arm to go greet him because she didn't want to go alone. So we end up in the back of his limo and he only spoke to Sheila pretty much with his back to me the whole time. My light for him went out right then and there.' (Lisa Janzen also remembers attending a *Saturday Night Live* recording with Sheila as the musical guest and realised she was sitting next to Bowie.)

Cat Glover recalls smuggling Bowie into an aftershow in Italy as Glass Spider was there at the same time as Prince.

So when Bowie's Glass Spider tour rolled into Minneapolis on 1 & 2 October 1987, it wasn't a total surprise that Prince would want to check out the show.

Black Entertainment Television's Video Soul presenter

Donnie Simpson and his longtime producer Jeff Newman were scheduled to be in Minneapolis to interview the Time.

David, a longtime advocate for more black artists on MTV, had, says Newman, 'made it a point to American EMI folks that he wanted to appear at BET.'

After broadcast, he told Simpson:

'"You should come to the show."

So we made arrangements.'

These arrangements led to a seat '10-12 rows from the front' by the lighting board, where Simpson and Newman bumped into a lady. Simpson apologised: 'Excuse me, ma'am.'

This was a man.

'"I'm sorry, Prince."

'"I'm having a party tonight for David. You should come."'

The party was at Paisley Park, which had just opened, and Prince was keen to show it off.

'I assume everybody is a fan of David's and I would assume he was,' guesses his guitarist Alomar, who attended with a handful of the Glass Spider crew. Throwing a party in his honour would suggest this was a reasonable assumption. Alomar's memory of the party, at Prince's Eden Prairie warehouse, was that 'it looked like a prison, and there was a smorgasbord buffet.' Newman adds 'there was a bar but no one was drinking alcohol. Some food, veggies, everyone there was part of Prince's inner circle. There were no gawkers. He knew everyone else there. We saw Prince unguarded having a good time. He was giving the guided tour so he was more outgoing then.'

Not, of course, that Bowie's entourage and Prince bonded on the night. Prince and Bowie quickly disappeared for a one on one. 'The band takes a seat and do whatever it takes. If the stars want to talk, we let them talk,' notes Alomar.

One of Bowie's dancers, Viktor Manoel, who turned down

Madonna and Michael Jackson's *Bad* tour for Glass Spider, didn't want to go.

'David said, "You've got to go, he's seen the tour. He talks about you." I remember coming to the party and walking down a hall and feeling someone stare at me and it was Prince. It was my birthday, I was tired, I was going through stuff with my father, and I remember it felt like I had an apple in my mouth the way he was looking at me.

"Hi, nice to meet you, my name is Viktor Manoel."

"I know who you are. I've been watching you on tour."'

The two men had a brief chat, Prince dressed in a suit made out of hearts, with, recalls Newman, 'a heart-shaped mirror strapped to his forearm' (as he'd worn on the *Sign* movie.) Manoel told him that 'Just As Long As We're Together', from debut album *For You*, was his background for his start in street dance.

Then the evening took a competitive turn.

'As I was walking out, sure enough, the dance boys in the battle approached me and I was avoiding them. Cat, all these people, "C'mon, c'mon." I knew that's what they wanted. I remember a tall guy doing a fan kick over his face, a spin, dropping to side splits which nobody still does, and I crawled between his legs and pushed him out of my way.'

A dance battle may have been in Prince's mind, but not Manoel's. 'I went and sat in the van because I wanted to go home.'

Newman and Simpson brought an unlikely party companion, their friend Sugar Ray Leonard who was also in town, and enthusiastically responded to the invitation. They headed to Paisley 'midnight, 1 a.m.,' according to Newman, bumped into Bowie who was leaving, and had a ten-minute chat.

Newman points out that Bowie 'would have ventured out an

hour from where he was staying to [Chanhassen] so that shows you what he thought of him [Prince].' There is no record of the two meeting outside this evening. Simpson, Newman and the boxing champ stayed 'until at least four or five in the morning. There's maybe 15–20 people.'

They remember the DJ playlist featuring The Staple Sisters' 'I'll Take You There', plenty of Sly and the Family Stone and snippets of *The Black Album*, which, says Newman, 'wasn't out yet. Deep cuts from Prince's other stuff. It could have been Madhouse.'

The producer asked about the predominantly 'instrumental and funky' playlist and was told by one of Prince's team: 'He could have recorded this ten years ago or he could have made it this morning and you will never hear it again.' The Video Soul crew got the guided tour, with the sound stages, and an impromptu basketball game in the loading bay. There had been an earlier screening of what they think was the Sign movie before they arrived. Of the party Simpson reflects 'even for musicians, it was a cool hang.'

For Glover, the party had cosmic significance. 'Prince asked me to be in his band on a Friday and I got offered the Glass Spider on the Saturday. The same weekend. So I decided to go with Prince which was hard as I loved Bowie. But because they were a dancer down I got Constance Marie who played George Lopez's wife on the Lopez show to take my place. Prince had a party at Paisley, and Bowie was there and Constance was there too. There was Prince and Bowie. Prince was saying, "That's my girl," about me and Bowie said, "No, she was supposed to be with me on my tour first," and it kinda went like that. It was fun but I was there looking at these two who I loved musically for years and they are talking about me – a dancer from Chicago. Crazy.'

Prince and Bowie had other similarities beyond their admiration for Cat. The dynamic use of visuals and versatility in music. They broke out of the straitjacketed expectations audiences might have of white rock stars and black soul musicians. Bowie went on *Soul Train*. Prince headlined rock festivals and appeared on the cover of *Kerrang!* magazine. Both would call other musicians late at night, for example Bowie got in touch with Nina Simone and Damon Albarn, Prince with George Michael and Anita Baker. Both men had that other-worldly quality which means their names are dropped into chat shows, memoirs and documentaries to add allure, glamour and musical heft to the storyteller for having entered their orbit.

As befits men who crossed over to cinematic success, they liked to keep the cameras rolling.

Where Prince would film his band for musical precision, Bowie would film his off-duty to shape their onstage characters, says Manoel. 'He would video me doing interesting things, like eating, talking and stretching. He would video everything and then come back and say, "Could you put this on that song?" So everybody's character was already set. Mine was in progress all the time. To me he was like a big brother. At the end of the tour, everybody wanted his autograph and I didn't want one.' Bowie still scribbled something. *'To whatsisname, from an old timer to a new timer, I hope you get everything you want.'*

Manoel admits the way they used their dancers 'as storytelling', like Prince did with Cat in the *Sign* movie, was similar. 'It was basically a theatre piece – reality versus rock 'n' roll. They had that in common.'

For all his *Man Who Fell to Earth* stage persona, Bowie was one of the guys offstage, suggests the dancer. 'Even with Madonna and Michael Jackson it's the same way. These people wanted to be super-mega. David was never like that.

'He always asked, "What do you think? What do you think?" He loved collaborating. I can't say that about Prince.' (Many Prince interviewees, particularly his female colleagues, disagree, maintaining that Prince would seek their opinion, particularly as he got older.)

Prince and Bowie both had their own signature looks as well as alter egos. Just as Ziggy Stardust, Major Tom, the Thin White Duke and the Blind Prophet were all one bloke from south London, so Joey Coco, Alexander Nevermind and Camille emerged from a shy boy from Minneapolis.

'All of these characters are so transformative they kind of reinvent themselves,' argues Alomar. 'There's a natural quality to how they do it.'

Both men had strong visual imaginations, from their own fashion templates to pop videos and stage presentation. 'He visualises everything like David,' adds Alomar.

Producer Dan the Automator, who has worked with Depeche Mode, RZA and the Black Keys, collaborated with Damon Albarn and his own cartoon alter egos on the first Gorillaz album. He draws a distinction between Prince's and Bowie's personality shifts. 'David Bowie is inhabiting a new character altogether. Prince is adding new personalities to his existing character, a bit like a sports personality giving himself a new name – he's still that guy.' Even as Tracy in *Under the Cherry Moon* or The Kid in his two other movies, or his writing aliases like Joey Coco or Alexander Nevermind, the producer feels 'it's Prince with a Hollywood mask. Even in the *Purple Rain* movie, it's still Prince.'

Bowie could disappear into the Thin White Duke or Aladdin Sane but disappearing at a party, that was trickier.

What most present at the Minneapolis party agree on is that Prince and Bowie shared private conversations about the challenges of their own personae. Walking into a room and instantly being the most stared-at person would be tricky for anyone, let alone the CEO and frontperson of a very public business with your name on it.

'David Bowie is not a regular guy,' argues Carlos Alomar. 'He's constantly putting out a probe to feel you out. Don't you think when you go out as Prince or Michael Jackson or David Bowie, everybody wants to talk to you?' They both had to learn the skill of elusiveness. It's better to take the attention off yourself. It's not comfortable.'

Like Prince, Bowie was learning about AIDS and discussed the subject with Manoel.

'David was not competitive,' recalls Manoel. 'He would introduce me to rock stars in full make-up to see what their expression was. He thought it was humorous. I used to hate him for that.'

Glass Spider was proof of Bowie's grand ambition, adds Manoel. 'His long dream was to do a Broadway play and he constructed his Glass Spider tour in regards to that. Even in auditions, we had to tell a joke and I didn't because I said I didn't find life funny, and he found that very cool.'

Bowie was dancing between the demands of commerce and art, as Prince was. 'Little Red Corvette' was included on the *Sign* movie – but no other hits outside that album were. The challenge between rolling out the hits and making an artistic statement with their live shows – both were in that place in 1987.

'The whole construction of the show changed to the Best of Bowie when we got to Vancouver, which he didn't want to do,' explains Manoel. 'He had a meeting not with all the dancers but with me. My song was cut. That's what he said to me – not to take business or art personally. Know when to walk in, know when to walk out. He also told me, "Never become a cartoon of yourself. Never give people what they want. Unless it's business. Because people are always finicky about what they want from you.'"

Carlos Alomar feels Prince's conversation with Bowie involved advice on straddling the hits and finding a new path to filling out sports arenas and stadia. 'Hell, yeah! We had gone into a place where we had the returns from promoters, everything is 60,000–80,000, the numbers became huge. How do you manage that? Every artist wants to talk to an artist who's already done it. You don't get a better mentor than David Bowie. A musician works in collaboration, knowing they can only go higher if they work with other people.

'If you get a chance to meet a person like that, your curiosity is pretty high. Both of these artists are at the top of their game.'

'It seems that David Bowie and Prince were extremely curious individuals. It's a redeeming characteristic. It keeps you young. You have so many artists that stagnate in their own realm comparing themselves to everybody. They want a certain curiosity. Greatness doesn't stay great by staying great [in one place]. There are going to be one or two artists who just say, "The hell with it." When you do meet somebody that does that, don't you want to find out more? We have something that you like. We call it a signature look.'

Bowie discovered Luther Vandross singing back-up on *Young Americans* with Alomar on guitar, and encouraged him to sing lead. He was an early champion of North American alternative acts Arcade Fire and TV On The Radio.

Prince's gift, says his video producer from 1979 to 1987, Simon Fields, was new not existing talent. 'What he was so good at was putting in new faces who hadn't been anywhere else. It was all fresh.'

Prince and Bowie would respect the unique voice. Both also

worked with Chic's Nile Rodgers. Bowie used him for two albums (*Let's Dance* and *Black Tie, White Noise*) as a producer, Prince performed 'Le Freak' onstage. Rodgers guested with Prince at the Essence Festival in New Orleans in July 2014. The song? 'Let's Dance'.

Prince would also perform 'Heroes' twice on his Piano and a Microphone tour in 2016 after Bowie's death in January of that year. Three months later, Prince would be gone.

One other thing that connected Bowie and Prince was their foresight in trends.

Bowie, demonstrating his characteristic foresight and imagination, famously said in a 1999 interview with the BBC's Jeremy Paxman: 'The potential of what the internet is going to do to society, both good and bad, is unimaginable.' Bowie sold his music on the stock exchange, Prince sold it through giveaways with concert tickets, via newspapers like the *Daily Mirror* and *Mail on Sunday*, and online through his NPG Music Club.

Eleven years after Bowie's pronouncement, Prince told the *Daily Mirror* in 2010, 'The internet's completely over.'

He didn't mean that, not if his private correspondence was anything to go by.

In his 3rdEyeGirl period in the mid-teens, he often privately messaged fans and friends, including on his 'Princestagram' as well as a Facebook page, the validity of which school friend Carla Dove had to check. (He sent her unreleased music to prove it was him.) Hayley Drinkall would send him artwork he then reposted on Instagram. And on Twitter, Mari Maupin saw his mischievous side as they exchanged memes. He would send a few, popularised by others. One of himself staring lasciviously from *Under the Cherry Moon*. Another Prince pose from 2006's 'Black Sweat' video. 'And the funniest, one of Mike Tyson and it said "Printhe".'

Prince. Funny how?

One quality attributed to Prince by friends and colleagues was his sense of humour.

Just as with jazz musicians, Prince had obvious areas of kinship with comedians. They would size up a room, from an arena to a cellar in a club, and know how to work it. They would pick up a hook or refrain, freewheel away from it and return to it, just as jazzers do. Timing and taste are key parts of their armoury, with bravery another required element.

Photographer Mathieu Bitton who worked on Prince's twenty-first-century re-issues, as well as shooting Dave Chappelle on his tours, argues that Prince loved comics "because they're free. He respected freedom. They could say whatever they wanted to say, do whatever they wanted to do. You can decide to be in the audience or you can decide not to be in the audience. There's nobody telling them what they can and can't say."

Prince hung out with comics. He would go rollerskating with Eddie Murphy in the middle of the night. Murphy revealed to Jimmy Fallon that Prince had skates which would light up because of course they did. Cedric The Entertainer was another favourite. 'Cedric could scan the situation and look for the comedy,' recalls Prince's musical director Morris Hayes. The moment at a Clive Davis Grammys party where the organ intro for Leona Lewis' performance of *Bleeding Love* kicked in and Cedric leaned over to Prince and whispered 'Dearly beloved' especially tickled him.

They met after Cedric played Target arena in Minneapolis and 'did a whole joke about the pants with the ass out. I talked about my nephews going through my old clothes, and how you come up with the idea about getting your ass out.' Prince was present, and amused. When they spent time together, 'the part that surprised me was that he loved to laugh. He was such a normal person. To talk to him would be like talking to a regular dude. He was very calm.'

Other comedians who would make Prince laugh on a private basis include Bernie Mac, Chris Rock, George Lopez, Sinbad and Arsenio Hall. Chappelle was another favourite. His early 21st century sketch programme *Chappelle's Show* featured a skit where *Purple Rain*-era Prince would cook Eddie Murphy's brother Charlie pancakes after schooling them at basketball.

In 2014, producer Dylan Dresdow worked with Prince and was told: 'that was true except for my butler makes the pancakes.'

Chappelle's image of the singer holding pancakes would be commandeered by Prince for the cover artwork of his 2013 single 'Breakfast Can Wait', something Chappelle described to talk show host Jimmy Fallon as 'a Prince judo move.' He was not in a position to object. Prince's own comedic style was a double-edged sword, on occasion an uncomfortably sharp one, as close confidant LeRoy Bennett noticed. "He had a dark sense of humour. He was very shy and because of that, he was very self-conscious, and anybody who is very self-conscious like that, they have a tendency to be a little sharp with people because they're protecting themselves."

His humour with staff, including bodyguard Harlan "Hucky" Austin could occasionally stray into the unkind. On one instance Austin entered the video set of 'Gett Off' in a bandana.

'Prince says *"Stop, stop… man, you know who you look like – Harriet Tubman."* My feelings were crushed to say the least.' There wasn't an apology forthcoming, or not an overt one. 'The very next day, he was wearing a yellow bandana.

"I thought you said I look stupid."

"I make this look sexy."

'He was hilarious,' recalls Jimmy Jam. 'He was courtside at the

Minnesota Timberwolves. Dennis Rodman kicked a cameraman and Prince riffed on it for about half an hour. He got kicked in the private area and Prince was re-enacting this whole event.'

Prince's sense of humour could often be goofy – calling up Jay Leno's *Tonight Show* switchboard pretending to be one of his staff, or for Bryant Gumbel's last day on NBC's *Today* in 1987, surprising him in full Bryant Gumbel costume.

Getting to know him helped to understand his humour. 'He was a funny guy but you wouldn't know that until you were around him to get to know him,' offers his record sleeve designer Laura LiPuma Nash. 'He liked to mimic others.' Make-up artist Robyn Lynch saw him 'get up and do impressions of me walking.'

He would occasionally sneak in a playful dig such as when asked at a press conference about will.i.am. 'I like the way he sees the world, he's very technology-driven, but let's remember… he did write "My Humps".'

DJ Rashida once dropped 'Short But Funky' by Too $hort into her set. 'He sent me a note via one of his bodyguards – "keep playing this and your next cheque is going to be too $hort!"'

On stage, he would occasionally quip. For instance after 'Purple Rain', he performed 'I Wanna Be Your Lover' on the *Parade* tour, recalls his video producer Tim Clawson. 'The music starts to play and he says "you might remember this from 1979" [Song lyrics] "Ain't got no money", and he says "that's a lie."'

When performing 'How Come You Don't Call Me Anymore' with Alicia Keys at the 2011 Inglewood, CA dates, he joked while tinkling the intro, 'Swizz Beatz [the father of Keys' children] might have something to do with it.'

He could even be self-deprecating, as dancer Nandy McClean remembers just before some lifetime achievement tribute. 'There was a film giving him accolades and we were under the stage waiting to go up on the elevator and he said "did they just say I was short?"'

Prince even sprinkled his playfulness into his concert presentation, including one memorable March 1993 gig at Florida's Sunrise Theatre where he invited his friend Les Garland, one of the creative forces behind MTV and The Box.

'A driver showed up to get me and off we go. Showtime eight o' clock. The driver gets lost.'

Prince tells his band he's not going on until his friend arrives.

'When we come rolling up to the backstage door, I felt like Dick Clark. They got a closet, two brooms like janitors, and they got a DAT machine and a mic and he wants me to record it. "Ladies and gentlemen... [Mayte added da-da-dah!]... Ladies and gentlemen, without further ado..." We did one take and they ran to the board and here's my voice introducing Prince, and the band starts playing.'

Garland later recorded a different announcement in a bathroom at a Radio City Music Hall gig for a prank.

'We switched it out to the soundboard and he never knew and that ended up being on the rest of the tour. My voice introduced him on the tour.

'Little did I know [what it was] he heard in my voice but he wouldn't go on stage until I got there and did that. That's the sense of humour. It's professional, it's humorous, it's artistic.'

There was the occasional sense of humour failure. For his 1999 album *Midnite Vultures*, Beck recorded the song 'Debra', allegedly inspired by 'Adore' (as well as David Bowie's 'Win') and felt by critics to be something of a pastiche. 'He didn't understand people like Beck,' remembers engineer Hans-Martin Buff. 'Prince heard "Debra".

"How can you listen to something like this?"

"It's meant to be funny. Trying to re-enact a mood."

'He didn't see himself as being perceived like this.'

Apart from his own material, there was plenty Prince did find funny. As befits the working title of *Under The Cherry Moon* soundtrack material sent to orchestrators Clare Fischer and son Brent, the Marx Brothers Project, Prince loved comedians. The more anti-establishment, the better.

Dave Chappelle's disdain for authority chimed with Prince's to the extent he wrestled with walking away from a $50m contract with Comedy Central at one point. Prince's advice at the time? 'Whatever it is, you're right.' (A variant on the words of Prince's own bedroom mirror, 'Everything U Think Is True'.)

'Dave tells the story of how when he quit Comedy Central,' reveals his long-term photographer and friend Mathieu Bitton, 'and the first phone call he got was Prince saying how proud he was of him and he had his back at a time everyone else was telling him he was crazy.'

Prince once sampled a section from one of Chappelle's TV specials, which led to contact from HBO's lawyers. Hayes details the response. 'He called Dave and had him come to Paisley Park to do the whole set and recorded it and sampled that.'

Prince didn't even meet him that night but spoke over the tannoy. 'I have got everything I need.' The comedian and his wife Elaine left Paisley Park not having met Prince but having done everything he wanted.

Another Prince judo move.

CHAPTER 16

ADORE

Up to the end of (his) time, Prince was circling home ...
Retail is detail ... 'Play what I sing' ... 'Adore ' ... Radio
could be a black and white affair ... Here in my car ... Eat,
sleep, record, repeat – but mainly the last two ... After Prince

Up to the end of (his) time,
Prince was circling home

On 16 April 2016, Prince cycled to The Electric Fetus and bought six vinyl albums. *The Best of Missing Persons*, whose singer Dale Bozzio had signed to Paisley Park Records in 1988, gospel music from the Chamber Brothers and Swan Silvertones and three albums from acts at the centre of his musical core – from childhood, through career peaks and now five days before his passing – *Talking Book*, *Hejira* and *Santana IV*. Stevie, Joni, Carlos. These three artists who, as well as James Brown, were never far from Prince's musical sweet spot.

Two days prior to that, in his second Piano and a Microphone show at the Fox Theatre in Atlanta he included a snippet of 'Linus and Lucy' from Vince Guaraldi's music for Charles Schulz's *Peanuts* cartoon.

His first public performance had been a school talent show aged six where the kid with the Afro had played the *Batman* theme on the piano.

Circling back, coming around again, going home, call it what you like, some Prince observers noticed this pattern in 2016. He rarely strayed far from the music that made him fall in love with it in the first place. After *Sign o' the Times*, this had even been one of the criticisms made against him – that he didn't stray far enough away from it.

Prince released thirty-nine studio albums before his death.

Even the most die-hard Prince devotee would not claim that albums ten to forty (*Welcome 2 America*, recorded in 2010, was released posthumously in 2021) had the impact of albums three to nine.

Sign o' the Times was only album number nine. Some records after *Sign* sold better. *Batman* sold somewhere over 4.5 million copies. Being attached to a £288 million-grossing movie couldn't hurt. *Diamonds and Pearls* (1991) boosted by a world tour sold three times *Sign*'s one million copies. It did not however leave anything like the same cultural footprint.

Common consensus suggests there were somewhere between four and six creative mountain tops Prince reached with studio work – the minimalism of his third album *Dirty Mind* which got music tastemakers discussing him, fifth record *1999*'s innovative future pop with its title track and 'Little Red Corvette' breaking him on MTV before he made himself into the biggest star in the world with the follow-up, *Purple Rain*. Then there's *Sign o' the Times*. Some fans love *Around the World in a Day*, a detour to get him off the stratospheric cloud he had built for himself on *Purple Rain*, and others love the playfulness of *Parade*, the album which Eric Leeds calls '*Sign o' the Times* Part One'. But very few people (apart from a select band of

Lovesexy aficionados) peg their favourite Prince record as one he recorded after 1987.

Why?

Alan Leeds has a suggestion.

'It's simple. He had defined himself. Every artist at some point defines themselves. They've reached a peak and after that basically exhausted much of what they can do.'

Leeds, who worked with James Brown, sees the fans running out of reference points after his peak. 'This is a great song, it reminds me of "Controversy"; this is a great song, it reminds me of "Do Me, Baby". James Brown ran out of ideas from the mid-'70s until his death – nobody wants those records. They were what he had done before. Nobody collects Miles Davis' last albums even though [1986's] *Tutu* was a good album.'

Christian McBride, who worked with James Brown, as well as being a fount of knowledge on him, agrees. 'James Brown's greatness ended in 1975. Everything after 1975 is not really good.'

There are other suggestions. Wendy & Lisa were strong creative foils for him in the studio and even on occasion stood up to him. Matt Fink and Bobby Z knew him from way back when in Minneapolis. They played together live and in TV studios but not over a sustained session making a record, and 1987, or even earlier, was arguably the last time Prince was surrounded by people he'd grown up with who could say no. Jimmy Jam suggests Terry Lewis was invaluable for calling Prince out when they disagreed and once that incarnation of the Time was out of his immediate circle, things changed. He adds that Morris Day, who did the same, never recovered from the band's line-up changing.

Prince had discussed writing a Broadway show, but he didn't branch out of the album-tour-album treadmill as much as, say, Patrice Rushen, who worked with Prince early in her career, and who moved into film music composition or music director for three consecutive Grammy Awards. 'He would have been one of my first choices to collaborate with. "Have you thought about an opera; have you thought about a ballet?" With the sensibilities of what he brought to the table, setting a high aesthetic and making music for the people, it would have been interesting if that collaborative moment with me had happened.'

Therese Stoulil takes a different view – that he diversified too much away from music. She worked with him as his assistant from just after the *Sign* era until the '90s, when she noticed burgeoning collaboration with non-musicians. 'Just watching from afar, when I started, the music was the utmost thing. It was 24/7. The music – honing it, changing it, perfecting it. As my years went on, it was interesting – the dynamic of Prince changed. When I started it was calling the best engineers, then getting [string arranger] Clare Fischer; when I left, we were calling people like [former Paramount & 20th Century Fox CEO] Barry Diller and people from Revlon as he wanted to do perfumes. Our priorities had changed – just his focus. If you get to that pinnacle of your career, you just want to roll. When I started, every tape had to be multi-tracked. When I left, [many of] these songs had one or two solos to it.'

Prince always produced himself – only Joshua Welton shares production credits on albums thirty-seven (*Art Official Age*) and thirty-eight (*HITnRUN Phase One*). Producer Andrew Watt feels that the desire to collaborate with other musicians keeps artists and their work evolving, referencing his own work with Sir Elton John.

'I truly believe that music is meant to be a collaborative art form. Take someone like Paul McCartney who could play every instrument on every record and he had his great albums and less than great albums. I feel like in music it's very important to change your collaborators. To take energy from younger people and to take energy from older people. [At time of writing] Elton's seventy-eight and I'm thirty-four and we got in a room and it's like two school kids. I feel it's important to change your collaborators and change your ways. You're eventually at some stage going to hit a wall and if you're not going to let people in, that's going to affect you. But I don't think that bothered Prince. I don't think he ever said, "I think I'm going to get some help."'

Former Paisley Park records president Craig Rice remembers himself and Prince 'watching TV and Nirvana's "Smells Like Teen Spirit" came on ... The lack of the video. We were spending hundreds of thousands on music videos and that was just raw. That was a game changer.'

By that stage, Prince wasn't the best at accepting constructive criticism, as Rice admits after a 1991 discussion around *Diamonds and Pearls*.

'I would tell him what I thought; I wouldn't criticise him out of cold-bloodedness.

"You have got a lot of stuff going on with this record."

"How many hit records have you got?"

"I have got none and you know that."

'I think he generally wants to know, but he likes praise.'

The school of thought that a creative person needs to be 49 per cent self-critic and 51 per cent advocate didn't always apply to Prince. Hans-Martin Buff engineered Prince's records in the late '90s, a point when observers could have detected a lack of confidence after a commercially fallow period. In fact, the reverse was true. 'I have never met a bigger Prince fan than Prince. He thought all his stuff was awesome. Stuff like

Sign o' the Times, there wasn't a difference between ten years ago and yesterday.'

In other words, most critics might regard Prince's classic albums as being confined to the '80s. As Buff heard, everything from *Lovesexy* to *HITnRUN Phase Two*, to Prince's ears anyway, was in the same league. 'Every last bit of it was just great. I have heard many, many times [from him] how great the stuff he did was. It was never … "weelll… meh." Never. *Crystal Ball* (1998) he gets out all these fan favourites. A remix or a demo. That's when I realised, he just thinks it's all fabulous.'

Prince himself was astute enough in 2006 to describe *Purple Rain* to the *Observer* as 'too successful, and no matter what I do, I'll never top it. It's my albatross and it'll be hanging around my neck as long as I make music.'

But the path he plotted in the studio – as a live performer he remained a hot ticket until his death – never seemed to delight critics or fans quite the way it had after *Sign*.

Another theory is that because so much was riding on *Purple Rain*, Prince took extra care over every track. *Purple Rain* 'forced patience' on him, his drummer and friend Bobby Z told *Backspin*. 'He had to let the songs stew.' *Sign o' the Times* tracks were mostly rerecorded to replace the Revolution's playing, requiring a different kind of reappraisal of every track. He had to whittle a triple into a double. Again, more effort in sequencing and programming. No album after that, when Prince could release from his own label, online, via a supermarket chain or free with a newspaper, would demand that Prince take anything like the same amount of care over it. If he wanted to write, record and release an album in a week and cut a deal with a newspaper or retail chain to put it out into the world, who was going to stop him?

Retail is detail

The twenty-first-century challenges of the internet and streaming meant releasing a new record had less promotional fanfare than in the 1990s. Sony created a 32-foot-tall statue of Michael Jackson which sailed down the Thames for the 1995 London release of *History*.

Around that time, Prince bypassed the record company and the music press too.

Sam Jennings helped set up the online NPG Music Club, which was just one way of shifting his albums. 'He was never going to stick with one way of doing things. We'd sold music through the internet. We'd sold music through Universal and Sony, and he just wanted to try something else.

'We would talk a lot and a big topic for him was the music industry and musicians' relationship with the music industry and music industry people. He didn't want them telling him how he should distribute his music. He didn't want to get advice from people who were glorified accountants in his mind." That didn't make any sense to him. "I'm the musician, I'm the one who owns it and makes all the decisions." They're not the people who are going to make the best decisions for him.'

Bill Stephney, the president of Def Jam records at the time of *Sign*, approved of the deals with Target supermarket, selling his *Planet Earth* album as part of a concert ticket and his *20TEN* record free via UK newspapers. 'I thought that was great from a retail standpoint, from a liquidity standpoint. Napster and YouTube killed it. He figured out stuff to come out with a new business model.'

Dylan Dresdow, who worked with other big stars like The Black Eyed Peas, Madonna and Britney Spears, said, 'With no radio play, without even knowing when a record came out, he's in the top 10 of the Billboard chart. They had to change the rules of how they did the charts; he changed the game.'

It's reasonable to assume that the music industry would not have rejoiced in any success which circumvented them.

Dave Hampton reflected to his friend Scottie Baldwin that 'the thing that scared the music industry more than anything was that he was a truly free black man.'

Many of his closest confidants like Alan Leeds feel the end of the road was foreshadowed. 'There's a case to be made that in the last year of his life he had become increasingly lonely and he was aware that he had run out of gas. Anything he was going to accomplish career-wise was going to be redundant.

'The fact that he had agreed to do the one-man show (his final tour, Piano and a Microphone) was an interesting choice. I don't think he was being challenged any more. Nobody was really anticipating his new music any more; they hadn't been for two decades. It was still an elite level but for him, it was nothing new. You can make a case that he was done.'

Adrian Crutchfield, the saxophonist who worked on Prince's last studio band project, *Black Is the New Black*, agrees. 'From a spiritual standpoint, I don't know, but from a musical standpoint, yeah.'

Morris Hayes, the man for whom Prince built a house across the road from his, thinks his friend 'had done all he was supposed to do in this world'.

Mari Maupin, as The Golden Hippie, worked on *Art Official Age*, his third-last recorded album before his final albums *HITnRUN Phases One* & *Two*. She sees the three as being chock-full of sign-off clues. They sampled lyrics and sounds from *Purple Rain*, *Parade* and *Sign o' the Times*, but more than that, songs like 'Breakdown' and 'June' portray a man in a contemplative state.

'When you look at the last three records before he passed away, you can consider those being last words in many ways that were pieced together as a body of work. And when you listen to those works with that in mind, you can hear the pain in a lot of it. You can hear the release in a lot of it. The elation of transcending in a lot of it. You can hear him letting go. He did leave us in that way. I think you can hear that now. He said those words to me as well as another person who worked with him: "Having done all he came to do."'

For someone who seemed aware of his own legacy, making these nods to his heritage, it seems unusual he didn't write a will. 'It was weird,' agrees Maupin. 'There are a lot of things that we don't know.'

He had asked his friend Les Garland years previously in the '90s to manage his affairs as Jack Douglas had managed Jimi Hendrix's, but his schoolmate Paul Mitchell is unsurprised. His childhood friend argues a lack of will was 'because of his whole lack of trust of people knowing anything personal about him. Obviously he didn't plan the way he died, but when he passed away, he was alone and in an elevator in his house. That says a lot.'

Jimmy Jam points out he paid attention to his own will when children arrived, a blessing Prince was not granted for long.

Bassist Josh Dunham, like others, had heard news of Prince's private plane making an emergency landing in Moline, Illinois and reports over the radio of an 'unresponsive' passenger – the plane owner himself – in the early hours of 15 April. Later that week, he checked in with Morris Hayes.

'I sat in my truck and called Paisley Park and the phone was ringing and I knew I have got to leave an answering machine message. The phone is ringing and I hear …

"Hello."

"This is Josh. I was just calling to check on you. Did I call you at a good time?"

"I'm just having some lunch."

"I just wanted to check on you to make sure you were good. You take care."

'My buddy texted me the next day: "You OK? Look at the news. Prince died."'

Prince died on 21 April 2016 two months shy of his fifty-eighth birthday with a fatal amount of fentanyl in his body. Minnesota health officials relayed it to NBC News as an 'accidental overdose' suggesting he had meant to take Vicodin.

When he died, Prince didn't have children, his second wife Manuela had filed for divorce almost a decade to the day earlier (May 2006) and if he went out socially, it would almost always end up with music.

His last public performance in Minneapolis was entering from the rear of the stage and playing a ninety-second guitar solo during 'Let the Good Times Roll' for a Ray Charles tribute on 12 March. He left before the second act started.

The venue was the Chanhassen Dinner Theatre, the venue that had donated the sets for the *Sign o' the Times* album cover.

'Play what I sing'

The final track of the double album illustrates a gift which, because of his guitar and piano playing, is often overlooked. 'Adore' showcases Prince's four-octave range.

What kind of a singer was Prince? Any kind of singer you wanted, or, more to the point, he wanted.

For a man who did his own backing vocals and sampled his own voice, being versatile couldn't hurt.

Often critics will praise a new artist for finding their voice, or an established artist for finding a new voice. This record sees Prince sourcing all sorts of voices. Having written and played the instruments on an album for an all-girl band wasn't enough by '86/'87. He had to pass himself off as a female artist.

The unreleased *Camille* album, recorded around that time, was intended to be Prince masquerading under his latest alter ego, and featured 'Strange Relationship', 'If I Was Your Girlfriend' and 'Housequake'.

'Housequake' also squeezed, sampled and distorted his voice via the Fairlight, which might explain Prince's admiration for Ohio funk band Zapp, whose leader Roger Troutman used computerised vocals and joined him and the Time for the Controversy tour. Similar vocal distortion can be heard on snippets of Prince's final project, *Black Is the New Black*.

He intended his voice to be flexible in relation to his chart rivals. When they went low, he would go high. Not that he would react competitively to them as much as himself.

The tender ballad 'Adore' [original title – 'Adore (Until the End of Time)'] was recorded two weeks before the deep and foreboding 'Bob George' from *The Black Album*, believed to be a composite pot shot at his manager Bob Cavallo and music writer Nelson George. It was recorded on the Publison Infernal Machine, a pitch-changing device, supervised by Coke Johnson. 'He could sing in his normal register and we could transpose it up or down. He could sing in his falsetto and it was such a pure tone.

'With the *Camille* stuff, harmonisers were getting really big and he would sing into that in real time and I would split it out in a different octave or different key. He could sing in four or five different octaves so he could reach up there. There wasn't autotune or pitch change back then.

'These voices were not just a rejection of his own natural

voice but a reaction to Warner Brothers who were trying to slow his productivity,' Johnson added. 'That's when he was trying to experiment. They only wanted one album a year and he was looking to create another artist so he could put his stuff out there under a pseudonym. The grooves were definitely Prince.'

It's hard to say whether all these styles meant Prince was becoming comfortable with his voice or the opposite.

He played the piano, but didn't sing, in his early school talent shows.

Part of the reason for his high voice was his admiration for the female voice. He told TV interviewer Tavis Smiley, 'I'm not a fan of male vocalists. Usually when I do ballads, I use my higher register because I love the female voice doing slow music.'

He once advised his late '00s protégé Bria Valente to 'try to do something which is not happening today. Try to get into a niche. You've got a beautiful voice but you've got to do something with it that you don't hear.'

This may well explain his professed admiration for, among others, Amy, Joni, Aretha, Björk and Mary J Blige as well as Anita Baker, Mavis Staples, Dolly Parton, The Cocteau Twins' Liz Fraser and Patrice Rushen, who says of him, 'I would say he was able to manipulate his voice to be a vehicle for the songs he wrote. These were choices he would make for the song to come through. His best instrument was songwriting.'

The Grammy award-winning soul singer Anthony Hamilton, no vocal slouch himself having worked with Buddy Guy, Mark Ronson, Gorillaz and Al Green, thinks, 'He had a falsetto like nobody and then to have that chest voice was just as memorable. He could do all of that.'

Elisa Fiorillo, in the rarefied position of having been produced by him as a lead vocalist as well as having sung backing vocals in his band, was not alone in marvelling at his lack of sleep.

'You definitely need sleep to get a high voice and this man never slept; I don't know how he did it. His chords must have been made of steel.'

For a man with a high singing voice, his speaking voice was on occasion reminiscent of the Low Talker, whom Jerry Seinfeld memorably had trouble hearing in one episode. 'He spoke to you very softly,' remembers Laura LiPuma Nash. 'I always dreaded his phone calls at work because I worked in an art department which was noisy and he would talk in a whisper. It was very difficult to say to Prince "What?!? What?"'

When he introduced himself to Scott Thurston at the Rock & Roll Hall of Fame gig, Tom Petty's bassist for the night says, 'I always thought he spoke like a preacher. Low, Midwestern.' As someone who rarely did interviews, Prince wanted to be remembered for what he recorded. He stayed away from the more usual vocal booth. Sunset's Studio 3 was already a pretty big space. 'It's very unusual to do a vocal in the control room,' admits Sunset's current owner Paul Camarata. 'You have got to turn the monitors down so you don't get feedback.'

Vocals unusually were recorded on his own, first into the Neumann U-47 microphone and then a Sennheiser MD441, a recommendation from Stevie Nicks. There was discomfort in being watched while singing, which could in turn have led to the story, denied by some, confirmed by others, that he was not under any circumstances to be looked straight in the eyes. (Many interviewees who enjoyed productive, lengthy working relationships with him often first introduced themselves by looking straight at him.)

'He wanted that privacy so he could speak directly to his listeners,' reasons Susan Rogers.

His *Sign*-era soundman Rob 'Cubby' Colby sees Prince's singing as an intimacy he demanded from his working family.

'We were all so close in the trenches with him that he did have the sense of "I need to do this privately so that I can be this expressive person that I need to be". Maybe he was being distracted.'

When it came to singing at Paisley Park, an assistant engineer around the *Sign* era, Mike Kloster says, 'We would set him up in a control room and leave him to it. His attitude was very independent and so he didn't like being in the booth. We set him up in a little box.'

Ambience was important. Another engineer Todd Herreman remembers him cutting 'Slow Love'. 'Sometimes the lights would be down and he would get a vibe and have candles, something like that to create the mood. He would do what he needed to do. When he cut vocals, often the lights would be turned way down.'

Cousin and drummer in his first band Grand Central, Chazz Smith remembers the early days in the studio where he sang over a drum pattern. 'I would hear this rhythm in his voice and he would tell me, "Play what I sing." Nobody else does that.'

Jack DeJohnette, the drummer who helped Miles Davis redefine his sound on *Bitches Brew*, has a favourite Prince track, the very spare 'Mary, Don't You Weep' from the 1983 *A Piano and a Microphone* recording. 'His voice goes through different things. He sings like Stevie, he sings like James Brown, he goes through a lot of different pitches. The live playing is really great. His feet stomping is right on it. When he started doing tracks without a bass, he turned his snare drum down low. It filled in the space where the bass was not happening.'

He was detail-oriented. Wendy Melvoin told author Liz Jones he included guidelines for vocals – 'every lick, every breath, every sigh, no question'.

'Adore'

For all that he wrote 'The Beautiful Ones', 'Nothing Compares 2 U', 'Love Thy Will Be Done', 'Diamonds and Pearls', 'She Loves Me 4 Me' and 'The Most Beautiful Girl in the World', 'Adore' remains for many fans the most romantic song Prince ever recorded.

Anthony Hamilton, known for navigating his own way around love songs, sees its power as 'one of those songs that seeps into you. It's the sweetest way to speak to a woman. The energy of adoring a woman, it can even feel better than loving. That's what he did to the song vocally. He had a falsetto like nobody.' Hamilton's praise of Prince's range and a 'chest voice [which] was just as memorable' did not deter him from his own version.

Hamilton would segue into a snippet of 'Adore' at the end of his own 'The Point of It All'. The reaction is 'always *aaaaaah. He didn't just sing "Adore" by Prince?!?* It's always pandemonium and a bunch of women screaming. They love it.

'They understood what it was and what it meant to women and it's something that changed the way people listen to music and produced music, like D'Angelo.'

Artists like Hamilton, D'Angelo, Eric Benet (who would go on to marry Prince's second wife Manuela Testolini) and Maxwell – all of whom covered 'Adore' – would herald a new kind of soul music (sometimes called neo-soul) leading to a new kind of male vulnerability, the bridge between Teddy Pendergrass and Al Green via Luther Vandross and Alexander O'Neal to Frank Ocean, Miguel, and Gabriels' Jacob Lusk. Prince's ballad, considers Hamilton, 'made people rethink how it should be and how it kicked sound. It had blackness all over it, it had some church, it had a mysterious sweetness to it that was a different kind of sexy. You just knew it felt good.'

Award-winning gospel singer Mary Griffin, who has worked with Patti LaBelle and Anita Baker, recorded a version and 'absolutely adored singing it. Doing "Adore" changed my perspective on what we do on my show. The words of it are a poem about God one day striking him blind ... at the end, that's church!'

Prince knew that the song's imprint went deep. His remark to Scottie Baldwin on seeing Maxwell sing this ballad was 'like watching home movies.'

Model Devin DeVasquez, dating Prince in the mid-'80s, allows herself a smile when she hears it now.

'When I first heard *Sign o' the Times*, he played "Housequake" and "Adore". I didn't think of it at the time but now I listen to the lyrics and think, "This song is about me!" My *Playboy* cover had come out and I don't think he had been friends with a girl like me. There was safety in the relationship. I could really be me around him.'

The most frequently expressed view is that 'Adore', like most of the rest of the album, is Susannah-inspired. The lyrics refer to her as an ingénue and she was nineteen when she met him. Susan Rogers 'had no doubt in my mind that she was the inspiration for that. She was such a huge presence in his life at the time that so much of his material does reflect his love for her. They were very tight at that point.'

The session has some soft brass courtesy of Eric Leeds and Atlanta Bliss, the name Prince gave trumpeter Matt Blistan, who had been house sharing with Leeds. (He's actually from Pittsburgh.)

'Blistan and his wife and I had been sharing a house in Atlanta, and we were in the process of moving (finally) to Minneapolis in November of '86,' remembers Leeds. 'They had found a house and I had found an apartment. We were in Atlanta packing up for the move when Prince needed us in LA for a session. So we left Atlanta on an early flight, got to LA and went straight to Sunset Sound. We put the horns on "Adore" and all the additional horns on "Beautiful Night" (on the live Paris track). We got out of the studio about 9 p.m., caught the red-eye back to Atlanta and got in about 5 a.m. That's what I remember about it. The session itself is just a blur.'

The session often was a blur, unless you were Prince and clear-minded about what you wanted to achieve.

Radio could be a black and white affair

On completion of 'Adore', Prince leaned back on the console and said to Susan Rogers: 'That one's for black radio.'

Some context.

The calendar year of 1987, the biggest selling album in the USA dated back to the previous year, Bon Jovi's *Slippery When Wet*.

1988's biggest seller was also released the previous year and hailed from an unlikely source: the son of a Greek restaurateur and English dancer who grew up in the suburbs of Bushey just outside north London.

George Michael's success was built on strong songwriting and his golden voice and the effervescent pop sunshine of Wham! with Andrew Ridgeley.

He added stubble, a leather jacket and grown-up soul to *Faith*'s breakthrough to a new American audience which had another enormously important foundation – support from black radio. Ray Parker Jr., no stranger to crossover success on white and black radio, notes that 'George Michael had a sound that was pleasing to both ears.'

Just as Michael's friend Elton John was said to have chosen

to release 'Bennie and the Jets' as a single in 1974 after support from black radio, the singer made sure to thank the same stations from the stage when *Faith* won three American Music Awards in 1989. It was those radio outlets that had hammered 'Father Figure', 'I Want Your Sex' and 'One More Try'.

While black music would freely admit the influence white rock had on it, Bill Stephney considers the early '80s after the disco backlash to be 'the most racially defined era since the 1950s'.

The then Def Jam president recalls one-way traffic for black artists. 'White pop music in the '80s was so protectionist. Black radio were playing Malcolm McLaren.'

Rock radio would play R&B hits by The System, Cherrelle and Marvin Gaye – but only after they were covered by Robert Palmer.

Stephney recalls the early days 'on tour with the Beastie Boys, with Anthrax, with U2. We were sampling Slayer, and there is no Public Enemy without me seeing The Clash at Bonds International Casino. Return of the Magnificent 7.'

Black artist videos in the early days of MTV were rare. 'I was convinced we needed to widen our vision,' says Les Garland. With 'Michael Jackson there was never even a question of whether we would play him or not.

'Michael Jackson and Prince were so important because if you're going to identify the most important artists of that time, they were among the most important artists on the planet. They had their own category.'

Once Prince and Michael Jackson broke down the doors, Lionel Richie, Janet Jackson, Whitney Houston followed. Then there was hip hop. Run-DMC in the '80s were massive. The first hip hop band to have a gold record, their own film, perform after Black Sabbath on Live Aid, and be on the cover of *Rolling Stone* levels of massive.

Ever since 'Little Red Corvette', Prince had chased the appeal of rock radio but was conscious of losing that audience.

Stephney admits before Public Enemy served up their Clash-inspired soundscape that Prince's support from rock radio around the time of *1999* had been a game changer for him. '"Lady Cab Driver" got played by the more progressive stations.'

The price to pay for a huge rise in white audiences picked up from crossover hits like '1999', 'Purple Rain' (a country-rock ballad designed for a mainstream Hollywood movie) and 'Raspberry Beret' was that the urban department of Warner Brothers' excitement around *Dirty Mind* was a distant memory.

'Don't make me black,' he had told Lenny Waronker before his first album *For You* came out in December 1977, in order to challenge a label largely staffed by white employees and their narrow lens of what a black recording artist could accomplish. Prince made this easier for artists in subsequent eras.

Frank McComb remembers a conversation with Prince at a *3121* party. 'He told me he hated R&B especially at the beginning of his career. He told me he wanted to play rock and this is from his lips to my ears: "They had us all in slots and boxes."'

By the time he recorded 'Adore', he was receiving criticism, as Sly Stone had in the past and Michael Jackson was around that time, for overly catering to a white audience, from his band members to his choice of girlfriends. It would be naive to pretend he wasn't aware of it.

This support from black radio for white artists – everyone from Sex Pistols manager Malcolm McLaren to George Michael – did not translate the other way round.

'*Sign o' the Times* comes after the marriage of Aerosmith and Run-DMC,' notes Stephney, so Prince was in a position to expect support from both.

Those two acts had clearly defined fan bases who created a new one.

It was a trick Prince would pull off – creating genres and audiences unique to him – throughout his working life.

Here in my car

In 2011, seven-time Formula One champion Lewis Hamilton, before he was knighted, paid $100,000 at a charity auction for Prince's gold Fender Stratocaster which he'd played on tour. It would be nice to think this would have tickled Prince.

First, he was super-competitive.

Second, he was a petrolhead.

In his music, the clues are there. The 'Little Red Corvette' (actually written in Lisa Coleman's 1964 pink Mercury Montclair); limousines namechecked in that hit as well as 'A Love Bizarre' and Vanity 6's 'Nasty Girl'; Mayte raps that her favourite car is a green Rolls-Royce in 'Love 2 The 9's' from 1992; and he namechecks father John's Thunderbird in 'Alphabet Street'. He also had a three-quarter-size fibreglass Thunderbird replica lifted onto the stage for the *Lovesexy* tour.

And in 'Adore', the woman he is impossibly in love with to the end of time itself, the one who invokes the image of choral angels in heaven, is allowed to burn up his clothes but he draws the line at her smashing up his ride.

He references the BMW in the Time's 'Jerk Out', and in real life, that was Prince's recurring motor of choice, normally the 7 Series, a car he bought with his first pay cheque. 'He loved cars,' agrees ex-girlfriend Devin DeVasquez. 'He picked me up in his purple BMW. He had this old car which had suicide doors; it was the car that was in "Sign o' the Times".'

Another ex, Maneca Lightner, remembers being picked up in

a limo or classic Rolls-Royce when in LA but in Minneapolis, 'He would come and get me.'

There were two things he would do on purchase. Danny Soltys recalls him buying an 850 Series 8 yellow BMW. 'When he bought it, BMW gave him a special paint job. He had that car painted gold. I drove that car a lot.' A gold BMW was not equipped for the Minnesotan snow, so Soltys got him a Jeep Cherokee too.

The second thing Prince would do on buying a new car? Turn the music up.

'He had me put the stereo in it, an $8,000 stereo, and he said, "Not enough." I took the back seat out and put speakers in it. The acoustics in a car are even better than a recording studio.'

Danny's brother Mike also worked at Paisley in the early days and on tour as a bass and guitar tech. He remembers having records printed when Prince worked at Sunset in LA, Bernie Grundman's mastering plant just off Hollywood Boulevard.

'There was a facility three blocks down that would stamp records. When Prince was done, he would listen to it back on the speakers and he also wanted to listen to it on the record so he had a turntable. They would stamp a reference and he would play it on the turntable. We would mix it into a cassette and listen to it in the car. That was brilliant of him. Where do people listen to their music? In their car! So he would make sure you could hear the kick drum on the cassette version.'

And the music Prince would play in his car, according to driver and valet Robbie Paster? 'Mostly his own.'

He drove automatic.

His *Under the Cherry Moon* co-star Emmanuelle Sallet and bodyguard Gilbert Davison, squeezed in the back seat, found this out the hard way. 'There was a scene in the movie where he had to take off in a car that was stick shift but didn't know how to drive standard so he asked me to teach him in my convertible Porsche Carrera, and Gilbert, Prince and I went off to the Cannes Port's parking lot where I attempted to teach him ... we all had a very big laugh as he kept stalling or making the Porsche jump too fast ... that was pretty scary.'

'You could always tell where his head was at depending on what colour his car was,' adds Bennett. 'He drove a purple one [BMW] during *Purple Rain*. It was originally black and it was painted purple, and then he had a 7 series he painted purple. He never drove a peach car. Always, always a new car and a new colour.'

Sal Greco, who worked with Prince from the late '80s to the early '90s remembers a peach BMW and a green one. Others remember yellow, robin egg blue and, most frequent, black.

Danny Soltys remembers a splurge after *Purple Rain* on a 1985 Cadillac limo and a Prowler as well as a spot of envy when bassist Mark Brown went car shopping and his boss told him: '*I* don't even have a Ferrari.'

Around the *3121* era, musician Frank McComb remembers lifts in a 'big suburban' Mercedes-Maybach and Rolls-Royce Phantom, both black.

In 2009, writer Ann Powers suggests Prince had given one of his cars, a low-slung black sports vehicle (she didn't specify model) a nickname – Miles Davis.

Then there is the blue Pontiac front end on *Sign*'s sleeve.

Cars were important to him because his music was.

'He always liked to listen to stuff in a car and on a really cheap boom box because that's what the kids were listening to,' recalls his merchandise man Bruce Huisinga, who recalls his first listen of the 1995 single 'Eye Hate U' loud in Paisley Park's parking lot. 'That would influence how he would mix a record.'

There were times when Prince's determination to make the

car sound good enough to play his music had the opposite effect. Sal Greco shudders at one memory. 'We weren't allowed to sit in the car with him but he rolled the window down. He had a yellow customised BMW and he says, "There's something wrong with the car." He goes into the parking lot and rolls down the window and there does seem to be real noise. We say, "It's coming from the trunk," and the back of the BMW fell off and we had to torque all the back of the car together. The sub-woofer was rattling it.' The speakers had been installed but that meant a loose trunk lid and faulty tail lights. The rear of a top of the range BMW had to be reassembled. Prince didn't just suffer for his art. His cars would too.

Eat, sleep, record, repeat — but mainly the last two

He loved to drive, but mealtime was often seen as an interruption. He had cooks but 'I never saw him eat' is heard as often from interviewees as 'I never saw him sleep'.

In the 1980s, he loved junk food like Doritos (plain flavour), popcorn (Orville Redenbacher's brand), doughnuts (Winchell's), cookies (Famous Amos), cake (lemon), soft drinks (Five Alive), 'big into lollipops … Tootsie Pops' (Marylou Badeaux), his favourite cereal as a child was Cap'n Crunch, he drank Earl Grey and he enjoyed soul food from Maurice's Snack 'n' Chat on Pico and Fairfax in LA and ribs from Rudolph's in Minneapolis, a favourite of Quincy Jones when he was in town. Kim Basinger made him popcorn.

Peggy McCreary, the engineer in the early to mid-'80s for many of his hits, suggests that as well as 'honey and lemon lozenges all the time' for his voice, he did drink coffee. She learned a valuable lesson in the process. 'Small Styrofoam cup. Two thirds white, sugar, Cremora stuff and that's what he would go on. If you wanna go home, don't get him a fresh pot of coffee. Let him deal with cold coffee because it's lost its caffeine.'

His valet around the *Sign* era Robbie Paster recalls fetching chicken and broccoli dishes from the local Chinese restaurant and making him pancakes and omelettes in his Paris apartment around the time of *Under the Cherry Moon*. Prince and his dad would share Chinese meals together. Occasionally, but not often, he would have a glass of red, perhaps a Cabernet Sauvignon. 'I never saw him finish a glass,' says ex-girlfriend Devin DeVasquez.

Tina and Melissa Huntsberry Kahn remember him at the height of *Purple Rain* ordering a Blue Hawaiian cocktail, and Robia Scott teased him for his '90s choice of drink when they were out socially. 'A piña colada should only be purchased poolside. That is not a drink you order in a nightclub.'

When he had housekeeper Michelle Schwartzbauer, he would go healthier before turning vegetarian and then vegan in later life. 'Fettucine Alfredo with vegetables was one of his favourite things to eat. Broccoli, carrots, it was a staple in his home. Comfort food.'

He was funny about whom he would let cook for him. When she was dating him around 1990, Elisa Fiorillo offered to cook. 'He was obviously vegetarian and vegan. He was very scared to have people poison him with food. I remember when I was nineteen and I tried to cook for him and he said, "I don't let people cook for me."'

He could be picky. Accountant Donnie Graves noticed a dessert trolley and a $35 bottle of Sonoma Au Contraire wine with around 5 per cent taken from all the portions and the bottle.

Peggy McCreary has an explanation. 'He had obesity in his family. He was terrified of being obese.'

Sometimes, says Carole Davis, who hung out with him in the

Big Apple between *Purple Rain* and *Sign...*, the menu choice was due to a different kind of vanity.

'When we went out in New York, he would order pea soup and tea. He never ordered anything other than soup and we went to many, many restaurants – the fanciest. Soup and tea. He didn't want anyone to see him chewing or see salad stuck in his mouth. We went to Tavern on the Green for a Christmas Day lunch. He was wearing a silk see-through onesie. You could see the hair in his ass. And still the napkin would come up, because God forbid you could see a bit of salad in his teeth.'

The thought that food would get in the way of his music creation might explain these decisions.

After Prince

His choice of cars and menu may have varied but a 24/7 music schedule was a constant.

Prince always had one eye on his musical legacy, the way he would ultimately want to be judged.

Instant reaction after the news of his death broke saw landmarks around the world including Wembley Stadium, the Eiffel Tower and even Egypt's pyramids lit up in purple, the internationally recognised colour (if not by him) of Prince. As Madhouse drummer Dale Alexander recalls: 'When he died, even the astronauts had some purple stuff on their ship.'

People's opinions on how Prince will be remembered will always be personal to them, but most recall the music. 'One hell of a songwriter, badass superhero of a musician,' says singer Anthony Hamilton. 'He's up there.'

Miles Davis' son Erin feels that 'the funny thing about Prince is that there aren't many people who will say, "I don't like him." Everybody likes at least one song. With Prince, there are going to be so many artists that derive from him. Whether it's his falsetto or songwriting, nobody can write like that. There is always going to be someone trying to be like Prince in some way. That's his legacy.'

Producer Bob Power argues: 'Like Mozart, Prince is one of the very few consistently jaw-dropping greats. The breadth of his vision, fearless over-the-edge expressiveness, always compelling, virtuosic, at times notably original, prolific … I'm running out of superlatives. And he skilfully bridged the gap between rock and R&B, and brought soul music into the twenty-first century in ways that no one had done before.'

Randy Newman hopes 'he's remembered as one of the best people who ever did this [pop music]. The Beatles would have to be there, maybe Stevie Wonder and he would be up there.'

Producer Andrew Watt says, 'Unilaterally, one of the greatest of all time. He's a cultural icon; he's a style icon. An artist could look at his outfits, you're not even listening to his music, and he's influencing culture.'

Frank McComb says, 'Prince was music,' engineer Ian Boxill calls him 'a MusiGod', Monique Mannen, the dancer from the 'Kiss' video, says he'll go down in history as 'Your Royal Badness'.

Gloria, Princess of Thurn and Taxis, the German noblewoman who gave him the guitar which graces the cover of *Welcome 2 America*, argues he will be remembered 'as one of the great musicians of his time'.

As well as referencing *Purple Rain* and his symbol for a name, engineer Michael Koppelman probably speaks for many with his answer. 'Prince would say, "I'm a guitar player." That would be one of the things people remember about him.'

Former girlfriend Mi-Ling Stone Poole puts it simply: 'He's the GOAT. Little did I know that he would be this huge star. The thing I always remember about Prince is his smile. And that big bold laugh when he could just be himself. That's one of the things I will cherish. The real Prince.'

Singer Lizz Wright, whose own gig at Minneapolis jazz club The Dakota on 19 April 2016 is thought to be the last Prince attended, recognises his desire for privacy. 'He is always going to be wrapped in mystique.'

Some interviewees maintain the importance of his estate keeping his work alive.

His front of house soundman Scottie Baldwin told a stranger that he had worked with Prince for many years. Her response: 'Which one ... William or Harry?'

For some fans, the memory will linger. For others, Prince's music challenges the idea that he will be remembered in another way. 'He *is* remembered,' corrects drummer Jack DeJohnette. Rapper Talib Kweli expands: 'I don't think he's going anywhere. All these ways Prince connected to all of us. I just watched *Sing 2* with my kids and the first song in it is "Let's Go Crazy".'

His influence is felt by his former colleagues with the Time, says Jimmy Jam as he and Terry Lewis produce music.

'Prince's influence is every day but as big as the day he left us. Terry and I live by it.

'*"Would Prince like this?"*

'*"What would Prince do?"*

'His impact is always going to be felt and that for me is his biggest legacy.'

Make-up artist Cheryl Ann Nick was speaking at a Prince panel when approached by a woman who 'comes up to me and says, "I can't tell you how important Prince's music was to me. He was like my solace. Prince helped me get out of my depression."'

'Ultimately, he was just popular,' adds country singer Toby Lightman. 'People just like anything that he did. His music will speak for him. His music speaks for itself. He will always have a mystery around him in the public eye. Just like so many legendary icons, there's always going to be a space in music and the world that he will fill.'

His former manager Ruth Arzate feels that 'Prince should be remembered as a pioneer. He wasn't the first musician to produce his first album – Shuggie Otis and others had – but he would take the attempts and create a bigger feat. If Prince was in a relay race with other musicians, instead of handing it to the next musician, he would take their baton too. He would run the race by himself. This was a singular person who wrote and composed. He had so many incredible visions for his own music. He was constantly, constantly creating. He should be remembered as a consummate musician. He did more "doing" than most of us do in our lifetime.'

Mari Maupin feels his activism and philanthropy broaden how he is considered. 'He will be remembered … whether it's [as] the greatest guitar player, the greatest musician, a fire starter in the industry, a songwriter, justice activist, human life advocate, a planet earth advocate, that's what he will be remembered for – he definitely was that way.'

Country singer Rissi Palmer is not alone among interviewees calling him 'always ahead of his time. So many people are stuck in the old model rather than trying to succeed in what is to come. For now, it's figuring out how to make a living in the era of streaming. If Prince was here now, he would have really strong feeling and advocacy for artists dealing with the AI model.'

Ani DiFranco thinks he will be remembered 'by each person in their own way. That's what he offered. He offered a rainbow and you pick your own frequency.'

Les Garland, a pivotal figure in the development of both MTV and The Box, argues: 'I think he will go on being discovered as time goes on. Somewhere around fifty years from now, what happens when the younger generation discovers classic rock and blues and R&B and James Brown? What is it going to be like for that person? The greatest artists, books, movies, TV shows; that renaissance period in art was the peak. Prince is one of those artists that people will keep falling in love with. The song is what is memorable to people. That's when they become acquainted and in love with the artist. You remember things like that. That's very powerful emotionally. That's why music is the language of emotion. "It's a great music video." Prince was all of that. He could sing, he could write, he could perform, he could play every instrument, he could produce; he did it all. Everything about him is what made him such a once-in-a-lifetime artist who is in his own space. I don't know who would be in there with him. He was all-in.'

Another of his female engineers Sylvia Massy says: 'He was a short kid with a big Afro who found a way to be important.'

Prince's video director and tour manager Craig Rice looks at Prince as 'someone that was authentically who he was. It's nice when an artist can soundtrack the times you're living in. That's a part of what an artist is supposed to do but it's only a part of what an artist does.'

Jacqui Thompson, who has worked as an executive in the music industry for decades and ran Paisley Park in the '90s thinks that 'eventually, people will come to the realisation that he is a black man. A lot of the fans don't think of him like that. He was very much into Black Lives Matter and black power and ownership and uniting. I know that for a fact. He was serious about it. Unification of black folks.

For younger black musicians like Sananda Maitreya and The Roots guitarist Kirk Douglas, Prince's desire to free himself from categorisation held weight.

'Just because I was a mixed man of colour,' says Maitreya,

whose breakthrough Grammy-nominated debut *Introducing the Hardline…* was released in the same year as *Sign*, 'I didn't have to choose to follow one type of path or genre for my music, but could mix all of them as having equal claims on my spirit. He was therefore a revelation that showed me the way, and that the vacuous and limited notion of "race" needn't be an obstacle in how I constructed my own burgeoning vision of music.'

'Prince provides a touchstone for me as a black person that plays guitar,' adds Douglas. 'For people who see me play in concert, they can look at Prince and there's this mental understanding, "you know what this is," beyond what were regular expressions for making music.

'When you think of what the standard is for a black man making music in modern times, it's very difficult to separate that from hip hop and R&B. Prince always went rock 'n' roll in a way that we haven't seen since Hendrix. For that to happen in the '80s was super-important. As a songwriter who makes people feel things and centres emotions would cut, already diffuse and makes people dream and aspire and all that stuff, he helped all of us do that. As a black person, it's such a beautiful thing I have Prince. An artist expressing what they have inside of them. He gave his view on the way the world was. He gave us *Sign o' the Times*.'

ACKNOWLEDGEMENTS

Definitive.

When writing a biography, that word is often a useful target.

Prince blurred so many of his working and professional relationships to the extent that start and end dates can be tricky to locate. Much of his recorded work remains buried away from public access. His rare interviews often contained fibs or offhand jokes to throw the reader off target. So definitive is tricky.

With fans too, their interpretations of him vary. As Ani DiFranco observes in the last chapter, he is remembered 'by each person in their own way. He offered a rainbow and you pick your own frequency.'

This is one book about him and if it has one aim, beyond being fair to its subject, it's to suggest the frequency of him as the '*Sign o' the Times* guy' over 'the *Purple Rain* fella' on the motorbike. The other starting point is that the most basic analysis of Prince's career shows not so much the picture of a multi-talented musical virtuoso – although he met this description – as much as the fact his success was rooted in hard work. Only then, after getting the right people around him and following his instincts, would the results you heard on record and saw on stage materialise.

Looking at the history of any musician, even Prince couldn't do it alone. He surrounded himself with phenomenally talented bandmates, stylists, photographers, dancers, managers – some of whom were kind enough to make this book better by giving their contributions. Even for someone who played many instruments to elite level, he had to ask for help.

So, I realised that for *Prince: A Sign o' the Times* to get to the stage you find it, it would require hard work plus team contributions, with a slice of good fortune. There are many people to thank.

First, BBC music editor Mark Savage who, after a chat about Prince in a Manchester pub in 2017, commissioned an article marking the 30th anniversary of *Sign o' the Times*, which sparked the idea for this book. What happened after publication of this in March 2017 was… very little. The seed had been planted but with a day job far removed from one two decades previously in the music press, impostor syndrome won out over productivity.

In March 2020, my beloved dad, also John, a retired classics teacher and crossword compiler for *The Glasgow Herald*, was fading fast. Sitting on his deathbed, there was something of a growing voice in my head, suggesting that I should write the book, and it was time to do so. My wife Liz Ford, a successful writer and journalist to her very bones, was warned that the book may take time and effort, publication was not a given, nor were copy sales. Her support never wavered. That support and advice have kept me going from March 2020 until July 2025 when the book was finally completed.

For those familiar with Liz's own work, it combines a determination to tell the story as directly, and powerfully, as possible, with justice running through it like writing on a stick of rock. These principles served as a North Star throughout writing. Thanks too to Liz for understanding that a tome about an era-defining album from 1987 would centre around *Sign o' the Times* rather than her preferred choice of Def Leppard's *Hysteria*.

Gratitude is owed to published author friend, Iain Martin, who at the start of the process suggested completing the work before going to publishers. This turned out to be good advice, giving me the freedom to keep writing and researching the book I wanted to write until I was happy. Stories like Prince's are only ever unfolding, never really complete.

Prince famously said 'the truth is, you are either here to enlighten or discourage' and it was a rich blessing to receive plenty of enlightenment and not too much discouragement. The sadder note of passing or illnesses meant that some contributors are no longer with us. For those familiar with this era of Prince's career, Cat Glover was front and centre of the *Sign* and *Lovesexy* imagery. The *Sign* era, particularly the movie, is inconceivable without her. To all those missing her, I hope her involvement in this book gives comfort, and thanks to Hayley Drinkall for her help and own wise counsel on Prince.

Others who were a big part of the story like Ian Boxill, who was interviewed, and Wally Safford and Mo Ostin who weren't, died during the writing of the book, while Dave Hampton's recent setbacks did not disguise what a sharp and analytical mind someone who worked with Herbie Hancock and Joni Mitchell had about Prince. I am very grateful we spoke when we did. For everyone who said yes to talking Prince, you could write your own book – and some have or will – but the kindness of giving up your time led to a deeper understanding of the musician and man.

A total of 220 people said yes to discussions or emailed

answers and each one helped me – and I hope you, the reader – to understand Prince a little better.

Thank you to Jason Agel, Dale Alexander, Zaheer Ali, Carlos Alomar, Don Amendolia, Eric 'Statik' Anest, Ruth Arzate, Nick Atkins, Harlan 'Hucky' Austin, Simon Austin, Dan The Automator, Marylou Badeaux, Roald Bakker, Scottie Baldwin, Lisa Barber, Allen Beaulieu, Brenda Bennett, LeRoy Bennett, Steven Berkoff, Spencer Bernard, Mathieu Bitton, Brian Blade, Michael Bland, Matt Blistan, Ian Boxill, Greg Boyer, Greg Brooks, Hans-Martin Buff, Tom Butsch, Paul Camarata, Lisa Chamblee, Terry Christian, Spencer Churchill, Tim Clawson, Heidi Clemence, Rob 'Cubby' Colby, Patrick Collins, Charles Coplin, Margie Cox, Adrian Crutchfield, Harald Michael Danker, Carole Davis, Erin Davis, Jack DeJohnette, Devin DeVasquez, Ani DiFranco, Rose Ann Dimalanta, Elizabeth Dorr, Kirk Douglas, Carla Dove, Dylan Dresdow, Hayley Drinkall, Josh Dunham, Nathan East, Cedric The Entertainer, Greg Errico, Steve Ferrone, Matt 'Dr' Fink, Elisa Fiorillo, Simon Fields, Brent Fischer, Allen Flowers, Marie France, Mychael Gabriel, Joel Gallen, Eva Gardos, David Garibaldi, Les Garland, Tom Garneau, H.S.H. Princess Gloria von Thurn und Taxis, Cat Glover, Jeff Gold, Buzz Goodchild, Andrew Gouche, Donnie Graves, Jay Graydon, Sal Greco, Mary Griffin, Susan Hale, Anthony Hamilton, Dave Hampton, Jody Hannon, Todd Herreman, Helen Hiatt, Terra Hinrichs, Murielle Hodler-Hamilton, Morris Hayes, Doug Henders, Chuck Hermes, Dale Hughes, David Hogan, Karin Hogsander, Adam Holzman, Michiel Hoogenboezem, Bruce Huisinga, Melissa Huntsberry Kahn, Tina Huntsberry Kahn, Terrance 'Terry' Jackson, Jimmy Jam, Chris James, Lisa Janzen, Sam Jennings, Coke Johnson, Cynthia Johnson, Jellybean Johnson, Kathleen Johnson, Shelby Johnson, Skip Johnson, Lisa Jordan, David Kahne, Gary

Kazanchyan, Mike Kloster, Bill Konersman, Karen Krattinger, Michael Koppelman, Cos Kyriacou, Edgar Kruize, Talib Kweli, Matt Larson, Alan Leeds, Eric Leeds, Toby Lightman, Maneca Lightner, Laura LiPuma Nash, Scott Litt, Peter Lodder, Tonjia Lowe, Pamela Ludwig, Steve Lukather, Robyn Lynch, Albert Magnoli, Tony Maiden, Sananda Maitreya, Monique Mannen, Viktor Manoel, Brad Marsh, Tom Marzullo, Jeff Mason, Sylvia Massy, Mari Maupin, Christian McBride, Nandy McClean, Frank McComb, Peggy McCreary, Bob Merlis, Eddie Miller, Paul Mitchell, Ana Moura, Michael Nelson, Jeff Newman, Cheryl Ann Nick, Randy Newman, Andy Newmark, Novi Novog, Alexander O'Neal, Rissi Palmer, Lenka Paris, Ray Parker Jr, Glenn Parsons, Robbie Paster, Don Peake, 'St.' Paul Peterson, Ricky Peterson, Max Pinnell, Bob Power, Robin Power Royal, James Poyser, Steve Purcell, Martha Quinn, Nick Raphael, DJ Rashida, Bill Reeves, Bevla Reeves, Craig Rice, Robyn Riggs, Ebet Roberts, John 'JR' Robinson, Susan Rogers, David Rule, Dave Rusan, Patrice Rushen, Eric 'Vietnam' Sadler, Roger Sadowsky, Emmanuelle Sallet, Jeymes Samuel, Michelle Schwartzbauer, Robia Scott, Taja Sevelle, Afshin Shahidi, Jeff Sharp, Elfar Sigmundsson, Donnie Simpson, Rhonda Smith, Charles 'Chazz' Smith, Danny Soltys, Mike Soltys, Norbert Stachel, Bill Stephney, Mi-Ling Stone Poole, Therese Stoulill, Erik Stroeve, Ashley Tåmar, Bret Thoeny, Dwayne 'MonoNeon' Thomas Jr., Jacqui Thompson, Scott Thurston, David Tickle, Sotera Tschetter, Steve Vai, Lenny Waronker, Andrew Watt, Mark Webster, Nik West, Vince Wilburn Jr., Lizz Wright, Jeff Young, Kara Young, David Z. (Rivkin) and Chuck Zwicky. If you are a Prince fan who enjoyed this book, you have these people who gave their contributions freely as a big reason why.

Nick Raphael, thank you for use of the anecdote and breakfast. Thank you to Liz's friend Tia Jeewa who invited me to her birthday dinner where I met interviewee Nick Atkins. (We spoke about Barbara Dickson before discovering Nick worked on sound for the *Sign* tour.) Thank you to all credited who offered images for the book plates inside, particularly Tom Butsch who sketched the 1975 *Guys and Dolls* set which twelve years later would become the album backdrop.

Thanks to Colin Paterson, who was kind enough to introduce me to the aforementioned Mark Savage, and lent me his interview with Herbie Hancock for the BBC. Colin's brother Michael, another dear friend, mentioned the book to author friend Rob Hutton who put me in touch with his agent Sally Holloway, who provided invaluable advice including joining the Society of Authors.

The main reason you read this through Bonnier is due to Pete Selby, the publisher behind Nine Eight's collection of music books, saying yes. He is a visionary, not because he greenlit this, but because he has birthed music books of all stripes into the world. His excitement helped fuel mine in the home strait of writing.

James Lilford offered a sympathetic edit and no little encouragement. Nige Tassell with his copy edit offered tougher love and a sharp eye, as did Ian Greensill, which were no less valuable. (Turns out Jack White and Jack Black are two very different people.)

Thank you to Joe Hallsworth at Bonnier for taking everything home with the images, copy and launch and Ben Pester for help with publicity.

There was so much goodwill from my family including my mum Lorna, siblings Andrew, Jane, David and Polly, mother-in-law Janice and brother-in-law David Ford and wife Karen, and too many friends and sympathetic ears in the Prince universe to mention but all of whom made a difference.

As did Natalie Balmain, Jon Bennett, Simon Blackmore, Fiona Cairns, Lee Dainty, Chris Elwell-Sutton, Nigel Hart, Peggy Hayes, James Hogan, Simon Kaston, Douglas Martin, Paul McKenzie, Rebecca McKie, Joanne McKie, Nicki Murphy, Casey Rain, Kenny Ritchie, Ally Ross, David Shaw, and Julian Stockton. Thank you.

This was written on the shoulders of some insightful books about Prince – works by Benoit Clerc, Jason Draper, Mayte Garcia, Alex Hahn, Dave Hill, Barney Hoskyns, Liz Jones, Per Nilsen, Ronin Ro, Matt Thorne, Duane Tudahl, Touré, as well as Prince's own memoir with Dan Piepenbring, *The Beautiful Ones*, and too many music biographies to mention. They all informed this book, as did podcasts from The Current in association with Prince's estate, Michael Dean and Red Bull Music Academy. Another vital checklist was the Prince Vault website. As much as was feasible, if a comment was used outside of author interviews, all efforts have been made to credit external sources. Key facts or statements about Prince were, where possible, drawn from more than one interviewee or source.

Another work by Prince enthusiast and music writer Alan Light was a touchstone. Not the obvious choice of Alan's book on the making of *Purple Rain's* movie and soundtrack, but another book on Leonard Cohen's song, *Hallelujah, The Holy or The Broken*. The granular detail on how one song can ripple out into the world, with the cover versions and influence over music and wider culture, was a useful roadmap in how *Sign…*'s sixteen songs could be expanded to paint a broader picture of Prince.

Final thanks must go to Prince for creating the *Sign o' the Times* album and movie which stand as a fitting testimony to his talents. His career was full of dazzling moments but as records go, neither the double album nor live concert is a bad place to start. 'If you want to know me, listen to my music' is another of his most famous comments and listening to the album or watching the movie remains a pretty good time capsule memory of Prince. If this book encourages you to check either film or record out, or check them out again if you are well-versed, then it was worth the effort.